To Fred,

with thanks

for coming to Western

[illegible]

A SIMPLE COMMON LAWYER

Michael Taggart was the Alexander Turner Professor of Law in the University of Auckland, New Zealand until his retirement in 2008. He has worked extensively on public law, in particular administrative law, privatisation and the public/private law divide as well as on legal history. He has visited and taught at the Universities of Melbourne, New South Wales, Toronto, Cambridge, Paris II, Victoria at Wellington, Saskatchewan, Western Ontario, Queen's University at Kingston and Osgoode Hall Law School. This book of essays, dedicated to him by a group of his friends, including academic colleagues, practitioners and judges, marks his enormous contribution to the common law.

A Simple Common Lawyer

Essays in Honour of Michael Taggart

Edited by

David Dyzenhaus, Murray Hunt and
Grant Huscroft

•HART•
PUBLISHING

OXFORD AND PORTLAND, OREGON
2009

Published in North America (US and Canada) by
Hart Publishing
c/o International Specialized Book Services
920 NE 58th Avenue, Suite 300
Portland, OR 97213–3786
USA
Tel: +1 503 287 3093 or toll-free: (1) 800 944 6190
Fax: +1 503 280 8832
E-mail: orders@isbs.com
Website: http://www.isbs.com

Hart Publishing Ltd, 16C Worcester Place, Oxford, OX1 2JW
Telephone: +44 (0)1865 517530 Fax: +44 (0)1865 510710
E-mail: mail@hartpub.co.uk
Website: http://www.hartpub.co.uk

British Library Cataloguing in Publication Data
Data Available

ISBN: 978-1-84113-923-4

Typeset by Columns Design Ltd, Reading
Printed and bound in Great Britain by
TJ International Ltd, Padstow, Cornwall

Contents

Foreword

The moment I was asked whether, in any circumstances, we might consider publishing a book of essays in Mike's honour was a bittersweet one. While there was never any doubt about what my answer would be, I could only wish that the circumstances had been different.

I first encountered Mike in the late 1980s when the book of essays he co-edited *Judicial Review of Administrative Action in the 1980s: Problems and Prospects,* published by OUP in Auckland, was beginning to make an impression in the UK. Mike wrote me patient letters from Auckland suggesting that OUP in Oxford might like to do a bit of marketing; I regret to say that not much happened. Despite that, or perhaps because of it, the book kept cropping up everywhere; much later I realised that it was rather special, the first of a series of books inspired, edited and partly written by Mike which charted and changed the face of administrative law in the common law world. Today Mike is widely regarded as one of the towering figures of the common law, a legend.

In his Preface to Mike's *Private Property and the Abuse of Rights in Victorian England,* Brian Simpson playfully describes Edward Pickles, the farmer who provoked Bradford Corporation into launching what would become a famous law suit, as "the archetypal Yorkshireman" who "surely wore a cloth cap". Reading the book recently I expected to come across confirmation that Pickles was indeed the epitome of Yorkshire masculinity. But, as Mike says, virtually nothing is known about Pickles the person besides what emerges from the public record. Where Brian used his poetic licence, Mike, ever the brutally honest scholar, refused to go in for the archetype. It's not his style. Which is a shame because I have always thought of Mike as being very close to the archetypal New Zealander (as Brian Simpson might have said "he surely wore a replica All Black shirt").What characteristics make him the archetypal Kiwi, the Ian Kirkpatrick or Zinzan Brooke of the common law? It's a short list: physical and mental strength; curiosity about the world coupled with an obvious love of home; visceral honesty – no airs and graces, no bullshit; the attractive blend of self-confidence and modesty; a great capacity for friendship and hospitality; and of course, not being Australian. Others in this volume are better placed to judge, but in my view one obvious attraction of Mike's academic work is that it reflects the man. It is direct and honest, and, in the best traditions of the common law, learned, judicious, critical, wryly amusing, lucid, fully engaged with practical problems but with one eye to the larger theoretical picture.

Hart Publishing was two days old and I was in my office waiting for the phone to ring when Mike e-mailed me from Saskatchewan to say that he had a manuscript which could be ready in a matter of weeks. It became *The Province of Administrative Law,* our second book (and rather successful at that). In the years since we have remained in close contact about Mike's work, about rugby (sadly mostly lamenting our respective teams' failures at World Cups), about Festschriften, about our many mutual friends, and about academic life in general. In all our dealings Mike has displayed the same fearlessness and generosity which I am sure originally inspired him to put his trust in an unknown and unproven publishing house.

How do I sum up the man? We are all defined by our public achievements, whether they are measured in educational honours, books written, battles won, empires built, or prizes awarded. But in life, as in the law, there is a public-private divide and the public record tells us less than half the story. There is a separate realm, the interior life, where achievements are not recorded publicly but where the far more important and sustaining achievements occur; where love is nurtured, where friendships are forged and honed, where intellectual and emotional support is given and received. As anyone who knows him will tell you, Mike's life has been one of quite daunting public achievement, but it is his mighty human spirit that marks him out from other mortals. It has been my great good fortune to be able to call Mike a friend, my great privilege to have been invited to publish these essays.

Richard Hart
Oxford
17 December 2008

Contributors

Mark Aronson is Emeritus Professor of Law at the University of New South Wales

David Dyzenhaus is Professor of Law and Philosophy at the University of Toronto

Dame Sian Elias is Chief Justice of New Zealand

Carol Harlow is Emeritus Professor at the Law Department, London School of Economics & Political Science

Murray Hunt is the Legal Adviser to the UK Parliament's Joint Select Committee on Human Rights

Grant Huscroft is Professor of Law at the University of Western Ontario

Martin Loughlin is Professor of Public Law, London School of Economics & Political Science

Sir Anthony Mason is a former Chief Justice of the High Court of Australia

P G McHugh is a Reader in Law at Sidney Sussex College at the University of Cambridge

Janet McLean is Professor of Law at Dundee University

David Mullan is Emeritus Professor of Law at Queen's University

Paul Rishworth is Dean and Professor of Law at the University of Auckland

Cheryl Saunders is Professor of Law at the University of Melbourne

Sir Stephen Sedley is a Lord Justice of Appeal

AW Brian Simpson is Charles F and Edith J Clyne Professor of Law at the University of Michigan

1

Introduction

MIKE TAGGART WAS born and raised in Auckland, and educated at the University of Auckland where he completed his LLB (Hons). He and his friend Ron Paterson were the top students in the class of 1977, and on graduating Mike served as Judges' Clerk at the Auckland High Court for two years.

He attended Harvard University as a Fulbright Scholar, from 1979–80, and on graduating accepted a position as Assistant Professor at the University of Western Ontario. There was a risk that he might stay in Canada, becoming another of New Zealand's great academic exports. Fortunately for New Zealand the pull of home was strong and in 1982, after two years at Western, Mike returned to New Zealand to take up a position at his *alma mater.*

Progress through the academic ranks was usually slow and incremental. One began as a lecturer and proceeded in annual steps toward applying for senior lectureship. If lucky enough to be appointed Senior Lecturer, most would expect to rise to "the bar", a level in the Senior Lecturer's scale that was considered a career grade. There were few chairs (full professorships in law) and these were beyond reach of most.

Not so for Mike. He was promoted to Senior Lecturer in 1987 and within a year of that was appointed to a chair, a story that was national news. At 32, Mike Taggart was the youngest full professor in Auckland history.

Mike has gone on to have the sort of career to which most academics aspire. His courses have been demanding, but he is beloved by a generation of students for his enthusiasm and commitment, and was awarded the University of Auckland Distinguished Teaching Award in 2000. His work has been published in the world's leading law journals and by the best presses, and he has been honoured by the New Zealand Legal Research Foundation with the JF Northey Memorial Prize (best law book) on two occasions, along with the Sir Ian Barker Prize (best published article). He has waved the Auckland flag around the world, participating in conferences and colloquia, delivering public lectures and teaching courses at leading law schools in the UK, the United States, Canada, France, and Australia. The University of Auckland recognized Mike's contributions to the law by naming him the first Alexander Turner Professor in Law in 2004, the only research chair in the Faculty of Law.

Throughout, Mike has led by example. He has poured heart and soul into his research and teaching and his work rate has been prodigious. He is the only teacher of law we know who can frankly announce to his students that teaching is what he has to do to earn the time in which to research, his real reason for being in the job, and still maintain the devotion of the students because of the complete commitment displayed in this teaching. The same is true of his attitude to administration. He never wanted to do it, but when he did it was with complete commitment and with a willingness to take stands on issues of principle whenever needed.

His research has addressed the leading issues of the day, exploring issues like the public/private divide; the implications of internationalization; and the constitutionalization of administrative law. He has also demonstrated his skills as a legal historian, researching the stories behind leading common law cases.

Mike's interest in the *Festschrift* genre is a good demonstration of his academic character. Some years ago, Mike noticed that high quality academic research was being overlooked because it was being published in books honouring other academics rather than in journals. Mike set out to fix that situation, discussing the *Festschrift* in an article in the *Oxford Journal of Legal Studies*, and establishing an index to common law *Festschriften*, first published as an electronic database that ensures legal research will be disseminated widely in future (*http://www.library.auckland.ac.nz/databases/learn_database/public.asp?record+iclf*) and subsequently published by Hart as a book.

Quite apart from his body of work, a defining feature of Mike Taggart's scholarship is his generosity. Mike has helped numerous colleagues become established as legal academics and has always been there with advice and encouragement. Scholars around the world have benefited from Mike's willingness to read and comment on their work over the years, even if they braced for the criticism (and the bad puns) that would be written in the margins.

It would be easy to think that Mike has done nothing but work, but this would be far from the truth. He is the consummate family man. He and Nicky have raised four children, Lisa, Sarah, Richard, and Danny. The Taggart house is a bewildering locus of activity to the observer. There is a level of commitment to each other, to frankness and decency, but above all to play and mischief, that has left more than one visiting parent feeling inadequate. In a way, the family and Mike's academic life mirror each other.

It is fitting that Mike Taggart be honoured with a *Festchrift*, and it is our great honour to have edited this collection. We are grateful to those who have contributed on very short notice, and sorry that we could not include the many others who would like to have contributed. As always, it has been a pleasure to work with Richard Hart, whose enthusiastic support (including taking on the task of copy editing the manuscript) made publication of this book possible in a tight time frame without compromising its quality.

Introduction

Mike's academic career has been cut short by illness, and we are all the worse for that. For those who have come to know him well, an academic world without Mike is unimaginable. He has always disdained the trappings of success while setting for himself and others the highest standards. No matter where you work or your educational credentials, no matter the subject matter on which you work, whether doctrinal, theoretical, or historical, Mike would say you must aspire to be a 'world class scholar' because only that aspiration will make you into a decent scholar. The title of this collection of essays is another quotation from Mike, his own self-description. It comes from the heart. His academic life has been devoted to understanding the common law and he has never had more ambition than to be a 'simple common lawyer'. But as his work has displayed, there is a characteristically mischievous element to the description. To understand the common law one has to understand a tradition of reasoning that is, warts and all, one of the most sophisticated and enduring of all human constructs. Mike is one of a handful of scholars in the world who is able to speak with confidence about that tradition in a way that commands international attention.

Mike Taggart has thus left a mark on legal scholarship, at the University of Auckland and internationally. Most of all, he has left a mark on all those whose lives he has touched, and especially those fortunate enough to be able to call him a friend.

Grant Huscroft
David Dyzenhaus
Murray Hunt

2

Process, Quality, and Variable Standards: Responding to an *Agent Provocateur*

MARK ARONSON*

Introduction

OVER THE YEARS, Mike Taggart has offered some remarkable and remarkably well-researched insights into the law of judicial review of administrative action as it operates in Australia. For the purposes of this essay, I want to focus on his most recent attack on the Australian High Court: "Australian Exceptionalism' in Judicial Review'.[1] This is a provocative read, mixing analytical brilliance and comparativist insight with personal opinions, *cris de coeur* and denunciation. And it is fun. Amongst those of us working in the trenches, who could honestly deny the secret pleasure of reading a witty attack on their court system's tallest poppies? Mike's other work spans the judicial review laws of several other countries, and his critiques of their doctrinal puzzles can be just as forthright, but not quite as critical. Australian judgments, he says, deserve special criticism for being 'exceptionalist' in a number of respects.

I will focus principally on only one of the issues he discusses in his exceptionalism article. Mike has long advocated a modification of judicial review's qualitative standards of review, in particular, the *Wednesbury* unreasonableness standard, which is so strict that the only decisions that it condemns are those that may properly be described as either crazy or morally indefensible.[2] He wants to

* Thanks go to Sean Brennan, Matthew Groves, Murray Hunt, Carol Harlow, Martin Krygier, Andrew Lynch, Keith Mason, Linda Pearson, Lorne Sossin, and Brian Tamanaha. They even go to Mike Taggart, who was as generous as ever with his help.

[1] (2008) 36 *Federal Law Review* 1 [Taggart, 'Exceptionalism'].

[2] Lord Diplock spoke of an 'outrageous … defiance of … accepted moral standards': *Council of Civil Service Unions v Minister for the Civil Service* [1985] 1 AC 374 at 410.

replace *Wednesbury*'s lunacy standard with a test of variable intensity, a test that would become ever stricter as the threat to human rights or fundamental freedoms increases.[3]

Mike rarely stays in the trenches, and his 'exceptionalism' article is no exception. I think that he under-estimates the intellectual strength of his enemy's position at several points, and even where he does succeed in storming the enemy lines, he sometimes leaves me wondering where *exactly* he wants to go to next. But that is both his point and his methodology. Mike is a seasoned *agent provocateur* who charms us out of our comfort zones to enter his more difficult territories. He is uncomfortable with the verbal labels that stand for the different grounds of judicial review. He is particularly critical of Australia's retention of a multiplicity of specific grounds; Australia's judicial review landscape is filled with labels. He sees their manipulable boundaries (their 'porous' quality in his terms) and their tendency to overlap each other as proof that more generalised grounds should replace them.

'Jurisdictional error' used to be a more generalised ground, but it has become a conclusory term in Australia, where it stands for any one or more of the grounds which (if established) result in the judicial nullification of the impugned decision.[4] He is against conclusory terms because of the danger that people will not realise that they are indeed conclusory, particularly if they previously had different meanings. The danger then is that people might go hunting for the terms' own separate meanings, creating confusion in the process. He is especially against the idea of a distinction between jurisdictional and non-jurisdictional errors of law because it lacks the power to explain why the courts cut more slack to some decision-makers than to others when it comes to their interpretations of the governing law. He prefers the more nuanced notion of 'deference' to 'slack', and thinks that it stands a greater chance of principled and contextual elaboration than Australia's labels, especially 'non-jurisdictional' error of law.[5]

These are the defining features of Mike's *modus operandi.* Judicial review's grounds will always be porous, always flexible, and we need to articulate the underlying forces that prompt restrictive applications in some contexts, thereby cutting more slack to the administration. The other side of that coin is of more immediate interest to Mike. He seeks to articulate the underlying forces that in

[3] Taggart, 'Exceptionalism' above n 1 at 11–12. It is his principal focus in M Taggart, 'Proportionality, Deference, *Wednesbury*' [2008] *New Zealand Law Review* 423 [Taggart, 'Proportionality']. 'Exceptionalism', however, represents his most sustained analysis of Australia's resistance to doctrinal change across a number of judicial review topics.

[4] M Aronson, 'Jurisdictional Error Without the Tears', in M Groves and H Lee (eds), *Australian Administrative Law: Fundamentals, Principles and Doctrines* (Melbourne, Cambridge University Press, 2007) Ch 21; M Aronson, B Dyer and M Groves, *Judicial Review of Administrative Action* (Sydney, Thomson, 4th ed, 2009) at [1.85]-[1.90] and [10.05]-[10.10] [Aronson et al, *Judicial Review*]; and *Commissioner of Taxation v Futuris Corporation Ltd* (2008) 247 ALR 605 at [129]-[134], Kirby J.

[5] He and I differ on this point; as he said in his 'exceptionalism' article: 'We have been in conversation about this and disagreeing for years, long may it continue': Taggart, 'Exceptionalism', above n 1 at 8.

most countries prompt more expansive applications of judicial review's grounds in other contexts (for example, where human rights or fundamental values are at stake), and roundly condemns Australia's exceptionalist position to the contrary.

The courts of other countries openly acknowledge that they increase the level of judicial scrutiny in the protection of human rights and fundamental freedoms,[6] and even 'fundamental values' in Canada's case.[7] Most importantly, their acceptance that judicial review's grounds (or standards) are applied with variable intensity applies in Canada's case across the board to review of errors of fact, law and discretion, and in the case of England and New Zealand to errors of fact and discretion. 'Unreasonableness' may therefore be seen as a variable standard in all three countries. Alternatively (and especially in Canada), it is a single standard that is applied with variable intensity according to context, the variability factors being grouped together beneath headings such as 'deference' or 'margin' or 'political judgment'. Proportionality review is self-evidently variable, although its availability and meaning beyond the area of constitutional or statutory human rights instruments are still hotly contested. The 'substantive unfairness' ground is also variable, although it is available only in England. Mike is a variability enthusiast, but only in the protection of fundamental rights that are either enshrined in statutory or constitutional Charters or well-recognised at common law.

Process and Quality

Like courts elsewhere, Australia's High Court sets lower barriers to invalidity where fundamental rights or freedoms are at risk, but its technique is strictly limited. In essence, it is as prepared as courts elsewhere to read down statutes that are an affront to civil liberties or fundamental rights or freedoms. Periodically it fillets savage privative clauses,[8] and apparently savage coercive powers are routinely read down, sometimes quite brilliantly.[9] But the court has not yet taken the

[6] *R v Secretary of State for the Home Department; Ex parte Bugdaycay* [1987] AC 514 at 531 [*Bugdaycay*]; and *R v Secretary of State for the Home Department; Ex parte Simms* [2000] 2 AC 115 at 130 and 144; and *Powerco Ltd v Commerce Commission* [2006] NZHC 662 at [23]-[24].

[7] *Baker v Canada (Minister of Citizenship and Immigration)* [1999] 2 SCR 817 at 855 [56], per L'Heureux-Dubé (for the majority): '[T]hough discretionary decisions will generally be given considerable respect, that discretion must be exercised in accordance with the boundaries imposed in the statute, the principles of the rule of law, the principles of administrative law, the fundamental values of Canadian society, and the principles of the *Charter*.'

[8] *Plaintiff S157/2002 v Commonwealth* (2003) 211 CLR 476 (the Act protected 'decisions' from review, but that had no effect on jurisdictionally flawed decisions); and *Batterham v QSR Ltd* (2006) 225 CLR 237 at 249 [26] (it seems that an Act protecting *purported decisions* is similarly ineffective). See also Aronson et al, *Judicial Review*, above n 4, Ch 17.

[9] *Coco v R* (1994) 179 CLR 427 at 436–38; *Plaintiff S157/2002 v Commonwealth* (2003) 211 CLR 476 at 492; *Daniels Corporation International Pty Ltd v Australian Competition and Consumer Commission* (2002) 213 CLR 543 at 553 and 592–93; and *Gypsy Jokers Motorcycle Club Inc v Commissioner of Police (WA)* (2008) 242 ALR 191.

next step of cutting the Executive less slack by tightening the screws of the 'qualitative' standards of review – *Wednesbury* unreasonableness being the most obvious.

Whilst recognising that the distinctions might be 'porous', this essay will divide judicial review's grounds into two categories: the grounds that focus on issues of process belong to the first category, and the second category covers grounds that focus on issues of quality.[10] Distinguishing rules of process and substance is a game that never ends because the distinctions vary between contexts. For all of its difficulties, I will adapt a distinction that Professor Martinez has drawn in a different context, namely, the rules applied by courts.[11] Like Martinez, I will distinguish between rules that seek to prescribe the things that an administrative decision-maker can do, and rules that seek to control how the decision-maker is to go about doing those things.

Martinez was seeking to understand the reasons, both good and bad, that the American courts kept dodging the substantive issues raised by challenges to some of the Executive excesses in its war on terror. She listed five different uses of 'process'. These were 'process as avoidance' of the hot substantive issues, 'process as signalling' the likely outcomes if the courts were pushed to deciding a substantive issue, 'process as substance', 'substance disguised as process', and 'process as housekeeping'. Judicial review doctrine commonly treats process as substance, partly for instrumental reasons[12] and partly for dignitarian and legitimacy reasons.[13] It occasionally disguises substance as process; given the choice, most courts will nominate process grounds for quashing a decision rather than *Wednesbury* unreasonableness. And with an eye to keeping their own house in order, the courts frequently test whether a challenge is really made on merits grounds by asking how much evidence it has to consider.

For the purposes of this essay, the process grounds check that administrative decision-makers have gone through all the right motions. In a sense, they are check-list grounds, because decision-makers can tick them off their lists as they go. But the qualitative grounds look beyond check-lists, asking not *whether* the decision-maker performed each requisite motion, but *how well* each was performed. The qualitative grounds sometimes boil down to a question of values,

[10] See G Weeks, 'The Expanding Role of Process in Judicial Review' (2008) 15 *Australian Journal of Administrative Law* 100.

[11] J Martinez, 'Process and Substance in the 'War on Terror'' (2008) 108 *Columbia Law Review* 1013 at 1020–21.

[12] For example, the natural justice rules are designed in part to improve the accuracy of decision-making. The requirements to discard forbidden and irrelevant considerations, and to consider relevant and mandatory factors, are designed to focus the decision-maker's mind on the governing law's essential criteria for decision-making.

[13] For example, the natural justice rules are designed in part to accord equal respect to those immediately affected by individualised decision-making, and in part to secure acceptance (however grudging) of unfavourable administrative determinations.

asking whether the decision-maker strayed too far from accepted moral standards.[14] I make these distinctions for more than mere analytical convenience.[15] I think that the amount of slack that the courts accord to administrative decision-makers tracks the distinction between process and quality fairly closely. The process grounds are more readily seen as 'objective', with the result that their application is less likely to result in charges of the judiciary usurping the administration's functions.

The process grounds include errors of law, breach of mandatory statutory procedures, acting in the absence of factual or other preconditions for making valid decisions, making orders beyond the decision-maker's statutory functions, and failing to consider relevant factors that the governing law stipulated as mandatory considerations. The process grounds can all be squeezed more or less comfortably beneath the headings of 'jurisdictional issues' or 'jurisdictional rules'. Speaking at a fairly high level of abstraction, jurisdictional issues mark out the limits of or boundaries to an administrative decision-maker's powers (almost in a spatial sense),[16] and jurisdictional rules dictate the procedures to be observed. Most of these issues or rules can be identified before the decision-making process gets under way.

In terms of the very legitimacy of judicial review, the process grounds are typically the least troublesome for the courts, because their application usually does not turn on any assessment of the degree to which (if at all) the court's view of the process requirements differs from the decision-maker's view. Put another way, the court has the last word on jurisdictional process rules *and* purports to cut no slack, the theory being that these sorts of questions have only one right answer.[17] Having said that, I readily acknowledge that even the process rules allow the courts to give some margin to the decision-makers, but this is done

[14] See above, n 2.

[15] Gummow J divided judicial review's grounds according to whether the law that they enforced '(i) determines the limits of the power in question [or] (ii) governs its exercise': *Minister for Immigration and Multicultural Affairs v Eshetu* (1999) 197 CLR 611 at 649 [*Eshetu*].

[16] In the context of review against human rights standards, Professor Allan spoke of 'A dubious 'spatial language of areas or margins of discretion', indicating exclusive zones of competence . . .'. See TRS Allan, 'Human Rights and Judicial Review: a Critique of 'Due Deference'', [2006] *Cambridge Law Journal* 671 at 672, quoting in part from M Hunt, 'Sovereignty's Blight: Why Contemporary *Public Law* Needs the Concept of 'Due Deference'', in N Bamforth and P Leyland (eds), *Public Law in a Multi-Layered Constitution* (Oxford, Hart Publishing, 2003) 339. In even earlier times, the language was less spatial than chronological, with jurisdictional issues being those which were 'preliminary', 'essential preliminaries' or 'collateral'. 'Essential preliminaries' appeared in *Colonial Bank of Australasia v Willan* (1874) LR 5 PC 417 at 443. Professor Craig calls this the 'commencement theory of jurisdiction': PP Craig, *Administrative Law* (London, Thomson Sweet & Maxwell, London, 6th ed, 2008) 14–038. The chronological tinge still makes the occasional appearance in Australia (eg, *Project Blue Sky Inc v Australian Broadcasting Authority* (1998) 194 CLR 355 at 389 and 391 [*Blue Sky*]), although usually with some sense of its inadequacy (eg, *Woolworths Ltd v Pallas Newco Pty Ltd* (2004) 61 NSWLR 707 at 718).

[17] See R Williams, 'When is an Error not an Error? Reform of Jurisdictional Review of Error of Law and Fact' [2007] *Public Law* 793. Canada's Supreme Court denies review for some 'reasonable' interpretations of a regulator's 'home statute' even if the court would have reached a different

indirectly. There is considerable room for debate, for example, as to whether a statutory procedure is mandatory or directory,[18] or whether a factual prerequisite is jurisdictional or non-jurisdictional,[19] and it has long been recognised that the actual content of the procedural fairness rule of natural justice varies enormously according to context.[20]

If there were no other review grounds than those dealing with process, then judicial review would be a very black-and-white affair, in which the reviewing courts would cut no slack whatsoever on jurisdictional issues and show no interest whatsoever in any remaining issues which would, by definition, constitute 'the merits'. In such a binary world, non-jurisdictional issues become black holes into which the courts cast no light.[21] There are other grounds, however, and it is convenient to categorise them as turning on the quality of the decision. So-called *Wednesbury* unreasonableness provides the easiest example, because it is not confined in its application to pre-defined 'jurisdictional issues'. It looks at everything, although in Australia, this is done usually in only a cursory manner, so as to catch only the most obviously unreasonable decisions. Proportionality review belongs equally obviously to the category of qualitative grounds. Proportionality review in Australia is confined to cases arising under statutory Charters of Rights, and there is no such Charter at the national level.[22]

One might debate how many other grounds are properly characterised as 'qualitative' review grounds, but categorisation *per se* is not the point of this essay. For present purposes, I will include only two more, and each is highly uncertain and even contested. The first is a requirement in some Australian cases that decision-makers do more than just tick off all relevant and mandatory considerations; the quality of the consideration which must be given is 'proper, genuine and realistic'. If that were to be generally accepted (and that is far from clear), then it would have transformed a process ground into a qualitative ground. Similarly, there are a couple of intriguing High Court cases that have the

interpretation. Its starting point is that interpretation is a matter of judgment, which is the same in that respect as fact-finding and policy-laden decision-making: *Dunsmuir v New Brunswick* [2008] 1 SCR 190 [*Dunsmuir*].

[18] *Blue Sky*, above n 16. *Blue Sky* declared its distaste for the 'mandatory' and 'directory' labels, because they are conclusory: at 390–91. They are useful conclusions nonetheless, so they remain in use, but in quotation marks or with an explicit nod to *Blue Sky*; see, eg, *PM v R* (2007) 232 CLR 370 at 381; and *Ayles v R* (2008) 232 CLR 410 at 419. The House of Lords has adopted a similar position: *Robinson v Secretary of State for Northern Ireland* [2002] UKHL 32 at [13] and [82]; *R v Soneji* [2006] 1 AC 340; and *R v Clarke* [2008] 1 WLR 338.

[19] England's term is 'precedent' facts, and they rarely arise in that country. They have all but vanished in the United States and do not appear to be a big feature in Canada. See Aronson et al, *Judicial Review* at [4.280]-[4.350].

[20] *Russell v Duke of Norfolk* [1949] 1 All ER 109.

[21] See: See: D Dyzenhaus and E Fox–Decent, 'Rethinking the Process/Substance Distinction: *Baker v Canada*' (2001) 51 *University of Toronto Law Journal* 193; D Dyzenhaus, 'Constituting the Rule of Law: Fundamental Values in Administrative Law' (2002) 27 *Queen's Law Journal* 445; and M Taggart, 'Reinventing Administrative Law' in N Bamforth and P Leyland (eds), *Public Law in a Multi-Layered Constitution* (Oxford, Hart Publishing, 2003) Ch 12, 311 at 333.

[22] Aronson et al, *Judicial Review* above n 4 at [6.225]-[6.240].

potential to transform the process focus of the procedural fairness rule into something more qualitative.[23] The court has said that decision-makers must not only provide affected persons an opportunity to put their case; they must also pay attention and remember at least the outlines of what was put.

Unreasonableness

Before discussing how *Wednesbury* unreasonableness operates in Australia, it is necessary to give a brief account of a recent terminological development (although it should be of no real substantive moment for the purposes of this essay).

Wednesbury unreasonableness has divided itself into two grounds in Australia, which is indeed exceptionalist in this respect. But the reason for the division was good; it was to outfox a savage Act. As in many common law countries, immigration decisions dominated Australia's judicial review case-load for around 15 years. For roughly a decade of that period, Australia's migration laws banned unreasonableness challenges to migration decisions in the Federal Court, although they could still be brought in the High Court's original jurisdiction. This resulted in what was called a 'bifurcated review process' over migration matters,[24] with challengers filing originating process simultaneously in the Federal Court and the High Court. The Federal Court challenge would usually be heard first. If that failed, the challenger would then appeal to the High Court, which would entertain the appeal and the matter lodged in its original jurisdiction at the same time. The pressures on the High Court were enormous,[25] and one cannot help suspecting that the Ministers were hoping that the High Court would react by restricting the reach of judicial review's grounds. But to its credit, the court stood its ground.

Eventually, the High Court devised a way around the problem. It adopted a restricted interpretation of the ban against unreasonableness challenges, so as to strip it of all effect. The court accepted that the ban applied to *Wednesbury* unreasonableness, but it gave that ground a very narrow scope. *Wednesbury*

[23] *Dranichnikov v Minister for Immigration and Multicultural Affairs* (2003) 197 ALR 389; and *NAIS v Minister for Immigration and Multicultural and Indigenous Affairs* (2005) 228 CLR 470.

[24] *Eshetu*, above n 15 at [104], Gaudron and Kirby JJ.

[25] For example, 300 judicial review applications were commenced in the High Court in the year ending 30 June 2002. Of these, 287 (96%) were immigration matters, and the 'bifurcated jurisdiction' scheme prevented the court from remitting the vast bulk of these to other courts for hearing. The matter was made worse by the huge increase (to 2855) in applications for special leave to appeal from other courts, and by the fact that 40% of all High Court filings were by unrepresented litigants, almost all of them attempting to litigate hopeless cases. See High Court of Australia, *Annual Report 2001–2002* (Canberra, 2002), p 7. Immigration matters continue to dominate the filings for special leave to appeal, but most of them are now dealt with on the papers. Full Court decisions on judicial review matters commenced in the court have dramatically reduced (to 2 in the reporting year 2006–2007) since the end of bifurcation: High Court of Australia, *Annual Report 2006–2007* (Canprint, Canberra, 2007) pp 17 and 89.

applied only to an exercise of discretion based on what an older judgment had rather quaintly called 'a matter of opinion or policy or taste'.[26] It is convenient to treat these as matters of 'pure discretion', and the court distinguished them from other matters which I might for the sake of convenience call matters of 'judgment'.[27] The latter included states of mind (such as 'satisfaction') that certain facts were established. The court initially indicated that matters of judgment could be subjected to 'reasonableness review'.[28] But when it had to deal squarely with interpreting the ban on *Wednesbury* in the Federal Court's migration caseload, it understandably adopted a different label. 'Reasonableness review' of matters of judgment was rebadged to become review for 'serious irrationality or illogicality', whilst the scope of *Wednesbury* unreasonableness was retracted to cover only the exercise of pure discretions.[29]

Judicial review for unreasonableness in administrative law preceded the *Wednesbury* case[30] by at least half a century, although it did not always use the label of 'unreasonableness'. Lord Halsbury LC said in *Sharp v Wakefield*[31] that discretionary power must be exercised

> according to the rules of reason and justice, not according to private opinion...; according to law, and not humour. It is to be, not arbitrary, vague, and fanciful, but legal and regular. And it must be exercised within the limit, to which an honest man competent to the discharge of his office ought to confine himself.

The parallel with American review for 'arbitrary and capricious' agency action is striking.[32] 'Arbitrary and capricious' seems to have made its legal début in

[26] *Buck v Bavone* (1976) 135 CLR 110 at 119, Gibbs J.

[27] Gummow J's major distinctions were between jurisdictional requirements turning on (i) the objective existence of facts; (ii) the decision-maker's subjective decision (usually expressed in terms of 'satisfaction') as to the existence of facts; and (iii) public interest, policy or values (what I am calling 'pure discretion'). The court itself has not spoken with one voice, although Gummow J's structured approach to judicial review matters appears to have caught on. My thumb-nail sketch in this paragraph summarises his Honour's development of a structured approach in three cases: *Eshetu*, above n 15; *Re Minister for Immigration and Multicultural Affairs; Ex parte Applicant S20/2002* (2003) 198 ALR 59 [*Applicant*]; and *Minister for Immigration and Multicultural and Indigenous Affairs v SGLB* (2004) 207 ALR 12 [*SGLB*].

[28] *Eshetu*, above n 15 at at 648–57, esp at 656 [145].

[29] *Applicant* above n 27 at [34]; and *SGLB*, above n 27 at [38]. This summary is contentious. Several cases have refused to accept that what I call 'serious irrationality or illogicality' has been hived off from *Wednesbury*. Unless one has to pick one's way around a poorly drafted legislative attempt to exclude specific review grounds, that particular debate scarcely matters, because whatever the badge, it is clear that the test (or tests) are as demanding as ever. See Aronson et al, *Judicial Review* at [4.405]-[4.435] and [5.65]-[5.75]. For the purposes of this essay, the badge is less important than the intensity of judicial scrutiny that it permits.

[30] *Associated Provincial Picture Houses Ltd v Wednesbury Corp* [1948] 1 KB 223.

[31] [1891] AC 173 at 179, references omitted. Similarly, subordinate laws would be invalid for unreasonableness if they were 'partial and unequal in their operation as between different classes; if they were manifestly unjust; if they disclosed bad faith; if they involved such oppressive or gratuitous interference with the rights of those subject to them as could find no justification in the minds of reasonable men . . .': per Lord Russell CJ in *Kruse v Johnson* [1898] 2 QB 91 at 99–100.

[32] 28 USC § 706(2)(A).

Blackstone's Commentaries,[33] and it first appeared in the law reports in the context of discussions as to the breadth of a trustee's discretionary powers.[34] At the time of its cross-over into the *Administrative Procedure Act* 1946 (US), it was a well-established review standard in American judicial review law.

Australia's first major recognition of what would now be called 'unreasonableness' review preceded *Wednesbury* by four years, and the standard was extremely demanding. That was in *R v Connell; Ex parte Hetton Bellbird Collieries Ltd*,[35] which strung several adjectives together. The exercise of a discretionary power must be neither 'arbitrary nor extravagant'; it must be exercised 'according to the rules of reason and justice' and could not be 'vague or fanciful'. It was always understood that only the most extreme cases would qualify for those sorts of epithets, and the High Court continues to this day to issue warnings against confusing *Wednesbury* unreasonableness with a judge's purely personal disagreement, however 'emphatic'.[36] That might partly explain why *Hetton Bellbird* slid between on the one hand using its adjectives as standards in their own right, and on the other, using them as bases for inferring errors of law, improper purpose, or failing to give attention to mandatory considerations.

That set the tone for many years to come. Whilst the High Court frequently said that statutory functions were not to be exercised arbitrarily, capriciously or unreasonably, the standard approach was to conclude that decisions as bad as that must have involved some sort of legal error or a failure to take account of relevant and mandatory considerations.[37] So long as the court was dealing with tight-lipped administrators under no obligation to give reasons, it had a choice whether to strike down manifestly unreasonable decisions because they were unreasonable, or because there must have been some misunderstanding as to the governing law. Given the choice, it was entirely understandable that it chose the option that looked less intrusive. There was no 'exceptionalism' in this.

England's *Wednesbury* standard was initially so strict that it, too, was a plea of last resort; the unreasonableness had to be so extreme as to be almost lunatic.

[33] Modern reprints usually include Chicago University's '*-page' marginal reference to the pagination of the 10th edition, London, 1793. Using that edition and pagination system, vol 4, *-353 explains an accused person's right of 20 peremptory challenges to jurors, saying that because the challenges can be for no cause at all, they can be 'arbitrary and capricious'.

[34] *Milsington v Musgrave* (1818) 3 Madd 491 at 493 (Vice-Chancellor Sir John Leach).

[35] (1944) 69 CLR at 430–31, Latham CJ, referencing cases dating back to *Sharp v Wakefield* [1891] AC 173 at 179.

[36] Gleeson CJ gave the most frequently repeated warning in *Eshetu*, above n 15 at 626: 'Someone who disagrees strongly with someone else's process of reasoning on an issue of fact may express such disagreement by describing the reasoning as 'illogical' or 'unreasonable', or even 'so unreasonable that no reasonable person could adopt it'. If these are merely emphatic ways of saying that the reasoning is wrong, then they may have no particular legal consequence.'

[37] The leading example is Dixon J's judgment in *Avon Downs Pty Ltd v Federal Commissioner of Taxation* (1949) 78 CLR 353 at 360. *Avon Downs* has sometimes been treated as part of the court's 'unreasonableness' canon; see, eg, *Minister for Immigration and Ethnic Affairs v Wu* (1996) 185 CLR 259 at 275–76; *Enfield City Corporation v Development Assessment Commission* (2000) 199 CLR 135 at 150; *Minister for Immigration and Multicultural Affairs v Jia* (2001) 205 CLR 507 at 532.

America's equivalent was similarly understood in that period.[38] The level of lunacy originally required to establish *Wednesbury* unreasonableness appears to have been the principal argument in England against according it recognition as a separate review ground in its own right. Professor de Smith argued that almost all decisions that were so unreasonable as to meet *Wednesbury*'s standard could more easily be attacked for having ignored relevant and mandatory considerations.[39] Of course, it was not the fact that the grounds overlapped that drove de Smith's opposition to unreasonableness review *per se*, but a fear of where reckless judges might go with unreasonableness if it were to be a truly independent review ground.

The English developments are too well-known to warrant more than a brief discussion here. Briefly, it is now the fashion to revile *Wednesbury*'s original 'lunacy' standard as just one part of a greater picture of a servile (or complacent)[40] judiciary bending its knee to an all-powerful state. Those eagerly awaiting a 'Wednesburial'[41] argue that the case should have become a dead letter after the European Court of Human Rights[42] instructed the English Courts that *Wednesbury* did too little in the protection of the rights enshrined in the *European Convention for the Protection of Human Rights* 1950. The context was the English Court of Appeal's rejection of a challenge to the UK's ban on gays serving in the armed forces.[43] The English court had itself thought that the ban was ridiculous and was prepared to treat *Wednesbury* as a floating standard, to be applied with 'anxious scrutiny' in a case such as this because human rights were at stake. It nevertheless rejected the claim that *no* reasonable person could have supported the ban, because the evidence showed that the ban had the support of the military's top brass, the Cabinet, and a majority of MPs. There are practical limits to the number of leading figures a court can tar with the *Wednesbury* brush of madness.

Wednesbury debates are no longer necessary in England to the extent that the *Human Rights Act* 1998 (UK) (*HRA*) has coverage. Proportionality review replaces *Wednesbury* to that extent, and proportionality testing is said (albeit with varying degrees of credibility) to require the courts to give effect to their own

[38] KC Davis and RJ Pierce Jr, *Administrative Law Treatise* (Boston, Little, Brown and Co, 3rd ed, 1994) vol 1, § 7.4, p 311: 'This version of the arbitrary and capricious test demands virtually nothing of an agency except a lawyer with enough creativity to identify a plausible justification . . .'.

[39] JM Evans, *de Smith's Judicial Review of Administrative Action* (London, Stevens, 4th ed, 1980) 348.

[40] Servility is the usual accusation. Stephen Sedley adds complacency, resulting from the judges and the top echelons of the public service all coming from the same tightly-defined upper class, combining to defeat both egalitarian impulses, and meritocratic reforms of the lower levels of the public service. S Sedley, 'Sounds of Silence: Constitutional Law Without a Constitution' (1994) 110 *Law Quarterly Review* 270 at 277–78. However, the 'complacency' theory has problems handling *Wednesbury* itself, in which elected local councillors had made the decision under challenge.

[41] R Harrison, 'The New Public Law: a New Zealand Perspective' (2003) 14 *Public Law Review* 41 at 56.

[42] In *Lustig-Prean v United Kingdom (No 1)* (2000) 29 EHRR 548.

[43] *R v Ministry of Defence; Ex parte Smith* [1996] QB 517.

views.[44] The English cases are now debating whether some sort of proportionality test should apply in *all* areas of judicial review, along with the factors that should go into the respect that the courts will afford to the government as a counter-weight to the adoption of such a radically intrusive review standard. Areas not covered by the *HRA* still use *Wednesbury*, but the standard now incorporates so many of proportionality's features that it is sometimes 'not possible to see daylight between the two tests'.[45]

Interestingly, Mike opposes a wholesale switch to proportionality review.[46] He would make the switch in only two areas, in each of which he thinks that 'rights' are 'trumps'. His first area is easily identified; statutory (or constitutional) charters of rights leave no option but to adopt the methodology of proportionality. His second area is more debateable, and sees him in his *agent provocateur* role. He urges the judiciary not to abandon its common law tradition of rights protection just because the right in question lies beyond a charter's reach. At the same time, he is opposed to the deployment of variable intensity review whenever a judge is so inclined. His challenge is for the courts to identify fundamental common law rights lying beyond a charter's reach, so that infringements of these (and only these) common law rights might also receive variable intensity review such as proportionality review. The right to property has, curiously, been omitted from some of the leading human rights instruments, and it might be a candidate for characterisation as a fundamental common law right in Mike's scheme.

The common law certainly treats some of its rights as being more important than others, but that is in the context of determining the extent to which statutes can override those rights without using clear words. Mike is right, though, that the common law lacks an authoritative catalogue of rights which might be called 'basic', 'fundamental' or 'constitutional' in a common law sense.[47] Lord Rodger candidly acknowledged that common law 'constitutional rights' were an 'heroic' judicial invention to achieve the benefits of the *European Convention on Human Rights* 1950 before the incorporation of that Convention into domestic law by the *Human Rights Act* 1998 (UK). The heroics, he said, were no longer needed.[48] Australian precedents suggest a similar difficulty in seeking to use the idea of the common law's fundamental rights beyond the context of determining whether

[44] See: *Huang v Secretary of State for the Home Department* [2007] 2 AC 167; *Belfast City Council v Miss Behavin' Ltd* [2007] 1 WLR 1420; and *Doherty v Birmingham City Council* [2008] 3 WLR 636 [*Doherty*].

[45] *Doherty*, ibid at [135], Lord Mance, quoting from an extra-curial speech given by Lord Hoffmann.

[46] I rely in this paragraph on two articles: M Taggart, 'Reinventing Administrative Law', in N Bamforth and P Leyland (eds), *Public Law in a Multi-Layered Constitution* (Oxford, Hart Publishing, 2003) Ch 12, 311; and Taggart, 'Proportionality', above n 3.

[47] *Watkins v Secretary of State for the Home Department* [2006] 2 AC 395 at 408–09 (Lord Bingham), 418–20 (Lord Rodger) and 423 (Lord Walker).

[48] Ibid at 420.

they have been overridden by statutory implication.[49] Mike argues that 'variable intensity unreasonableness' is really proportionality review,[50] and that proportionality review is intelligible only where Charter or common law fundamental rights have *prima facie* precedence over the public interest; unless they are specially protected, there is no way of balancing a person's private rights against the public's interests. Where no such pre-eminent rights are at stake, Mike believes that the only qualitative ground of review should be *Wednesbury* unreasonableness in its originally strict form. He prefers the more determinate content of the process grounds, and maintains that their growth and the prevalence of a right to reasons mean that there is simply less need to resort to strict 'unreasonableness', because decision-makers' reasons will almost always reveal that there were specific legal errors underlying insanely unreasonable outcomes.

Proper, Genuine, and Realistic Consideration

It is more than 20 years since Gummow J said that decision-makers must give 'proper, genuine and realistic consideration to the merits of the case', suggesting that failure to do so would warrant judicial review.[51] The case report was heavily edited, and several people understandably took his Honour's remarks as a significant expansion of the 'relevant considerations' grounds of review, from process (or check-list) grounds to qualitative review. It later transpired that Gummow J's remarks had been designed only to explain one of the consequences of the judicial review principle that decision-makers should be prepared to give individual consideration to matters that come before them, rather than exercise their discretions according to fixed (and informal) policy rules.[52] But the cat was out of the bag by that stage, and it remains at large despite some fairly severe ridicule.[53] In the longer term, the odds are against the emergence of a separate ground of review for instances of decision-makers failing to give issues 'proper, genuine and realistic consideration'. However, that level of inadequate consideration might end up being seen as amounting either to *Wednesbury* unreasonableness or its off-shoot of 'serious irrationality or illogicality'.[54]

[49] *Electrolux Home Products Pty Ltd v Australian Workers' Union* (2004) 221 CLR 309 at 328–29 and 357–58; and *Evans v New South Wales* (2008) 168 FCR 576 at 593–96.

[50] The standard that dared not speak its name until the enactment of statutory rights charters: Taggart, 'Proportionality' [2008] *New Zealand Law Review* 423.

[51] *Khan v Minister for Immigration, Local Government and Ethnic Affairs* (1987) 14 ALD 291 at 292.

[52] *Broussard v Minister for Local Government and Ethnic Affairs* (1989) 21 FCR 472 at 483.

[53] *Minister for Immigration and Multicultural Affairs v Anthonypillai* (2001) 106 FCR 426 at 442 (Full Federal Court).

[54] See: *Re Real Estate and Business Agents Supervisory Board; Ex parte Cohen* (1999) 21 WAR 158; and *Notaras v Waverly Council* [2007] NSWCA 333. The analogy is with Mason J's view in *Minister for*

One can understand concerns to avoid qualitative review overreaching, but it is difficult to understand how one might defend, say, a tribunal decision that ticked all the requisite 'considerations' boxes, but in a merely cursory way. Like anyone else, administrative decision-makers are bound to make mistakes and fail to grasp the real significance of something. But surely they should at least *try*. As Jordan CJ said in a much-cited passage more than 60 years ago, 'there are mistakes and mistakes'.[55]

Pay Attention and Remain Focused

If 'proper, genuine and realistic' fails to catch on in the land of labels, then it is inevitable that people will start pushing the boundaries of the more established grounds. The High Court offered the tantalising observation in *Dranichnikov v Minister for Immigration and Multicultural Affairs*[56] that an asylum tribunal had breached the procedural fairness rule of natural justice because it had failed 'to respond to a substantial, clearly articulated argument relying on established facts'. The tribunal's mistake had been to misunderstand the nature of the 'particular social group' (in terms of refugee law) that was allegedly being persecuted by the Russian authorities. Mr Dranichnikov had sought to persuade the tribunal to recognise businesspeople who went public with their complaints about officially condoned corruption and violence, whereas the tribunal had thought that he had depicted his 'group' as comprising anyone who made those complaints. The High Court has not yet returned to the subject, and it would be easier to characterise the tribunal's mistake in *Dranichnikov* as an error of law.[57]

If there were to be resistance to *Dranichnikov*'s stretch of procedural fairness into a qualitative review ground, another tactic might sometimes be available. The tribunal in *NAIS v Minister for Immigration and Multicultural and Indigenous Affairs*[58] had conducted two oral hearings roughly 3½ years apart, and then taken

Aboriginal Affairs v Peko-Wallsend Ltd (1986) 162 CLR 24 that *Wednesbury* is the appropriate review ground where the complaint is not that a mandatory consideration was entirely overlooked, but that it was given inadequate consideration.

[55] *Ex parte Hebburn Ltd; Re Kearsley Shire Council* (1947) 47 SR (NSW) 416 at 420.

[56] (2003) 197 ALR 389 at [24], Gummow and Callinan JJ. Hayne J agreed at [95]. Gleeson CJ dissented on the facts, but not on the legal principles.

[57] The case commenced in both the Federal Court and the High Court in the days of a bifurcated review process. Gummow and Callinan JJ suggested that 'error of law' may well have been a statutory ground available in the Federal Court, but it was more trouble than it was worth to pursue that possibility: (2003) 197 ALR 389 at [33]. *Wednesbury* unreasonableness was unavailable in the Federal Court when Mr Dranichnikov commenced suit. Failing to give thought to relevant and mandatory considerations was not a ground in its own right in the Federal Court, although *Minister for Immigration and Multicultural Affairs v Yusuf* (2001) 206 CLR 323 said that it could be repackaged in the guise of two available grounds, namely, that the decision-maker 'did not have jurisdiction', and that the decision was not 'authorised': ss 476(1)(b) and 476(1)(c) respectively of the *Migration Act* 1958 (Cth). Those provisions have since been repealed as part of the unwinding of the scheme for a bifurcated review process.

[58] (2005) 228 CLR 470.

another year to deliver its decision. That decision depended to a considerable extent on a comparative assessment of the demeanour of witnesses at the two hearings without, it seems, resort to contemporaneous notes or tapes. The mistake in *Dranichnikov* had been that the tribunal did not listen closely enough. The tribunal's mistake in *NAIS* was that it very probably forgot what it heard; it had 'disabled' itself from an opportunity to consider the evidence, which was just as much a breach of procedural fairness as if it had denied the asylum-seeker an opportunity to present evidence.[59]

There is considerable uncertainty as to how one might apply the rulings in *Dranichnikov* and *NAIS*. Even though the tribunals' errors were characterised in procedural terms, they raise questions of degree that amount to questions as to the quality of the decision-makers' reasoning processes. In each case, the court took care to emphasise that it was intervening only because the errors were extreme; momentary inattention (*Dranichnikov*) or forgetfulness on a less extreme scale (*NAIS*) would not have warranted judicial review. That is entirely appropriate; otherwise, the court would indeed be engaged in a full appeal process. What is intriguing, however, is why the court thought it necessary to dress up its qualitative review in the garb of process – substance disguised as process, in Martinez' terms.

It will be recalled that in order to outflank a legislative restriction on Federal Court review for *Wednesbury* unreasonableness, the High Court gave a new label to reasonableness review where the subject matter of challenge was a decision-maker's 'judgment' (or 'satisfaction') as to factual issues. When the challenged decision is a matter of judgment, rather than an exercise of 'pure discretion', there will be review for 'serious irrationality or illogicality'. Even there, two judges emphasised that they were reviewing a reasoning process, rather than measuring the tribunal's factual conclusions against the whole of the evidence, and one of those judges went so far as to italicise the distinction.[60] There was a semblance of credibility to their characterisation. Speaking in overall terms, there was ample evidence to support the tribunal's findings. However, the challenger's complaints were that the tribunal had given no credence to his corroborating witnesses because it had determined prematurely that he was a complete liar, and that it had made that determination without considering that his evidence was corroborated. At a stretch, one *might* say that these were 'process' complaints; but they are more easily characterised as qualitative complaints.

[59] Ibid at 526, Callinan and Heydon JJ.

[60] *Applicant*, above note 27 at [7] (Gleeson CJ), and [132]-[132] and [146] (Kirby J, with the italics at [132]).

Federal Court Resists Variable Intensity

Australia's Federal Court has refused to treat *Wednesbury* unreasonableness (and its off-shoot of review for serious irrationality or illogicality) as variable standards whose intensity increases in the face of threats to fundamental rights or freedoms.[61] It prefers to wait for the green light from the High Court. To be fair, the Federal Court has acknowledged that the application of *Wednesbury* unreasonableness and 'serious irrationality' will 'always be a matter of degree',[62] but that was probably not to be understood as the equivalent of treating unreasonableness as a floating standard of review, to be varied according to the gravity of the context. The overwhelming bulk of Australian decisions treats *Wednesbury* unreasonableness as the last resort of desperate counsel; to be *that* unreasonable, the impugned decision must have been quite mad.

The Federal Court's reasons were rooted in precedent. Fundamental human rights and freedoms typically underlie most of the litigation involving asylum claims. Those claims have dominated the High Court's judicial review case-load in recent years, without any clear indication from that source that the standards are variable. Not only that, but the English precedents for using *Wednesbury* with heightened scrutiny could be put down to the effect of the *European Convention on Human Rights*, and latterly to the incorporation of that convention into UK law.

Mike's 'exceptionalism' article suggests that the Federal Court's position was unduly cautious, but that court has far less room for manouevre than the High Court, whose judicial review precedents seem to have considerably longer shelf-lives than those from the highest courts in New Zealand, England, and Canada. I discuss below a new development in Australia's precedent system, a development that some predict will make it extremely difficult for a State appeal court to disagree with the decision of any mid-level appellate court somewhere else in the federation.[63] If that is correct, then only the High Court can depart from the Federal Court's position.

[61] See: *SZADC v Minister for Immigration and Multicultural and Indigenous Affairs* [2003] FCA 1497 at [23]–[24]; *SHJB v Minister for Immigration and Multicultural and Indigenous Affairs* (2003) 134 FCR 43; and *STKB v Minister for Immigration and Multicultural and Indigenous Affairs* [2004] FCAFC 251.

[62] *SHJB v Minister for Immigration and Multicultural and Indigenous Affairs* (2003) 134 FCR 43 at 50, per Carr, Finn, and Sundberg JJ.

[63] See below, text to n 92.

Disowning Considerations of Justice

Kirby J has long been the High Court's 'great outsider';[64] in 2007, his Honour dissented in over 40% of the cases in which he participated.[65] His dissents range across most areas and exhibit a number of features. His judicial review judgments became increasingly normative, increasingly angry with outrageous results. Time and again, his judgments accepted doctrine as a general rule, but with the proviso that exceptional cases (he often used the word 'extreme') called for exceptional departures. In his view, the rule of law itself demands these departures. He explained himself thus:[66]

> Our legal system commonly rejects absolute or rigid categories. It does so out of a recognition of the requirement to secure justice in the particular case wherever possible. The residual category of unidentified error in discretionary decisions is such a case. Appellate correction of factual findings that are 'glaringly improbable' or 'inconsistent with facts incontrovertibly established' or 'contrary to the compelling inferences' is another. In administrative law, extreme irrationality and serious illogicality represent yet further examples of the same *genus*. The primary rule remains intact. Courts of appeal and review do not generally disturb discretionary decisions, factual conclusions at trial and administrative evaluations of the facts and merits of a case. But, subject to the Constitution or the applicable legislation, they reserve to themselves the jurisdiction and power to intervene in extreme circumstances. They do this to uphold the rule of law itself, the maintenance of minimum standards of decision-making and the correction of clear injustices where what has occurred does not truly answer to the description of the legal process that the Parliament has laid down.

Kirby J's philosophy is in marked contrast to the majority's need for something more specific than 'extreme'. The High Court's standard reference point[67] in judicial review is a judgment of Brennan J given almost 20 years ago. Its disavowal of a judicial warrant to cure administrative injustice can be read consistently with judgments rendered in comparable jurisdictions, but its very articulation was comparatively unusual two decades ago. Nowadays, the English courts say that they can intervene in cases of administrative 'unfairness and abuse of power', although they admit that:[68]

> The excoriation of these vices no doubt shows that the law's heart is in the right place, but it provides little guidance for the resolution of specific instances.

64 A Lynch and G Williams, 'The High Court on Constitutional Law: the Statistics' (2008) 31 *University of New South Wales Law Journal* 238 at 246.

65 Ibid at 245, Table D(1). The Gilbert + Tobin Centre of *Public Law*, at the Law Faculty of the University of New South Wales, collects and analyses High Court statistics on an annual basis. The measurement criteria are the same each year. The measurements started for 1998, and all of the annual surveys appear in *University of New South Wales Law Journal*.

66 *Re Minister for Immigration and Multicultural Affairs; Ex parte Applicant S20/2002* (2003) 198 ALR 59 at [161], references omitted.

67 Except for Kirby J: Ibid at [170].

68 *R (Bhatt Murphy) v The Independent Assessor* [2008] EWCA Civ 755 at [28], Laws LJ.

Brennan J said:[69]

> The duty and jurisdiction of the court to review administrative action do not go beyond the declaration and enforcing of the law which determines the limits and governs the exercise of the repository's power. If, in so doing, the court avoids administrative injustice or error, so be it; but the court has no jurisdiction simply to cure administrative injustice or error. The merits of administrative action, to the extent that they can be distinguished from legality, are for the repository of the relevant power and, subject to political control, for the repository alone.
>
> The consequence is that the scope of judicial review must be defined not in terms of the protection of individual interests but in terms of the extent of power and the legality of its exercise. In Australia, the modern development and expansion of the law of judicial review of administrative action have been achieved by an increasingly sophisticated exposition of implied limitations on the extent or the exercise of statutory power, but those limitations are not calculated to secure judicial scrutiny of the merits of a particular case.
>
> There is one limitation, '*Wednesbury* unreasonableness' . . .. Properly applied, *Wednesbury* unreasonableness leaves the merits of a decision or action unaffected unless the decision or action is such as to amount to an abuse of power . . .. The limitation is extremely confined.

This is classic Brennan.[70] The comparativist reader might need reminding that his Honour was one of the key figures in the Australian High Court's so-called 'swing jazz period'[71] of innovation across a range of areas, from the recognition of native title[72] to the radical expansion of the scope and depth of the rules of natural justice. It was abundantly clear to every observer that his Honour was profoundly concerned to avoid 'administrative injustice'. Whilst he *said* that its avoidance was a mere by-product of the implementation of legislative will, it was nevertheless a by-product that his Honour's judgments happily produced with remarkable consistency. He had no difficulty in reconciling judicial review's expansionary tendencies with a rejection of common law constitutionalism; 'increasingly sophisticated' implications were a well-established way around that issue. But he was decidedly uneasy about the proximity of *Wednesbury* unreasonableness to merits review. In this last respect, he has been typical of almost all Australian judges for the last 20 years.

[69] *Attorney-General (NSW) v Quin* (1990) 170 CLR 1 at 35–36.

[70] See the essays in R Creyke and P Keyzer (eds), *The Brennan Legacy: Blowing the Winds of Legal Orthodoxy* (Sydney, Federation Press, 2002).

[71] See G Orr, 'Verbosity and Richness: Current Trends in the Craft of the High Court' (1998) 6 *Torts Law Journal* 1.

[72] *Mabo v Queensland [No 2]* (1992) 175 CLR 1 at 42 per Brennan J: 'The common law does not necessarily conform with international law, but international law is a legitimate and important influence on the development of the common law, especially when international law declares the existence of universal human rights. A common law doctrine founded on unjust discrimination in the enjoyment of civil and political rights demands reconsideration. It is contrary both to international standards and to the fundamental values of our common law . . .'.

No-one could fault the High Court's attention to the fine detail of legal rules, but rules cannot operate by themselves. They need the coordination functions provided by the development and articulation of legal 'principle, policy, values and justice in adjudication'.[73] If one can distinguish between 'bottom up' and 'top down' reasoning, the point is that judicial review needs both,[74] and as importantly, their combination involves no repudiation of the common law's incrementalist method of development.

Mike Taggart's legal passions are as a top-downer, as one would expect of someone who is either a comparativist or a writer of the intellectual history of administrative law scholarship, and he is famous for being both. The High Court, on the other hand, has become increasingly suspicious of the top end, not just in judicial review, but across the board.[75] Its suspicions would surely be valid if directed at a judicial method that is *solely* top down, just as Mike is right to criticise attempts at reasoning that is *solely* bottom up. However, Australia has no judge who even comes close to the parody of operating *only* at the top end. Nor does Australia have any Lord Dennings, cynically boasting of their ability to manipulate judicial review doctrine to suit their predetermined outcome.[76] Those are straw men, and the High Court has something more tangible in mind.

The court's judgments over the last decade or so have become markedly more reluctant to accept invitations to reshape general common law principles, markedly more content to fine-tune the existing common law principles. It is in the nature of any precedent system that change is resisted, and rightly so, but the resistance is stronger now than, say, 20 years ago. This is not a development that applies with equal intensity across all substantive areas,[77] nor even a development that applies consistently to judicial review. It is evident nevertheless, and its most

[73] Taggart, 'Exceptionalism' above n 1 at 7.

[74] S Gageler, 'The Underpinnings of Judicial Review of Administrative Action: Common Law or Constitution?', (2000) 28 *Federal Law Review* 303 at 305; B Selway, 'The Principle Behind Common Law Judicial Review of Administrative Action – the Search Continues' (2002) 30 *Federal Law Review* 217; M Aronson, 'Is the *ADJR Act* Hampering the Development of Australian Administrative Law?' (2004) 15 *Public Law Review* 202 at 203 and 216–19 [Aronson, 'Hampering the Development']; and K Mason, 'What is Wrong with Top-down Legal Reasoning?' (2004) 78 *Australian Law Journal* 574.

[75] See: *McGinty v Western Australia* (1996) 186 CLR 140 at 232, where McHugh J quoted with evident agreement the astonishing proposition that the 'top-downer and the bottom-upper do not meet'; *Roxborough v Rothmans of Pall Mall Australia Ltd* (2001) 208 CLR 516 at 544–45; *Tanwar Enterprises Pty Ltd v Cauchi* (2003) 217 CLR 315 at 324; *Australian Broadcasting Corporation v O'Neill* (2006) 227 CLR 57 at 154–55; and *Lumbers v W Cook Builders Pty Ltd (In Liq)* (2008) 232 CLR 635 at 662.

[76] Lord Denning said in *Pearlman v Harrow School* [1979] QB 56 at 69–70 that he could (and would) manipulate the distinction between jurisdictional and non-jurisdictional errors of law as he pleased. This was a 'cynical dictum' according to D Dyzenhaus, 'The Politics of Deference: Judicial Review and Democracy', in M Taggart (ed), *The Province of Administrative Law* (Oxford, Hart Publishing, 1997) 291.

[77] By four votes to three, *Brodie v Singleton Shire Council* (2001) 206 CLR 512 overturned the old rule that had held highway authorities free of negligence liability for injuries resulting from 'non-feasance'. *Brodie* would have gone the other way if Heydon J had been on the court: JD Heydon, 'Judicial Activism and the Death of the Rule of Law' (2003) 47 *Quadrant* 9 at 20, also published at

noticeable manifestation in the court's judicial review judgments has been an increasingly refined discussion of the common law's existing grounds of review, especially those focused on process. This is in marked contrast to decisions of the highest courts in New Zealand, Canada, and England over the same period, although the contrast in terms of actual outcomes for comparable legal issues is much smaller.

Precedents and the Rule of Law

Mike's 'exceptionalism' article lays a good deal of the blame for the High Court's bottom-up approach on the court's revisionist conception of precedent, and on its 'formalist' legal style.[78] Mike is keeping excellent company. Kirby J agrees that Australia's common law principles of judicial review have stagnated to the point where they risk being so particularist as to lack any underlying principles, although his Honour did not single out 'formalism' as a prime cause.[79] Professor Pierce wrote from the perspective of a political scientist and he, too, emphasised the court's reversion to the legal 'formalism' of Sir Owen Dixon's time.[80] Pierce's grand conclusion was that for a brief period under Mason CJ, the court had become 'legal realists', by which he meant a combination of features, including a more relaxed view of the force of precedent and a willingness to acknowledge the law-making capacity of the appellate judiciary.[81]

I have a vague idea of what most critics mean when they charge the court with the sin of 'formalism', but it is no more vague than the usual charge. Aside from Professor Pierce's criticisms, I suspect that the formalist's principal sins are a lack of style and transparency. The court would have to plead guilty to a lack of style, but that is surely no federal offence. As for opacity, the implication is that the judges hide their real values behind a smoke screen of easily manipulated rules, so that readers cannot see how the rules work out in practice. Unless the charge is of actual dishonesty (which seems unlikely), I think that it is no more difficult to detect an Australian judgment's underlying value preferences than it is to decode the preferences of judgments from elsewhere. In judicial review, at least, the

(2004) 10 *Otago Law Review* 493. Legislation quickly overturned *Brodie* in most Australian jurisdictions; see M Aronson, 'Government Liability in Negligence' (2008) 32 *Melbourne University Law Review* 44 at 73.

[78] Taggart, 'Exceptionalism', above n 1 at 7–8.

[79] *Applicant*, above note 27 at [122] and [156]-[168]. See Aronson, 'Hampering the Development', above note 74.

[80] JL Pierce, *Inside the Mason Court Revolution: the High Court of Australia Transformed* (Durham North Carolina, Carolina Academic Press, 2006).

[81] Ibid at 69–75 and 147.

charge of 'formalism' therefore appears to be just another way of saying that Australia's judicial review grounds should be more directly normative or principles-based.[82]

Pierce saw the High Court during Mason CJ's time as having shifted focus from formalist concerns for legal certainty of doctrine to more pressing concerns for justice, a search for over-arching principles, and an impatience with legal labels and categories that had outlived their usefulness. He saw the post-Mason court as reverting to type. In each case, his reasons were many and complex, but at least one of them does not work for me, at least in administrative law cases. That might be in part because Pierce appeared to equate public law with constitutional law.[83] Tracking the Mason-period rise and post-Mason fall of interveners and *amici curiae* in High Court cases, Pierce said that the court had reverted to a private law model of adjudication, focusing on solving bipolar private disputes. But the fact is that the post-Mason court's non-constitutional judicial review case-load peaked well after Sir Anthony Mason's departure. All the evidence points to the court's unbroken sensitivity in those cases to the pressing interests of non-parties, and an uninterrupted sense that Australia's separation of powers doctrine severely limits the judicial capacity to adopt review grounds that require a balance to be struck in individual cases between private interests and government policies.[84]

There can be no doubting the proposition that the present High Court is more 'formalist' in Pierce's sense than it was in the 1990s, but one must question whether the High Court *ever* had any judges who seriously doubted that they made law.[85] The real debates concern the permissible extent of that exercise and, more importantly, the occasions which call for it. Specifically, opinions differ markedly as to whether greater law-making is called for to break political deadlocks; to modernise language; to amalgamate and reconfigure categories whose separation appears intellectually incoherent; or to produce a better fit between doctrine, function or (dare one say it) community values or expectations. Measured by the responses to these criteria, Pierce may well be right that the court has become noticeably more conservative, although I would not categorise that in terms of a departure from legal realism. Furthermore, I do not

82 See C Forsyth, 'Showing the Fly the Way Out of the Flybottle: the Value of Formalism and Conceptual Reasoning in Administrative Law' (2007) 66 *Cambridge Law Journal* 325.

83 He made no analysis of the High Court's judicial review work in non-constitutional matters. See also JL Pierce, *Inside the Mason Court Revolution,* above n 80 at p 12 for the astonishing proposition that: 'British judges have exercised judicial review over administrative decisions since 1982, but not until [the *Human Rights Act* 1998 (UK)] were they equipped to review the substance of parliamentary statutes.' One reviewer thought that Pierce failed to read the cases and listen to their authors, and failed to draw on his interview material to present a thorough-going analysis of the cultural outlook of the judicial elite: D Robertson, 'Book Review' (2006) 6 *Oxford University Commonwealth Law Journal* 237.

84 M Groves, 'Judicial Review of Administrative Action in the High Court of Australia' (2008) 33 *Queen's Law Journal* 327.

85 See B Tamanaha, 'The Bogus Tale About the Legal Formalists' St John's Legal Studies Research Paper No: 08:0130, posted on ssrn, abstract 1123498.

see Mike's critique as a call for legal realism so much as a call for two things – a greater infusion of normativity, and a conscious effort at doctrinal simplication. As regards simplication, one might compare Australia's judicial review jurisprudence with the judgments and extra-curial contributions of another Kiwi, Lord Robin Cooke, who long argued that judicial review's principles could be boiled down to requiring decision-makers to act 'in accordance with the law, fairly and reasonably'.[86] And Cooke wanted no qualifications of 'reasonably'. Apart from saying that it was never to be equated to *Wednesbury*'s lunacy standard, he thought that it was to be treated as a variable term that could be safely entrusted to the judges.[87]

Whatever meaning one might ascribe to 'formalism', Australia is in the midst of a prolonged and depressingly acrimonious debate amongst the judiciary and the profession about the very nature of legal precedent. The antagonists all swear by the precedent system, but they have radically different takes on what that means. That should come as no surprise, because no-one has ever succeeded in nailing down the precise differences between rationes and dicta. Nor have any judges yet succeeded in banishing their personal values from their judicial role; the idea is nonsense. It is inevitable that one person's attempt to make sense of a mass of precedents will strike some others as unwarranted judicial creativity. Similarly, people have different tolerance levels for doctrinal conflict or even incoherence, and different views as to when it is the judge's role or the legislature's to tackle such problems. None of that is new. What is relatively new (for Australians, at least) is the invective that now accompanies some of the narrower prescriptions for a properly functioning precedent system.[88]

[86] R Cooke, 'The Struggle for Simplicity in Administrative Law', in M Taggart (ed), *Judicial Review of Administrative Action in the 1980s* (Auckland, Oxford University Press, 1986) at p 2.

[87] D Knight, 'Simple, Fair, and Discretionary Administrative Law' (2008) 39 *Victoria University of Wellington Law Review* 99.

[88] McHugh J said that Kirby J's approach to constitutional interpretation would produce 'a 'loose-leaf' copy of the Constitution': *Al-Kateb v Godwin* (2004) 219 CLR 562 at 595. Kirby J was a favourite target of attack, from judges, practitioners, politicians and journalists. His return fire pulled few punches, but he refrained from the *ad hominen* rancour of some of his attackers. He did, however, devote considerable space to establishing that judges make law, as if there were judges and lawyers who thought otherwise. See, eg: M Kirby, 'Judicial Activism: a Riposte to the Counter-Reformation' (2005) 11 *Otago Law Review* 1; and M Kirby, 'Judicial Activism: Power without Responsibility? No, Appropriate Activism Conforming to Duty' (2006) 30 *Melbourne University Law Review* 576. Gleeson CJ was always more discreet about his 'activism'. He wrote several well-polished papers in the style of 'on the one hand, but on the other . . .', but was generally seen as harking back to the Dixonian era of high 'legalism'. See, eg, AM Gleeson: 'Legal Oil and Political Vinegar' [1999] *The Sydney Papers* 51; 'Judicial Legitimacy' (2000) 12 *Judicial Officers' Bulletin* 41; and 'A Core Value' (2007) 8 *Judicial Review* 329 at 340. Crennan J rejected any immediate relevance of Lyotard, Derrida and Foucault without declaring her own position: SM Crennan, 'Scepticism and Judicial Method' (2008) 82 *Australian Law Journal* 169. French CJ doubts the utility of labels such as 'activist'. On the proviso that the judge's methods are broadly accepted by his or her professional audience (and therefore conform to the 'legal model'), he appears to be agnostic about the impact of personal attitudes. See: *NAAV v Minister for Immigration and Multicultural and Indigenous Affairs* (2002) 123 FCR 298 at 410–18; and R French, 'Speaking in Tongues: Courts and Cultures' (2008) 17 *Journal of Judicial Administration* 203 at 208–09.

In a highly personal attack, Justice Heydon famously inveighed against the excesses (as he saw them) of the High Court in its Mason era, accusing it of threatening the rule of law itself.[89] He wanted the court to return to the era of 'strict and complete legalism'[90] that had been its proud boast in the 1950s. He was against 'activist' judges, whose pathologies could be easily identified, but whose names for the most part he left to his readers' fairly easy guesswork. They were the judges whose footnotes pretended to too much erudition, posturing to the legal academy in vain attempts at doctrinal immortality. They were the judges who thought that a legal rule's age might sometimes count as a reason for changing it. They were the judges who would justify changes to bring the common law into conformity with their highly personalised and inevitably fallible senses of the Australian community's 'contemporary needs and aspirations', 'contemporary values', 'relatively permanent values', or 'enduring values'. They were the judges whose judgments contain '[e]xcessive and self-indulgent surveys of the law' better left to the academy, which is itself at fault for downgrading its professional connections and over-emphasising a 'critical analysis of the merits of legal rules'.[91] But above all, and this has been a consistent theme in his judgments since his appointment to the High Court, they were the judges who stated law in broad and general terms. That method of law making should be left to the politicians, who could act on better evidence and advice, and who had a more grounded (less patrician) sense of their communities' values and aspirations.

Heydon J thought that things were worse in the United States, Canada and New Zealand, an interesting list in light of England's absence. Overall, his Honour thought that judges should stick to precedent, defined as the smallest legal proposition necessary to sustain and explain the actual result of a case. Anything more would be no less than an assault on the rule of law, which requires the legal certainty of stable rules.

It is regrettable that what are really only differences of degree concerning acceptable judicial method should have been so exaggerated, let alone portrayed as posing a stark choice between bottom-uppers on the one hand and on the other, an all-out assault on the rule of law. But the bottom-uppers currently have

[89] JD Heydon, 'Judicial Activism and the Death of the Rule of Law' above n 77.

[90] After noting that non-lawyers were prone to misconstrue the nature of the High Court's role so far as it was engaged in determining Constitutional challenges to the validity of legislation or Executive action, Sir Owen Dixon said 'that close adherence to legal reasoning is the only way to maintain the confidence of all parties in Federal conflicts. It may be that the court is thought to be excessively legalistic. I should be sorry to think that it is anything else. There is no other safe guide to judicial decisions in great conflicts than a strict and complete legalism': 'Swearing in of Sir Owen Dixon as Chief Justice' (1952) 85 CLR xi at xiii-xiv. It is a favourite Australian legal pastime to debate what Dixon meant by that passage.

[91] Justice Gummow went a little further; W Gummow, 'Conclusion' in S Degeling and J Edelman (eds), *Equity in Commercial Law* (Sydney, Thomson Lawbook, 2005) 515: '[I]n Australia rather too much modern academic writing is an exercise in the promotion of the writer's view of what the law ought to be without prior analysis of how the law came to be in its present state.'

the High Court ascendancy, even if they do not all subscribe to all of Heydon J's reasoning. A five-member court delivered a joint judgment sharply rebuking the New South Wales Court of Appeal for having taken precedent too lightly.[92] Speaking generally, the overall sin of that court had been to confound the settled expectations of most of the profession by adopting a radically new slant on an area of commercial law. If the common law had to engage in radical change, then that was a job that should in future be left to the High Court. More specifically, the Court of Appeal was said to have erred in a number of ways. These included the discounting of seriously considered High Court dicta on the ground of their age, and according insufficient weight to the contrary views of the intermediate appellate courts of other Australian States. This has been taken as an 'assertion of a High Court monopoly in the essential development of the common law'.[93] That may well be its practical effect. It has always been hard to persuade intermediate appellate courts to overturn one of their own precedents, and now it will be almost as hard to persuade them to disagree with a precedent from a coordinate court in another State or Territory. The Australian precedent system has become more constricted for courts beneath the High Court. If that is correct, we might expect the increments by which Australia's common law evolves to become somewhat smaller.

One of the striking features of the debate about precedent is that some of its protagonists view top-downers as a threat to the rule of law. Of course, there never was a High Court judge who knowingly set out to attack the rule of law; activists and strict and complete legalists alike routinely declare their affection for it. But they are in thrall to different conceptions – the bottom-uppers to the dream of legal certainty that they hope will ensue from small rules tightly defined, the top-downers to the dream of uniting law and justice. To put this another way, their differences are about judicial discretion; broad-based justice principles inevitably allow more discretion to the judges, and that in itself produces uncertainty.

It is fundamental to note that this is not a debate about *administrative* discretion; its sole focus is *judicial* discretion. Bottom-uppers and top-downers alike are perfectly content with broad-based administrative discretions. Indeed, for the purposes of ensuring the constitutional separation of judicial and Executive powers, the fact that a statutory power allows room for policy-based discretions contributes to its characterisation as administrative rather than 'judicial'.[94] The result is a paradox. The bottom-uppers' preference for rules over principles translates in judicial review to an aversion to qualitative review

92 *Farah Constructions Pty Ltd v Say-Dee Pty Ltd* (2007) 230 CLR 89 at 148–52.

93 Mason P, speech on the occasion of his retirement, 30 May 2008, accessed via <www.lawlink.nsw.gov.au>.

94 E Armson, 'Judicial Power and Administrative Tribunals: the Constitutional Challenge to the Takeovers Panel' (2008) 19 *Public Law Review* 91, commenting on *Attorney-General (Cth) v Alinta Ltd* (2008) 242 ALR 1.

grounds, typified by an aversion to *Wednesbury* unreasonableness. The paradox is that the bottom-uppers purchase their idealised legal certainty at the expense of leaving what I have called 'pure discretions' almost entirely unconstrained, and matters of 'judgment' constrained only by process considerations. Clarity of judicial doctrine is achieved at the expense of uncertainty in the administrative arena. Administrative discretion used to be *the* question of administrative law.[95] Process constraints can be only part of the answer.

Evidentiary Consequences of Variable Intensity

Most Australian judges share Brennan J's discomfort[96] with *Wednesbury* unreasonableness. That is because unreasonableness review[97] so obviously requires a merits assessment, albeit a light-touch assessment designed to catch only the most obviously ridiculous decisions. Even the Canadian judges acknowledge that unreasonableness review of the outcome of a decision (as opposed to the processes leading to it) involves a gear-change:[98]

> At this point, judicial review shifts gears. When the applicant for judicial review challenges the substantive *outcome* of an administrative action, the judge is invited to cross the line into second-guessing matters that lie within the function of the administrator. This is controversial because it is not immediately obvious why a judge's view of the reasonableness of an administrative policy or the exercise of an administrative discretion should be preferred to that of the administrator to whom Parliament or a legislature has allocated the decision, unless there is a full statutory right of appeal to the courts, or it is otherwise indicated in the conferring legislation that a 'correctness' standard is intended.

In Australia, only Kirby J wants to follow the English decision[99] to relax *Wednesbury*'s lunacy standard where human rights or fundamental freedoms are at risk, and the Federal Court understandably prefers to leave that issue to the High Court.[100] Apart from its reluctance to create a precedent, the Federal Court's most telling reason was the forbidding quantity of evidence that the challenger wanted the court to examine:[101]

> Counsel for the appellant then took us through, mainly by reference to detailed written submissions, what we think it is fair to describe as a minute examination of the

[95] C Reich, 'The New Property' (1964) 73 *Yale Law Journal* 733; KC Davis, *Discretionary Justice: a Preliminary Inquiry* (Urbana, University of Chicago Press, 1969); and HWR Wade, *Administrative Law* (Oxford, Clarendon Press, 1st ed, 1961) p 1.

[96] *Attorney-General (NSW) v Quin* (1990) 170 CLR 1 at 35–36; see above, text to n 69.

[97] Or its off-shoot of review for serious irrationality or illogicality.

[98] *Dunsmuir*, above n 17 at [130], Binnie J (emphasis in original).

[99] Specifically, *Bugdaycay*, above note 6.

[100] See above, n 61.

[101] *SHJB v Minister for Immigration and Multicultural and Indigenous Affairs* (2003) 134 FCR 43 at 48–49, Carr, Finn and Sundberg JJ.

> evidence which was before the Tribunal and the evidence upon which it relied. The purpose of that examination was said to be to demonstrate that the Tribunal's decision was unreasonable by reference to 'relative reasonable satisfaction'.
>
> The appellant denied that this led to merits review. However, in our opinion, an examination of the last eight pages of the appellant's written submissions exposes it as both an exercise in merits review and a scrutiny of the Tribunal's reasons with an eye keenly attuned to error.

So long as the requisite standard of unreasonableness equates to lunacy, it will usually be obvious; any less-demanding standard requires more work, and it is worth pausing to speculate about the likely additional burden.

It appears from the reports that the challenge to England's ban on gays serving in the armed forces took up 5 hearing days before the Divisional Court and a further 4 before the Court of Appeal.[102] As noted above, the challenge failed, even though the court relaxed *Wednesbury*'s lunacy standard. As is usually the case in England, most (and perhaps all) of the evidence was in affidavit form. It is difficult to determine how much the volume of evidence can be attributed to the relaxation of the lunacy standard, and how much was the result of the court allowing 'fresh evidence' that was not before the Ministry at the time of the challenged decision. There seems to have been no objection to the reception of the fresh evidence, although its recency was said to show that it was reasonable for the Ministry to take more time to consider the issue afresh.[103]

According to Weinberg J: 'Proceedings for judicial review are not, and should not, be regarded as, full-blown trials.'[104] That, however, was said in despair. His Honour had presided over an 11-day hearing which had amounted to a battle between the experts – in this case, between a number of leading economists who were in fundamental disagreement with one another. The parties led mountains of affidavit evidence (some of it 'fresh' in the sense that it was not before the original decision-maker)[105] and conducted a good deal of cross-examination. His Honour frankly acknowledged that some of the more abstruse mathematical modelling left him completely bamboozled,[106] and it seems reasonably clear that he took comfort in the fact that *Wednesbury*'s lunacy standard excused him from having to improve his maths.[107]

[102] *R v Ministry of Defence; Ex parte Smith* [1996] QB 517.

[103] [1996] QB 517 at 558.

[104] *Australian Retailers Association v Reserve Bank of Australia* (2005) 148 FCR 446 at 596. Mason CJ said much the same thing in *Australian Broadcasting Tribunal v Bond* (1990) 170 CLR 321 at 341, in the context of comparing fact review in a merits appeal tribunal with judicial review.

[105] There is a strong case to be made against the reception of evidence that is 'fresh' in that sense, although I accept Weinberg J's criticism that I went too far in previously maintaining that fresh evidence is 'never' received: *Australian Retailers Association*, ibid at 584–85. See now Aronson et al, *Judicial Review* at [4.355]-[4.365].

[106] *Australian Retailers Association v Reserve Bank of Australia* above n 104 at 569–70.

[107] Ibid at 585.

I suspect that oral evidence is taken more frequently in Australia's judicial review litigation than in England's, even though the latter's judicial review standards demand more of government. Even so, lengthy factual disputes are not meant to be a feature of Australia's judicial review cases. There is always some formal evidence, showing what was decided, and possibly how the decision was reached. Beyond that, however, the evidence should be limited because the grounds are limited. Judicial review is not about proving 'errors' per se, nor about proving factual errors per se. In Australia, at least, it is certainly not about falsifying the decision-maker's factual assumptions or conclusions by adducing evidence in contradiction that was not before the decision-maker.[108] That usually leaves limited room for evidence, but the potential for more evidence must expand as the grounds of review expand.

Pushing the Boundaries

Squeezing the precedent system is a bit like squeezing a tube of toothpaste – something is bound to come out, if not at the top, then from a burst seam. I have already noted the attempts in the leading case to characterise review for serious irrationality as focusing on process, not outcome.[109] In Martinez' terms, that was substance disguised as process. That is not the only distortion caused by the reluctance to engage openly with the qualitative grounds of review. Martinez spoke of 'process as signalling', whereby a court might issue some fairly strong signals on a substantive matter at the same time as stating that it will not formally resolve the debate. The High Court does a lot of signalling,[110] although none so far as to whether unreasonableness review is a standard of variable intensity. The Federal Court is understandably more cautious, but there has been more spilt toothpaste of late, and some of the cases seem to be pushing the boundaries that rope off qualitative review.

The pressure in the Federal Court is greatest in cases challenging decisions of the Refugee Review Tribunal, which has had to churn through the cases under

[108] The position might be otherwise in England: *E v Secretary of State for the Home Department* [2004] QB 1044. Section 5(3)(b) of the *Administrative Decisions (Judicial Review) Act* 1977 (Cth) provides a review ground not found in Australia's common law, namely, that the challenged decision was 'based … on the existence of a particular fact, and that fact did not exist'. The High Court has read that ground very narrowly, but its exact meaning remains unclear: *Minister for Immigration and Multicultural Affairs v Rajamanikkam* (2002) 210 CLR 222.

[109] See above, n 60.

[110] *Re Minister for Immigration and Multicultural and Indigenous Affairs; Ex parte Lam* (2003) 214 CLR 1 signalled the death of *Minister for Immigration and Ethnic Affairs v Teoh* (1995) 183 CLR 273 without formally overruling it, and signalled its refusal to tread the English path of enforcing substantive legitimate expectations (as in *R v North and East Devon Health Authority; Ex parte Coughlan* [2001] QB 213), once again, without formally deciding the issue. *Farah Constructions Pty Ltd v Say-Dee Pty Ltd* (2007) 230 CLR 89 signalled the rejection of proposals to replace or extend the rule in *Barnes v Addy* (1874) LR 9 Ch App 244, whilst castigating the court below (see above, n 92) for having entertained the possibility.

enormous time constraints. Three examples will suffice. The tribunal in one case got an asylum-seeker's nationality right in its initial recital of the claim; he was from Pakistan. Further on in its reasons statement, however, the tribunal said that the appellant was Indonesian, and it concluded by saying that it was safe to return him to China. The court overturned the decision, largely on the basis that the Tribunal had failed to take a mandatory consideration into account.[111] The court summed up the tribunal's relevant obligation thus:[112]

> The obligation to undertake an un-distracted, focussed and deliberative assessment of only those facts and circumstances referrable to the case of the appellant is an essential element of the discharge of the [tribunal's] review function.

That is not a long way from stating the obvious, namely, that the tribunal had paid far too little attention.

In my second example, Weinberg J set aside a tribunal decision because its hypercritical treatment of the applicant's evidence demonstrated a failure to give it proper, genuine and realistic consideration.[113] An asylum claimant had told his story to officials and tribunals on seven different occasions over the space of four years, and the tribunal concluded that the claimant had changed his story on each occasion. Weinberg J said that the tribunal was plainly wrong in detecting some of the alleged differences between the claimant's various statements. Also, the tribunal did not explicitly acknowledge that the passage of time might have provided an innocent explanation for differences of historical recall. None of those errors by themselves would have warranted intervention, but their totality showed that the tribunal had committed a jurisdictional error, whether that be characterised as considering impermissible factors or failing to take account of mandatory considerations, or failing to give proper, genuine and realistic consideration to the claim, or breach of natural justice. His Honour acknowledged that the courts generally cannot intervene for mere factual error, but added:[114]

> However, every case must be considered in the light of its own particular circumstances, and there comes a point at which it may fairly be said that the tribunal has not discharged its statutory function.

That bears a remarkable resemblance to variable qualitative review.

The tribunal in another case had rejected a written witness statement because it was still in draft; its maker had to have its translation double-checked by a certified interpreter before signing it, and that was taking some time to arrange in Albania. The court overturned the decision on a number of grounds, one of them being that the tribunal's approach to its fact-finding functions had been so slap-dash as to show that it had failed to understand its fact-finding role.[115]

[111] *SZIFI v Minister for Immigration and Multicultural and Indigenous Affairs* (2007) 238 ALR 611.
[112] Ibid at [44], Greenwood J.
[113] *SZIIF v Minister for Immigration and Citizenship* (2008) 102 ALD 366.
[114] Ibid at [66].
[115] *SBLF v Minister for Immigration and Citizenship* [2008] FCA 1219.

Conclusion

I do not understand anyone to assert that a 'reasonableness' concept could be anything *other* than variable in its application. Even if the standard were to remain the same, its application would necessarily vary enormously according to context. The real debate about variability in the context of judicial review is whether unreasonableness review should be more demanding of government where decision-making poses risks to a subject's most fundamental rights and freedoms than would otherwise be the case.

Australian judicial review doctrine is indeed exceptionalist, particularly in its failure so far to have countenanced any relaxation in the strictness of unreasonableness review. It has some good arguments. Judicial review does 'shift gears'[116] when it engages in qualitative review. If used unwisely, qualitative review can be a slippery slope towards merits review. The problem can usually be avoided because decision-makers arriving at extremely unreasonable conclusions have likely made reviewable process errors of one sort or another. Qualitative review is likely to require more work from the judge and allow for the reception of more evidence.

Nevertheless, it is submitted that the stronger arguments go the other way. Like countries elsewhere, Australia already has overtly qualitative review grounds, even though they are more rarely used. The resistance to the qualitative grounds plays out in the stretching of the process grounds of review in ways which are scarcely credible. Above all, one must question the credibility of refusing review where decision-makers entrusted with the power to make important decisions with enormous and serious ramifications on a person's future have simply not tried. The administrative state has long entrusted tribunals and bureaucrats with far-reaching powers on the assumptions that they will be exercised diligently and carefully. Judicial review can perform a useful role in ensuring that those assumptions are fulfilled.

[116] *Dunsmuir*, above n 17 at [130], Binnie J.

3

The Legitimacy of the Rule of Law

DAVID DYZENHAUS[1]

> Plainly these features of control by rule are closely related to the requirements of justice which lawyers term principles of legality. Indeed one critic of positivism has seen in these aspects of control by rules, something amounting to a necessary connection between law and morality, and suggested that they be called 'the inner morality of law'. Again, if this is what the necessary connection of law and morality means, we may accept it. It is unfortunately compatible with very great iniquity.
>
> HLA Hart, The Concept of Law[2]

[1] The argument of this chapter has been forged in discussions over the years with a 'simple' common lawyer, Mike Taggart, starting with the detailed comments he gave me in 1989 on the doctoral thesis that became my first book, through the seminar on the rule of law we taught in Auckland in 2002 and our latest joint essay, 'Reasoned Decisions and Legal Theory', and until his characteristic mix of supportive, subversive, corrosive and funny (in some respects unrepeatably so) comments on an essay I wrote on global administrative law earlier this year. Over this period, Mike became, without any intention of taking this role, my most important intellectual mentor. Not only has he been a constant source of frank, careful, and insightful critique always backed by an encyclopedic legal knowledge, he has also often suggested the ideas for my own research (and for conferences for me to organise).

The chapter explores an idea that Mike is both attracted to and deeply sceptical of—that the law necessarily contains moral resources. It began as a paper in 2006 for the Colloquium in Legal Philosophy run by Ronald Dworkin and Thomas Nagel at New York University's Faculty of Law. I am grateful to them and also to Jeremy Waldron for the privilege of being subjected to a several hour-long, withering critique. I also relied on my own Law Faculty's profound resources through presenting the initial draft of the paper to a Faculty Workshop and to a Graduate Student Workshop. I thank in particular Mary Liston, Arthur Ripstein, Horacio Spector, and Ernie Weinrib for illuminating conversations at these events and Rueban Balasubramaniam, Jonathan Horne, Robert Leckey, Cheryl Misak, Sean Rehaag and Lars Vinx for written comments. I also acknowledge my most recent debt to Mark Bennett and Kristen Rundle for many discussions of this chapter's general themes.

[2] HLA Hart, *The Concept of Law* (Oxford, Clarendon Press, 2nd edition, 1994) 207 [Hart, *Concept of Law*].

Introduction

THE RULE OF law or legality[3] is much in the news for 9/11 reasons. Faced with the threat of international terror, governments have used law to reduce or to do away with the legal protections associated with the rule of law, protections embedded in the ideas of natural justice and due process. Critics of such measures often rely on the intuition that the rule of law is a moral good. Government in accordance with the rule of law is legitimate so that the measures are unjustified. But many philosophers of law consider this intuition misleading. That a government complies with the rule of law is not a sufficient condition of legitimacy because government under the rule of law is compatible with evil, indeed such compliance can make evil worse. Nor is compliance a necessary condition, because it might be impossible to achieve certain worthwhile political aims within the scope of the rule of law. This position is associated with the tradition of legal positivism and its Separation Thesis that there is no necessary connection between law and morality.[4]

I will argue that positivists are wrong: the rule of law is made of principles which amount to what Lon L Fuller called an 'internal' or 'inner' 'morality of law'.[5] Hence, government under the rule of law is always to some significant degree legitimate. In making this argument, I hope to show that one can take forward the debate between legal positivists and Ronald Dworkin, their leading contemporary critic. Dworkin's argument is based on the role of judges in deciding 'hard cases' in which there is reasonable disagreement about what the law requires. According to positivists, that argument founders because it confuses the lawyer's parochial question, 'What does the law of my legal order require?', with the philosopher's general and conceptual question, 'What is law?'[6] My discussion suggests that principles of the rule of law provide a bridge between philosophical questions about the nature of law and lawyerly questions about the law. That bridge deflects the charge of parochialism because it helps to explain why immanent in particular legal orders are moral resources on which judges may and should rely in deciding hard cases.

[3] I treat these as synonyms.

[4] It has become fashionable among legal positivists to assert that no member of their camp has ever held to such an absurd idea as the Separation Thesis. This is not the forum to try to show the absurdity of that assertion or that the thesis itself is far from absurd. I do address these issues briefly through my discussion in the last section of the place of a 'transmission' account of legality in legal positivism and more fully in David Dyzenhaus 'The Genealogy of Legal Positivism' (2004) 1 *Oxford Journal of Legal Studies* 39 [Dyzenhaus, 'The Genealogy'].

[5] LL Fuller, *The Morality of Law*, revised edition (New Haven, Conn, Yale University Press, 1969) [Fuller, *Morality of Law*].

[6] For a recent extended statement of this claim, see J Gardner, 'The Legality of Law', (2004) 17 *Ratio Juris* 168.

'Law' v 'The Law'

According to positivists, a law is a law of a legal system if it would be certified as such by whatever criteria for validity exist in that legal system. In 1961, Hart proposed that we understand such criteria as located in a rule of recognition,[7] the 'ultimate'[8] rule of a legal system. Because the rule is ultimate, its existence cannot be certified by any other rule. Hart argued that it is manifested in the practice of those officials who have authority to make determinations of validity and who perpetuate that practice because they accept the rule of recognition as a 'critical common standard of behaviour.'[9] On this account, while each legal system will have a rule of recognition, these rules will be different in terms both of their complexity and of the kinds of criteria of validity they prescribe. A legal order in which there is a tradition of Parliamentary supremacy has a different rule of recognition from one that has an entrenched bill of rights. Not only is the content of the rule of recognition contingent on the history of the particular legal order, but so also is the content of its laws. An entrenched bill of rights can help to guard against the enactment of morally obnoxious law, but how it is interpreted will depend to a large extent on contingent features—the character of the judges, the mood of the times, and so on.

In sum, since the law of a particular legal system is simply the law that is valid by the criteria of that system, and since the moral content of that law is determined by contingent features of the society in which the legal system is to be found, any claim that there is a necessary connection between law and morality fails. Moreover, since in any particular society the law that rules will be the valid law of its legal system, any connection between the rule of law and moral goodness is contingent on the content of the law, just as the connection between law and morality is contingent in this way.

Thus, in 'Positivism and the Separation of Law and Morals',[10] Hart claimed that John Austin had shown that there is no connection between particular laws and morality. He quoted the passage in which Austin gives the example of a man who is convicted of a crime punishable by death when the 'crime' was in fact trivial or even beneficial. The man objects to the sentence that it is 'contrary to the law of God' and therefore invalid. But the 'inconclusiveness' of his reasoning, Austin says, is demonstrated by the 'court of justice' by 'hanging [him] up, in pursuance of the law of which [he had] impugned the validity.'[11]

Hart saw clearly that this kind of objection, *the wicked law objection*, responds only to a claim about a connection between the law (particular valid laws) and

[7] Hart, *Concept of Law*, above n 2 at 94.

[8] Ibid at 105.

[9] Ibid at 117. Hart has 'standards' in the original as he is referring at this point to all secondary rules of which the rule of recognition is but one.

[10] In HLA Hart, *Essays in Jurisprudence and Philosophy* (Oxford, Clarendon Press, 1983) 49.

[11] Ibid at 73.

morality. A different kind of claim is made when the connection is asserted between law understood as referring to legal systems and morality.[12] He suggested that one of the reasons why this second kind of claim seems plausible is that we might 'attach to a legal system the minimum meaning that it must consist of general rules.' That brings in the principle of treating like cases alike, which is '*one* essential element of the concept of justice.' Such justice is

> justice in the administration of the law, not justice of the law. So there is, in the very notion of law consisting of general rules, something which prevents us from treating it as if morally it is utterly neutral, without any necessary contact with moral principles. Natural procedural justice consists therefore of those principles of objectivity and impartiality in the administration of the law ... and which are designed to ensure that rules are applied only to what are genuinely cases of the rule or at least to minimize the risks of inequalities in this sense.[13]

So there is more to the rule of law than the rule of particular valid laws; there are also the principles that seem to be present by necessity in every legal order.

Hart, however, did not think that the Separation Thesis is impugned through recognising justice in the administration of the law. His reason was that 'a legal system that satisfied these minimum requirements might apply, with the most pedantic impartiality as between the persons affected, laws which were hideously oppressive ...',[14] a point which he repeated in the epigraph to this chapter. His view was that the procedural rules of the administration of justice do not constrain the substance or the content of the positive law; and so the wicked law objection serves to deal with the claim about a connection between legal systems and morality or law in general, since with enough wicked laws we get a wicked legal system.

Exactly the same point is the burden of Joseph Raz's response to Fuller, the most important proponent of the claim that a connection between law and morality emerges out of an understanding of the internal morality of legality. Fuller argued that inherent in legal order are the principles of generality, publicity, non-retroactivity, intelligibility, non-contradiction, possibility of compliance, constancy through time, and congruence between declared rule and official action.[15] In perhaps the most influential account of the rule of law of the last 50 years Raz responds, following Hart, that Fuller is right that there are principles intrinsic to the idea of government under the rule of law. But Raz argues that these are not moral principles—they merely make the law into a more effective instrument.[16]

[12] Ibid at 78.

[13] Ibid at 81.

[14] Ibid.

[15] Fuller, *Morality of Law*, above n 5 at 33–91, and the section replying to critics at 187–253.

[16] J Raz, 'The Rule of Law and Its Virtue', in J Raz, *The Authority of Law: Essays on Law and Morality* (Oxford, Clarendon Press, 1979) 210 [Raz, 'The Rule of Law'].

It is worth recalling that Dworkin, in one of his earliest publications, joined in this kind of critique of Fuller.[17] Moreover, in his later work, Dworkin seems to equate fairness with either the democratic reasons that require judicial deference to legislative intent[18] or with due process, which for him is a matter of finding the 'right balance between accuracy and efficiency in enforcing some part of the law.'[19] So we find here a point of agreement between Dworkin and the positivists. The process of making law and of justice in the administration of the law is neutral with respect to substance or content. Hence, if a connection between law and morality is to be established, one should look elsewhere than the law-making process and the administration of justice. The natural candidate is the content of the law.[20] As I will now show, the focus of legal philosophy on that candidate has resulted in what positivists regard as their victory.

Victory in Philosophy of Law

Dworkin argues that a connection between law and morality emerges through an understanding of the adjudication of hard cases.[21] Judges do and should decide such cases through finding a conclusion to the legal question that not only fits with relevant legal materials, but also shows them in their best possible light. In this way, judges seek to show that their interpretation supplies the best possible justification for the coercion of the law.

Positivists think that the wicked law objection suffices to deal with Dworkin's position. Even if for the sake of argument one grants Dworkin's description of hard cases, whether the best possible justification is also moral will depend on the history of the legal order. For example, in the apartheid legal order where the

[17] R Dworkin, 'Philosophy, Morality, and Law: Observations Prompted by Professor Fuller's Novel Claim' (1965) 113 *University of Pennsylvania Law Review* 668 [Dworkin, 'Philosophy, Morality, and Law']. Dworkin did suggest that the more pertinent of Fuller's arguments are those about what Dworkin called (his emphasis) '*invasions* of legality'; at 682. My argument to come explores the consequences of what happens when there is what Dworkin referred to as a 'recognizable shift in the geometry of our concepts'; at 683. Dworkin has adverted to this idea in later work, when responding to the wicked law objection. Thus, he has said that he would be prepared to conclude that a legal order could cease to be a legal order. See R Dworkin, 'A Reply', in M Cohen (ed), *Ronald Dworkin & Contemporary Jurisprudence* (London, Duckworth, 1984) 258–60.

[18] R Dworkin, *Law's Empire* (London, Fontana, 1986) 340–1, 364–5 [Dworkin, *Law's Empire*].

[19] Ibid at 166–7. Though see R Dworkin, 'Principle, Policy, Procedure', in Dworkin, *A Matter of Principle* (Cambridge, Mass, Harvard University Press, 1985) 72 at 101–3 [Dworkin, *Matter of Principle*].

[20] See Dworkin's response to J Waldron, 'The Rule of Law as a Theatre of Debate' in J Burley (ed), *Dworkin and his Critics* (Oxford, Blackwell, 2004) 319 at 387–8. Waldron argues that Dworkin's conception of the rule of law is procedural because of Dworkin's emphasis on the way in which the content of the law is produced by debate about what the law requires, on its best interpretation. Dworkin responds by saying that the content of all the law, including procedural rules, is to be settled by such debate. In other words, he seems to resist the suggestion that his theory of law should be proceduralised.

[21] Dworkin, *Law's Empire*, above n 18.

statute book was full of particular racist laws, the best possible justification in any hard case about the interpretation of a particular racist law was, positivists suggest, likely one that advanced the cause of racism. Dworkin's position is thus said to be viable only in legal orders which happen to have a preponderance of morally good particular laws.[22]

At most, positivists conclude, Dworkin offers a theory of adjudication, a theory of how judges should decide hard cases, and not a theory of law. Moreover, that theory is parochial in two respects. It is institutionally parochial in that it is most plausible in legal orders where judges have a central role, including judicial review of statutes, so that there is the possibility to declare invalid morally obnoxious statutes. It is morally parochial in that it is tied to liberal democratic political orders in which there is an overlap between the value content of the positive law and liberal democratic morality. In sum, Dworkin does not offer an account of law, but of how judges should interpret the positive law of liberal democratic legal orders, especially those orders in which there is an entrenched bill of rights.

If positivists are right in this claim, it could be and is said that the problem in the debate between positivists and Dworkin is that they are not in fact engaged in debate. Positivists are interested in answering the philosopher's question, 'What is law?', while Dworkin is interested in answering the lawyer's question, 'How best should judges in this jurisdiction decide hard cases?'

Moreover, when positivists grant Dworkin's account of hard cases, they do so only in order to argue that Dworkin's account fails on its own terms to establish a necessary link between law and morality. Their main and analytically distinct response arises out of their claim that in hard cases, judges have to exercise a quasi-legislative discretion. Law is a system of rules and if the rules do not determine a result in a case because there is more than one reasonable answer to the question of law, judges have to exercise a discretion that cannot, by definition, be determined, by the law. Dworkin has emphasised that the claim about judicial discretion is at odds with the fact that judges regard their decisions in hard cases as fully determined by law, where law includes 'the law', that is, the relevant legal materials, and 'law', a more abstract understanding of the principles that give point to the exercise of justification.[23] But because of the alleged contingency of his theory of adjudication, the choice in philosophy of law seems a Hobson's one between a parochial theory and a descriptive general one, even if the latter requires us to discount judges' own understanding of their practice. As I will now show, the terms of debate change subtly once one enters the terrain of the rule of law.

[22] J Raz, 'Authority, Law, and Morality' in Raz, *Ethics in the Public Domain: Essays in the Morality of Law and Politics* (Oxford, Clarendon Press, 1994) 194 at 208 [Raz, "Authority, Law"].

[23] Dworkin, *Law's Empire*, above n 18.

The Rule of Law and Rule by Law

On the positivist distinction between philosophical and legal inquiry, the question 'What is the rule of law?' looks philosophical rather than lawyerly. It is about 'law' not 'the law'. Of course, if one rejects this distinction, one might suppose that the route to answering 'What is the rule of law?' is via 'What is the rule of *the* law?', and Dworkin has given the impression at times that there is little more to an understanding of the rule of law than getting right what we have when the law rules.[24] We have the rule of law when judges interpret the law correctly, in accordance with the moral principles that by hypothesis underpin the positive law of their jurisdiction.

Positivists do not equate the rule of law with the rule of the law. Put differently, they accept that there is a difference between government by law and government in accordance with the rule of law. The former exists when all acts of public power have a basis in some positive legal authorization to act. The latter exists when public power in addition to being authorised has to be exercised in accordance with principles which together make up the rule of law. So, for example, Raz says that the rule of law is 'an ideal', a 'standard to which the law ought to conform but which it can and sometimes does violate most radically and systematically.'[25] Raz also agrees with Fuller that no legal system could violate 'altogether' 'most of the principles of the rule of law.'[26]

Does this agreement lead to the conclusion that positivists now accept at least a weak version of natural law through the idea that rule of law contrasts favourably with the arbitrary rule of men? It might seem so, because Raz uses as the epigraph to his essay FA Hayek's famous description of the rule of law:

> stripped of all its technicalities this means that government in all its actions is bound by rules fixed and announced beforehand—rules which make it possible to foresee with fair certainty how the authority will use its coercive powers in given circumstances, and to plan one's individual affairs on the basis of this knowledge.[27]

Hayek's claim is that the rule of law requires that any exercise of public power has to be authorised in advance by a clear or a determinate law and that makes it possible for individuals to plan ahead, which is a moral good.

[24] Consider, for example, Dworkin's description of his 'rights' conception of the rule of law as not distinguishing between the 'rule of law and substantive justice'; R Dworkin, 'Political Judges and the Rule of Law', in Dworkin, *Matter of Principle,* above n 19 at 11–12. In more recent work, Dworkin has started to indicate that the idea of legality has to be taken seriously in its own right, but his treatment of it still, in my view, threatens to collapse the ideal into his account of adjudication. See R Dworkin, 'Hart's Postscript and the Character of Political Philosophy' (2004) 24 *Oxford Journal of Legal Studies* 1 at 23–35 and 'Introduction: Law and Morals' and 'The Concepts of Law' in *Justice in Robes* (Cambridge, Mass, Harvard University Press, 2006) 1 and 223.

[25] Raz, 'The Rule of Law', above n 16 at 223.

[26] Ibid with the addition in n 11 at 223.

[27] FA Hayek, *The Road to Serfdom* (Chicago, University of Chicago Press, 1944) 80.

Raz accepts this claim and adds that the ability to plan, and thus the rule of law, is essential to liberal democratic society. But he also says that a society can have the rule of law and be neither democratic nor liberal.[28] For example, in a slave-owning society in which the institution of slavery is meticulously created and regulated by the law of a despot, everyone (presumably the slaves as well) can plan their lives with great certainty. Indeed, such a society might be morally worse than a slave-owning society which is not so strictly governed, because in the less ruly society slaves might find more space to make their lives somewhat less oppressive.[29]

Raz concludes that the rule of law is a political ideal, but one that competes with others that may not be realisable through the rule of law. It does not guarantee moral goodness and it is compatible with great evil. It does reduce arbitrariness, but reduction of arbitrariness is not necessarily a moral good and can make things morally worse. In addition, Raz argues that while the rule of law does reduce arbitrariness, the arbitrariness it reduces is the arbitrariness that law itself—rule by law—makes possible through facilitating the concentration of power in the hands of those with authority to make law.[30]

The upshot is, in my view, bewildering. On the one hand, there is the apparent concession that law has to conform at least to some extent to the rule of law and that such conformity is a moral good. Rule by law requires some degree of conformity with the rule of law, a political and moral ideal. It follows that there is a necessary though rather weak connection between law and morality. On the other hand, there are the claims that the ideal has to compete with others that cannot be realised in conformity with the rule of law, and that conformity with it can make life morally worse for those subject to it. It follows that there is no necessary connection between law and morality.[31]

The root of this problem resides in the fact that at the same time as Raz seems to make a concession to Fuller, he withdraws it by adding that the principles of the rule of law follow Hart's conception of law, rather than Fuller's. The principles are derived from the 'basic intuition' that, 'if the law is to be obeyed *it must be capable of guiding the behaviour of its subjects*.'[32] Raz's list is: All laws should be prospective, open and clear; laws should be relatively stable; the making of particular laws (particular legal orders) should be guided by open, stable, clear, and general rules; the independence of the judiciary must be guaranteed; the principles of natural justice must be observed; the courts should

[28] Raz, 'The Rule of Law', above n 16 at 211.

[29] In later work, Hayek seemed to rethink this aspect of his argument. He suggested that delegated authority could conform sufficiently with the rule of law as long as it could be 'controlled by the possibility of a review of the substance of the decision by an independent court'; FA Hayek, *The Constitution of Liberty* (London, Routledge, 1993) 213.

[30] Raz, 'The Rule of Law', above n 16 at 224.

[31] For an illuminating treatment of this tension in legal positivism, see N Simmonds, *Law as a Moral Ideal* (Oxford, Oxford University Press, 2007) 69 (ch 3 'Evil Regimes and the Rule of Law').

[32] Raz, 'The Rule of Law', above n 16 at 214–19.

have review powers over the implementation of the other principles; the courts should be easily accessible; the discretion of the crime-preventing agencies should not be allowed to pervert the law.[33]

The principles of the rule of law are not then moral principles. Rather, they make the law into a more effective instrument for guiding the action of those subject to the law and the 'virtue' of the rule of law is exhibited through law living up to these principles. That virtue, Raz says, is like the virtue of a sharp knife. Whether it issues in moral goodness or not will depend on the purposes to which the instrument, law or the knife, is put.[34] The rule of law helps to make the law into a better vehicle or instrument for transmitting the actual judgments of those who have authority to make law. It also helps to ensure implementation of those judgments. I will call this the *transmission account* of the rule of law.

As I will now argue, the transmission account fails to support even the principles on Raz's list. Moreover, in seeing that failure we can see why the thought Raz takes from Fuller—that there must be some minimum conformity by law with the rule of law—is, albeit ambiguously, a significant concession to Fuller's claim that there is an internal morality of the rule of law.

Validity and Illegal Law

Hayek of course knew that there have been societies that legalise slavery. Indeed, his arguments about the rule of law were part of a polemic against the welfare or administrative state, which he thought put individuals into a condition akin to serfdom. As he pointed out, the delegation of public power to the officials of the administrative state necessarily gives them discretion over the lives of the individuals subject to their decisions and that discretion is not, in Hayek's view, controllable by law. The administrative state substitutes for the rule of law the rule of administrative officials.

Since Hayek was a proponent of free market capitalism, he equated the rule of law with the preservation of that kind of economic order. For him this equation was justified because any extensive intrusion by the state into the market requires establishing the administrative state and thus the arbitrary rule of administrative officials. This equation leads Raz to a different objection. Although it might be true that to some significant extent state interventions in the market require sacrifices in the rule of law, whether such sacrifices are justified is a question to be settled by political or moral argument, not philosophy of law, for there are political ideals that compete with the rule of law.[35]

However, Hayek's claim about the rule of law and the free market is not well answered by saying, for example, that state interventions in the free market are

[33] Ibid at 214–19.
[34] Ibid at 225–6.
[35] Ibid at 228–9.

justifiable, hence, sacrifices in the rule of law are justifiable. The better answer is that the administrative state can be made subject to the rule of law, just as the state itself is subject to that rule, indeed, has authority as a state only in so far as its exercises of power comply with the rule of law. It is only if one equates the rule of law with the rule of the determinate contents of valid law that there is by definition a sacrifice in the rule of law whenever the positive law does not have a content that tells an official what to do.

On that view of law and its rule, as Hayek rightly saw, the administrative state requires so great a sacrifice in the rule of law that one should conclude that it gives rise to a society no longer governed by law. However, no such sacrifice is required when the rule of law is conceived differently, as rule in accordance with principles of legality that go beyond the idea of law as transmitted content. As long as officials make their decisions in accordance with the principles of the rule of law, and on the basis of a reasonable interpretation of what the substantive law of their regime requires, there is no sacrifice in the rule of law.[36] More importantly, the ideal of the rule of law precludes making any sacrifices of it. It requires not only that the law authorise any official act, but also that the act comply with the rule of law. To suppose that the state can act outside of the rule of law is to give up on the ideal that seeks to ensure that exercises of public authority will be counted as such when and only when they comply with law.

Consider, to begin, two kinds of privative clause, provisions adopted by legislatures to oust or inhibit judicial review of administrative action. General privative clauses are those that say bluntly that judges are not entitled to review the decisions made by the officials who purport to be exercising the powers delegated to them by the statute. What I call 'substantive privative clauses' are provisions that leave intact the judges' authority to review, but explicitly preclude judges from reviewing on particular rule-of-law grounds, for example, on natural justice grounds.

In all Commonwealth legal orders, judges have found creative ways to avoid understanding general privative clauses literally, variations on a theme that parliament, in delegating authority to an official by statute, must intend that the official stay within the limits of his authority. These limits are set not only by the terms of the statute, but also by the principles of the rule of law. Parliament is taken to intend that both sets of limits have to be respected because to think otherwise would be to attribute to it the intention that the officials may act in an arbitrary fashion. A substantive privative clause, however, makes plain an intention that the officials may act arbitrarily, in that judicial review is explicitly excluded on the basis of particular principles of the rule of law.

[36] The idea of reasonable interpretation is what distinguishes this view from Hayek's later view, described in *Constitution of Liberty*. That is, Hayek's view presupposes a correctness standard for judicial review of officials' decisions.

Now these principles are in part the reason why judges have a general review authority.[37] So it might seem that if judges are entitled to sidestep a literal reading of a general privative clause, they should also be entitled to avoid an explicit substantive privative clause. But as a matter of fact, judges have been reluctant to do so and there is no inconsistency in their stance.

In the general privative clause, the legislature sends a mixed message to judges. Their constitutional responsibility is to resolve the problem by applying a presumption that the legislature must be taken to intend its statutes to be governed by legality. That presumption entitles the courts to interpret the privative clause as if the legislature intended it to work other than by excluding either positive or rule-of law limits. But it is another thing to say that when specific limits are explicitly excluded that Parliament did not mean what it said. Judges would have to invalidate such a provision, not sidestep it. That judges seem reluctant or unable to take this step in the absence of the authority of a written constitution shows that a law that is valid by all the criteria of validity of a legal order can survive despite the fact that it is offensive to principles of the rule of law.

Validity's victory over principle fails, however, to show that there is no necessary connection between law and the principles of the rule of law. That conclusion follows only if one equates legality with validity. That judges may have to uphold a substantive privative clause does not exhaust the resources of their legal vocabulary. They can and should point out in their judgments that the statute, although valid, suffers from a deficit of legality: their legislature has chosen to govern outside the reach of the rule of law. They are in effect doing what section 4 of the Human Rights Act (1998) requires judges in the United Kingdom to do by declaring incompatible with the Act statutory provisions that violate its substantive protections. Section 4 simply formalises the requirement that applies to all judges who understand their duty to uphold the rule of law.

Judges who adopt this path force a government with control over legislation to make public its intention to govern free of the rule of law. This result is not trivial. If judges say that because the substantive privative clause is valid, official action under it is thereby in accordance with legality, they confuse legality with validity. That confusion permits the government to claim that it operates under the rule of law, even though it has used a statute as a brute instrument to escape the constraints of such rule. This gap between legality and validity is acknowledged by all those who argue that there are principles intrinsic to the rule of law and that gap is generated by the principles on both Raz's and Fuller's lists. The point about judicial duty stems from the fact that among the principles of the rule of law is that those principles furnish grounds for judicial review. But the

[37] Only in part because the limits that parliament itself set in the statute have also to be observed, as well as written constitutional limits if any, and any limits set by the administrative agency itself, if it has authority to do so.

transmission account of the rule of law mischaracterises what judges do to safeguard their review power when confronted with privative clauses.

As we have seen, Raz's principles of the rule of law are supposed to be derivable from the aim of ensuring that law is applied with the content it in fact has to the legal subject. But in the case of the general privative clause, the judicial duty to interpret statutes in the light of the principles of the rule of law inclines a judge to reinterpret the specific instruction not to review contained in that clause. And in the case of the substantive privative clause, the principles of the rule of law do not help us to gain access to the content of the law in Raz's sense; rather they stand as legality's rebuke to the content the law in fact has.

The problem here is not that law is necessarily rendered incapable of performing its task when that task is conceived as providing a content that can guide the legal subject. It might be that the officials who administer a regime protected from judicial review altogether by a literally interpreted general privative clause, or from review on particular rule-of-law grounds because of a substantive privative clause, develop a consistent practice that permits those subject to the law to know exactly where they stand. For example, individuals of Arab origin who have taken flying lessons and seek to travel by plane on a one-way ticket might know that it is highly likely that they will be detained indefinitely as 'enemy combatants'. Rather, the problem is that the principles of the rule of law outrun a description of the task of law when that task is confined to transmitting content capable of guiding conduct.

This argument establishes that law has to conform to the rule of law more substantially than Raz acknowledges and that even his list of principles is not well explained by the transmission account. It does not yet show that substantial conformity with either that list or another must exhibit a connection with morality. I have not yet argued that a requirement that law to be such must conform substantially to the rule of law means that law is inherently moral. This point brings us back to the wicked law objection—that substantial conformity with the rule of law is compatible with great iniquity and can even make iniquity worse.

However, the Separation Thesis is undermined by a concession that there is a necessary connection between law and the rule of law. That concession becomes especially powerful when it is combined with the principle, which we have seen Raz adopts as one of the principles of the rule of law, that judges should have review powers over officials to check that the other rule of law principles have been observed. For it follows from the principle of judicial review that a judge faced with a statute that seems problematic must try to make it compatible with legality.

Notice how different the problem I just identified for the transmission account of law looks if one's starting point is not the idea of guidance, but Fuller's idea that the rule of law helps to ensure that a relationship of reciprocity exists between ruler and ruled which works in the interests of the latter.[38] On this view, the principles of the rule of law are in the service of the interests of the individual, so that their point is not to help ascertain a predetermined content of the rules of the positive law and to ensure that that content is accurately applied. Rather, the content of positive law is to be ascertained in the light of the principles, guided by the overarching aim of serving the interests of the individual.

Consider in this regard an example from the apartheid legal order, a legal system that we have seen is thought by positivist philosophers to be a refutation of Dworkin's theory because the preponderance of racist law would require judges, on Dworkin's account of adjudication, to further the cause of racism. South Africa's highest court—the Appellate Division—had to interpret a provision in the Group Areas Act, a statute that authorised officials to reserve areas for the exclusive use of one racial group. The areas were designated in ways that greatly favoured the minority white population and the designations were challenged on the ground that the discretion had to be exercised reasonably, that is, in accordance with a principle of rough equality.

The judge who first heard the matter upheld the challenge, holding that the statutory discretion given to officials to set aside areas for residence by one racial group had to be exercised reasonably or in accordance with a principle of equality, so that the areas set aside for whites could not be vastly superior to those set aside for other races.[39] Put differently, he held that the Group Areas Act was a law that applied in very general terms to white and black South Africans. It clearly contemplated that official decisions would be taken that would segregate the racial groups. But the law said nothing about how that segregation was to be implemented, which he took to mean that the legislature must have intended that segregation would take place in a roughly equal fashion.

The Appellate Division held that legislators who initiated the social experiment contemplated by the Group Areas Act must have contemplated that it could be implemented in ways that created vast inequalities.[40] No doubt, as a matter of fact, the court was right. But the question the judge who first heard the matter asked was not how the statute was best interpreted as an instrument that transmitted a certain content from rulers to ruled, nor did he ask whether the public officials who were implementing the law were doing so in a way that

[38] As TRS Allan notes, Fuller did not always make this perspective clear: *Constitutional Justice: A Liberal Theory of the Rule of Law* (Oxford, Oxford University Press, 2001) 54–6.

[39] Fuller did not mention equality in setting out his principles of the rule of law. But the formal equality principle in play here, that a statutory authorization cannot be exercised in an unreasonably discriminatory fashion unless the official is given explicit authority so to discriminate, is I would venture, a principle that would figure on any list of rule-of-law principles and is implicated in the principle of generality.

[40] *Minister of the Interior v. Lockhart* 1961 (3) SA 587 (A), discussed in detail in D Dyzenhaus, *Hard Cases in Wicked Legal Systems: South African Law in the Perspective of Legal Philosophy* (Oxford, Clarendon Press, 1991) 79–83 [Dyzenhaus, *Hard Cases*]

revealed a content capable of guiding those subject to the law. To ask either of those questions would have led to the answer the Appellate Division gave that, as a matter of fact, the officials were authorised to do as they did, or at least were creating legal regimes that could effectively guide those subject to them. It follows that the judge's understanding of the rule of law principles he took to be relevant could not be as resources to give him access to content in that sense. Rather, the principles provided him with a resource to wrestle the content of the law into a form that could make some sense of a picture of the point of law as serving the interests of all those subject to it.

It was of course likely that a decision upholding the lower court's judgment would have provoked a legislative response that explicitly permitted officials to act unreasonably by allocating land in a way that favoured whites. But that legislative response would at least have had the virtue of forcing the government to explicitly declare in its legislation that it was not willing to abide by a central principle of the rule of law. Here the principle of publicity does real normative work because at the same time as the legislature is forced to declare its lack of commitment to principles of legality, so the principle of intelligibility—that legal subjects should be able to understand the law—is imperilled.

For intelligibility—at least on Fuller's account but I would argue on any account—has to do not with mere understanding.[41] It also has to do with communication by legal authority to legal subject in a way that makes sense to the subject of her subjection to the law; that is, her subjection is necessary to establish the relationship of reciprocity that serves the interests of the subject. A law that says one can be deprived of liberty without justification, or that one is not equal before the law because of one's race, is not intelligible on this understanding of intelligibility, because one's subjection to the law is so manifestly against one's interests. Law has become—to use Fuller's expression—a mere 'one-way projection of authority originating with government and imposing itself on the citizen.'[42]

In fact, a system of legalised racial discrimination that falls short of declaring the oppressed group to be slaves provides more grist to a Fullerian mill than to positivism.[43] In a slave-owning society, the slaves are no more subject to the rule of law than is my computer.[44] Only human beings are subject to the rule of law and slaves are deemed to be non-human by law, a deeming that removes them from the protection of the rule of law.

[41] So much is surely conceded by Hart when he says if the rules of a legal system fails to satisfy the minimum requirements that he recognizes are part and parcel of legality, the system 'would sink to the status of a set of meaningless taboos'; Hart, 'Separation of Law and Morals', above n 10 at 82.

[42] Fuller, *Morality of Law*, above n 5 at 207.

[43] See Dyzenhaus, *Hard Cases*, above n 40 and Fuller, *Morality of Law*, above n 5 at 159–62.

[44] Complications will of course emerge if slaves are given protection against cruelty or access to other sorts of legal protections—see WW Buckland, 2nd edition, *A Text-Book of Roman Law from Augustus to Justinian* (Cambridge, Cambridge University Press, 1932) 62–6. Slaves differ from computers in that they are reasoning creatures who can use the law to guide their actions. But this fact

In contrast, black South Africans during apartheid were in a twilight zone between slavery and full humanity. Some racial groups were given a status closer to whites and sometimes distinctions were made within some of these groups. The result was a nightmare from the perspective of the rule of law. But it also gave to judges minded to do so an opportunity to use the fact that all South Africans were officially under the protection of that rule to temper rule by law with the rule of law. In addition, the cost of making racist intentions ever plainer in statutes was not only that the moral obnoxiousness of the regime was exposed.[45] As indicated above, with such exposure the claim becomes ever weaker that everyone in the society is governed in accordance with the rule of law. For while 'separate but equal' might be rejected as a slogan by all liberal accounts of equality, it is still an interpretation of the value of equality that can plausibly be represented as a conception of the principle that all those subject to the law are equal before the law.[46] In contrast, 'separate and unequal' is not an interpretation of equality, but a violation of the idea of equality on any account, and so also of the idea of equality before the law.

Moreover, reflection on the differences between a slave-owning society and a society in which there is something akin to serfdom help to show why the wicked law objection is inapt when it comes to the rule of law. Recall that the wicked law objection to a Fullerian account of the rule of law depends on the claim that the rule of law is not only compatible with great iniquity, but also in fact can make iniquity worse by ensuring its meticulous administration.

Suppose, however, that the free in the slave-owning society are governed in accordance with law that reflects the basic principles of liberal democratic morality. While this society is deeply unjust, the free are governed justly. So although there is a gross tension at the core of this society, this tension stems from the fact that the free are governed justly. The complaint about such a society is the unjust exclusion of a group from the just order.[47] In other words, the fact that a realm of morality can coexist in the same society with a realm of great iniquity because a group is deemed beyond the reach of morality leads to tension, not to the conclusion that the realm of morality is not moral.

about them, that they can react as deliberately as any other human being to the law, does not place them within the scope of the rule of law's protection.

[45] See Dworkin, 'Philosophy, Morality, and Law', above n 17 at 672, criticising Fuller on the basis that this is all publicity does.

[46] I believe it is the case that some egalitarian Americans who are thoroughly disillusioned by the aftermath of *Brown v Board of Education* 347 US 483 (1954) argue that separate but truly equal education might have served the African-American community better.

[47] It is of course the case that the free benefit from the injustice to the slaves and we might therefore think it odd to say that the free are governed justly. But suppose that it is true both that Canada is one of the more just societies in the world and that Canada, like other such societies, benefits from the existence of less just societies. Here we get duplicated the situation where a realm of morality coexists with a realm of immorality and those who live in the former benefit from the exploitation of those who live in the latter. The difference is that when two such realms coexist in the same society, it is likely that the exploitation will be formalised by law. And that, as I argue in the text, heightens the tensions.

Of course, it is law that creates the institution of slavery, which is why such a society is used as an example by positivists against the likes of Fuller. But the example cuts both ways, since one feature of this society that heightens the tension is that a vast exception is created to the generality of the law that gives to the free the benefits of liberal democracy. As we have seen, one way of describing the requirement of generality is as the requirement of equal treatment by the law—the principle that like cases must be treated alike, often called the principle of formal equality. On this description, the tension manifests itself as a tension within the legal order. I mean by this not simply that there are positive laws that deliver contradictory moral messages. The point is that when the law is used to create a wholesale and harmful exception for a class of people to one or several of the principles of legality, including the principle of generality, the result is tension in the order's claim to respect the rule of law.[48]

Raz rejects this kind of argument. He says that the requirement of generality is 'sometimes assumed' to be 'of the essence of the rule of law' and that 'the rule of law is particularly relevant to the protection of equality and that equality is related to the generality of law.' This 'last belief', he asserts, is 'mistaken. Racial, religious, and all manner of discrimination are not only compatible but often institutionalised by general rules.'[49] But again the problem is Raz's determination to show that principles of the rule of law are instrumental to transmitting the content of valid law, which leads to distortion of the way in which such principles operate when judges fulfill their duty to uphold such principles.

My last example is a hypothetical one, a riposte to Hart's reliance on Austin's claim about the validity of the law that requires the execution of a man for a trivial offence. Imagine a society that lives up to all the principles of the rule of law, on either Fuller's or Raz's list, but has a very different understanding from ours of the kinds of substantive interests which should be protected by the rule of law. For example, suppose that those charged with infractions of the building code punishable by minor fines are given full due process rights, while those who are convicted of non-regulatory criminal offences from petty theft to murder are punished by life imprisonment or execution and are given no or little due process. The existence of such a society would be a better counterexample to a

[48] I thank Joanna Langille for reminding me of the evocative passage in *The Philosophy of Right* on this point: But the science of positive law at least cannot be very intimately concerned with definitions since it begins in the first place by stating what is legal, i.e. what the particular legal provisions are, and for this reason the warning has been given: *omnis definitio in jure civili periculosa*. In fact, the more disconnected and inherently contradictory are the provisions giving determinate character to a right, the less are any definitions in its field possible, for definitions should be stated in universal terms, while to use these immediately exposes in all its nakedness what contradicts them—the wrong in this instance. Thus in Roman law, for example, there could be no definition of 'man', since 'slave' could not be brought under it—the very status of slave indeed is an outrage on the conception of man; it would appear just as hazardous to attempt a definition of 'property' and 'proprietor' in many cases. GWF Hegel, *Philosophy of Right* (Oxford, Oxford University Press, 1967) 14–15.

[49] Raz, 'The Rule of Law', above n 16 at 215–16.

theory such as Fuller's than a slave-owning society, since it would subject everyone to a criminal law that flagrantly violated their interests.

But that this counterexample has to be produced largely by our imaginations reminds us that the political struggles for the rule of law were not directed at placing an even more effective instrument of government in the hands of ruling elites.[50] Rather, they were aimed at ensuring that, when the elites exercised power, the power they exercised was in accordance with law, not only with the law, but with an abstract conception of law framed by rule-of-law principles designed to protect our most important interests—notably liberty and equality. That is why a society in which these principles protect quite different interests seems bizarre. It is also why in all societies that have principles of the sort that figure on lists of principles such as Raz's and Fuller's, the positive law will also to some significant extent protect interests such as liberty and equality.

Although this line of thought would need much elaboration to be fully convincing, that elaboration would be primarily historical and sociological, not philosophical. But from it I think we can draw two tentative conclusions. First, Dworkin's account of adjudication is hardly as contingent as positivists think. As long as legal orders are orders that aspire to live up to the rule of law, including the principle of judicial review, Dworkinian accounts of adjudication will have a toehold in the positive law.

The second conclusion is that we need to re-evaluate more than Hart's response to natural law arguments based on the rule of law. We should also revisit that section of his response where he dealt with the claim that legal systems inevitably make provision for certain human interests, for example, the interest in being protected against violence. Hart used a divide and conquer strategy when responding to natural law, treating each argument he detected as distinct from the others.[51] But, as we have seen, he also responded to the claim about interests by relying on the wicked law objection—a legal order might always protect some of its subjects from harm but need not protect all, for example slaves.[52]

[50] I say 'largely' because Tony Blair and George Bush both took steps towards creating such a society. Emilios Christodoulidis argues that the further one goes in this direction, the more Dworkin's idea of integrity will find itself faithful to the animating values of the security state: '"End of History" Jurisprudence: Dworkin in South Africa' in Francois Du Bois (ed), *The Practice of Integrity: Reflections on Ronald Dworkin & South African Law* (Lansdowne, South Africa, Juta, 2004) 64 at 84–5. See Dworkin's response, ibid at 16.

[51] For detailed treatment of Hart's strategy in dealing with Fuller, see J Waldron, 'Positivism and Legality: Hart's Equivocal Response to Fuller' (2008) 83 *New York University Law Review* 1135.

[52] Hart proposed another response—that those who based natural law arguments on a list of objective human interests the law has to address failed to see that it was only as a matter of contingency that law has to address such interests. That is, if human beings had a hard carapace like crabs, the law would not have to address the kind of vulnerability that attaches to our delicate skins; Hart, *Concept of Law*, above n 2 at 194–5. It would seem odd to infer from this that for Hart the concept of law has to be one detached from facts about human beings, that is, that the 'wider' scope he sees in positivism's concept of law (209–10) is to be recommended not only because it covers wicked as well as good human societies, but also societies produced by some science fictional thought experiment.

In seeing how rule-of-law principles are inevitably associated with a list of what we can think of as objective human interests, we can see why the divide and conquer strategy should be rejected. For we see that law, the rule of law, and the interests on that list of principles of the rule of law are connected in ways that resist radical rearrangement, since any such rearrangement of the interests to which rule-of-law principles attach, or of deeming classes of human beings not to have such interests, will have consequences for our views about whether we have law, the rule of law, and so on.

So my claim is that Raz's list of the principles of the rule of law pull in two different directions. The principles themselves, taken as a package, pull in the direction of a Fullerian account of law, by which I mean an account in which law and the rule of law are best understood as serving the interests of those who are subject to law's rule, and in which the list of principles will look more like Fuller's than like Raz's.[53] But the point Raz ascribes to rule-of-law principles, the point of making the law into a better instrument for transmitting content, is not consistent with even his own list. Notably, the principle of generality, understood as requiring formal equality before the law, the principles of natural justice, and the principle that judges should have a review authority over the other principles are principles that will in many cases outrun the idea that the point of the principles of the rule of law is to help to determine transmitted content. As my examples show, the idea of transmitted content and these principles will be in tension in those situations where rule by law is used explicitly to put the rule of law under stress. And, as I will now show, the other direction in which Raz's account is pulled, the idea that the rule of law is about making the law into a better instrument for transmitting content, leads to a conception of legal order in which the rule of law has no independent role as a check on arbitrary power. Indeed, one should doubt whether this conception is genuinely one of legal order.

The Rule of Law in Legal Theory

There is an explanation of why the tensions arise in Raz's account of the rule of law, tensions that explain why Hart's remarks about legality in the epigraph to

[53] Indeed, in a later essay on the rule of law, Raz advances an account of the rule of law that goes beyond Fuller to a position closer to Dworkin's. This account insists, *inter alia*, 'that judicial decisions should not only be faithful but also principled' because 'the function of law is to facilitate the integration of particular pieces of legislation with the underlying doctrines of the legal system'. In this way, judges ensure 'coherence of purpose in the law' because they mix 'fruits of long-established traditions with the urgencies of short-term exigencies'; Joseph Raz 'The Politics of the Rule of Law' in J Raz, *Ethics in the Public Domain* 354 at 359–60. The only difference that Raz might see between his account and Dworkin's (if, that is, he thinks that Dworkin would endorse the model of the rule of law Raz calls the model of community law (355)), is that Raz claims that his account has a 'greater emphasis on the role of legislation' (358). In addition, Raz is keen to emphasise from the outset that this later essay is an account of the rule of law in one society, the United Kingdom in which there is parliamentary supremacy, tempered by the rule of law as interpreted by judges (354).

this chapter are uncharacteristically ambiguous. Suppose that one understands one's task in constructing an account of the rule of law not as a conceptual inquiry that unpacks the constitutive concepts of our practices. Rather, one starts with rough agreement about what the features of those practices are and then tries to make sense of them through a political argument about the ideals into whose service one's conception of law is to be pressed. The principles of the rule of law are then a bridge between one's ideal (though practice based) understanding of law and the kinds of artifacts that will be recognised as the law, given that ideal. In other words, the principles of the rule of law are principles chosen because they will produce a certain kind of artifact. Suppose further that one's political ideal is that of a majoritarian democracy where the judgments made by the majority are transmitted in as unadulterated a form as possible from the legislature to the public, and implemented according to that form, in order to avoid other institutions attempting to substitute their judgment for that of the legislature.

A rule-of-recognition account of law is suited to this ideal, especially if its criteria for valid law are confined to manner and form type criteria. Such criteria attest to the fact that a law is in fact a law properly made by the legislature, but they do not in any way make validity dependent on moral considerations and arguments.[54] The principles of the rule of law that will figure on the list of majoritarian democracy will be those principles that will help officials to determine and implement transmitted content. Omitted from the list will be principles that might lead officials to suppose that content is not transmitted content; for example, principles of the sort that led to the first court in the Group Areas case deciding that the statute has to be interpreted as excluding creation of vastly unequal areas would be off the list.

In such a society, one will need highly trained officials to staff the administrative regimes created by the statutes and a hierarchy within the regimes to ensure definite answers to conflicts about what the law of the regime requires. One might also need a body with review powers over all the regimes in order to deal with conflicts in the positive law between the administrative regimes that make up the law. But there is no reason to make that body into a court, or to give it the authority to make binding decisions. It might be much more in keeping with the political ideal to have a Benthamite system of reference from the body to a parliamentary committee when the body detects a problem.[55]

So an independent judiciary with inherent jurisdiction to ensure that rule of law principles are observed is not needed, for it is a threat to this majoritarian ideal, especially if its decisions are treated as legally binding beyond the particular

[54] This is exclusive legal positivism, properly so called. See Dyzenhaus, 'The Genealogy', above n 4 at 44–5.

[55] See G Postema, *Bentham and the Common Law Tradition* (Oxford, Clarendon Press, 1986) ch 12.

dispute. Such a judiciary is what I have called elsewhere an 'institutional mistake' from the perspective of this ideal because its very existence will tend to subvert the ideal.[56]

In the rule-of-recognition legal order, the regime that administered the criminal code would be designed to ensure that offenders were punished when and only when they contravened the content of a provision in the code. But there is no necessity for that regime to adopt procedural principles that we take for granted, notably natural justice/due process or rules about improperly obtained evidence. There might be and probably are far more efficient ways of ensuring an accurate determination of whether an offence has been committed than the elaborate protections associated with the tradition of due process. The issue of what procedures to adopt would be no different for the drafters of the criminal code than for the designers of the building code.

In addition, while each regime would be governed by a highly determinate set of internally consistent set of rules, and while conflicts between the positive law of different regimes would be ironed out, there would be no attempt made to ensure that all the regimes lived up to constitutional requirements, judicially enforced or not, that might pull the officials of a regime away from their duty to ascertain and apply the transmitted content of the law of their regime. Finally, there would be no requirement that rules be general or intelligible in the more normative sense sketched in the last section.[57]

This legal order is more than morally unattractive. It is also legally flawed, flawed from the perspective of the rule of law. It is, however, the legal order most appropriate to the thought that our basic intuition about law is that, if the law is to be an effective guide, it must be understood as law that transmits content. But, whatever its flaws, it is deeply interesting to a debate about the rule of law and about the place of that rule in the more general debate about law.

First, the idea that there could be an illegal law, a valid law that is suspect from the perspective of the rule of law, does not exist in it, because the whole energy and design of the legal order, including its vision of the rule of law, are exclusively directed at producing and implementing particular valid laws. The authority of law resides in the particular valid laws and it is legitimate not only *de facto* authority, since the content of these laws is determined by the legislature.

Put differently, this legal order assumes a necessary connection between law and morality at one level: particular laws must be applied and obeyed because they transmit morally justified decisions—that is, the decisions of the democratically elected, law-making body. But at other levels it requires versions of the Separation Thesis since, in determining the content of particular laws, officials

[56] Dyzenhaus, 'The Genealogy", above n 4 at 62. It is for this reason that Hobbes and Bentham (in his later work) wanted judges stripped of any authority beyond deciding the dispute before them.

[57] Compare Fuller, *Morality of Law*, above n 5 at 208–9.

must exclude reliance on their own moral convictions, while subjects must take the law's judgment about how to act as (morally) definitive of what they should do.[58]

Second, this legal order can be justified by other means than an appeal to majoritarian democracy. It can be justified by a Hobbist argument that any order is preferable to chaos and that to avoid the slippery slope to chaos one needs to understand one's political sovereign along the lines of, to use Hart's expression, an 'uncommanded commander'.[59] The only difference is that the commander understands that to be really effective, to have his commands be truly instrumental of his judgments, a rule of recognition is necessary.[60] In addition, such a legal order is justified by any position that views law as the transmitter of judgment.

Third, the rule-of-recognition legal order in which the transmission account is nested is not the kind of legal order that well serves a liberal society. In a liberal society, one would expect to see rule-of-law principles that go beyond aiming to make the law into a better instrument, that is, principles that help to ensure that rule by law conforms to a more generous conception of the rule of law. Indeed, one can make exactly the same point about democracy. Even democrats who would like to see much more attention given to the role of the legislature in legal theory, and who, correspondingly, wish to diminish the hold that judicial review has on both our practices and our legal imaginations, do not advocate exactly this rule-of-recognition legal order or its transmission account of the rule of law.[61]

In conclusion, Hart and Raz's accounts of the rule of law are ambiguous because they are caught between two positions. On the one hand, there is the rule-of-recognition position that regards rule-of-law principles as designed to serve the transmission of the content of positive law. On this position, valid law by definition is law that lives up to the ideal of the rule of law, an ideal that is politically plausible though both unattractive as a moral ideal and in conflict with our current rule-of-law practices. On the other hand, there is the position articulated by Raz in his essay on the rule of law. This second position articulates a moral ideal of the rule of law closer to a Fullerian position. And this ambiguity arises because the positivist conception of law is defined by reference to a

[58] Indeed, what Hart in 1958 called Bentham's 'general recipe for life under the government of laws' —'*To obey punctually; to censure freely*', does not, as Hart seemed to think, support the Separation Thesis. (Hart, 'Positivism and the Separation of Law and Morals' 597, quoting J Bentham, *A Fragment on Government*, JH Burns and HLA Hart (eds), in JH Burns, *The Collected Works of Jeremy Bentham: Principles of Legislation* (London, Athlone Press, 1977) 393, at 399 (emphasis in original.) Rather, the slogan supports a general moral duty to obey the law.

[59] Hart, 'Positivism and the Separation of Law and Morals', ibid at 603. I say Hobbist because Hobbes himself did not argue for this position. It is instructive that Raz, when he admits to ways in which there might be some necessary connection between law and morality, lists precisely this kind of connection: Raz, 'Authority, Law', above n 22 at 211.

[60] Howard Warrender explained just why Hobbes must allow for rule of recognition type constraints before Hart had articulated the idea for which his legal theory is famous: H Warrender, *The Political Theory of Hobbes: His Theory of Obligation* (Oxford, Clarendon Press, 1957) 258–63.

[61] Most notably, J Waldron, 'Can there be a Democratic Jurisprudence? <http://www.law.nyu.edu/newscalendars/2003_2004/legalphilosophy/waldron.pdf>

different ideal, more accurately, to whatever ideal can justify the conception of law as the transmitter of judgments from ruler to ruled.[62]

In contrast, a Fullerian, moral ideal of the rule of law provides us with a wider conception of legality than that of transmission account.[63] A transmission account does not aspire to anything more than being as effective an instrument as possible. From its own perspective, there are no further points along what we can think of as the continuum of legality once the order in which it is located is as close to perfection in ensuring a transmission belt for authoritative judgments as it can be. To go further is to step off the continuum, because any further step involves adopting principles that organize order in a way that potentially disrupts transmission.

In contrast, from the perspective of a moral ideal of the rule of law, a rule-of-recognition legal order can be seen as a step onto a continuum of legality because it insists on non-arbitrariness in the sense that no official may act unless there is a warrant in a valid law. It is but a step since a full realisation of the rule of law requires observance of principles beyond those that derive from a rule of recognition. That is, to go further along the continuum of legality one will need, on a Fullerian or Dworkinian account, judicial review in order to ensure that law lives up to the ideal of the rule of law. Indeed, all liberal democratic legal orders are so much further along the continuum that it might seem that the rule-of-recognition legal order is at best an embryonic form of legal order, rather than on the continuum of legality.

[62] Raz, of course, gets to his understanding of the rule of law by a conceptual, not a political route. But the conceptual unpacking he does is not of some neutral concept of law; it is of the conception of law in Hobbist and Benthamite political theories that need to understand law as the transmitter of determinate judgment. At base, Raz's is not a theory of law but a theory of authority, in which law has a conceptually determined role. His account of the authority of law starts with what he takes to be a central feature of law, the fact that law claims authority over its subjects. On his view, law is capable of having authority precisely because law can be an effective transmitter of judgment from lawmaker to legal subject. But the law will have authority when and only when the judgment it transmits is correct. Thus law itself never has authority. Rather, *the* law contingently has authority when the content of the law's directives is such that those subject to the law serve their interests better by complying with the law's judgment rather than their own. Raz, then, equates the authority of law with the authority of the valid law of a (morally good) legal system. Law's claim to be authoritative is a feature of particular valid laws. As a result, Raz excludes the possibility that law's authority, that is, its authority *qua* law, is based on the extent to which it lives up to an aspiration to comply with a moral ideal—the ideal of legality or the rule of law. But he excludes that possibility precisely because the ideal of the rule of law is not, in his view, a moral one. See generally, Raz, 'Authority, Law', above n 22.

[63] See Hart, *Concept of Law*, above n 2 at 209–12, for his reasons to prefer a wider concept of law.

4

Righting Administrative Law

SIAN ELIAS

Professing Administrative Law

SCEPTICISM AND PASSION thread through Michael Taggart's writing about administrative law. It is never ordinary, often subversive, and always illuminating. It is scholarship deeply attentive to method, both academic and judicial. The passion arises from recognition that administrative law is:[1]

> the space where the State (and its emanations) and the subject/citizen/rights-bearing individual come into contact – and sometimes clash – and the maintenance of a relatively free and democratic society depends on the fair and orderly resolution of those disputes.

The scepticism is the discipline mature scholarship brings to what matters. It is a discipline earned by research, often historical and always contextual. Attention to ugly facts, while antidote to 'creation stories' and other mythology,[2] does not in Taggart seem to diminish faith in the power of organising principles and belief in the virtue of law. He is concerned that principles of administrative law be integrated with thinking developed in other fields, particularly political theory, and has expressed disappointment that such insights from other disciplines are so neglected by administrative lawyers. Taggart takes evident pleasure in the 'footlights of footnotes' that illuminate sources of thought in scholarly writing.[3] And he is generous with such illumination in his own writing. (When I have a spare six months I hope to read my way through the footnotes in *Private Property and Abuse of Rights in Victorian England*.[4])

[1] M Taggart, 'Prolegomenon to an Intellectual History of Administrative Law in the Twentieth Century: The Case of John Willis and Canadian Administrative Law' (2005) 43 *Osgoode Hall Law Journal* 223 at 233 [Taggart, 'Prolegomenon'].

[2] Ibid at 231.

[3] Ibid at 255.

[4] M Taggart, *Private Property and Abuse of Rights in Victorian England: The Story of Edward Pickles and the Bradford Water Supply* (Oxford, Oxford University Press, 2002).

Similar attention to their methodology is shown in Taggart's critical assessments of administrators and judges, prodding awareness that muddled pragmatism is not good enough. The 'fair and orderly resolution' of disputes between the state and the individual depends in part upon the space available to each in the balance of public interest values with legitimate self-regarding behaviour.[5] Where the balance is struck in any legal system reflects its own history and traditions and shifts over time. Invoking Quentin Skinner,[6] Taggart is clear that who strikes the balance, and according to what values and methodological framework, are critical questions for the scholar.[7]

Today, such questions are often addressed in the context of the subset of administrative law concerned with human rights. At one time, when human rights legislation was new in jurisdictions such as Canada, the United Kingdom, and New Zealand, a number of administrative lawyers, including Taggart,[8] feared that administrative law might come to be swamped by human rights. With some years of experience with such legislation, there is some reason to think that the methodology required by human rights litigation has been beneficial in administrative law more generally.

Human rights adjudication, drawing on broad values expressed as fundamental, throws a spotlight on institutional legitimacy and judicial methodology. These challenges necessitate better focus on public law values and the space between public interest and self-regarding behaviour. Such space, as Taggart has pointed out in a number of articles,[9] has been an area of contest in Anglo-American law between legal centralists and pluralists. A combination of Diceyan insistence that there is one law which applies to citizens and government and the pull of the *Marbury v Madison*[10] view that it is the province of the courts of general jurisdiction to say what the law is, may have blunted appreciation that administrative law has traditionally accommodated a degree of pluralism.

Claims for greater plurality through which the modern state can operate may have been too readily dismissed as prompted by political preferences (and hostility to 'judge & co'), at least in countries lacking federal systems of government or without developed separation of powers.[11] The expansion of the

[5] Taggart, 'Prolegomenon', above n 1 at 233.

[6] Q Skinner, 'What is Intellectual History?' (1985) 35:10 *History Today* 50 at 51.

[7] Taggart, 'Prolegomenon', above n 1 at 227–8.

[8] M Taggart, 'Tugging Superman's Cape: Lessons from Experience with the New Zealand Bill of Rights Act 1990' (1998) *Public Law* 266 at 277.

[9] See, for example, M Taggart, '"The Peculiarities of the English': Resisting the Public/Private Law Distinction' in P Craig and R Rawlings (eds), *Law and Administration in Europe, Essays in Honour of Carol Harlow* (Oxford, Oxford University Press, 2003) 107 and M Taggart, 'Lord Cooke and the Scope of Review Doctrine in Administrative Law' in P Rishworth (ed), *The Struggle for Simplicity in the Law* (Wellington, Butterworths, 1997) [Taggart, 'Lord Cooke'].

[10] 5 US 137 (1803).

[11] As Taggart has emphasised, American development of techniques of deference has been neglected in Commonwealth jurisdictions, at least until the important decision of the Canadian Supreme Court in *CUPE v NB Liquor Corporation* [1979] 2 SCR 227. That case has, however, 'run into the sand' because of its continued use of jurisdictional error: 'Outside Canadian Administrative Law'

supervisory jurisdiction of the courts in modern law, with abandonment of the blunt instruments of jurisdictional review and irrationality and their replacement by error of law and varied intensity scrutiny for unreasonableness, may have occurred without sufficient attention to the reasons why preserving some space for pluralism may be desirable. Such reasons may be found when wide discretion effectively delegates legislative power to specialist administrative agencies.

Taggart has suggested that, in the absence of a more calibrated system of deference to replace jurisdiction and irrationality, we are throwing the baby of pluralism out with the bathwater.[12] In recent case law arising out of human rights there may be signs of such a more calibrated response. I offer some thoughts on these lines. My perspective is inevitably that of a New Zealand judge. It is an honour indeed to contribute to this well-merited festschrift for someone who has so generously contributed to the genre and whose industry has made these 'gardens' of scholarship bloom.[13]

A Little Historical New Zealand Context

Taggart has gently queried the 'creation story' of the development of administrative law.[14] Under it, the light did not arrive to allow order and structure to develop until the English judges, in the late 1960s, realised 'how much had been lost'.[15] As someone who studied the new distinct subject of administrative law in 1968 at Auckland (some years before a much younger Michael Taggart), my perception however is that the 'gloom' described by Sir William Wade was real enough.

Duties to act judicially and jurisdictional error were the mainstays of Professor Northey's course taught by the new, and alarming, case method system. The indigenous highlight of the casebook was a decision of the New Zealand Court of Appeal in *New Zealand Dairy Board v Okitu Co-operative Dairy Co Ltd*.[16] Although two of the judges considered whether natural justice applied on the technical but conventional basis that a 'lis' was present, Finlay J cut to the chase by asserting that a decision concerning the zone in which a dairy company could

(1996) 46 *University of Toronto Law Journal* 649 at 652 [Taggart, 'Outside Canadian']. In Australia, another federal jurisdiction, a rigid adherence to jurisdictional error preserves scope for such pluralism, but at what is perhaps a very high cost: see M Taggart, '"Australian Exceptionalism" in Judicial Review' (2008) 36 *Federal Law Review* 1.

[12] M Taggart, 'Lord Cooke and the Scope of Review Doctrine in Administrative Law' in Rishworth (ed) *The Struggle for Simplicity in the Law* (Wellington, Butterworths, 1997).

[13] M Taggart, 'Gardens or graveyards of scholarship? Festschriften in the Literature of the Common Law' (2002) 22 *Oxford Journal of Legal Studies* 227; and (in answer) M Taggart, *An index to common law festchriften: from the beginning of the genre up to 2005* (Oxford, Hart Publishing, 2006).

[14] Taggart, 'Prolegomenon', above n 1 at 231.

[15] W Wade and C Forsyth, *Administrative Law* (7th ed) (Oxford, Clarendon Press, 1994) 16.

[16] [1953] NZLR 366.

operate inherently required natural justice. The zoning Board was not, he thought, entitled 'to act autocratically and in defiance of the fundamental principles of fairness'.[17]

But this was one swallow only and spring was some years off. *Ridge v Baldwin*[18] was decided that year, too late to be included in Professor Northey's casebook. *Anisminic*[19] was in the future. Even then, its implications were not fully realised in New Zealand until the decision of the Court of Appeal in *Bulk Gas*.[20] As Taggart has noted,[21] *Bulk Gas* was anticipated by a new High Court Judge in 1973 in *Car Haulaways NZ Ltd v McCarthy*.[22] There, in a blow for Diceyan centralism, Cooke J held that, in considering a privative clause, courts of general jurisdiction should be slow to think that Parliament intended to give a tribunal authority to determine conclusively the meaning of its constitutive statute. Cooke J was overturned by a Court of Appeal who thought the approach insufficiently deferential to the tribunal,[23] but later as President of the Court of Appeal was able to turn the tables.[24]

For the most part, until the 1970s, administrative law in New Zealand still languished in the state which, in England, had shocked the distinguished American administrative lawyer, Kenneth Culp Davis, in 1961. In New Zealand at the time, we were just emerging from what has been described as a period of 'slavish imitation' of English law.[25] Davis, reviewing SA de Smith's *Judicial Review of Administrative Action*, expressed dismay about the future of judge made public law in England.[26] In particular, he criticised the failures to grapple with policy and the abdication of responsibility to ensure procedural fairness. He expressed the view that judicial review, properly limited, does not weaken but strengthens the administrative process. He was 'often shocked by the extent to which English courts refused to enquire whether serious justice has been done in the administrative process'.[27] That, he said, was wholly unsatisfactory in building the 'giant

[17] Ibid at 407.

[18] [1964] AC 40.

[19] *Anisminic Ltd v Foreign Compensation Commission* [1969] 2 AC 147.

[20] *Bulk Gas Users' Group v Attorney-General* [1983] NZLR 129.

[21] Taggart, 'Lord Cooke', above note 9.

[22] High Court, Auckland, A8/73, 8 August 1973.

[23] *Attorney-General v Car Haulaways (NZ) Ltd and Anor* [1974] 2 NZLR 331 (CA).

[24] Taggart's tracing of this important development in New Zealand law to *Car Haulaways* is of interest to me since the hearing was my first as counsel and I was required to argue the law for the plaintiff (senior counsel preferring, perhaps wisely, to concentrate on the facts). I do not imagine that any counsel ever made a more nervous debut, but the points were old hat and not at all novel to the Judge.

[25] Characterised by J Cameron as 'legal cringe' in 'Legal Change over 50 Years' (1987) 3 *Canterbury Law Review* 198 at 198.

[26] KC Davis, 'The Future of Judge Made Public Law in England: A Problem of Practical Jurisprudence' (1961) 61 *Columbia Law Review* 201.

[27] Ibid at 207.

structure' of public law that had to be built during the coming century.[28] What he was looking to was a changed culture in law, in better response to the needs of 'living people'.[29]

Davis's call for a change in 'culture' was met, in the view of Sir William Wade. He considered that the judges responded to 'the public mood'[30] that administrative injustice had become too strong to be ignored. A similar cultural shift occurred from the 1980s in New Zealand. Whether this describes a 'creation story' or an inevitable repositioning in a longer progression is a question to be addressed in the intellectual history of administrative law that remains to be written.

A Climate of Open Government Meets Human Rights

The cultural shift can be attributed to a number of influences. One rightly identified by Taggart is the increased professionalism of the teaching of law.[31] But particularly important have been changes in popular perceptions of government and law. They have been influenced in particular by a new climate of openness in government and by human rights standards.

In many jurisdictions, modern administration is now conducted under freedom of information requirements and human rights standards. Freedom of information legislation was enacted in 1982 in New Zealand.[32] In addition to providing for access to official information, it enables anyone affected by an administrative determination to obtain reasons.[33] The work of the courts in judicial review therefore comes to be undertaken in a climate of openness and justification in public administration.

A statutory bill of rights, the New Zealand Bill of Rights Act (NZBORA), was enacted in New Zealand in 1990. It proceeds on the basis that the rights and freedoms were already part of New Zealand law and that the legislation is declaratory of them. Nor does it purport to be an exclusive statement of fundamental rights and freedoms. It makes it clear that their expression does not exclude other rights and freedoms that are part of New Zealand law. The statute refers explicitly to the International Covenant on Civil and Political Rights as its principal source.

The Covenant, and the Universal Declaration of Human Rights that preceded it, admitted legal systems like New Zealand, with no tradition of rights beyond those immanent in the general law, to a developed body of comparative and international case-law. All were able to benefit from what Anthony Lester has

[28] Ibid at 220.
[29] Ibid at 219.
[30] Sir William Wade, *Constitutional Fundamentals* (revised ed) (London, Stevens, 1989) 78.
[31] Taggart, 'Prolegomenon', above note 1 at 228.
[32] Official Information Act 1982.
[33] Official Information Act 1982, section 23.

described as the 'Overseas trade in the American Bill of Rights'.[34] In New Zealand, increasing attention is now being paid to North American case law and legal writing, after years of neglect.[35]

One of the aspirations of those who promoted the NZBORA was that it would become part of the political and social discourse, as well as a source of vindication through courts. It was to be a 'set of navigation lights'[36] for legislators, and a standard by which executive power, particularly in the exercise of discretion, could be measured and, if necessary, checked. It was to be an accessible statement of shared values that would raise public consciousness about constitutional fundamentals and the level of civil discourse about such values.

The new climate of openness in government and human rights justification has had a transforming effect on administrative practice and law. First, the processes of government have been profoundly affected. Sir Geoffrey Palmer, who as Attorney-General promoted the NZBORA, has described it is a 'parliamentary bill of rights' that relies principally upon the processes of government, rather than court decisions, to protect human rights.[37] In saying this, he does not minimise the 'significant and sometimes dramatic' effect of the 'weak form of judicial review' provided by the legislation. He makes the point however that the case law may not be the most important result of the Act.

Even in jurisdictions with strong judicial review, the same conclusion may be drawn. There is no doubt that in New Zealand the success of the NZBORA is not principally to be gauged from reading court decisions. It has permeated the processes of power, as appears from the Cabinet Manual down. It would be cynical to doubt that the observance of human rights by public agencies has not greatly improved as a result, although the risk of degeneration into a 'tick the box' mentality remains a reason for additional supervision. Such supervision is provided by Parliament as well as the judiciary.

Parliamentary Supervision for Compliance with Human Rights

The NZBORA applies 'to acts done … by the legislative, executive, or judicial branches of the government of New Zealand' as well as to those done 'by any person in the performance of any public function, power, or duty conferred or

[34] Anthony Lester, 'The Overseas Trade in the American Bill of Rights' (1988) 88 *Columbia Law Review* 537.

[35] Jeremy Finn has described the declining use of American precedent from World War I in 'New Zealand lawyers and 'overseas' precedent 1874–1973 – lessons from the Otago District Law Society library' (2007) 11 *Otago Law Review* 469.

[36] *A Bill of Rights for New Zealand* (1985) AJHR A6 at 6 [*White Paper*].

[37] Foreword to A Butler and P Butler, *The New Zealand Bill of Rights Act: A Commentary* (Wellington, LexisNexis, 2006) v.

imposed on that person or body by or pursuant to law'.[38] The Attorney-General is required by section 7 to report to Parliament any provision in a Bill that appears to be inconsistent with the rights and freedoms in the Act. It has been claimed that the existence of the vetting procedure contributes significantly to the creation of a 'rights culture that [is] sufficiently robust to protect rights'.[39] But the provision provides less scope for reporting to Parliament than is required under the equivalent United Kingdom and Victorian provisions, which require certificates of compliance.[40]

Since 2003, the Attorney, most commendably, has adopted the practice of publishing the legal advice relied upon in making section 7 reports. There have been 17 such reports since 2003. In eight cases of reported infringement of the NZBORA, the legislation was nevertheless enacted. In by no means all of these cases did the House debate the appropriateness of the Bill in the light of the report.

Significantly, reports are not considered necessary when the legal opinions obtained are that any encroachment on rights is justifiable under section 5. This conforms to guidelines adopted by the Legislation Advisory Committee[41] on the basis, recently endorsed by the Supreme Court after some doubt,[42] that rights are not infringed, triggering report, if the infringements can be justified in a free and democratic society under section 5. In 2007 and 2008, 13 of the bills introduced into Parliament were considered by the government lawyers to contain limitations justifiable in a free and democratic society, and were therefore not the subject of section 7 report.[43] The judgment that a limitation is demonstrably justifiable in a free and democratic society is often highly contestable. The legal advice obtained by the Attorney-General may effectively preclude the close Parliamentary scrutiny that seems to be behind the policy of the reporting provision.

The Challenges to Judicial Method in Human Rights

If it is right that judicial enforcement is not the principal method of protecting human rights, it may be that what is most important in the judicial contribution to human rights is its method of justification. Ultimately, whether human rights are observed depends upon whether they are valued and understood by the wider community. The role of the courts may, however, be critical in explaining the

[38] NZBORA section 3.

[39] J Heibert, 'Rights Vetting in New Zealand and Canada: Similar Idea, Different Outcomes' (2005) 3 *New Zealand Journal of Public and International Law* 63 at 65.

[40] Human Rights Act 1998 (UK), s 19; Charter of Human Rights and Responsibilities Act 2006 (Victoria), s 28.

[41] Legislation Advisory Committee Guidelines (May 2001) 110–19.

[42] *R v Hansen* [2007] 3 NZLR 1 (SC).

[43] As at October 2008.

application of human rights values in particular contexts. The deliberative and open processes of courts are not the only means by which rights and their limitations are demonstrated. But it is in this demonstration of human rights in action that the principal contribution of the courts to legislative statements of human rights is to be found.

That view accords with the discourse ethics associated with Jürgen Habermas[44] and, especially in connection with human rights, Sir Stephen Sedley[45] and Yash Ghai.[46] It suggests that the universality of human rights lies less with substantive ethical precepts than with the provision of a shared framework for the political and cultural accommodations that diverse societies must reach. The view has implications for judicial method.

There are a number of challenges in judicial enforcement of human rights: how the courts identify the values they apply in human rights cases, including those which may be used to limit rights; the techniques used in accommodating values of comparable weight but which are otherwise incommensurable; and what deference or margin of appreciation courts should permit the primary decision-maker in supervising for human rights compliance. All these stretch both judicial method and judicial legitimacy.

A number of commentators have expressed the view that the adjustment required by human rights is revolutionising our understanding of law.[47] If so, I am not sure that the implications have yet been fully absorbed. Pragmatic, unintellectual habits of judicial reasoning are not good enough. If we are not to 'sleepwalk' through the changes brought through human rights, we need to engage not only with the international and comparative case-law but with the intellectual scholarly tradition it draws on, little of it judge-made.

Identification of Values

We do not start in very good shape. The legal historian, Holdsworth, considered that a consequence of the hold of positivism on law has been the impoverishment of ethical reasoning caused by strict separation of morals from law in our legal tradition.[48] He thought that, as a result of this ethical impoverishment, utilitarianism had filled the gap. A utilitarian calculus, though appealing to judges schooled in positivist tradition, is unequal to human rights adjudication.

[44] J Habermas, *Justification and application: remarks on discourse ethics,* translated by Ciaran Cronin (Cambridge, Polity Press, 1993).

[45] Sir Stephen Sedley, 'Are human rights universal and does it matter?' The Holdsworth Lecture, 25 November 2005, University of Birmingham.

[46] Y Ghai, 'Universalism and Relativism: Human Rights as a Framework for Negotiating Interethnic Claims' (2000) 21 *Cardozo Law Review* 1095.

[47] See, for example, M Loughlin, *The Idea of Public Law* (Oxford, Oxford University Press, 2003) 127.

[48] WS Holdsworth, *Some Lessons from our Legal History* (New York, MacMillan, 1928) 158.

One of the consequences of the enactment of a statement of 'fundamental rights and freedoms' that does not purport to be exclusive, and which contains references to values not captured in the statements of rights and freedoms, is that courts need to develop a sense of the bedrock values within the legal system. How are these values to be identified with legitimacy by courts?

The structure and internal indications in the legislation itself are the obvious starting point. They lead directly to the International Covenant on Civil and Political Rights, which the Act fulfils in domestic law. For the most part the rights identified in the NZBORA are widely expressed without internal qualifications. Instead, in the manner of the Canadian Charter of Rights and Freedoms, rights are expressed to be subject to such reasonable limits prescribed by law as may be justified in a free and democratic society.[49] Although the Act does not adopt the qualifications expressed in respect of each right in the Covenant, the Covenant qualifications are clearly relevant in interpreting the limitations that may be justifiable. Chief Justice Barak points out that the same values underlie both rights and their limits:[50]

> Human rights and the limitations on them derive from the same source, and they reflect the same values. Human rights can be limited, but there are limits to the limitation. The role of the judge in a democracy is to preserve both of those limitations.

It is surprising that until relatively recently there has been relatively slight use of the Covenant and the general comments made by the United Nations Human Rights Committee in New Zealand case law. Starting with *Baigent*[51] (a case concerning effective remedy) more use of the international materials has been apparent.[52]

Apart from the text of the Act and the international statements and law it invokes, judges have to draw on wider constitutional values in identifying the scope of rights and their limitations. Since the Act and the Covenant invoke the standard of a 'free and democratic society', protecting the processes of democracy would seem to fit within the values that are fundamental. So too, since the enjoyment of rights and freedoms is only possible in organised society, protecting the social structure would also seem to be a fundamental principle. Other principles too may be fundamental. The NZBORA does not contain a general right to equal treatment beyond the right not to be discriminated against on one of the prohibited grounds.[53] But the White Paper that preceded enactment of the

[49] Section 5 of the NZBORA is modelled on section 1 of the Canadian Charter.

[50] As Lorraine Weinrib suggested in relation to the Canadian Charter in 'The Supreme Court of Canada and Section One of the Charter' (1988) 10 *Supreme Court Law Review* 469 at 482. See A Barak, *The Judge in a Democracy* (Princeton, Princeton University Press, 2006) 84.

[51] *Simpson v Attorney General [Baigent's Case]* [1994] 3 NZLR 667 (CA).

[52] See, for example, the use made of such material in *Taunoa v Attorney General* [2008] 1 NZLR 429 (SC).

[53] NZBORA section 19.

legislation maintained that equality was an aspect of the rule of law,[54] itself a fundamental value in the constitutional order as the Supreme Court Act 2003 now makes clear.[55] Such fundamental values immanent in the legal order may need to be brought into human rights evaluations. To date, in New Zealand there has been little exploration of these values.[56]

More controversial is the question whether human rights can be limited to protect values or principles that advance social or government policy, but which cannot be ranked as fundamental or as human rights in themselves. Some commentators assume that the values advanced in limitation of rights must be of the same rank, thus setting up 'intra-constitutional conflict'.[57] In a number of New Zealand cases justifiable limits have been assumed to arise from interests not equivalent to human rights or fundamental constitutional principles. Professor Ashworth has criticised decisions in the United Kingdom that seem to favour 'broad balancing' of rights against other less fundamental public interests.[58] Jeremy Waldron, on the other hand, accepts that many conflicts between rights and utility as well as between rights are properly addressed by balancing—although he stresses the need for care, context, and relativity in time and place.[59] Competing governmental objectives that are the basis for limitation of rights can usually be taken back to equivalent rights or values, but it is impossible not to be left a little uneasy at the lack of conceptual clarity.

Balance

Where rights and other important values conflict, striking the balance is difficult. Justice Scalia memorably commented once that constitutional balancing is sometimes 'like judging whether a particular line is longer than a particular rock is heavy'.[60] There is no clear formula for dealing with 'incommensurability' where there is no common scale upon which to weigh and measure disparate rights.

It would be wrong to see the justification required in such cases simply as at-large balancing. Objective correctness in outcome is very often the standard

[54] *White Paper*, above n 36 at 86.

[55] Supreme Court Act 2003 section 3(2).

[56] Privacy is an exception: see, for example, *Brooker v Police* [2007] 3 NZLR 91 (SC) and *Lange v Atkinson and Australian Consolidated Press NZ Ltd* [1997] 2 NZLR 22 (HC) and [1998] 3 NZLR 424 (CA).

[57] A Stone Sweet and J Matthews, 'Proportionality Balancing and Global Constitutionalism' (2008) 46 *Columbia Journal of Transnational Law* 1 [Stone Sweet and Matthews, 'Proportionality'].

[58] A Ashworth, *Human Rights, Serious Crime and Criminal Procedure* (London, Sweet & Maxwell, 2002) 62–64, citing *Salabiaku v France* (1988) 13 EHRR 379 [Ashworth, *Human Rights*].

[59] J Waldron, 'Rights in Conflict' in *Liberal Rights* (Cambridge, Cambridge University Press, 1993) 203 at 223 and 'Security and Liberty: The Image of Balance' (2003) 11(2) *The Journal of Political Philosophy* 191.

[60] *Bendix Autolite v Midwesco Enterprises* 486 US 888 (1988) at 897.

the courts can and should apply. The problems of incommensurability can be exaggerated. And, in any event, as Rivers points out:[61]

> [W]e probably do not believe in complete incommensurability between constitutional values. Few would view with indifference a massive loss of liberty for a marginal gain in national security. Our problem is not that the values are incommensurable but that relative assessments can only be carried out in a crude manner.

To similar effect, in the ultimate balancing of incommensurable values, Robert Alexy says that '[t]he greater the degree of non-satisfaction of, or detriment to, one principle, the greater must be the importance of satisfying the other'.[62] This is an appeal to rationality. And it may be that, in context, it requires optimisation. That is consistent with the dominant methodology of proportionality.

Such approach is value-driven rather than driven by utility. It is also not acceptable if based solely on assessments of majority preference. Ronald Dworkin says that it is 'surely controversial' that what rights an individual has should be determined by history or by the application of an inferred community standard.[63] He points out that, since there is likely to be a range of views in the community, such assertions simply mask in many cases the Judge's preference. Jeffrey Jowell and TRS Allan have also emphasised that in the end the content of individual rights is not a matter for majoritarian determination. If so, invocation of 'community standards', without more, is insufficient justification where rights are engaged.

Alec Stone Sweet and Jud Matthews have referred to the proper reluctance of courts to develop a hierarchy of rights, effectively 'constitutionalising' winners and losers.[64] I do not disagree with the view that rights cannot be prioritised in some abstract hierarchy. But perhaps some ranking may properly be given effect in a particular case:

> where it builds on the qualifications and priorities explicit and implicit in the human rights statements and the wider constitutional values of the society; or
>
> when the particular context requires weighting as a matter of rationality.

The structure of rights instruments themselves may impose some discipline. The architecture of the European Convention on Human Rights, for example, constrains and defines the degree to which competing interests may limit rights. Non-derogable rights on this view do not give way to other public interest considerations. Qualified rights may be subject to interference only if one of the stated grounds apply. In between the two are what Ashworth calls 'strong

[61] J Rivers, 'Proportionality and Variable Intensity of Review' (2006) 65 *Cambridge Law Journal* 174 at 201.

[62] R Alexy, 'Constitutional Rights, Balancing and Rationality' (2003) 16 *Ratio Juris* 131 at 136.

[63] R Dworkin, 'The Judge's New Role: Should Personal Convictions Count?' (2003) *Journal of International Criminal Justice* 4 at 8.

[64] Stone Sweet and Matthews, 'Proportionality', above n 57 at 10.

rights'—those that are derogable but not specifically qualified.[65] This is the sort of analysis that a conscientious court needs to bring to the determination of whether limitations are permissible or justified.

In balancing incommensurables, it is necessary to weight the conflicting values according to a variable and contextual analysis. And, if the value judgments are necessarily crude, such crudeness should not be exacerbated by the 'underwriting' of conclusions. Justification of limitations on rights requires careful exposition.

Deference and Human Rights

Institutional deference to the political branches risks not only vindication of rights (and therefore their efficacy) but also the vindication of official conduct that is substantively compliant with human rights by a disinterested and independent judiciary. Providing such legitimacy is a principal contribution of legal process to the rule of law. It is not delivered through supervision for procedural exactness that avoids the issue of substantive compliance. Perfunctory judicial performance in bill of rights litigation may lead to unjustified relaxation in human rights vigilance by the political actors and the public.

The debate over the weight to be given to the assessment of the primary decision-maker has not yet produced a substantial body of case law in New Zealand. In the United Kingdom, the Courts have acknowledged frankly that they are feeling their way. In *R (ProLife Alliance) v British Broadcasting Corporation* Lord Walker said that the whole area was one where domestic jurisprudence was still developing:[66]

> So the court's task is, not to substitute its own view for that of the broadcasters, but to review their decision with an intensity appropriate to all the circumstances of the case.

In *R (SB) v Denbigh High School*, the House of Lords took the view that whether human rights have been infringed is always a matter for objective determination by the court.[67] In *Miss Behavin' Ltd v Belfast City Council*, Lord Hoffmann criticised an administrative review approach as a 'tick the box' check for rationality in process potentially destructive of human rights. He also thought it 'quite impractical':[68]

> What was the Council supposed to have said? 'We have thought very seriously about your convention rights but we think that the appropriate number of sex shops in the locality is nil'? Or: 'Taking into account art 10 and art 1 of the First Protocol and doing the best we can, we think that the appropriate number is nil' Would it have been

[65] Ashworth, *Human Rights*, above n 58 at 97.
[66] [2004] 1 AC 185 at para [139].
[67] *R (SB) v Governors of Denbigh High School* [2007] 1 AC 100.
[68] [2007] 1 WLR 1420 (HL) at para [13].

> sufficient to say that they had taken convention rights into account, or would they have had to specify the right ones? A construction of the 1998 Act which requires ordinary citizens in local government to produce such formulaic incantations would make it ridiculous. Either the refusal infringed the applicant's convention rights or it did not. If it did, no display of human rights learning by the Belfast City Council would have made the decision lawful. If it did not, it would not matter if the councillors had never heard of art 10 or the First Protocol.

The court is not concerned with whether the decision-maker took human rights into account and came to a decision that was rational. But in considering whether a limitation is demonstrably justified in a free and democratic society, the reasoned views of the primary rule-maker may be given weight. A margin of appreciation may be appropriate if the assessment is one of judgment and the rule-maker has addressed the question and offered adequate justification for the conclusion reached. On the approach taken by Lord Bingham in *Huang v Secretary of State for the Home Department,*[69] close assessment by the courts will be necessary if the decision-maker has not properly addressed the human rights dimension. The court does not undertake a 'secondary, reviewing function', but must itself be of the view that rights have not been infringed. The judgment of the primary decision-maker is however 'always relevant and may be decisive'.[70]

The topic of deference in human rights has unsurprisingly attracted a great deal of academic comment. TRS Allan has argued that a doctrine of judicial deference is 'either empty or pernicious'.[71] If prompted by separation of powers concerns it is 'empty' because 'that separation is independently secured by the proper application of legal principles defining the scope of individual rights or the limits of public powers'.[72] A doctrine of deference is 'pernicious' if it:[73]

> permits the abdication of judicial responsibility in favour of reliance on the good faith or good sense or special expertise of public officials, whose judgments about the implications of rights in specific cases may well be wrong. In its latter manifestation, judicial deference amounts to the abandonment of impartiality between citizen and state: in acceding to the supposedly superior wisdom of the public agency (or of Parliament), the court is co-opted into the executive (or the legislature), leaving the claimant without any independent means of redress for an arguable violation of rights.

[69] [2007] 2 AC 167 at 183.

[70] Ibid at 184.

[71] TRS Allan, 'Human Rights and Judicial Review: A Critique of Due Deference' (2006) 65(3) *Cambridge Law Journal* 671 at 675.

[72] Ibid.

[73] Ibid at 675–76.

Allan's conclusion is that deference-talk short-circuits proper analysis and that its suggestion of a 'direct linkage between deep-level constitutional theory and the resolution of particular rights-claims' generates 'only confusion and misunderstanding'.[74]

In New Zealand, we have fluctuated in our approach. In the *Moonen* litigation, the Court of Appeal focussed on the process followed by the Film and Literature Board of Review in making its classification that a publication was 'objectionable'.[75] In the first case, the Court held that the Board had failed to weigh the right to freedom of expression in its determination. It remitted the classification for further consideration. In the second case, after such reconsideration, the Court refused to supervise more closely than to consider whether there was evidence before the Board upon which it could have come to its conclusion and whether the determination was reasonably open to it. This approach is similar to that taken in the English Court of Appeal in *Denbigh High School* (and repudiated by the House of Lords) and is similar to the approach taken by the minority in the Supreme Court of Canada in *Multani v Commission Scolaire Marguerite-Bougeoys.*[76]

As these opinions show, such reasoning exerts some attraction. It is the tug of pluralism. But the centre still holds. The later cases in the United Kingdom and Canada make it clear is that it is one thing for the courts to find the reasoning of the primary decision-maker convincing, and it is quite another thing to defer to that agency unless its conclusion is irrational.

It may be that we will see a more nuanced approach develop in which there is further room to respect the assessment of the primary decision-maker, depending on the nature of the decision and the relative institutional competencies of the court and the primary decision-maker. It is possible that where discretionary decisions are effectively subordinate legislation, especially when they are entrusted to specialist bodies, more deference is available. And in socially controversial cases, those that William Eskridge has described as amounting to 'culture wars',[77] the significance of the political view may be seen as more important, justifying a wider margin of appreciation. These themes of relative institutional competence in the context of decisions about incommensurable values have been explored by a number of legal philosophers, in theory that is not

[74] Ibid at 676. See also TRS Allan, 'Fairness, Equality, Rationality: Constitutional Theory and Judicial Review' in C Forsyth and I Hare (eds) *The Golden Metwand and the Crooked Cord, Essays on Public Law in Honour of Sir William Wade QC* (Oxford, Oxford University Press, 1998) 15 at 29.

[75] *Moonen v Film and Literature Board of Review* [2000] 2 NZLR 9; *Moonen v Film and Literature Board of Review (No 2)* [2002] 2 NZLR 754.

[76] [2006] 1 SCR 256 (Deschamps, Abella and Le Bel JJ).

[77] W Eskridge, 'Pluralism and Distrust: How Courts Can Support Democracy by Lowering the Stakes of Politics' (2005) 114 *Yale Law Journal* 1279 at 1298.

for the light-headed.[78] I allow some attraction to the view that where the content of human rights in context turns on what Cass Sunstein has referred to as the 'qualitative actual experience and self-understanding within a society',[79] the promotion of human rights may be best served by accepting that the courts are not always best-placed to make that assessment.

Purists may take the view that the courts, which are themselves bound to observe the Bill of Rights Act in what they do, cannot avoid concluding objectively whether rights have been infringed. I am not unattracted to that view (and think it may have particular force in respect of particular determinations, not properly seen as rule-making), but do not think it prevents the court giving the weight it thinks appropriate in the circumstances to the conclusions of the agencies primarily responsible. The reasons they give will be key to the courts having confidence in their conclusions. If they do not give convincing reasons why the human right should yield, the courts will have to undertake close scrutiny and make the determination unless there are reasons why the decision-making body should have to reconsider the matter. And it may be that the question of deference, even in human rights cases, will need to be considered in the light of any statutory indication as to the role of the primary decision-maker, as Taggart has suggested in relation to judicial review of administrative action more generally.[80]

It is possible that deference may have more scope in consideration of remedies for breaches of rights. Sunstein has suggested that in considering remedies the courts should bear in mind that the question of crafting a remedy may be better left to the political branches:[81]

> When a democracy is in moral flux, courts may not have the best or the final answers. Judicial answers may be wrong. They may be counterproductive even if they are right. Courts do best by proceeding in a way that is catalytic rather than preclusive, and that is closely attuned to the fact that courts are participants in the system of democratic deliberation.

Our case law has barely stirred these waters to date.

[78] See, for example, C Sunstein, 'Incommensurability and Valuations in Law' (1994) 92 *Michigan Law Review* 779; J Alder, 'The Sublime and the Beautiful: Incommensurability and Human Rights' (2006) *Public Law* 697; R Alexy, 'Balancing, constitutional review, and representation' (2005) 3 *International Journal of Constitutional Law* 572.

[79] Sunstein, ibid at 856.

[80] Taggart, 'Lord Cooke', above n 9 at 199 making the point that privative clauses are not 'boilerplate', unthinkingly inserted in statutes, and that courts should not be dismissive of the direction they are intended to give.

[81] C Sunstein, 'Leaving Things Undecided' (1996) 110 *Harvard Law Review* 4 at 101.

Administrative Law Method

Even if the scope for plurality is circumscribed where human rights are in issue, a consequence of the greater focus on methodology in human rights cases benefits wider administrative law. Identifying the restraints that identify and control discretion is principally an exercise in statutory interpretation in which the courts act as 'junior partners' to the legislature.[82] The task of the courts in such cases is not merely to ensure accountability. It includes promoting good administration and ensuring that the law is fit for changing circumstances.

Just as is the case with human rights litigation, judicial process resolves controversies sometimes through vindication of claim of legal right in public law but also, and more frequently, through approval of administrative conduct which is substantively compliant with legal obligations, including obligations of fairness and reasonableness. Again, providing such legitimacy is a principal contribution of legal process to the rule of law.

A climate of openness and an emphasis on reasons cannot help but effect a change in the way administrative law operates beyond the area of human rights. In such climate, controversies are not stilled through supervision for procedural exactness but unquestioning deference in matters of substance. It creates expectations of justification and rationality of outcome. Nor does such deference permit contribution to wider civil discourse.[83] Full exposition is a benefit of the deliberative process of litigation that is valuable in itself. Sometimes in patient examination of claims dismissed out of hand in less deliberative, less disinterested processes there are important gains irrespective of formal outcome.[84] Expression of the values that bear on the outcome promotes understanding and participation.

In a climate of justification, people want to know the reasons why official action is taken that affects them. It is an aspect of human dignity. Reasons facilitate participation and prevent human beings being regarded as objects. And if people are given the dignity of reasons, they want them to justify the outcome. As David Dyzenhaus, Murray Hunt, and Taggart have remarked, a culture of justification means that reasons must be 'good' reasons. A culture of justification therefore entails 'substantive commitments'.[85] Sir William Wade once explained judicial review for error of law on the face of the record, on the basis that it was

[82] DC Pearce, 'Statutory interpretation in Australia' (1974) 148; and see Sir David Williams, citing E Freund in 'Statute Law and Administrative law' (1984) *Statute Law Review* 157 at 163 [Williams, 'Statute Law].

[83] See S Fredman, 'From Deference to Democracy: the Role of Equality under the Human Rights Act 1998' (2006) 122 *Law Quarterly Review* 53.

[84] As Sir Neil MacCormick has long argued. See N MacCormick, *Legal Reasoning and Legal Theory* (Oxford, Clarendon Press, 2nd ed, 1994).

[85] D Dyzenhaus, M Hunt & M Taggart, 'The Principle of Legality in Administrative Law: Internationalisation is Constitutionalisation' (2001) *Oxford University Commonwealth Law Journal* 5 at 29.

more than judicial flesh and blood could bear.[86] Such reaction is not a judicial response only. Decisions that are clearly wrong are more than human flesh and blood can bear.[87] Clear error of material fact is as offensive as clear error of law.[88] Substantive unfairness rankles as much as substantive unreasonableness. And in real life an unreasonable decision is not understood as one so unreasonable that it is wholly irrational.

A Repositioning of Administrative Law?

The new culture of justification, with its emphasis on reasons, is effecting a repositioning of administrative law. Old boundaries, always porous, between law and policy, fact and law, process and substance, private and public, legislative and administrative, and the other categories with which we have tried to provide bright lines and rules themselves have to be justified. In such climate there may be no alternative but to focus on administrative law values and ends, as Taggart has long urged. In the identification of such 'public law values',[89] he suggests that the starting point is where 'self-regarding behaviour' ends and 'public-regarding behaviour' starts.[90] It may be that greater emphasis on the values of public law—both constitutional and administrative values—may also lead to re-evaluation of the spaces for pluralism and the development of new rules of deference which are respectful of agency expertise (where such deference is earned through conscientious effort to engage with public interest ends), private space, and democratic choices. If so, we may be better able to address the ends of good government and the meeting of individual aspirations to autonomy as a general and shared responsibility rather than the preserve of one institution of government to the exclusion of another.

In such a setting, judicial supervision must be highly contextual. Felix Frankfurter thought that in administrative law it was necessary to be on guard against 'an undue quest for certainty, borne of an eager desire to curb the dangers of discretionary power'.[91] Although there are fields of legal control where the mechanical application of fixed rules is attainable, 'there are other fields where

[86] M Aronson, B Dyer & M Groves, *Judicial Review of Administrative Action* (Sydney, Thompson Legal and Regulatory Group, 3rd ed, 2004) 104, citing W Wade and C Forsyth, *Administrative Law* (Oxford, Clarendon Press, 7th ed, 1994) 306. This passage was dropped from the current edition of Wade.

[87] As is illustrated by the history of a number of vexatious litigants, a topic Taggart has considered in 'Vexing the Establishment: Jack Wiseman of Murrays Bay' [2007] *New Zealand Law Review* 271 [Taggart, 'Vexing the Establishment'].

[88] As Cooke P saw in *Daganayasi v Minister of Immigration* [1980] 2 NZLR 130 (CA).

[89] M Taggart, 'The Province of Administrative Law Determined?' in M Taggart (ed) *The Province of Administrative Law* (Oxford, Hart Publishing, 1997) 1 at 3.

[90] See Laws J in *R v Somerset County Council ex parte Fewings* [1995] 1 All ER 513 (QBD).

[91] F Frankfurter, 'The Task of Administrative Law' (1926) 75 *University of Pennsylvania Law Review* 614 at 619.

law necessarily means the application of standards' if it is to meet 'the infinite variety of life'.[92] And he considered administrative law, which must meet the needs of living people and evolving government, was such a field where fixed rules are unattainable.

Taggart has rightly cautioned against wholly contextual methodology in administrative law, while always himself paying close attention to context.[93] And it is true that without principles and values, contextual evaluation may not rise above conclusionary assertions that mask political choices. But context, if not everything, comes close to it. Sir David Williams suggests that, in the long term, the courts would help in the development of a more ordered legal system if they intervened 'where intervention is constitutionally desirable'.[94] Knowing when intervention is constitutionally desirable requires close attention to the principles of the constitution, as well as to the principles of administrative law. Similarly, Professor Louis Jaffe is cited by Taggart[95] for his suggestion that judges must intervene when convinced that one reading of a statute is the only correct one, or that one application of an administrative discretion is the only faithful one. They should abstain from intervening if the agency's preference is 'reasonable'. Such simplicity may yet be the best policy.

Conclusion

It is not necessary to throw the baby out with the bathwater. Judicial review does not entail the court substituting its judgment for that of the primary decision-maker, although in cases concerning fundamental values there may rightly be no space for discretion that is not justified convincingly. The courts in their supervisory jurisdiction cannot simply defer to assertions of 'plenary political authority, promotion of the public good, fidelity to traditional moral values or social roles, or financial constraints'.[96] Their supervision must be purposive and substantive. Proportionality methodology is rationality in operation. While the values of human rights are more well developed, its methodology is appropriate to administrative law more generally, as Paul Craig has argued.[97] In substance, it may not differ greatly from variable intensity reasonableness review.[98] But if the sequencing of considerations encourages focus upon

[92] Ibid at 619.

[93] Taggart, 'Prolegomenon', above n 1 at 227.

[94] Williams, 'Statute Law', above n 82 at 168.

[95] Taggart, 'Outside Canadian', above n 11 at 652.

[96] L Weinrib, 'The Postwar Paradigm and American Exceptionalism' in S Choudhry (ed), *The Migration of Constitutional Ideas* (Cambridge, Cambridge University Press, 2006) 84 at 96.

[97] P Craig, *Administrative Law* (London, Thomson-Sweet and Maxwell, 5th ed, 2003) 630.

[98] As Lord Cooke argued: see, for example, 'The Struggle for Simplicity in Administrative Law' in M Taggart (ed), *Judicial Review of Administrative Action in the 1980s: Problems and Prospects* (Auckland, Oxford University Press in association with the Legal Research Foundation, 1986) 1 at 5.

constitutional and administrative values and their exposition, as the culture of justification requires, administrative law will come of age.

When that happens, Mr Pickles[99] and Jaws[100] and all who exercise power over others will join administrators under a principled rule of law. Mr Wiseman will have full reasons.[101] AV Dicey will have some space, but so will good government. And judges will never avert their eyes from serious injustice caused by administrative process. The intellectual history to be written of administrative law may then reveal that the subject was oviferous indeed.

[99] M Taggart, *Private Property and Abuse of Rights in Victorian England: The Story of Edward Pickles and the Bradford Water Supply* (Oxford, Oxford University Press, 2002).

[100] See Sir Stephen Sedley, *Freedom, Law and Justice* (50th series, The Hamlyn Lectures) (London, Sweet & Maxwell, 1999) 38.

[101] Taggart, 'Vexing the Establishment', above n 87.

5

The 'Hidden Paw' of the State and the Publicisation of Private Law

CAROL HARLOW*

Macavity's a Mystery Cat: he's called the Hidden Paw –
For he's the master criminal who can defy the Law.
He's the bafflement of Scotland Yard, the Flying Squad's despair:
For when they reach the scene of crime – *Macavity's not there*!

T.S. Eliot, Old Possum's Book of Practical Cats.

The Province Of Administrative Law Revisited

TOWARDS THE END of the century that gave birth to the 'administrative state' and just as New Right government was about to lose its charm for the United Kingdom, Michael Taggart organised a conference in Canada to consider the 'province of administrative law'.[1] As a group, Taggart felt that lawyers had been slow to appreciate the impact of 'the profound changes brought about by deregulation, commercialisation, corporatisation, public sector downsizing, privatisation and globalisation'. Fifteen-plus years after the 'New Right' revolution,[2] they had not come to grips with the paradigm shift. Indeed, Mark Aronson noted a flight of administrative law scholars, more especially in the US, 'to the new Jerusalem, which beckons with responsive regulation, regulatory negotiation and regulation by performance outcome and through economic

* I am as ever grateful to Mark Aronson and Richard Rawlings for their help and advice.

[1] M Taggart (ed), 'The Province of Administrative Law Determined' in M Taggart (ed), *The Province of Administrative Law* (Oxford, Hart Publishing, 1997) [Taggart, *Province*] at 2.

[2] D King, *The New Right, Politics, Markets and Citizenship* (Basingstoke, Macmillan, 1st edn, 1987) [King, *The New Right*] dated the New Right revolution to the early 1980s, linking it to the rejection of Keynesian economics after the oil crisis of the 1970s and to Margaret Thatcher's Government in the UK (1979–90) and Ronald Reagan's US Presidency (1981–89). In the US, M Tushnet, *The New Constitutional Order* (Princeton, New Jersey, Princeton University Press, 2003) characterised the changes as 'constitutional'. In the UK, to which this paper is limited, John Major took over from Margaret Thatcher in 1990 and Major's Conservative Government gave way to Tony Blair's New Labour Government in 1997, inaugurating 10-plus years of New Labour rule.

incentives'.[3] Would we see control by lawyers and law courts in the name of the rule of law replaced by the values and, more importantly, processes of regulators and auditors?[4] Was the future of administrative law to become merely a subset of regulation?

Liberalism, argued Roger Scruton, sees the state as means to the end of individual freedom. It is therefore 'bound to consider the civil society as absolutely separate from the state, and to require of the latter only that minimum of interference in the life of society which the aim of freedom requires.'[5] Many public lawyers felt differently. The more radical were dismayed by the destruction of the state industrial sector under the pretence that privatisation 'hands back, to the people of this country, industries that have no place in the public sector'.[6] Concern was expressed at the lack of *constitutional* protection in common law countries for public goods.[7] Others, committed to a 'New Deal' ideology, feared the demise of the welfare state, which they saw as largely beneficent, under the impact of radical conservatism.[8] They deplored the nostrum that 'less government is good government'[9] and the consequential attack on the administrative state. The 'new public management' started from the assumption that the administrative state was too large and costly and that centralised or rule-oriented solutions were part of the problem. Its logo was 'the Three Es' of efficiency, economy, and effectiveness; it was concerned, as H. Wade MacLaughlan put it, with flexibility, experimentation, responsiveness, cost-effectiveness, cost cutting and performance.[10] The fear was that the concept of public service would be washed away on a tide of contracting out and managerialism.[11]

The Province reflects the traditional preoccupation of public lawyers with the state and state power.[12] The state seemed to be shrinking. It was being 'hollowed

[3] M Aronson, 'A Public Lawyer's Responses to Privatisation and Outsourcing', in Taggart, *Province*, above n 1 at 43.

[4] See M Power, The *Audit Society, Rituals of Verification* (Oxford, Oxford University Press, 1997).

[5] R Scruton, *The Meaning of Conservatism* (London, Penguin Books, 1980) at 45.

[6] J Moore, 'Why Privatise?' in J Kay, J Moore and D Thompson (eds) *Privatisation and Regulation: The UK Experience*, (Oxford, Clarendon Press, 1986) at 93 [Moore, 'Why Privatise?'].

[7] T Prosser, 'The State, Constitutions and Implementing Economic Policy: Privatization and Regulation in the UK, France and the USA' (1995) 4 *Social & Legal Studies* 507; C Graham and T Prosser 'Privatising Nationalised Industries: Constitutional Issues and New Legal Techniques' (1987) 50 *Modern Law Review* 16.

[8] See King, *The New Right*, above n 2 at 49–53; R Goodin, 'Vulnerabilities and Responsibilities: An Ethical Defence of the Welfare State' (1985) 79 *American Political Science Review* 775.

[9] Moore, 'Why Privatise?', above n 6. For the international spread of the New Deal ideology amongst administrative lawyers, see *Administrative Law Today: Culture, Ideas, Institutions, Processes, Values*, Special Issue in honour of John Willis (2005) 55 *University of Toronto Law Journal* 31- 890.

[10] H Wade MacLaughlan, 'Public Service Law and the New Public Management' in Taggart, *Province*, above n 1 at 118 [MacLaughlan 'Public Service'].

[11] M Freedland and S Sciarra (eds), *Public Services and Citizenship in European Law, Public and Labour Law Perspectives* (Oxford, Clarendon Press, 1998).

[12] See M Loughlin, *Public Law and Political Theory* (Oxford, Clarendon Press, 1992) and *The Idea of Public Law* (Oxford, Oxford University Press, 2004).

out'[13] and losing power as public functions were hived off sideways to non-departmental public bodies or 'quangos' – an acronym designed to stress autonomy from government – with obvious implications for accountability and legitimacy. Though not strictly a 'hollowing out' of state power, central government was losing power to regional governments, assemblies and legislatures. Sovereignty became an issue[14] and the role of the nation state came into question as power was uploaded to institutions of transnational governance, notably for the UK, the European Communities.[15] On the one hand globalisation was seen as diminishing the power of the state and undermining its capacity to bring under control the engines of modern capitalism; on the other, it was, as Alfred Aman Jr saw matters, undercutting 'the move towards greater political participation and ultimately greater transparency of agency decision-making processes that typified modern administrative law in the 1960s and 1970s'.[16] Aman saw administrative law as a potential saviour, helping to create 'the institutional architecture necessary for democracy to work, not only within the institutions of government but also beyond them in the sphere where the private sector governs'.[17]

So the underlying theme of *The Province* was attrition, and the contributors' mood, though not entirely pessimistic, was protective. Public law, which concerned itself with the important matters of 'constitutional and near-constitutional values, with hierarchical order, with due process, rules and standards, with systemic coherence, and with the manners and sustainability of institutional practices',[18] was seen as threatened by the commercial values of neo-liberalism and the public choice attack on the 'public-regarding' premises of administrative law.[19] Public lawyers were sceptical of the capacity of private law to take on a control function generally associated with public law, and of private lawyers' willingness to mould it into an instrument for accountability. A 'contracting' state would allow private law to replace public law and thus erode the machinery for public accountability and control.[20] There was in consequence much 'skirmishing ...[over] the public/private divide'.[21] My argument in this chapter is that colonisation of the private by the public is the true characteristic

[13] R Rhodes, 'The Hollowing Out of the State: The Changing Nature of the Public Service in Britain' (1994) 65 *Political Quarterly* 138.

[14] See N MacCormick, *Questioning Sovereignty, Law, State and Nation in the European Commonwealth* (Oxford, Oxford University Press, 1999).

[15] See A-M Slaughter, *A New World Order* (Princeton, New Jersey, Princeton University Press, 2004) and 'Disaggregated Sovereignty' in D Held and M Koenig-Archibugi (eds), *Global Governance and Public Accountability* (Oxford, Blackwell, 2005).

[16] A Aman Jr, 'Administrative Law for a New Century', in Taggart, *Province*, above n 1 at 95.

[17] A Aman Jr, *The Democracy Deficit* (New York, New York University Press, 2004) at 136.

[18] MacLaughlan, 'Public Service', above n 10.

[19] Taggart, *Province*, above n 1 at 3.

[20] I Harden, *The Contracting State* (Buckingham, Open University Press, 1992). See also M. Freedland, 'Government by Contract and Public Law' [1994] *Public Law* 86.

[21] Taggart, *Province*, above n 1 at 4.

of contemporary government and that the state, far from ceding power to the public sector, was everywhere active behind the scenes.

In a concise and typically scholarly introduction to the published conference papers, Taggart noted two main responses to the perceived problems. The first was a 'self-conscious identification of public law values', with the object of 'distil[ling] the essence of administrative law for transporting to the newly deregulated and privatised areas'.[22] By and large these were values of liberal constitutionalism.[23] Taggart drew his list of openness, fairness, participation, impartiality, accountability, honesty and rationality from both constitutional and administrative law.[24] Dawn Oliver, in an exploratory conference paper, added to the classical administrative law principles that ground judicial review a new set of values based in human rights—dignity, respect, security and autonomy—as 'part of the climate' or 'background' in which judges operate.[25] The reference to judges is significant. Taggart saw this limb of the debate as essentially court-centred, focused on the legitimacy of judicial activism and the willingness and ability of the judges to propagate and disseminate public law values. Later, the values debate would blossom as a branch of a wider discourse of human rights by which it has largely been swallowed up.[26] Alongside, a secondary limb would dwindle into sterile disputes over common law constitutionalism.[27]

Taggart's second or 'bottom up' approach to privatisation was more empirical, focusing on public administration and what actually went on inside offices and bureaux.[28] This line of analysis, represented in the *Province* by studies of contracting out, new public management, intermediate or civil society associations and rulemaking in the police, has since been fleshed out by many studies of

[22] Taggart, *Province*, above n 1 at 3.

[23] As expressed in the work of Ronald Dworkin or TRS Allan, more particularly R Dworkin, *Taking Rights Seriously* (London, Duckworth, 1976); TRS Allan, *Law, Liberty and Justice, The Legal Foundations of British Constitutionalism* (Oxford, Oxford University Press, 1993) and *Constitutional Justice: A Liberal Theory of the Rule of Law* (Oxford, Oxford University Press, 2001).

[24] Taggart, *Province*, above n 1 at 3; M Taggart, ''The Peculiarities of the English': Resisting the Public/Private Distinction' in P Craig and R Rawlings (eds), *Law and Administration in Europe* (Oxford, Oxford University Press, 2003) [Craig and Rawlings, *Law and Administration*]; M Aronson, B Dyer and M Groves, *Judicial Review of Administrative Action* (Sydney, Law Book Co, 4th edn, 2008) at 1. See also J Freeman, 'Symposium: Public Values in an Era of Privatization: Extending Public Law Norms through Privatization' (2003) 116 *Harvard Law Review* 1285.

[25] D Oliver, 'The Underlying Values of Public Law' in Taggart, *Province*, above n 1 at 223, 240; D Oliver, *Common Values and the Public-Private Divide*, (London, Butterworths, 1999) [Oliver, 'The Underlying Values'].

[26] See C McCrudden, 'A Common Law of Human Rights? Transnational Judicial Conversations on Constitutional Rights' in K O'Donovan and G Rubin (eds), *Human Rights and Legal History* (Oxford, Oxford University Press, 2000).

[27] The substantial literature, which will not be re-visited here, is chronicled and critiqued by T Poole, 'Back to the Future? Unearthing the Theory of Common Law Constitutionalism' (2003) 23 *Oxford Journal of Legal Studies* 435 and 'Questioning Common Law Constitutionalism' (2005) 25 *Legal Studies* 142.

[28] Taggart, *Province*, above n 1 at 3.

the state's various administrative functions.[29] I see it as an essential step in theorising administrative law regimes and it is the approach followed in this paper.

To sum up, the new political order seemed to threaten public law in three main ways: first, by the substitution of private law (or liberal-economic) values for public law values seen as more liberal and humane; secondly, through the shrinking of its territorial domain. A third threat came from the 'hollowing out' of the state by a 'new world order', where 'governance', dominated by multinational corporations and conducted through amorphous networks of public and private transnational actors and bodies, was replacing 'billeted and bounded' government.[30] In all these areas, there was anxiety over the inability of private law to exercise control functions generally accepted as a major function of public law.

Twelve years later, a festschrift designed to honour Michael Taggart's substantial contribution to legal scholarship to which many of the original participants are contributing, seems the right time and place to re-visit some of these assumptions. In this paper, I shall argue that many were misplaced. The state has shown great regenerative power. Both at national and international level, where states remain the primary actors, the powers and influence of central government have burgeoned. In Part 2 of this paper I shall show regulation and contractualisation acting as mercenaries in a steady process of empowering a new regulatory state. I shall look too at the use of private law techniques to augment state penetration of the private sphere. In Part 3, I shall consider how, in the new cold climate of the post-9/11 world that contributors to *The Province* could hardly have foreseen, concepts of risk and security have underpinned and legitimated the growth of a powerful and uncontrolled surveillance state.

The Decentred State

A number of straws suggested that the wind might not be blowing so strongly in the direction of privatisation (using this term broadly to cover property, law and values). In *The Province*, Aronson expressed his doubts over the utility of the public/private distinction, arguing that 'mixed governmental methods fracture the old dichotomy between public and private power, into a trichotomy which recognises the sharing of governmental functions between organs of the state and organisations sourced in the private sector'; hybridisation was taking place,

[29] Particularly influential were J Freeman, 'Collaborative Governance in the Administrative State' (1997) 45 *UCLA Law Review* 1 and 'The Private Role in Public Governance' (2000) 75 *New York University Law Review* 543.

[30] M Shapiro, 'Administrative Law Unbounded: Reflections on Government and Governance' (2001) 8 *Indiana Journal of Global Legal Studies* 369; C. Harlow, 'Deconstructing Governance' (2004) 23 *Yearbook of European Law* 57.

although administrative law had only recently recognised the reality.[31] In similar vein, MacLean exposed the extent to which, largely unnoticed, a third non-governmental sector was growing up, composed of voluntary organisations such as housing associations and other organs of civil society that exercised public functions with the help of public funding.[32] In time, this third sector would be largely 'captured' by government through funding and regulation. At another level, Taggart argued that values were neither specifically public nor specifically private; they were simply embedded in the common law to be drawn on as appropriate in diverse situations. There was 'a synthesis or blending of public and private law principles' to which 'the artificial separation of common law and statute law, and the common law's innate superiority complex' was blinding us.[33]

In their 'bottom up' studies of privatisation, Cosmo Graham and Tony Prosser echoed Wolfgang Friedmann's earlier dismissal of the distinction between direct government control of nationalised industry and indirect control through regulation as largely nominal: 'The bulk of industry and business, which remains in private ownership, is subject to varying degrees of public supervision and regulation'.[34] They pointed out that nationalisation had started out with an 'arms length' relationship with government that had soon become much closer; 'political intervention became extensive' though it remained 'largely *ad hoc*'. Privatisation, they deduced, was likely to progress similarly:[35]

> The key question must be whether government possesses the tools by which it can successfully intervene in the affairs of privatised concerns. The answer to this must be a firm 'yes', and indeed it has taken care to provide itself with the necessary legal powers for intervention.

There were three tools at the disposal of government. In regulation (and licensing, a sub-set of regulation), government had retained important powers and the operation of regulatory bodies was to a large degree dependent on prior ministerial decisions. The 'golden share' enabled government to participate as the major shareholder in corporate decision-making. The third tool was contract. The authors foresaw too that privatisation alone would not be enough to resolve the characteristic problems of nationalisation; it would merely provide 'the opportunity for the design of fresh institutions which may or may not be superior to those of public ownership'. This prediction has been amply fulfilled.

[31] Taggart, *Province*, above n 1 at 5. See now P Cane, 'Accountability and the Public/Private Distinction', in N Bamforth and P Leyland (eds), *Public Law in a Multi-Layered Constitution* (Oxford, Hart Publishing, 2003).

[32] J Maclean, 'Intermediate Associations and the State' in Taggart, *Province*, above note 1 at 160.

[33] Taggart, *Province*, above n 1 at 5; Oliver, above n 25.

[34] W Friedmann, *Law in a Changing Society* (Harmondsworth, Penguin, 2nd edn, 1964), 273–74.

[35] C Graham and T Prosser, 'The Privatisation of State Enterprises' in C Graham and T Prosser (eds.), *Waiving the Rules: The Constitution under Thatcherism* (Milton Keynes, Open University Press, 1988) at 76–78 [Graham and Prosser 'The Privatisation'].

Transforming Regulation

In the special case of monopolies, regulation was initially envisaged as a temporary measure, a way to protect the public interest and the customers of utilities that would 'hold the fort' until markets replaced it with the free play of competition; like the state in Marxist theory (as Prosser cynically observed) regulation would then wither away.[36] Initially it was envisaged too that such regulation as was deemed necessary would 'operate with a light touch, based on a number of simple and stable rules which would be revised at set intervals.'[37] The first pretence (as Prosser pointed out),[38] 'had little correspondence with the reality of utility regulation in the UK, the EU, or indeed in the USA'. The direction in which things were really moving was demonstrated when the electricity supply industry came to be privatised in 1990. In its 1988 White Paper, the Conservative Government expressed the intention 'to lightly regulate' the industry, while leaving the privatised companies largely free to manage their affairs 'without the interference of government'.[39] The subsequent legislation, however, introduced a complex licensing system to be operated in parallel by the Secretary of State and a Director-General of Electricity Supply appointed by him 'to secure that all reasonable demands for electricity are satisfied' and with considerable influence over pricing. Both were able to issue licences, the difference being that, by section 6, the minister had to 'consult' the D-G while the D-G needed 'the consent' of the minister. As Blanche Sas observed, there appeared to be a centralisation of power in the minister—it was 'hard to conceive of a single power he has relinquished'—and the independence of the regulator was suspect:[40]

> Although described as an 'independent' regulator, the question can be posed as to exactly how independent is [the regulator]. Its Director is appointed by the Government, the number and quality of its staff are dependent on the agreement of the Treasury, for its investigations and enforcement of authorisation conditions it will be dependent on the [Monopolies and Mergers Commission] and so on. It could be said that in fact its independence appears to involve mainly the removal of [the regulator] from direct Parliamentary control, except in so far as its annual report is to be laid before Parliament.

Finally, the Government had played 'an active interventionary role' in the negotiation of all the private contractual arrangements between the privatised public electricity suppliers, the generators and the national grid company,

[36] T Prosser, 'Theorising Utility Regulation' [1999] 62 *Modern Law Review* 196 [Prosser, 'Theorising Utility'].

[37] C Veljanovski, *The Future of Industry Regulation in the UK* (European Policy Forum, 1993) at 59.

[38] Prosser, 'Theorising Utility', above n 36.

[39] DTI, *Privatising Electricity*, Cm. 322 (1988).

[40] B Sas, 'Regulation and the Privatised Electricity Supply Industry' (1990) 53 *Modern Law Review* 485, 491 and 497. The regulator, OFFER, has now been replaced by a super-regulator, OFGEM.

exposing the important role played by government in contract. The scheme amounted to a tacit admission of the central presence of the state in regulation. Decisively, this was the shape of things to come.

More generally, a 1998 White Paper exposed the fiction that responsibility for policy lay with regulators, confirming that 'the Government not regulators, should determine the social objectives of regulation.'[41] Statutory guidance was proposed, exposing the hand of government on the tiller, exposed again when the Cabinet Office set in place non-statutory 'guidance'.[42] Steady progression to juridification and state intervention has now culminated in the Legislative and Regulatory Reform Act 2006, which gave the soft law guidance a hard, statutory edge; and the Regulatory Enforcement and Sanctions Act 2008, which has introduced a new and toughened sanctions regime. Ministers are now authorised to confer on regulators by Order the power to administer civil sanctions, including fixed and variable fines, enforcement and stop orders. Noting with displeasure a 'general retreat from reliance on the criminal justice system alone as a means to control wrongdoing', the House of Lords Constitution Committee queried the compatibility of the new system with the rule of law. 'The scheme envisaged in the bill will enable the transfer, on an unprecedented scale, of responsibilities for deciding guilt and imposing financial sanctions (with no upper limit) away from independent and impartial judges to officials…The onus will be placed on the individual or company to seek first an internal review and then an appeal to the First-tier Tribunal.'[43] This is very much a manifestation of core state power.

Something very similar was taking place in the more obviously private field of self-regulation. During the nineteenth century, the professions had gained status and autonomy, bringing them powers of self-regulation. Under Margaret Thatcher, attacks on trade unions[44] were paralleled by assaults on the status and autonomy of the civil service, the medical and teaching professions, universities and the legal profession.[45] Intervention typically took the form of control through audit: the imposition of government standards, 'league tables' and requirements to publicise in the name of accountability. More recently, regulators

[41] DTI, *A Fair Deal for Consumers: Modernizing the Framework for Utility Regulation*, Cm 3898 (1998) [213–18] cited Prosser, 'Theorising Utility', above n 36.

[42] See now Better Regulation Task Force, *Principles of Good Regulation* (Cabinet Office, 2003).

[43] House of Lords Constitution Committee, 1st Report, Session 2007–08, *The Regulatory Enforcement and Sanctions Bill*, HL Paper 16 at para. 9. RESA actually implements recommendations of the Hampton Review, *Reducing administrative burdens: effective inspection and enforcement* (HM Treasury, 2005) and the Macrory Review, *Regulatory Justice: Making Sanctions Effective* (Better Regulation Executive, 2006). The 'first tier tribunal' is a new general purpose tribunal established by the Tribunals, Courts and Enforcement Act 2007.

[44] K Ewing, 'Trade Unions and the Constitution: the Impact of the New Conservatives' in Graham and Prosser, *The Privatisation*, above n 35.

[45] See M Burrage, 'Mrs Thatcher against the 'Little Republics': Ideology, Precedents, and Reactions', in T Halliday and L Karpik, *Lawyers and the Rise of Western Political Liberalism* (Oxford, Clarendon Press, 1997).

have been introduced: the complaints-handling function of the Law Society has, for example, been transferred to an Office for Legal Complaints and its regulatory functions hived off to a semi-autonomous Solicitors Regulation Authority, now supervised by the Legal Services Board,[46] while a Director of Fair Access to Higher Education appointed by the Minister oversees university entrance requirements and practice.

Elaborating the concept of 'decentred regulation' (terminology that unintentionally minimises the public dimension of the regulatory process) Julia Black postulated four modalities of state participation in self-regulation—mandated, sanctions, coerced and voluntary—in only one of which there was 'no active involvement, direct or indirect, in promoting or mandating self-regulation'.[47] Robert Baldwin and Martin Cave detected some form of state involvement in virtually all regulatory schemes, observing that self-regulation typically formed part of a wider regulatory scheme and, even where it appeared to lack any state involvement, might 'constitute a response to threats by government that if nothing is done state action will follow'.[48] For Black, there was a steady progression in 'decentred regulation' to a point where clear distinctions between public and private have broken down, freeing the state, with the aid of legal rules backed by (often criminal) sanctions, to act through private persons in pursuit of its goals.[49] She picked up the new interventionist edge of regulation in a significantly broad definition of regulation as 'the sustained and focused attempt *to alter the behaviour of others* with the intention of producing a broadly identified outcome or outcomes'.

In the UK, Michael Moran confirmed the picture of steadily increasing state intervention.[50] He linked the decline of self-regulation and emergence of a 'regulatory state' to the twin influences of globalisation and the rise of a powerful new regulator: the European Commission—whose role in pushing states towards privatisation has in this respect, I would argue, been considerably overstated.[51] Today, regulation in the UK has expanded as exponentially as state intervention in regulatory activity. The Hampton Review, for example, recorded 63 national regulators and 468 local authorities engaged in regulation, together employing

[46] The Legal Services Ombudsman was created by the Courts and Legal Services Act 1990 and replaced by the Office for Legal Complaints in the Legal Services Act 2007. The Solicitors Regulation Authority, set up after the Clementi *Review of the Regulatory Framework for Legal Services in England and Wales* (2004), was renamed in 2007, to underscore its autonomy. The Director of Fair Access to Higher Education was created by the Higher Education Act 2004.

[47] J Black, 'Constitutionalising Self-regulation' (1996) 59 *Modern Law Review* 24.

[48] R Baldwin and M Cave, *Understanding Regulation* (Oxford, Oxford University Press, 1999) at 126.

[49] J Black, 'Critical Reflections on Regulation' (2002) 27 *Australian Journal of Legal Philosophy* 1.

[50] M Moran, *The British Regulatory State: High Modernism and Hyper-Innovation* (Oxford, Oxford University Press, 2003) at 68–9, 92–3.

[51] See G Majone, 'The rise of the regulatory state in Europe' (1994) 17 *West European Politics* 77; B. Eberlein and E. Grande, 'Beyond Delegation: Transnational Regulatory Regimes and the EU Regulatory State' (2005) 12 *Journal of European Public Policy* 89.

upwards of 60,000 people.[52] Local government is itself increasingly regulated, with a transformation of the traditional British model of 'independent statelets' into an 'agency model' of subservience to central government and its policies.[53] Regulation, which came with audit by an admittedly independent though nonetheless centralising Audit Commission operating through the technique of 'Value-for-Money' audits, is now, despite the departmental rhetoric,[54] increasingly supplemented by central government directions and guidance, as a cursory look at the departmental website reveals.

More recently, regulatory centralisation has been augmented by the trend to 'super-regulators', responsible for the supervision of whole industries or activities, such as the energy regulator OFGEM, the Office of Communications (OFCOM) established by the Communications Act 2002 as regulator for the UK communications industries, with responsibilities across television, radio, telecommunications and wireless communications services, or the Equality and Human Rights Commission (below). In principle autonomous and independent of the state, these vast and powerful bodies, which are usually appointed by ministers and carry out what are obviously public functions, can be seen as taking up local government's erstwhile position of 'independent statelet'. This move is enhanced by increasing resort to criminal sanction,[55] an obvious hallmark of public power, and the new 'civil' sanctions package mentioned earlier. As summed up by Ian Bartle and Peter Vass the reality is[56]

> a distinct increase in the role of the state…evident in the regulation of many areas of modern life, including a wide range of economic, industrial, legal and financial areas, health, culture and sport. In addition, although late twentieth century Britain saw a rise in the ideologies of 'deregulation' and an aversion to state intervention, the privatisation and liberalisation of key economic sectors has been accompanied by an increase in regulatory rules.

Risk and Regulation

Citizens born in state hospitals and educated in state schools had come to believe that the state could and should wrap every citizen in a personal security blanket.

[52] P Hampton, *Reducing Administrative Burdens: effective inspection and enforcement* (HM Treasury, 2005) at 11–12.

[53] Terminology used by A King, *Does the United Kingdom still have a Constitution?* (London, Sweet & Maxwell, 2001) at 27. See now King, *The British Constitution* (Oxford, Oxford University Press, 2007), ch 7, 'The Ghost of Local Government'. And see M Loughlin, 'The Demise of Local Government' in V Bogdanor (ed), *The British Constitution in the Twentieth Century* (Oxford, Oxford University Press, 2003). Relationships are now semi-formalised in a Central-Local Concordat of 12 December 2007, published on the departmental website, currently the Department for Communities and Local Government.

[54] DCLG, *Strong and Prosperous Communities*, Cm 6939 (2006).

[55] See R Baldwin, 'The New Punitive Regulation' (2004) 67 *Modern Law Review* 351.

[56] I Bartle and P Vass, 'Self-regulation within the Regulatory State: Towards a New Regulatory Paradigm?' (2007) 85 *Public Administration* 885, 886.

This growing perception of the state as the main insurance against personal disaster could not easily be halted. The post-war 'cradle-to-grave' welfare state had nourished a risk-averse society, increasingly preoccupied with protection against risk. Elizabeth Fisher has styled risk 'the new buzzword of administrative governance', as the task of public decision-makers and the legitimacy of public decision-making is increasingly 'characterised in terms of the identification, assessment, and management of risk is also being evaluated on such a basis.'[57] The New Labour Government has always seen itself as a key actor, signalling its awareness in an early White Paper.[58]

Development by sociologists like Ulrich Beck of risk as a concept[59] has proved central to the growth of the regulatory state. Michael Power sees the 'risk management of everything' as the 'motif for one of the major public policy challenges of the early twenty-first century' and sets it 'at the centre stage of public service delivery and a model of organisation in its own right'.[60] He puts his finger too on a key characteristic: that, since the mid-1990s, risk management and private corporative governance agendas have become 'intertwined, if not identical'. To put this differently, having a broad and formal risk management programme is the central characteristic of being 'a good organisation', a desideratum that increasingly engages the efforts of both public and private sectors. Today, risk analysis is the core of *all* managerial and regulatory practices;[61] risk and impact assessments are a mandatory element in *all* forms of management and rulemaking.

This is a society in which security has become a key political value with the extended meaning of 'being protected from or not exposed to danger. This involves protection against unwanted and damaging change—loss of income, livelihood or home, for instance'.[62] Confronting claims running into many billions from disappointed customers of private insurance companies, employees facing the loss of their private occupational pensions, mortgagees, and shareholders of private banks, governments may reflect ruefully on a new form of public/private partnership in which profit is privatised while losses are underwritten by the state.[63] In this new context, state regulation seems inevitable and

[57] E Fisher, 'The Rise of the Risk Commonwealth and the Challenge for Administrative Law' [2003] *Public Law* 455.

[58] *Modernising Government*, Cm 4310 (1999); Cabinet Office, *Risk: Improving Government's Capability to Handle Risk and Uncertainty* (HMSO, 2002).

[59] See notably U Beck (trans Ritter), *Risk Society, Towards a New Modernity* (London, Sage Publications, 1992).

[60] M Power, *The Risk Management of Everything* (London, Demos, 2004) 10, 11 and *Organising a World of Risk Management* (Oxford, Oxford University Press, 2007). See also B Hutter, *The Attractions of Risk-Based Regulation* (London, Centre for Risk and Regulation, 2005).

[61] J Black, 'The Emergence of Risk-Based Regulation and the New Public Risk Management in the United Kingdom' [2005] *Public Law* 512.

[62] Oliver, 'The Underlying Values', above n 25 at 226.

[63] See, e.g., Parliamentary Commissioner for Administration, *Trusting in the Pensions Promise*, HC 984 (2006); Parliamentary Commissioner for Administration, *Equitable Life: A Decade of*

even the regulators are affected, as the UK Financial Services Authority found when asked to re-regulate in the aftermath of the failure of the Northern Rock building society/bank[63a]. The FSA, an independent non-governmental body financed by the financial services industry, which presents itself as 'operationally independent of Government', is in practice accountable to Treasury Ministers, who appoint the FSA Board, and through them to Parliament.[64]

Nationalisation, declared unthinkable when Railtrack, a group of private companies that owned the track etc of the British rail system, went into liquidation in 2001,[65] has crept back on to the agenda. In February 2008, 'a period of temporary public ownership' for the stricken Northern Rock bank was arranged, after negotiations for sale to private buyers were discounted. Emphasising that the bank would be 'run at arm's length and on a commercial basis', the Chancellor of the Exchequer appointed a new Executive Chairman and Chief Financial Officer. At the same time, legislation to provide 'for the first time a permanent statutory regime for dealing with failing banks' was passed and applied to Northern Rock and Bradford & Bingley.[66] In October, with the announcement of a bail out of British banks to the tune of some £37 billion, the British Government underlined its 'hands off approach'. A new arms length body would be created 'to manage the Government's shareholdings in recapitalised institutions on a professional and wholly commercial basis' and 'transparent arrangements [would] be put in place to ensure that any role for the Government in relation to investment decision-making is clearly defined.' At the same time the Government was negotiating a right 'to agree with boards the appointment of new independent non-executive directors' and was strenuously urging policy change in the shape of schemes to avoid repossession of homes, with restrictions on the remuneration of senior executives.[67]

In the United States, the Government of President Bush has gone rather further. 'Fannie Mae' and 'Freddie Mac', both government sponsored enterprise and public companies, were placed into the conservatorship of the Federal Housing Finance Agency, action described by the Director of the Federal Housing Finance Agency, James Lockhart, as 'one of the most sweeping government

Regulatory Failure HC 815 (2007/8) and on Northern Rock, statement by the Chancellor of the Exchequer, *Hansard*, col. 959 (18 Feb. 2008); Northern Rock plc Transfer Order 2008, SI 2008/432.

[63a] Financial Services Authority, *Retailing Banking Code of Practice*, CP 09/19, currently out to consultation.

[64] Financial Services and Markets Act 2000.

[65] See P Leyland, 'The Railtrack Case: Mainly on the Wrong Track' (2004–5) 14 *Utilities Law Review* 213.

[66] See section 3 of the Banking (Special Provisions) Act 2008; the The Bradford & Bingley plc Transfer of Securities and Property etc. Order 2008, SI 2008/2546; The Transfer of Rights and Liabilities to ING Order 2008, SI 2008/2666; and the Banking Bill 2008, at the time of writing before Parliament.

[67] HM Treasury, Press Release 105/08, Statement on financial support to the banking industry (13 Oct. 2008; Press release 114/08 New company to manage Government's shareholding in banks 03 November 2008.

interventions in private financial markets in decades'.[68] Shortly afterwards, Congress was asked to approve a 'bail-out' package to purchase distressed assets, especially mortgage-backed securities, from the nation's banks. The three-page draft coupled sweeping powers for the Treasury Secretary to buy and sell mortgage-related securities with a draconian preclusive clause barring agency oversight and review by the courts:

> Decisions by the Secretary pursuant to the authority of this Act are non-reviewable and committed to agency discretion, and may not be reviewed by any court of law or any administrative agency.

Rejected in this form, the Emergency Economic Stabilization Act of 2008, which authorises the Secretary of the Treasury to spend up to $700 billion to purchase 'distressed assets' from US banks, is effectively, and was widely seen by the American public, as a nationalisation of bad debts.

The Transformation of Contract

Implicit in the debate over contractualisation during the early 1990s was fear of the 'hollowing out the state' and a consequent diminution of the role of public law.

The common law of contract was considered inadequate both in the way it had dealt historically with government contracts and because of 'the absence of a framework of legal principles governing the growing role of contract in public administration'.[69] There was, as Nick Seddon observed, an inbuilt conflict with Taggart's list of public law values (above).[70]

> Contract contradicts these values almost perfectly, with honesty being the only value common to both contract and public law. Contract is traditionally about secrecy, no duty to act fairly, participation of the immediate parties but otherwise not concerned with third parties, no duty to act impartially, accountability only to the extent required by the contract and then only to the other party and no duty to act rationally. When traditional contract values are combined with the public purpose, the mix does not necessarily work very well... The safeguards for the protection of citizens' interests and wellbeing inherent in public law are simply absent with contract and there has been no adaptation of contract to fill the gap. Official reports and enquiries have pointed to the adverse consequences for public accountability of the use of contract by government but with little to show for such criticism.

In similar vein, Mark Aronson in his study of contract and outsourcing had predicted a general move away from the rule-bound world of K C Davis, which

[68] FHFA, Statement of the Director (7 Sep. 2008) available on line.

[69] P Vincent-Jones, 'Regulating Government by Contract' (2002) 65 *Modern Law Review* 611 [Vincent-Jones, 'Regulating Government']. And see Harden and Freedland, above n 20.

[70] N Seddon, 'The Interaction of Contract and Executive Power' (2003) 31 *Federal Law Review* 541 at 548.

had formed the blueprint for much post-war thinking in administrative law.[71] Aronson saw rules under attack 'as a hangover of the command and control mentality'; they were giving way to discretion as the mode of regulatory governance. The new rules were 'qualitatively and operationally different, with a heavy emphasis on regulatory flexibility. In many regulatory areas in which business interests prevail, the great project of turning discretion into rules has been turned on its head'.[72] While in one sense this prediction was mistaken—privatisation did not halt the onward march of juridification but contributed largely to it—the reminder of the state's tendency to 'retreat from legalism' in matters of financial policy was exactly right.

Two aspects in particular of 'governance by contract' attracted public lawyers' attention in the United Kingdom: the first (self-evidently) was government contracting, where the European Community would soon assume responsibility for setting in place a framework for public procurement, with the somewhat paradoxical outcome of a proliferation of ineffective regulation under the banner of market liberalisation.[73] The second was the use of contract as a tool for public administration, as functions previously exercised by government departments were hived off to agencies or outsourced by local government. This debate would later be re-formulated in terms of constitutionalism and accountability.[74]

A three-fold, functional model of contractualisation has been suggested:[75]

> *Economic contracts* or contractual arrangements directed at improving public services through competition and/or the devolution of management powers to public purchasing or commissioning agencies in a variety of hybrid forms beyond simple market or bureaucratic organisation;
>
> *Administrative contracts* or 'pseudo-contracts' designed to separate the political and managerial aspects of government, and to clarify bureaucratic roles through performance-based management systems. These have evolved into the standard way of modelling public institutional relationships and delivering public services;
>
> *Social control contracts* or adaptations of the contractual mechanism used in the regulation of relationships between individual citizens and state authority.

Here, where the theme is the publicisation of the private, the emphasis will be on the evolution of contract into a form of 'pseudo-regulation' and the use of 'pseudo-contracts' for purposes of social control.

[71] KC Davis, *Discretionary Justice: a Preliminary Inquiry* (Baton Rouge, Louisiana State University Press, 1969).

[72] Taggart, *Province*, above n 1 at 43. For the continuity of the practices return to J Winckler, 'Law, State and Economy: The Industry Act 1975 in Context' (1075) 2 *British Journal of Law and Society* 103.

[73] See M Chiti, 'Regulation and Market in the Public Procurement Sector' (1995) 7 *European Review of Public Law* 373; S Arrowsmith, 'The Past and Future Evolution of EC Procurement Law: From Framework to Common Code?' (2006) 35 *Public Contract Law Journal* 337.

[74] A Davies, *Accountability: A Public Law Analysis of Government by Contract* (Oxford, Oxford University Press, 2001).

[75] See P Vincent-Jones, *The New Public Contracting* (Oxford, Oxford University Press, 2006).

The big change in the structure of major infrastructure initiatives has been in the way they are financed. Private Finance Initiatives (PFIs) and public/private partnerships (PPPs), eagerly welcomed by the New Labour Government, have blossomed into a central feature of contemporary government. A public/private partnership (PPP) has been defined as 'a risk-sharing relationship between the public and private sectors based upon a shared aspiration to bring about a desired public policy outcome'.[76] A PPP may be carried through by a private finance initiative (PFI) which, according to Matthew Flinders, differs from privatisation in that 'the public sector *remains a key actor in the project*, usually as both the facilitator of the project and the main purchaser of services' (emphasis added).[77] Also included in the 'complex multi-layered networks' set in place to deliver PPPs are public interest corporations (PICs), whose core characteristics are, according to Flinders, that they deliver a public service and are legally independent of government but do not have shareholders (or if they do, are restricted in terms of profits); in short, they are hybrids—neither private nor public.[78] Freedland calls this 'public/private market-making role', where public services are provided by a mix of public and private market institutions with 'government assuming the role of the makers and maintainers of these public/private market institutions', a 'new role for the state'.[79] Figures from the Treasury in 2003 showed its extent: in 2002 alone, 451 projects had been completed delivering 600 facilities under 563 PFI contracts and there were 65 new projects at an estimated cost of £7.5 billion.

Central to the debate over PPPs are natural concerns over effectiveness, transparency, accountability and democratic values: more pertinent to my argument here, however, is the extent to which the state is a major player in the arrangements. Government still proposes the projects, plans, drives, and supervises them. They are public in the sense that government usually 'owns' them, retaining a reversionary interest after a long-term franchise expires. But government raises the capital in ways that avoid both the need for tax legislation, parliamentary scrutiny and scrutiny through public law freedom of information legislation. Essentially government operates as a mortgagor of specific assets, embodying the terms in complex mortgage documents.[80]

Behind the scenes, the footprints of the state are everywhere. First and foremost, the Treasury has a key role in overseeing the financial negotiations. Similarly, the role of central management in the purportedly regional National

[76] *Building Better Partnerships* (IPPR, 2004).

[77] M Flinders, 'The Politics of Public-Private Partnership' (2005) 7 *British Journal of Politics and International Relations* 215 at 220.

[78] Ibid at 219. See also P Maltby, *In the Public Interest? Assessing the Potential of Public Interest Companies* (London IPPR, 2003).

[79] M Freedland, 'Government by Contract Re-examined—Some Functional Issues', in Craig and Rawlings, *Law and Administration*, above n 24 at 128.

[80] I am grateful to Mark Aronson for this explanation of the way BOOT (Build, Own, Operate, and Transfer to government) contracts operate.

Health Service has been described as 'paramount both in establishing the general parameters of the contracting process and the approach taken to dispute resolution'.[81] Richard Rawlings describes the complexity of the legal arrangements for modernising the London Underground system as 'mind-boggling'; the original contractual documentation ran to 28,000 pages and over two million words; it included intricate mathematical formulae to calculate both bonuses and penalties or abatements.[82] In complexity and specificity these contracts approximate to regulations and their terms are regulatory in character. We should note too a growing general practice of submitting disputes, as in the London Underground case, to a *statutory* arbiter who is something more than an arbitrator though a little less than a regulator.[83] I am not of course arguing that this is really regulation, as pseudo-contracts are. There is a measure of equality in bargains typically negotiated with giants of commerce and industry. At the end of the day, however, government can always pull out its regulatory weapons.

Where projects operate at arms length from government it is not in fact easy for government to shuffle off responsibility. Just as failing banks impinge on the country's economy, so responsibility for railway accidents is inevitably laid at the door of government as the ultimate risk regulator. Metronet's cost overruns for the London Underground were in the region of £1.2 billion; to keep the capital's Underground running, government was forced to act as 'safety-net'. In the notorious *Three Rivers* litigation, £850 million in damages was (unsuccessfully) claimed by the liquidators from the Bank of England as regulator;[84] the Private Shareholders Action Group's (unsuccessful) claim against the Government after Railtrack went bankrupt was for £157 million in government compensation.[85] Not surprisingly, it is central rather than local government or any of the other manifestations of the disaggregated state that ultimately has to foot such bills.

So who has the whip hand? Many years ago, Terence Daintith described contract as a 'new prerogative', where government was a privileged party, able at any point to draw on its regulatory and legislative (public) powers while at the same time it was released from the burdens of public accountability.[86] Nearly

[81] Vincent-Jones, 'Regulating Government' above n 69 at 620.

[82] R Rawlings, 'Poetic Justice—Public Contracting and the Case of the London Tube' in L Pearson, C Harlow and M Taggart (eds), *Administrative Law in a Changing State* (Hart Publishing, 2008) 223 at 236.

[83] The Public-Private Partnership Agreement Arbiter was constituted under ss. 225–27 of the *Greater London Authority Act* 1999. Significantly, he serves both as PPP Arbiter and chairman of the Office of Rail Regulation.

[84] *Three Rivers District Council v Governor and Company of the Bank of England (No 1)* [2000] 2 WLR 1227 [HL].

[85] *Weir v Secretary of State for Transport* [2005] EWHC 2192 (Ch) was an action for misfeasance in public office by the Transport Minister for allegedly driving the company into liquidation with a view to re-nationalisation.

[86] T Daintith, 'Regulation by Contract: The New Prerogative' [1979] *Current Legal Problems* 41. The point was later illustrated in the family practitioner contracts litigated in *Roy v Kensington and Chelsea and Westminster FPC* [1992] 1 AC 624 (HL).

thirty years later, Vincent-Jones, re-interpreting contract by government in 'an alternative 'regulatory space' perspective', draws a similar conclusion:[87]

> The internal government contract may be viewed as an instrument of control of the provider by the purchaser, operating within a broader policy-driven regulatory framework in which the purchaser's capacities are themselves subject to regulation by central government.

Pseudo-Contract: Regulation and Responsibility

Over the last two decades, 'pseudo-contract' has increasingly been used to model relations between the state and the individual. Under Thatcher, the theme was of citizen as consumer, giving the illusion of the consumer as dominant partner. John Major's 'Citizen's Charter' made explicit the idea of 'entitlement' to public service and benefit in return for taxes or contributions that had been paid.[88] In parallel, pseudo-contract began to emerge as a technique of social control. The Job Seeker's Allowance replaced unemployment benefit and income support for the unemployed in an effort to focus the efforts of claimants on seeking work.[89] Within social services, behaviour modification schemes incorporating rewards and sanctions tailored to 'progress' and conditions or requirements for the use of care facilities proliferated.[90]

Under New Labour these practices have flourished, based on new doctrines of 'responsibilisation', of 'growing' individuals as self-determining and self-willing agents[91] and, within the criminal law, a new philosophy of 'the responsible subject'.[92] The welfare state has been re-defined in terms of 'a new contract between the citizen and the Government based on responsibilities and rights',[93] a process that would culminate in a Green Paper[94] that speaks of a 'benefit

[87] Vincent-Jones, 'Regulating Government' above n 69 and 'The Regulation of Contractualisation in Quasi-Markets for Public Services [1999] *Public Law* 304.

[88] *The Citizen's Charter, Raising the Standard*, Cm. 1599 (1991). And see N Lewis, 'The Citizen's Charter and Next Steps: A New Way of Governing?' (1993) 64 *Political Quarterly* 316.

[89] *Job Seeker's Allowance*, Cm. 2687 (1994) and ss. 1, 9 of the Jobseekers' Act 1995, noted Fulbrook, 'The Job Seekers' Act 1995: Consolidation with a Sting of Contractual Compliance' (1995) 24 *Industrial Law Journal* 395.

[90] D Nelken, 'The Use of 'Contracts' as a Social Work Technique' (1987) 40 *Current Legal Problems* 207, 215–16.

[91] N Rose, 'Government and Control' in D Garland and R Sparks (eds.), *Criminology and Social Theory* (Oxford, Clarendon Press, 2000).

[92] N Lacey, 'In Search of the Responsible Subject: History, Philosophy and Social Sciences in Criminal Law Theory' (2001) 64 *Modern Law Review* 350, 353.

[93] *A New Contract for Welfare: New Ambitions for Our Country*, Cm. 3805 (1998) at 1–2. And see S White, 'Social rights and the social contract: political theory and the new welfare politics' (2000) 30 *British Journal of Political Science* 507; P Larkin, 'The 'Criminalization' of Social Security Law: Towards a Punitive Welfare State?' (2007) 34 *Journal of Law and Society* 295.

[94] *A new deal for welfare – Empowering people to work*, Cm 6730 (2006) at 118, 120. See also Dept. of Work and Pensions, *Reducing dependency, increasing opportunity* (2007) (the Freud Review) and *No one written off: reforming the welfare state to reward responsibilities* (2008).

contract' between the state and the individual, framed in terms of an obligation to work for all those capable of working, in consideration for benefit backed by 'tougher sanctions'. Individual responsibility is explicitly stated to be 'at the heart of these reforms. For people to exercise responsibility, we need to increase choice.' What choice? The reality is a one-sided contract of which compulsion is the key component.[95]

Premised on a philosophy of 'respect', we find a systematic and highly instrumental use of pseudo-contract in the field of social work designed to foster clients' responsibility for their choices. The Anti-Social Behaviour Act 2003 empowered youth offending teams to 'contract' with the parents where there is reason to believe that a child or young person 'has engaged, or is likely to engage' in criminal conduct or anti-social behaviour. The Education and Inspections Act 2006 extended 'acceptable behaviour contracts' to cases of truancy and school exclusions; contract is also used to tackle deviance.[96] The Police and Criminal Justice Act 2006 gave similar powers to local authorities and housing associations. Contracts are highly specific: typically they list anti-social acts that will not be continued or specify positive activities that will help to prevent recurrence of bad conduct. Contract has been turned to the profit of the state and transmuted into a potent public law technique.

Although in principle compatible, the reality of parenting contracts, 'naming and shaming', the civil punishment of ASBOs and a punitive criminal law, is hard to reconcile with the Government's vision of a 'strategic and enabling state', in which 'citizens take joint responsibility with the state for their own well-being'.[97] It sounds benign to say that 'in order to address inequality adequately, child rearing must be repositioned as a public rather than a private concern and the state must take responsibility for inculcating the practice of good parenting.' To announce 'intensive care sin bins' for 'reckless and disruptive families' or 'pre-birth intervention' to identify 'the kids and families that are going to be difficult in the future' is less benign.[98] And paradoxically, since human rights were devised for the protection of individuals from the state, human rights have played a similarly ambiguous role in the state's empowerment. As affirmative concepts of human rights, which cast positive duties on the state, have become increasingly important, state intervention into areas of life previously considered private, such as sexual relationships and parental discipline, has been legitimated. The two

[95] See M Freedland and D King, 'Contractual Governance and Illiberal Contracts: Some Problems of Contractualism as an Instrument of Behaviour Management by Agencies of Government' (2003) 27 *Cambridge Journal of Economics* 465.

[96] A Crawford, 'Contractual Governance of Deviant Behaviour' (2003) 30 *Journal of Law and Society* 479 at 503–4.

[97] Cabinet Office Policy Review, *Building on progress. The role of the state* (May, 2007) at [1.10–1.15].

[98] Dept of Education and Skills, *Every Parent Matters* (2007). And see C. Henricson, 'Governing Parenting: Is There a Case for a Policy Review and Statement of Parenting Rights and Responsibilities?' (2008) 35 *Journal of Law and Society* 150.

faces of human rights are clearly present in the Equality Act 2006, which establishes a new 'super-agency', the Commission for Equality and Human Rights (EHRC). The EHRC is mandated to:

(a) promote understanding of the importance of equality and diversity,
(b) encourage good practice in relation to equality and diversity,
(c) promote equality of opportunity,
(d) promote awareness and understanding of rights under the equality enactments,
(e) enforce the equality enactments,
(f) work towards the elimination of unlawful discrimination, and
(g) work towards the elimination of unlawful harassment.

How benevolent! But, in fulfilling its broad and infinitely extensible mission, the agency is empowered to: conduct inquiries and investigations; issue 'unlawful act notices'; apply for the restraint of unlawful advertising, apply for injunctions and for judicial review and support legal proceedings by others. It can call for action plans from private bodies, approve them and see them implemented. It has rule-making powers. It matters not that these draconian powers are delegated to a supposedly 'independent' agency; behind them is the mailed fist of the state. The point is underscored by the fact that all appointments to the EHRC are made by a government minister,[99] who also must approve the appointment of the main executive officers. The minister has power to dismiss any member who is, in her opinion, unable, unfit or unwilling to perform his functions. Formal accountability is to the minister and only loosely, through a report laid by her, to Parliament.[100]

The State Resurgent

I indicated earlier that the twin concepts of risk and security have proved useful in the aftermath of 9/11 to legitimate the growth of a powerful new and uncontrolled 'surveillance state'.[101] I have space to follow this theme only briefly. My first point concerns what I see as a misuse of human rights, my second concerns the role of the European Union.

[99] Originally the Secretary of State for Communities and Local Government and now, since the Transfer of Functions (Equality) Order 2007 (SI 2007/2914) the Lord Privy Seal (Leader of the House, Harriet Harman).

[100] I have left out of account here the possibility of intervention by Select Committees, especially the House of Commons Communities and Local Government Committee (see, eg, 6th Report, Session 2006–07, *Equality*, HC468) and very proactive Joint Committee on Human Rights (see, eg, JCHR, 4th Report, Session 2005–06, *Legislative Scrutiny: Equality Bill*, HL Paper 89/HC 766).

[101] Information Commissioner, *Report by the Surveillance Studies Network on the Surveillance Society* (September 2006); *A Surveillance Society* (Nov. 2007); Home Affairs Committee, *A Surveillance Society?* HC 58 (2007/8).

Under the premiership of Tony Blair, the concept of 'security' contributed to a serious erosion of civil liberties. The broad but essentially benign definition of security discussed earlier as a 'condition of being protected or not exposed to danger'[102] has been subverted. Anti-terrorism legislation has become commonplace; since 9/11, three major changes to the terrorism legislation have been considered indispensable[103] and the UK, alone amongst European nations, has found it necessary to derogate from the European Convention on Human Rights.[104] When courts have intervened in defence of human rights, they have often met a frosty reception. After one such decision, Tony Blair publicly labelled the judge's ruling 'an abuse of common sense' and called on his Home Secretary to change the law 'to ensure the law-abiding majority can live without fear'.[105] For good measure he demanded a 'profound re-balancing' of the debate and warned of possible amendments to the Human Rights Act passed by his own Government in 1998, to require judges to balance the rights of the individual with public safety, which they 'do not always do'. 'The kinds of things terrorism laws do,' Conor Gearty has commented, are 'no longer embarrassing and compromising and to be endured for only so long as they are absolutely necessary—rather they are becoming essential saviours of our society, safeguards against an otherwise inevitable barbarism: in short the new common sense of our age'.[106] The packaging is significant. Through a 'redefinition of human rights the effect of which is to excuse repression as necessary to prevent the destruction of human rights values',[107] the state has secured significant new powers.

Equally, the role of the state has been enhanced by the programme of inter-governmental co-operation in the so-called 'Third Pillar' of the European Union (1992).[108] The Treaty of Amsterdam (1997) introduced the Utopian ideal of a European area of 'freedom, security and justice' in which the free movement of persons would be assured. With its proposal for a Charter of Fundamental Rights and Freedoms, the European Council at Tampere (1999) hinted at a

[102] D Oliver in Taggart, *Province*, above n 1 at 226.

[103] The Anti-Terrorism, Crime and Security Act 2001; Prevention of Terrorism Act 2005; and Terrorism Act 2006. A new Counter-Terrorism Bill, originally with provision for 42-days detention before trial until it was defeated in the Lords, is currently before Parliament: see Joint Committee on Human Rights, 21st Report, Session 2007–08, *Counter-Terrorism Policy and Human Rights (Eleventh Report): 42 Days and Public Emergencies*, HL Paper 116/HC 635. And see more generally, J. Hiebert 'Parliamentary Review of Terrorism Measures' (2005) 68 *Modern Law Review* 676.

[104] By the Human Rights Act 1998 (Designated Derogation) Order 2001, which derogated from ECHR Article 5 (liberty of the person) in terms of ECHR Article 15 (derogation in emergency situations). In *A and others v Home Secretary* [2005] 2 AC 68, the House of Lords held by a majority (Lord Hoffmann dissenting) that the issue of emergency was a matter on which the domestic courts would give great weight to the judgment of the Government and Parliament.

[105] Remarks provoked by the order of Sullivan J. in *R (on the application of GG and others) v SSHD* [2006] EWHC 1111 (Admin). See more generally, R Austin, 'The New Constitutionalism, Terrorism and Torture' (2007) 60 *Current Legal Problems*, 79.

[106] C Gearty, *Can Human Rights Survive?* (Cambridge, Cambridge University Press, 2006) 106–7.

[107] Ibid at 108.

[108] Now *The Hague Programme : strengthening freedom, security and justice in the European Union 5 November 2004* 16054/04 JAI 5591 (13 December 2004).

humane and expansive meaning for this soothing terminology. The proviso that the area would be developed 'in conjunction with appropriate measures with respect to external border controls, asylum, immigration and the prevention and combating of crime' would soon, however, lend a less generous connotation to these fine words. As commentators had foreseen,[109] 'freedom' could be translated as 'crime-free', 'justice' equated with criminal justice and law enforcement and the 'security' of the many could take precedence over civil liberties.[110]

Despite their expressed hostility to many Third Pillar programmes, British governments have been able to benefit from its processes to shelter activities that a national parliament might not have allowed. They have indeed been active in pushing forward policies while overtly declaring their unwillingness to participate. Gradually and secretly Member States have acquiesced in setting up 'a control system without a state'.[111] This has greatly enlarged the powers of national governments at the expense of national parliaments and courts.[112] Technically, it may be 'delegation' but it is less a 'hollowing out' than a second 'European rescue of the nation-state'.[113] National governments, acting at all times through the Council, have remained firmly in charge of policy and have indeed built up their own executive (the Committee of Permanent Representatives, or 'Coreper') for policy-development and implementation in the area.

The trend is an accelerating one. National governments have used the cover of Third Pillar programmes greatly to enhance the capabilities of the surveillance state. Substantial data banks, the Schengen Information System (SIS), have been built up, giving access to national resources by authorities in the twenty-seven Member States[114] and, to a limited degree, the United States.[115] Without any prior consultation of national parliaments or the European Parliament, Coreper and

[109] P Boeles, 'Introduction: Freedom, Security and Justice for All', J Crowley, 'Differential Free Movement and the Sociology of the "Internal Border"' and C Harlow, 'Endpiece', in E Guild and C Harlow (eds), *Implementing Amsterdam* (Oxford, Hart Publishing, 2000). See similarly S Douglas-Scott, 'The rule of law in the European Union – putting the security into the area of "freedom, security and justice"' (2004) 29 *European Law Review* 219.

[110] Epitomised in the decision of the European Court of First Instance in Case T-306/01 *Ali Yusuf and Others v Council and Commission* [2005] ECR II-3533 and Case T-315/01 *Yassin Abdullah Kadi v Council and Commission* [2005] ECR II- 3649, noted C Tomuschat (2006) 43 *Common Market Law Review* 537, happily reversed by the Court of Justice in Joined Cases C-402 and 415/05 P *Kadi v. Council and Commission* (judgment of 3 September 2008).

[111] T Mathiesen, *Lex Vigilatoria – Towards a control system without a state*? available on-line from the European Civil Liberties Network.

[112] See generally, S Peers, *EU Justice and Home Affairs Law* (Harlow, Longman, 2000).

[113] See A Milward, *The European Rescue of the Nation-State* (London, Routledge, 1992).

[114] For the 'availability principle', see European Commission, *Proposal for a Council Framework Decision on the exchange of information under the principle of availability* (COM (2005) 4090 final (12.10.2005).

[115] See the so called 'adequacy decisions' or agreements on the processing and transfer of PNR data by air carriers to the United States: Council Decision 2004/496/EC of 17 May 2004, OJ 2004 L 183, p 83, and Commission Decision 2004/535/EC of 14 May 2004, OJ 2004 L 235, p11. And see Joined Cases 317, 318/04 *Parliament v Council* [2006] ECR I-4721.

Commission officials acted through Member States in the Council' to create the 'technical capacity' for the new functions in SIS II and then 'activate' them later on'.[116] The end result was to build 'function creep' into the databases and present parliaments and civil society with a *fait accompli.* After the Heiligendamm meeting on the so called 'Prüm proposals' on data protection in the Third Pillar, the House of Lords European Committee complained of decision-making in small groups of compliant Member States. They also criticised the lack of transparency and accountability in justice and home affairs decision-making, especially Home Office failure in the instant case to issue a press notice or other information. The Committee had 'gleaned information from other sources, in particular from a statement issued after the meeting by the German Ministry of the Interior' and had otherwise to await a letter from the Home Secretary plus oral evidence from a junior minister, over three months after the meeting.[117] These are the tips of a titanic iceberg.

Conclusion

At the time of *The Province*, I suggest, the state was seen by most of the contributors as in the process of transformation through 'hollowing out'. This was largely regarded as a threat to public law and its values, though the changes might have been viewed more optimistically. A common theme in liberal democratic writing has been re-configuration of the state in terms of an open, pluralist and 'bottom up' society in which power and sovereignty are broken down and diffused, creating greater space for 'those who are governed to regulate their own behaviour'[118] under a less restrictive private law regime.

In this paper, I have drawn a rather different picture. Out of the crucible of privatisation came a 'new regulatory state', to John Braithwaite's mind[119] qualitatively different 'in its reliance on self-regulatory organisations, enforced self-regulation and other responsive regulatory techniques that substitute for direct command and control.' What has emerged over time from the tactics of regulation 'through compliance systems, codes of practice and other self-regulatory strategies' is not decentred regulation but a decentred state.

[116] B Hayes, *From the Schengen Information System to SIS II and the Visa Information (VIS): the proposals explained* (London, Statewatch, 2004), available on line.

[117] House of Lords EU Committee, 5th Report, Session 2006–07, *After Heiligendamm, Doors Ajar at Stratford-on-Avon*, HL Paper 32; *Behind Closed Doors: the Meeting of the G6 Interior Ministers at Heiligendamm*, HL 221 (2005/6).

[118] J Morison, 'Modernising Government and the e-government Revolution' in N Bamforth and P Leyland (eds), *Public Law in a Multi-Layered Constitution* (Oxford, Hart Publishing, 2003), citing M Foucault, 'Governmentality' and 'The Subject and Power', in J Faubion (ed), *Michel Foucault, Power: The Essential Works*, vol3 (London, Penguin Books, 2000).

[119] J Braithwaite, 'The New Regulatory State and the Transformation of Criminology' (2000) 40 *British Journal of Criminology* 222 at 223–24.

Government, rightly seen by John Griffith as inherently authoritarian,[120] has not discarded its controlling tendencies even if it has learned better to disguise them. Its boundaries have not, as Margaret Thatcher promised, been rolled back even if 'hollowing out' sideways to semi-autonomous agencies and upwards to transnational institutions has allowed the inexorable growth of public power to be obscured. In its welfare guise and under the cover of an enhanced night-watchman role the state remains profoundly interventionist, regulatory and often verges on the despotic. The state may have been reconfigured but it has not been greatly reformed. The footprints left by Macavity's hidden paw are an unrelenting bafflement for administrative law.

120 JAG Griffith, 'The Political Constitution' (1979) 42 *Modern Law Review* 1.

6

Against Bifurcation

MURRAY HUNT[1]

Introduction

IN THE DAYS before human rights law was considered part of the public law mainstream, administrative lawyers and human rights lawyers tended not to see eye to eye about the appropriate role of the courts in public law. Although some administrative lawyers supported a more interventionist role for judges than others, at least in the defence of certain interests, most would regard it as an incontestable article of faith that there were clear limits to judicial review of administrative and executive action. This flowed partly from recognition of the expertise of technocratic decision-makers in particular regulatory contexts and partly from a deeply held instinct that in a democratic society courts must acknowledge the limits to the legitimacy of their role. At least those who were sympathetic to the broad objectives of the administrative state, redressing the inequalities and other injustices that flowed from private ordering, were keen to preserve as much space as possible for the administration to achieve those objectives without the courts frustrating them by intervening to protect the private interests being regulated.[2] Human rights lawyers, on the other hand, were for the most part used to seeing the state as the enemy and the courts as the one institutional hope of protection against oppressive state practices such as torture, inhuman or degrading treatment, fair trial violations, or other flagrant interferences with liberty, free speech or personal autonomy. Judicial deference, for most

[1] I am grateful to David Dyzenhaus and Grant Huscroft for their comments on an earlier draft. The views expressed in this chapter are personal to the author and do not purport to represent the views of any Member, Officer or member of staff of either House of Parliament.

[2] This emphasis on judicial restraint was the defining feature of the so-called 'classic' model of judicial review: see C Harlow, 'A Special Relationship? American Influences on Judicial Review in England' in I Loveland (ed), *A Special Relationship? American Influences on Public Law in the UK* (Oxford, Clarendon Press, 1995), 79 at 83.

human rights lawyers, was the vocabulary of weak, executive-minded judges reluctant to defend the human rights of individuals against the powerful state.[3]

Mike Taggart's distinguished career as New Zealand's foremost administrative lawyer spans the shift of human rights law into the public law mainstream in most of the common law jurisdictions on which he has been such a peerless comparativist commentator: in Canada by the adoption of the Charter of Rights and Freedoms in 1982; in his native New Zealand by the enactment of the New Zealand Bill of Rights Act 1990; in the United Kingdom by the enactment of the Human Rights Act 1998; and, latterly, in Australia by the adoption of state-level charters of rights.[4] He began that career as an administrative lawyer with a broad sympathy for the objectives of the administrative state, and therefore an instinctive identification with those who would keep courts in their place, but also with a distinctively liberal concern for the inherent worth and dignity of the individual. This combination, together with his insatiable intellectual curiosity about what confers legitimacy in a modern democracy, has made it inevitable that he would be drawn again and again to think and write about one of the central issues for his generation of public lawyers: how to reconcile the apparently competing instincts of administrative lawyers on the one hand and human rights lawyers on the other about the appropriate role of the courts.

This chapter explores this recurrent theme in Mike Taggart's writing: the relationship between administrative law and human rights law and, in particular, the extent to which the apparently inexorable rise of human rights law in common law jurisdictions has transformed received understandings of administrative law. It argues that Mike's account of this relationship contains a number of important insights about the nature of public law today. Amongst the most crucial insights are the central importance of transparent justification and the need for some way of ensuring that 'democratic considerations' have a role to play in public law. It goes on to argue that, taken together, these insights point towards a more unified public law than Mike has himself been prepared to acknowledge in his writings. Those insights, it is suggested, in fact foreshadow the emergence in the coming decades of an entirely reconceived public law, rooted in the values that are recognised within the legal order as being fundamental, and organised around the central concepts of justification and due deference, thereby

[3] At the risk of charges of reductionism, it is suggested that a version of this tension lies at the heart of the fruitful collaboration over many years between Mike Taggart and David Dyzenhaus: Mike, the product of an established democracy with a relatively developed welfare state, instinctively more sympathetic to, but not untroubled by, the tradition of legal positivism; David from a wicked legal system in which courts offered the only real prospect of vindicating the rule of law.

[4] State level bills of rights have been adopted in Victoria and the Australian Capital Territories and are being actively considered in Tasmania, New South Wales and Western Australia: see G Williams, *A Charter of Rights for Australia* (Sydney, University of New South Wales Press, 2007). Consideration is now also being actively given to a federal bill of rights: in August 2008 the Attorney General announced a national consultation on the question.

according a meaningful role to the democratic branches in the definition and furtherance of those fundamental values.

The Relationship Between Administrative Law and Human Rights

Mike was amongst the first to appreciate that the adoption of a national human rights instrument such as the Human Rights Act in the United Kingdom or the New Zealand Bill of Rights Act 'fundamentally changes the traditional administrative law grounds for review of discretionary decision-making', because it makes the right the starting point of the inquiry and requires a balancing test to be applied—weighing the 'private right' against the public interest in limiting it.[5] He has also long been interested in the courts' increasing use of administrative law doctrines and techniques to give greater effect to international treaty obligations in domestic law, and in particular to human rights obligations.[6]

In his early consideration of these questions, Mike tended to explain the growing impact of human rights law in terms of received administrative law doctrines. He characterised the increasing role played by international human rights norms, for example, as their evolution to the status of 'mandatory relevant considerations', or 'decisive' relevant considerations in the case of those human rights norms given effect in a national human rights instrument (such as the International Covenant on Civil and Political Rights in New Zealand and the European Convention on Human Rights in the United Kingdom). By the time of his contribution to Christopher Forsyth's edited collection on *Judicial Review and the Constitution*,[7] however, Mike could scarcely conceal his impatience with the growing unreality of the traditional account of administrative law, according to which everything the courts do in administrative law is justified by reference to the intention of Parliament. 'The rule of law envelops and subsumes the *ultra vires* doctrine', he wrote.[8] *Ultra vires*, he concluded, 'appears increasingly beside the point.'[9] Constitutionalisation, internationalisation, privatisation, all were combining to undermine the traditional justification for the role of the courts in administrative law.

[5] See, eg, J McLean, P Rishworth and M Taggart, 'The Impact of the Bill of Rights on Administrative Law' in *The New Zealand Bill of Rights Act 1990* (Auckland, Legal Research Foundation Inc, 1992) 62–97; M Taggart, 'Tugging on Superman's Cape: Lessons from Experience with the New Zealand Bill of Rights Act 1990' [1998] *Public Law* 266.

[6] See, eg, M Taggart, D Dyzenhaus & M Hunt, 'The Principle of Legality in Administrative Law: Internationalisation as Constitutionalisation' (2001) 1 *Oxford University Commonwealth Law Journal* 5; M Taggart, 'The Tub of Public Law', in D Dyzenhaus, (ed), *The Unity of Public Law* (Oxford, Hart Publishing, 2004) [Taggart, 'The Tub of Public Law'].

[7] C Forsyth (ed), *Judicial Review and the Constitution* (Oxford, Hart Publishing, 2000).

[8] M Taggart, '*Ultra vires* as Distraction' in C Forsyth (ed), *Judicial Review and the Constitution*, ibid at 427.

[9] Ibid at 429.

Surveying the landscape in 2003, it no longer seemed appropriate to Mike to attempt to assimilate human rights law into the existing categories and doctrines of administrative law. In his important contribution, 'Reinventing Administrative Law', Mike argued that the central tenets of what he describes as the 'classic model' of administrative law are being undermined by constitutionalism from within and internationalisation from without, and by the 'constitutional methodology' that is an integral part of both of those developments.[10] The defining characteristic of the classic model of administrative law was judicial restraint. Standing to bring challenges was narrow, the grounds on which challenges could be brought were restricted, justiciability was narrowly defined, 'policy' issues were considered off-limits to the courts, factual questions could hardly ever be revisited, the threshold for intervention was high and there was no onus on decision-makers to provide any explanation of the reasons justifying their decision. All these features of the classic model, however, were now being subjected to considerable stress by the advent of human rights protection in the domestic legal system. In legal systems that lack 'a capital C constitution', such as the United Kingdom and New Zealand, rights-based adjudication mainly takes place through administrative law proceedings. As a result, British administrative law was in the process of being 'reinvented' to adjust to an enhanced, human rights protecting role.

In this sustained and evolving account of the relationship between administrative law and human rights, and many of his other writings, Mike has provided us with a wealth of insights about the nature of public law today. He has demonstrated the growing diversity in the sources of the norms that are in play in public law, including the increasing reception of international norms into national legal systems, the rediscovery of values considered fundamental by the common law, and the common law's capacity to evolve by distilling fundamental values from longstanding statutory commitments. He has insisted on the centrality of the idea of justification in public law: the importance of requiring administrative decision-makers to give a transparent account of the reasons for their decisions.[11] At the same time, he has correctly identified the need for public law to articulate better the notions of deference that lurk beneath so many of the doctrines of administrative law. In his work on the scope of review he has demonstrated the need for differential standards of review and the necessity of trying to map the varying intensity of review according to some principles or criteria with some normative, not merely functional, underpinning. He has consistently exposed the lack of any rigid distinction between public and private.[12] For many of us with a

[10] M Taggart, 'Reinventing Administrative Law' in N Bamforth and P Leyland (eds), *Public Law in a Multi-layered Constitution* (Oxford, Hart Publishing, 2003) 311 [Taggart, 'Reinventing Administrative Law'].

[11] See, eg, M Taggart, '*Osmond* in the High Court of Australia: Opportunity Lost' in M Taggart (ed), *Judicial Review of Administrative Action in the 1980s: Problems and Prospects* (Auckland, Oxford University Press in association with the Legal Research Foundation, 1986) 53.

[12] See, eg, M Taggart (ed), *The Province of Administrative Law* (Oxford, Hart Publishing, 1997).

tendency to focus too much on the latest pronouncements of the judges, he has been our conscience, reminding us not to take too court-centred an approach to law, insisting on the importance of history and context to an understanding of how law really works as a lived phenomenon, rather than as a disparate collection of abstract texts. He has rightly insisted that parliamentary control of the executive and administration is as important an object of study as judicial control in any proper conception of administrative law.[13] And yet throughout, he has, by his example, demonstrated the value of the methodology of the common law: combining particularism and contextualism with an unshakable belief that, in time, normative general principles emerge from the decision of individual cases in particular contexts.

One way of interpreting the significance of Mike's contributions to these debates is to read them as charting the growing 'constitutionalisation' of administrative law, that is, its recognition as a source of norms enjoying a higher status than other law. But this characterisation of the developments Mike has chronicled carries considerable risks. In liberal democracies we tend to have preconceived ideas about what constitutions do and what is a proper subject-matter for inclusion within a constitution. Although some modern written constitutions expressly include a constitutional right to fair and just administrative action,[14] this is very much the exception rather than the rule: we are used to constitutions that privilege a relatively narrow catalogue of rights as fundamental rights. Against this background, talk of constitutionalising administrative law is likely to lead to a bifurcated public law, in which rigid distinctions are drawn between that part of public law which concerns human rights on the one hand, and the rest of administrative law, which concerns a narrowly conceived set of grounds of illegality, on the other. This would be a seriously retrograde step in the development of public law: it would risk forfeiting many of the important insights about the nature of public law Mike's work has yielded, insights, it will be argued below, which point not to the bifurcation of public law, between 'constitutionalised' human rights and the rest, but towards a thoroughgoing reconceptualisation of public law as a more integrated body of interrelated norms, concepts and doctrines. First, however, there is a puzzle to solve: what explains Mike's own recent defence of bifurcation?

[13] M Taggart, 'From "Parliamentary Powers" to Privatization: The Chequered History of Delegated Legislation in the Twentieth Century' (2005) 55 *University of Toronto Law Journal* 575: an impassioned plea for the reintegration of administrative law and constitutional law, which have become disentwined because of administrative lawyers' preoccupation with courts to the neglect of other important institutions, including Parliament.

[14] Section 33(1) of the South African Bill of Rights, for example, provides 'Everyone has the right to administrative action that is lawful, reasonable and procedurally fair.' Intriguingly, a right to fair and just administrative action is one of the few 'additional rights' that the United Kingdom Government has indicated it is prepared to consider as a candidate for inclusion in any United Kingdom Bill of Rights: see report of the Joint Committee on Human Rights *A Bill of Rights for the UK?*, Twenty-ninth Report of Session 2007–08, HL Paper 165-I, HC 150-I at para 128. The UK process, however, seems most unlikely to lead to a new Bill of Rights in the foreseeable future.

A Bifurcated Public Law?

In 'Reinventing Administrative Law', in which he so clearly charted some of the significant departures from the classic model as a result of the twin pressures of constitutionalism from within and internationalisation from without, Mike entered an important qualification to the reach of his argument that administrative law is in the process of being reinvented.[15] His argument, he said, was limited to administrative law cases involving alleged infringements of rights recognised in domestic, regional or international human rights instruments or by the common law. He noted that there was an important debate, yet to be had in the United Kingdom, about whether or not British public law will bifurcate into human rights law and general administrative law, that is, the area left when you subtract rights-centred litigation. He foresaw that some would argue that the unreformed or classic model of administrative law should survive in the latter area. Though at that time he could see no advantage in maintaining an administrative law rump, cut off from developments in human rights law, he expressly left that as a matter for another day.

Returning to the issue in his contribution to David Dyzenhaus's edited collection of essays about the important decision of the Supreme Court of Canada in *Baker*,[16] Mike characteristically gave us a memorable metaphor to represent what he described as his growing realisation that the sub-disciplines of public law (constitutional law, administrative law and international law) are all in the same boat: they are the three men of the nursery rhyme, rub-a-dub-dubbing in 'the tub of public law.'[17] As Dyzenhaus commented in his introduction to the volume, the image of public law as a churning tub of fundamental values, in which no neat compartmentalisation is possible, seemed an apt way to depict the volume's central theme, that the 'unity' of public law is now beginning to emerge as the relationship between constitutional, administrative and international human rights law is increasingly subjected to scrutiny. As well as supplying the metaphor, Mike's essay seemed to confirm that his instinct remained what he had hinted at in 'Reinventing Administrative Law': that the cleavage of public law into constitutional law on one side and everything else on the other is 'not attractive'.[18] The imbrication of human rights was not only strengthening the tub of public law, it was 'unifying it'.[19]

[15] Taggart, 'Reinventing Administrative Law', above n 10 at 334, note 144.

[16] *Baker v Canada (Minister of Citizenshiop and immigration)* [1999] 2 SCR 817 [*Baker*].

[17] Taggart, 'The Tub of Public Law', above n 6 at 455. In a characteristic thrashing of the metaphor to within an inch of its life, Mike suggested that the 'rotten potato' of the nursery rhyme represented public law. It is too tempting not to observe, in the spirit of Mike's skill for metaphor-morphosis, that in the United Kingdom what has rotted the public law potato is the indigenous disease known as Sovereignty's Blight.

[18] Ibid at 467.

[19] Ibid at 479.

In his most recent piece on proportionality, *Wednesbury* and deference, however, Mike comes out very clearly in defence of a bifurcated public law in New Zealand ... at least for now.[20] In a masterly survey of the debate about proportionality versus *Wednesbury* unreasonableness as grounds for review, he argues for the embrace of proportionality in administrative law cases concerning fundamental rights, but not in cases concerning what he describes, following Stephen Sedley, as 'public wrongs'. Moreover, 'due deference' is regarded as the counter-balance to proportionality, and therefore it too should only apply in cases concerning fundamental rights. In all other cases, it seems, all the old grounds and dichotomies of the traditional model should continue to apply.

In defending bifurcation, Mike is in distinguished company. His position seems close to that of David Mullan, who has also recently defended a bifurcated public law in Canada, comprising, on the one hand, Charter adjudication in cases concerning Charter rights, where one set of principles applies, and, on the other hand, ordinary administrative law where more traditional administrative law principles continue to govern, largely unaffected by the constitutionalisation of the values in the Charter.[21] Mullan is unhappy that Canadian courts appear to be intervening on a correctness standard in cases where Charter rights and freedoms are not at stake, and being deferential in immigration cases such as *Suresh* where important rights such as the right to be free from torture are at stake.[22] Implicit in Mullan's position is that there ought to be a bifurcated approach, with less deference where Charter rights or freedoms are at stake, and more deference in the traditional administrative law sphere where such rights are not in play.[23]

Against the Bifurcation of Public Law

There are powerful arguments against accepting the bifurcation of public law. First, the distinction between 'rights' cases on the one hand and 'public wrongs' on the other is by no means straightforward. Mike acknowledges this, but argues that it is important to remember that 'most administrative law cases do not involve human rights. They involve maladministration or actions contrary to principles of good administration. The enthusiasm of human rights lawyers and the burgeoning literature can obscure this fact.' Although it may sound like human rights imperialism, or the over-enthusiasm of a human rights lawyer, there is a risk here of underestimating the reach of human rights. The catalogue

[20] M Taggart, 'Proportionality, Deference, *Wednesbury*' [2008] *New Zealand Law Review* 423 [Taggart, 'Proportionality']. Mike's reasons for his change of view are considered below.

[21] D Mullan, 'Deference from *Baker* to *Suresh* and Beyond – Interpreting the Conflicting Signals' in Dyzenhaus, *The Unity of Public Law*, above n 6.

[22] *Suresh v Canada (Minister of Citizenship and Immigration)* [2002] 1 SCR 3.

[23] For a similar defence of a bifurcated public law in the UK following the enactment of the Human Rights Act 1998, see Lord Irvine, 'The Development of Human Rights in Britain under an Incorporated Convention on Human Rights' [1998] *Public Law* 221.

of human rights covers a very wide range of values or interests that are important to people's lives, and regulating important aspects of people's lives is the very stuff of the administrative state. Licensing decisions, for example, often involve the right to pursue an occupation or a livelihood; disciplinary decisions likewise; planning decisions concern the right to the enjoyment of one's property, or the right of a third party to the enjoyment of their property without interference; financial regulation engages the right to peaceful enjoyment of possessions. While the ground for complaint in administrative law cases may often appear to be one of maladministration or public wrong, rather than breach of a human right, what brings the applicant in a judicial review case to the point of litigating is often that the decision has had an adverse impact on an underlying right or interest of fundamental importance to the affected person, and that underlying right or interest is often within the scope of what is recognised to be a fundamental right. This is even more likely to be the case if we treat the category of human rights as including the economic, social and cultural rights that are internationally recognised to be indivisible from the civil and political rights that more commonly find legal protection in national legal orders. So we cannot divide what Mike describes as 'the rainbow of review' so easily into a 'rights' side and a 'public wrongs' side.

Second, human rights are not the only substantive fundamental values that public law has increasingly come to be seen as protecting in recent years. Those values include, but are not confined to, human rights. They include other substantive principles such as consistency of treatment, non-retrospectivity and access to court to question the legality of a decision. In recent years, much of the progress that has been made in moving beyond the judicially manipulable *Wednesbury* standard has been as a result of identifying as the real grounds of review, not only fundamental human rights, but substantive principles of good administration.[24] Increasingly, courts deploy a proportionality-type methodology to assess the adequacy of the justification for an interference with these substantive principles. In legitimate expectations cases, for example, which are grounded in the substantive principle of consistency of treatment, courts regularly scrutinise decision-makers' justifications for departing from representations they have given in order to assess whether the departure from the principle of consistency is justified by sufficiently weighty considerations in the particular circumstances.[25] It is not clear why these substantive principles are not just as capable of anchoring the proportionality methodology as, in Mike's account, are fundamental rights.

[24] See J Jowell and A Lester, 'Beyond *Wednesbury*: Towards Substantive Principles of Administrative Law' [1987] *Public Law* 386.

[25] See, eg, *R (Highly Skilled Migrants Programme Forum Ltd) v Secretary of State for the Home Department* [2008] EWHC 664 (Admin) (8 April 2008), in which the High Court considered the Home Secretary's reasons for not adhering to the statements made to highly skilled migrants about the circumstances in which they would qualify for permanent settlement, and held (at para 61) that

Third, the bifurcation of public law appears to presuppose that a more intense scrutiny of justifications is always warranted in cases where fundamental rights are at stake. However, review of variable intensity is also necessary where fundamental rights are at stake. It is now well established, for example, that there is no room for notions of deference when applying the norm prohibiting torture. The prohibition is absolute and any court considering whether a minister's decision to return a person to a country where they may be tortured must satisfy itself, on all the evidence available, as to whether there is a real risk of torture in the receiving country.[26] However, when deciding whether an interference with the right to peaceful enjoyment of possessions is proportionate and therefore justified, a far less intense scrutiny is applied by courts, and the threshold of justification is accordingly lower. Similarly, in what the courts regard as the area of social policy the courts will frequently adopt a deferential approach to the scrutiny of justifications even where there is acknowledged to be a human right in play.[27] In short, there is a spectrum of intensity of review in *all* public law cases, and the intensity of review therefore does not necessarily correspond with the distinction between rights and non-rights cases. A non-rights case, for example about consistency of behaviour where departure from a representation would cause grave unfairness, may call for stricter scrutiny than a routine interference with a property right, such as an exercise of a regulatory power to enter and search, or a discriminatory eligibility criterion for a social benefit.

Fourth and finally, both the case for requiring decision-makers to provide transparent justifications for their decisions, in part to enable judicial scrutiny, and the case for courts explicitly taking 'democratic considerations' into account when they review administrative decisions, apply with equal force in all administrative law cases, not just those concerning human rights. Indeed, Mike himself accepts that due deference can do some useful work on what he calls the "public wrongs" part of the spectrum.[28]

there was not a sufficient public interest to outweigh the unfairness caused to those who had relocated their jobs, homes and families to the United Kingdom in reliance on the Home Secretary's statements.

26 *Saadi v Italy*, Application No. 37201/06, judgment of 28 February 2008 (Grand Chamber), in which the Grand Chamber of the European Court of Human Rights unanimously rejected, by 17 votes to 0, the argument of the UK Government (intervening) that the threat presented by the person to be deported must be a factor to be assessed in relation to the possibility and the nature of the potential ill-treatment. See also *AS and another (Libya) v Secretary of State for the Home Department* [2008] EWCA Civ 289.

27 See, eg, *R (RJM) v Secretary of State for Work and Pensions* [2008] UKHL 63 at paras 56–57 (22 October 2008): '[t]he discrimination in the present case was justified, in the sense that the government was entitled to adopt and apply the policy at issue. This is an area where the court should be very slow to substitute its view for that of the executive … The fact that there are grounds for criticising, or disagreeing with, these views does not mean that they must be rejected. Equally, the fact that the line may have been drawn imperfectly does not mean that the policy cannot be justified.'

28 Taggart, 'Proportionality', above n 20 at 457.

What Explains the Defence of Bifurcation?

Here, then, is a genuine puzzle. Why do administrative lawyers like Mike Taggart and David Mullan, who have done so much to move administrative law beyond the stultifying confines of the traditional model, appear to be so keen to preserve it outside the sphere of human rights? Were those long-running debates about the unreality of the ultra vires doctrine really just about accommodating human rights challenges by developing special rules for that particular category of case? Or were they about something much deeper, a shift to constitutionalism in a more profound sense, involving the recognition of a role for courts in the enforcement of fundamental substantive values including, but not confined to, human rights?

With characteristic intellectual honesty, Mike has given a detailed account of the reasons for his recent change of mind.[29] He is concerned that where rights are not in play there is no compelling normative justification for the more intensive review that in his view the proportionality methodology inevitably entails. He sees rights as the necessary anchor for that methodology, and without that important starting point he fears that proportionality is an indeterminate standard that will fail to confine judicial discretion when controlling exercises of administrative discretion. Outside of the 'rights' context, he argues, proportionality furnishes a 'determinate-looking structure' that in fact conceals unacceptable judicial discretion. There is already too much unconstrained judicial discretion in administrative law, and reverting to the traditional conception of *Wednesbury* unreasonableness, with its in-built notions of deference, in administrative law cases where no rights are at stake will better respect the institutional, functional and pragmatic limitations on judicial review. Accepting bifurcation should not be seen as a backward step, Mike argues: the appropriate advances have already been made in the expansion and refinement of the specific substantive grounds of review, and progress towards the emerging culture of justification will continue because of the well established and wide-ranging statutory duties to give reasons and the more recently emerging common law duties where statutes are silent.

Here we see exposed Mike's genuine and deep-seated ambivalence about the project of reconceiving law as justification and administrative law as scrutiny for adequate justification. In their recent account of the common law's 'pull of justification', Mike and David Dyzenhaus argue that the central idea of the common law tradition is that law is the expression of public reason, drawn from a public stock of those moral values that are thought to be fundamental to a society and therefore part of its legal constitution. Within the common law legal order, they argue, decisions derive their authority not from fiat, or command, but from the quality of the reasons offered in support of them. In the common law

[29] Ibid at 477–80.

legal order, 'the decision has authority if and only if it is also in accordance with reason, or, in other words, reasonable.'[30] The common law exhibits the pull of justification, meaning that public power is considered authoritative when and only when it justifies its exercise to those whom it affects.

Mike is instinctively uneasy with this conception of law as reason because of the risk of indeterminacy and in particular the risk of judicial discretion. In the common law tradition it appears to be up to the judge to decide what is reasonable. So Mike's unease with the implications of many of his own insights (for example, about the constraints on judicial identification of fundamental values, about judicial scrutiny of decision-makers' reasons for their decisions, about proportionality as a ground of review in administrative law, and about how constraining due deference doctrine really is), and with claims about 'the unity of public law', has a deeper underpinning in his unease about this conception of law as justification. Though his substantive rule of law credentials are not in doubt, he remains instinctively sympathetic to the Willis/Robson/Griffith critique of romantic common lawyers, that the common law does not sufficiently constrain the judges.[31]

Mike is of course right to be concerned about indeterminacy and judicial discretion. He is right to be suspicious of judicial moves to 'simplicity' and to be alert to the risk of judicial supremacy. In a democracy the greater claim to legitimacy by an elected politician compared to an unelected judge is simply a modern fact of life. One of the basic norms by which we order our societies is that the people who make decisions about how we should be governed should be accountable by being elected and required to submit themselves to re-election. It is futile to deny this: the common law simply has to find a way to accommodate it. This does not necessarily mean, however, that the common law must accommodate a command-based conception of authority. There may be a role to play for the second-order reasons why democratic decisions command authority that is not the same as a crude insistence on submission to those decisions because of the identity of the decision-maker. Authority could then still derive primarily from the quality of reasons, but, to avoid judges being the supreme decision-makers, at least some role could be played by considerations such as the democratic pedigree of the decision-maker, the extent to which affected interests have participated in the decision-making process leading to the decision, and the availability and effectiveness of other forms of accountability. To concede that there is some role to play for such considerations is not to concede that they should be determinative. The difficult question is exactly what role they should play, and how to describe and develop a methodology that acknowledges a role for them alongside many other factors. The question, in other words, is whether

[30] M Taggart and D Dyzenhaus, 'Reasoned Decisions and Legal Theory' in D Edlin (ed), *Common Law Theory* (New York, Cambridge University Press, 2007) 134 at 152.

[31] See also his unease with Lord Cooke's attempt to characterise the grounds of judicial review as reducing to fairness and reasonableness.

there is an account of the common law tradition that can accommodate any role for democratically constituted authority, not as a reason in its own right for submitting to decisions from that source, but as a factor that is relevant because of the democratic legitimacy of the decision-maker? This, in a nutshell, is what the theory of due deference has been trying to grope its way towards. Mike's conversion to bifurcation is the surest sign that so far those efforts have failed.

If there are powerful reasons against the bifurcation of public law, how do we address these concerns about unbridled judicial discretion that appear to drive even scholars like Mike and David Mullan towards accepting bifurcation? The key to avoiding bifurcation, it is suggested, lies in Mike's subtle appreciation of the important interrelationship between reason-giving, scrutiny for justification, proportionality and due deference, and of the essentially constitutional nature of all three.

The way Forward: Reasons, Justification, Proportionality and Due Deference

Mike himself has shown us the way forward from here in a number of ways. First, there is his work on the importance of decision-makers giving reasons for their decisions. No doubt influenced by his grounding in the administrative law of the United States, which boasts a longstanding duty to give reasons,[32] Mike has long championed the importance of a requirement that decision-makers publicly provide reasoned elaboration of their decisions.[33] The availability of such reasons is central to the idea of a culture of justification: it facilitates review by courts of the adequacy of a decision-maker's reasons for its decision, which are often crucial to determining the legality of that decision. For some, the very availability of detailed reasons is a dangerous invitation to courts to assess the adequacy of those reasons, which is likely to lead quickly to review for correctness. However, as Mike has also pointed out, the giving of detailed reasons for decisions is 'the start of deference as respect':[34] it provides courts with the reasons for a decision, to which the court must pay due regard when considering the lawfulness of the

[32] As Mike points out this duty first arose from the common law before being codified in the US Administrative Procedure Act: 'The Contribution of Lord Cooke to Scope of Review Doctrine in Administrative Law: A Comparative Common Law Perspective' in P Rishworth (ed), *The Struggle for Simplicity in the Law: Essays for Lord Cooke of Thorndon* (Wellington, Butterworths, 1997) 189 at 211 [Taggart, 'The Contribution of Lord Cooke']. In South Africa, everyone whose rights have been adversely affected by administrative action has a constitutional right to be given written reasons: section 33(2) of the South African Bill of Rights. The effect of the decision of the Supreme Court of Canada in *Baker*, above n 16, is similarly to provide a constitutional right to reasons. In the United Kingdom, although the courts have extended the circumstances in which reasons must be given, there is still no general duty to give reasons for administrative decisions, whether in common law or statute.

[33] See, eg, 'Osmond in the High Court of Australia', above n 11.

[34] Taggart, 'Proportionality', above n 20 at 463.

decision. In other words, the reasons are the starting point for any consideration of what degree of deference is due to the decision-maker.

Second, Mike's work on the concept of proportionality has provided us with the tools to resist its mischaracterisation as an indeterminate 'standard' or an open-ended ground of review that inevitably collapses into correctness review if the anchor of rights is removed. Despite the enormous literature, this basic fact about the concept of proportionality is still frequently overlooked. Proportionality does not pretend to be either a 'standard of review' with a determinate content, or a freestanding 'ground of review'. Rather, it is an intrinsically relational concept which, to be relied upon, must always be parasitic on some other right or interest or value: the nature of a complaint of disproportionality is that a particular decision or action or omission is unlawful, not because it is disproportionate in some abstract sense, but because it has a disproportionate impact on something that we value. To complain that a decision is disproportionate, without more, would be like complaining that a decision is too big.

Indeed, Mike's own exploration of the concept has shown that proportionality is not so much a standard or a ground of review as a *methodology* for ascertaining whether the impact of a decision, action or omission on something we value has been demonstrated to be adequately justified.[35] This is important because it shows that the proportionality methodology must always be anchored in some value regarded as being of fundamental importance. If there is always some such starting point, proportionality does not lose all its advantages of analytical rigour and transparency[36] in non-rights cases, and the concern about it collapsing into correctness review recedes. That concern cannot disappear completely, however, unless the proportionality methodology for assessing the adequacy of justifications also contains a notion of deference capable of preserving a meaningful space for the possibility of disagreement between the court and the decision-maker on the issue in question that does not render the decision unlawful.

This leads us to the third rich seam of Mike's work that provides us with the resources to resist bifurcation: his work on deference. Again deploying his great skill as a comparativist, in 1997 Mike drew on his knowledge of United States and Canadian administrative law to gently challenge the prevailing orthodoxy, both in New Zealand and the United Kingdom, that courts have a constitutional monopoly over the interpretation of statutes, and therefore have the power to overturn any administrative decision on the basis that the decision-maker has made an error of law.[37] With his usual keen eye for lack of judicial candour, and in particular for the judicial manipulation of labels and categories, Mike pointed out that, if you look at what judges do as well as what they say, 'notions of

[35] Ibid at 424.

[36] 'It is hoped and expected that proportionality would herald a more transparent, systematic, rigorous, evidence- and fact-based and principled process [than *Wednesbury* unreasonableness]. In short, a more scientific and determinate one.' Ibid at 459.

[37] Taggart, 'The Contribution of Lord Cooke', above n 32.

deference' in fact play an important role in the approach of the courts in both New Zealand and the United Kingdom, for example when classifying an issue as one of fact or law for the purposes of determining the appropriate scope of review. He argued that these notions of deference lurking in the doctrinal undergrowth of administrative law should be made explicit by 'the recognition and refinement of a doctrine or theory of deference.'[38] The public were entitled to expect open and honest explanation by the judges of what they were doing and why, and the explicit recognition of the role played by deference considerations would, it was hoped, lead to a more principled and predictable approach to when the courts would intervene to correct an administrative decision based on an interpretation of the decision-maker's statute. Although gently made, this was a radical argument, given the strength of judicial support for the orthodoxy in New Zealand and the United Kingdom that administrative interpretations of statutes are to be reviewed by courts on a correctness standard.

However, Mike's argument for deference, it is important to note, was essentially an argument for transparency: to make explicit the notions of deference already implicit in the approach of the courts. For, as Mike has demonstrated, many of the received doctrines of administrative law are underpinned by notions of deference. The concept of jurisdiction, for example, until its replacement by the doctrine of error of law, was a means of allocating interpretive authority between courts and administrative decision-makers, with questions the courts thought decision-makers were best placed to decide for themselves being characterised as 'within jurisdiction'. *Wednesbury* unreasonableness, which governed the exercise of statutory discretions, also contained in-built deference in its requirement that, to be unlawful, the exercise of discretion would have to be 'so unreasonable that no reasonable authority could ever have come to it.'[39] Just as the justification for the United States doctrine of deference lay in notions of legislative intent and agency expertise,[40] so, Mike pointed out, there were similar notions of deference in English administrative law, based on similar understandings of separation of powers and institutional competence.[41]

Now it is worth considering carefully the possible bases for a theory or doctrine of deference, because it will be suggested below that putting deference on a proper basis is the single most important way of avoiding the temptation of a bifurcated public law. In most jurisdictions that have developed an explicit doctrine of deference, two broad bases have tended to emerge from the judgments in which courts have explained why they are deferring to administrative decisions: legislative choice and relative institutional competence. In Canada, for example, David Mullan's account of the principles on which the courts do and

[38] Ibid at 202–3.

[39] *Associated Provincial Picture Houses Ltd. v Wednesbury Corporation* [1948] 1 KB 223 (CA) at 229–30 (Lord Greene MR).

[40] Taggart, 'The Contribution of Lord Cooke', above n 32 at 209.

[41] Taggart, 'The Tub of Public Law', above n 6 at 472.

should accord deference to statutory and prerogative decision-making[42] notes that the answer most commonly provided is that of respect for legislative choice of instruments for the performance of certain tasks. This is factored in by the court taking notice of specific indicia of legislative intention such as the presence or otherwise of an ouster clause, or the conferral of a discretionary power in broad, unstructured terms. But Mullan also notes that the matter is also often regarded by courts as one of 'institutional competence'. In certain domains, he says, courts do not have the expertise or the facilities to engage in matters already evaluated by a specialist tribunal or a member of the executive or administration. The question here is the relative competence of the court on the one hand and the designated decision-maker on the other in relation to the specific issue or issues that arises for determination.[43]

There are at least three significant problems with accounts of deference based on legislative choice or institutional competence, or some combination of the two. First, to rely on 'legislative choice' as a justification for deference is to retain a significant foothold in deference theory for the positivist reason for deferring: that courts should stay out because Parliament has told them to. Any approach that treats legislative choice as determinative amounts to deference as submission, a stance that pre-empts any meaningful review for justification.

Second, reliance on relative institutional competence as a determinative factor in deciding whether or not to defer to a decision-maker risks stripping deference theory of any normative dimension, by focusing narrowly on how institutions happen to be currently designed.[44] We cannot merely accept the institutions of legal order as they are if, according to deeply held convictions about the nature of a democratic society, it would not be correct for a court to defer to a decision-maker on grounds purely of institutional competence. We do not expect, for example, a judicial review court to defer on institutional competence grounds to a Secretary of State who has decided to deport a person who claims that they will face a real risk of torture on their return, even though the determination of the issue involves the determination of a number of factual questions about conditions in the country in question on which the Secretary of State has access to specialist advice. Because of the absolute nature of the right not to be tortured,

[42] D Mullan, 'Deference from *Baker* to *Suresh* and Beyond – Interpreting the Conflicting Signals' in Dyzenhaus, *The Unity of Public Law*, above n 6, 21.

[43] In the United Kingdom a number of commentators have argued that the only legitimate basis for judicial deference is relative institutional competence, not constitutional competence which has been settled by the Human Rights Act: see, eg, J Jowell, 'Judicial Deference: Servility, Civility or Institutional Capacity?' [2003] *Public Law* 592; Dyson LJ, 'Some Thoughts on Judicial Deference' [2006] 11 *Judicial Review* 103. For an account combining both institutional and constitutional reasons, see C A Gearty, 'Are Judges Now Out of their Depth?' [2007] *Justice Journal* 8.

[44] See M Hunt, 'Sovereignty's Blight: Why Contemporary Public Law Needs the Concept of Due Deference' in N Bamforth and P Leyland (eds), *Public Law in a Multi-layered Constitution* (Oxford, Hart Publishing, 2003), 337 at 350–51 for a fuller explanation of the argument that questions of institutional competence are inseparable from deeper normative questions of institutional design [Hunt, 'Sovereignty's Blight'].

we expect the reviewing court to ensure that it has available to it all the evidence and expert advice that was available to the Secretary of State, to enable the court to reach its own view on that question.

Third, and closely related to the first two, accounts of deference based on legislative choice and institutional competence do not give any role to the quality of the reasons relied upon to justify the decision. They may therefore pre-empt serious consideration being given to the quality of the justificatory reasons, because the stage of scrutiny may never be reached if the court decides to defer on grounds of legislative choice of decision-maker or relative institutional competence.

An alternative account of deference that seeks to escape these three basic problems with conventional deference theory has been developed elsewhere, and this is not the place to repeat that account in detail.[45] Mike has similarly argued for the articulation of a theory of due deference, with fine calibrations of democratic legitimacy, expertise and comparative competence.[46] In short, 'due deference' is based on the idea of deference as 'respect', where a court's respect for a decision has to be earned by a combination of the quality of the reasons for making it and other considerations that suggest that those reasons are 'good enough reasons' in a democratic society. Due deference requires courts to engage directly with the quality of the reasons offered as justifications for the decision, but also acknowledges a role for a range of other factors that are relevant to the court's determination of whether the quality of the reasons is 'good enough' in a democracy. These other factors include democratic considerations such as the degree of democratic accountability of the primary decision-maker, the extent to which other mechanisms of accountability are available, how well democratic mechanisms are working in practice and the extent to which those affected by the decision had an opportunity to influence the decision in the process leading up to it. The precise nature of the role played by the other factors is considered further below.

The due deference account confronts head on the fact that some critics of deference doctrine see it as being too strong, thereby encouraging judicial abdication, while others see it as too weak, providing no constraint on judges bent on correctness review. Any account of deference must have the resources within it to prevent it from collapsing into effectively a non-justiciability doctrine at one end of the spectrum, or offering so little counter-balance as to be merely a legitimating cloak for correctness review at the other end of the spectrum (other than in rare cases, such as torture cases, where the absolute nature of the

[45] See D Dyzenhaus, 'The Politics of Deference: Judicial Review and Democracy' in M Taggart (ed), *The Province of Administrative Law*, above n 12); D Dyzenhaus, 'Law as Justification: Etienne Mureinik's Conception of Legal Culture' (1998) 14 *South African Journal of Human Rights* 11; Hunt, 'Sovereignty's Blight', ibid at 349–54; D Dyzenhaus, 'Deference, Security and Human Rights' in B Goold and L Lazarus, *Security and Human Rights* (Oxford, Hart Publishing, 2007) 125.

[46] See, eg, 'Reinventing Administrative Law', above n 10 at 332.

fundamental norm requires review on a correctness standard). The concept of due deference, based on the notion of earned respect, distinguishes deference, following review of the adequacy of the justifications, from non-justiciability at one end of the spectrum. But it also distinguishes review for adequate justification from review for correctness at the other end of the spectrum, by preserving an important distinction between a democratically good enough justification and a justification that the reviewing court agrees with. The idea of a democratically good enough justification allows some space in which review for justification can take place between non-justiciability on the one hand and a correctness standard on the other.

'Due deference' has provoked some strong reactions. Trevor Allan, for example, regards due deference as an abdication of judicial responsibility for the protection of rights, a substitute for legal analysis of rights claims.[47] He argues that there are no general criteria or principles of deference because no coherent theory or doctrine of deference is feasible. The court's role is to decide, on a correctness standard, whether there has been a breach of an individual's right in the particular circumstances of the individual's case, and considerations such as the democratic nature or institutional competence of the decision-maker are external to the legal analysis of whether there has been a breach of the right. Due deference raises the spectre, for Allan, of a court reaching the conclusion that, on a proper legal analysis, an individual's right has been infringed, but bowing to the superior democratic authority or institutional competence of the decision-maker. It sanctions judicial capitulation to legislative or executive fiat. In Allan's view, the very quest for deference principles undermines the rule of law, the separation of powers and the neutrality and impartiality of the courts between the citizen and the state.

Much of Allan's critique of due deference is aimed at the Aunt Sally of non-justiciability. Due deference, he says, turns out on close inspection, to be 'non-justiciability dressed in pastel colours.'[48] But due deference is not a non-justiciability doctrine as Allan appears to suppose. On the contrary, it explicitly acknowledges that neither democratic arguments nor considerations of relative institutional competence must be treated as determinative of the justification question, that is, as reasons that pre-empt judicial involvement altogether, because the court would then be abdicating its task of properly scrutinising the reasons to decide whether adequate justification has been made out.[49] The idea of deference as respect requires active engagement with the quality of the reasons for the decision in question. Nor can the 'deference factors' or criteria properly be characterised as 'external' to the quality of the decision under review. Rather

[47] TRS Allan, 'Human Rights and Judicial Review: A Critique of "Due Deference"' (2006) 65 *Cambridge Law Journal* 671. See also TRS Allan, 'Common Law Reason and the Limits of Deference' in D Dyzenhaus (ed), *The Unity of Public Law*, above n 6 at 289.

[48] Allan, 'Human rights and Judicial Review' ibid at 689.

[49] Hunt, 'Sovereignty's Blight', above n 44 at 351.

those factors are integral to the determination of the question of compatibility with the right. It is the interaction of the quality of the reasons and the deference factors which enables the court to reach a view about compatibility: is the quality of the reasons good enough bearing in mind the relative expertise, institutional competence and constitutional position of the decision-maker? On Allan's account, it seems, a challenge by a resident to the compulsory purchase of his land to build a motorway, on the basis that it unjustifiably interferes with his right to peaceful enjoyment of his possessions,[50] must be treated by the court in exactly the same way as it treats a challenge to a deportation decision on the basis that there is a real risk of torture on return. Even if the compulsory purchase decision has been preceded by a lengthy inquiry in which the landowner had an opportunity to participate, the court must satisfy itself that the correct decision has been reached about the interference being justified, including, presumably, by apprising itself of all the relevant evidence that was before the original decision-maker. As Mike observes, "this is utterly implausible, to say nothing of undesirable."[51]

Allan's critique, however, has a certain resonance with the judiciary. English courts for the most part remain stubbornly resistant to any overt embrace of the idea of deference. As Mike charts in his recent New Zealand Law Review piece, prominent English judges, including many of those who write extra-judicially, have gone out of their way to denounce deference as amounting to an abdication of the judicial function.[52] This scepticism about deference is exemplified in the House of Lords' most recent consideration of the question in an immigration case called *Huang*.[53] The issue for decision in *Huang* was the approach to be taken by appellate immigration judges when deciding statutory appeals against refusals of leave to enter or remain on the ground that the refusal is incompatible with a Convention right. The House of Lords in *Huang* held that the task of the appellate immigration authority, on an appeal on a Convention ground against a decision of the primary official decision-maker refusing leave to enter or remain in the United Kingdom, is to decide whether the challenged decision is unlawful as incompatible with a Convention right or compatible and so lawful. It is not a secondary, reviewing, function dependent on establishing that the primary decision-maker misdirected himself or acted irrationally or was guilty of procedural impropriety.

The actual decision in *Huang* appears to be nothing more controversial than a correction of the mistaken approach of the lower courts to the nature of the function of the appellate immigration judges where the ground of appeal is

[50] Although not included in every national bill of rights, the right to property is protected by Article 1 Protocol 1 to the ECHR.

[51] Taggart, 'Proportionality', above n 20 at 456.

[52] Most prominently Lord Hoffmann and Lord Justice Sedley.

[53] *Huang v Secretary of State for the Home Department; Kashmiri v Secretary of State for the Home Department* [2007] UKHL 11, [2007] 2 AC 167 [*Huang*]. See M Amos, 'Separating Human Rights Adjudication from Judicial Review' [2007] *European Human Rights Law Review* 679.

breach of a Convention right, and to this extent it is a welcome clarification.[54] However, the House of Lords went on in *Huang* to give short shrift to the extensive argument they had heard about due deference and related concepts when deciding what the proper approach of the immigration appellate bodies should be to their task. They were critical of the tendency 'to complicate and mystify what is not, in principle, a hard task to define, however difficult the task is, in practice, to perform.'[55] The first task of the appellate immigration authority is to establish the relevant facts, which will always be important to their decision and often decisive. The authority will also wish to consider and weigh all that tells in favour of the decision being challenged, with particular reference to justification under Article 8(2) ECHR. These will include both general considerations that apply in almost any case (such as the general administrative desirability of applying known rules so that the system of immigration control is workable, predictable, consistent and fair as between one applicant and another) and particular reasons relied on to justify refusal in the particular case. The House of Lords, however, rejected the language of deference to describe the giving of weight to factors such as these:[56]

> The giving of weight to factors such as these is not, in our opinion, aptly described as deference: it is performance of the ordinary judicial task of weighing up the competing considerations on each side and according appropriate weight to the judgment of a person with responsibility for a given subject matter and access to special sources of knowledge and advice. This is how any rational judicial decision-maker is likely to proceed.

Mike has some harsh words for the House of Lords decision in *Huang*.[57] He argues that the House of Lords made 'a serious mistake' by its disparaging attitude to deference language and, by implication, to the attempts that have been made to articulate 'deference factors' and attempt to give them weight in different contexts. He criticises the 'vacuity' of their Lordships' definition of the right approach: that courts merely have to find the facts and weigh up the competing considerations, giving appropriate weight to the view of the decision-maker. As Mike rightly comments, this really provides no guidance whatsoever.

[54] The issue for decision in *Huang* was remarkably similar to the issue which the House of Lords decided in the earlier landmark case of *R (Daly) v Secretary of State for the Home Department* [2001] UKHL 26, [2001] 2 AC 532 in the early days of the Human Rights Act. In *Daly* the House of Lords was called upon to rule on the approach to be taken by courts in judicial review cases where the ground of review relied on was that the decision-maker had acted incompatibly with a Convention right. The House of Lords unanimously disapproved of the approach being taken by the lower courts, because it was couched in language too reminiscent of the traditional *Wednesbury* ground of review. Proportionality required a greater intensity of review than review for mere reasonableness of the decision-maker's conclusion. *Huang* concerned essentially the same issue, but in the context of a statutory appeal rather than a judicial review.

[55] *Huang*, above n 53 at para 14.

[56] Ibid at para 16.

[57] Taggart, 'Proportionality', above n 20 at 460.

As any simple common lawyer knows, when tasks are easy to define in principle but difficult to perform in practice it is usually a sign that insufficient thought has gone into the nature of the task. In recent years, much academic thought and energy has gone into attempts to theorise the proper delineation of the respective functions of courts and decision-makers where Convention rights are in play. The most disappointing feature of the House of Lords' judgment in *Huang* is the failure of the highest court to engage with these efforts. One needs the standing and authority of a Taggart to level the charges of vacuity, serious error and abdication of responsibility at a decision of a unanimous panel of Law Lords chaired by Lord Bingham. But these are well aimed barbs.[58]

The decision in *Huang* leaves a number of unanswered questions. First, where does it leave debates about the doctrine of due deference? The House of Lords may have liked to consign the concept itself to oblivion in the United Kingdom, an unnecessarily complicating and mystifying distraction from the straightforward task of judging. But, as I have argued elsewhere, this is the inescapable central question of public law in any legal system with a pretence to constitutionalism of any kind and, so long as UK public law maintains that pretension, it will not go away.[59] The label of due deference may not survive the decision in *Huang*, but this hardly matters. What matters is the substantive approach beneath the label: the explicit articulation of the sorts of factors that might make courts reluctant to substitute their own assessment of proportionality for that of the original decision-maker; the identification of the specific factors in play in a particular case; and a clear explanation of the reasons why some considerations are given more weight than others in the overall exercise of arriving at a determination of the compatibility question.

Second, what role is to be played by democratic considerations when courts are weighing the competing considerations that are relevant to determining whether a decision is compatible with human rights? Notwithstanding the general judicial scepticism about the aptness of the language of deference, it is clear that such considerations continue to play an important part in courts' reasoning in cases where challenges are made to executive or administrative decisions on human rights grounds.[60] Indeed, the relevance of democratic considerations was explicitly acknowledged in the judgment of the House of Lords in *Huang* itself. It is clearly envisaged to be part of the ordinary judicial task, for example, to accord

[58] Compare the detailed consideration given to the academic literature on these questions by the Supreme Court of Canada (see, eg, *Baker*, above n 16 at para 65) and the Constitutional Court of South Africa (see, eg, *Bato Star Fishing v Minister of Environmental Affairs and Tourism* [2004] B Const LR 687 at para 46).

[59] 'Sovereignty's Blight', above n 44 at 338.

[60] See, eg, *R (SB) v Governors of Denbigh High School* [2007] 1 AC 100 and *R (RJM) v Secretary of State* [2008] UKHL 63. And see the recent observation by Baroness Hale that when deciding whether a particular limitation upon an established right is 'necessary in a democratic society', courts are bound to give 'great weight to the recent and carefully considered judgments of the elected legislature and government': 'Law Lords at the Margin: Who Defines Convention Rights?' (Tom Sargant Memorial Lecture 2008, 15 October 2008).

'appropriate weight' to the judgment of a person 'with responsibility for a given subject matter.' Although the House of Lords gives no assistance at all on what will be the 'appropriate weight' to be given to such a factor, the claim to any weight at all presumably derives from the fact that this 'responsibility' for the subject matter will usually have been given by Parliament, in an allocation of decision-making power in a statute. The House of Lords also distinguished certain cases relied on by the Secretary of State, in which the courts had taken a deferential approach to the Secretary of State's view about the proportionality of an interference with human rights, in part on the basis that those were cases 'where Parliament had specifically excluded any right of appeal.'[61]

Most significantly, however, the House of Lords in *Huang* explicitly had regard to the democratic pedigree of the Immigration Rules as a relevant factor in determining the weight to be given to the Home Secretary's assessment of the proportionality of the interference with the applicants' right to respect for family life. The Lords were invited to do so by the Government itself which argued that 'the appellate immigration authority should assume that the Immigration Rules and supplementary instructions, made by the responsible minister and laid before Parliament, had the imprimatur of democratic approval and should be taken to strike the right balance between the interests of the individual and those of the community.' The House of Lords rejected the Government's argument because the Immigration Rules and supplementary instructions could not be said to represent 'a considered democratic compromise', not being the product of active debate in Parliament, where non-nationals seeking leave to enter or remain are not in any event represented.[62]

It is in Mike's response to *Huang* that he shows us the way to the future development of a doctrine of due deference:[63]

> it is precisely the articulation and application of deference in the particular context that should be encouraged. Only by the courts weighing up the relevant deference factors will they appropriately calibrate the intensity of review in the particular case and, as

[61] *Huang*, above n 53 at para 16, referring to *Samaroo v Secretary of State for the Home Department* [2001] EWCA Civ 1139, [2002] INLR 55 (weight given to the Secretary of State's judgment that deportation was a valuable deterrent to actual or prospective drug traffickers) and *R (Farrakhan) v Secretary of State for the Home Department* [2002] EWCA Civ 606, [2002] QB 1391 (weight given to Home Secretary's judgment that applicant posed a threat to community relations between Muslims and Jews).

[62] The Government had sought to rely on the analogy of housing legislation, in light of the decision of the House of Lords in *Kay v Lambeth London Borough Council* [2006] UKHL 10, [2006] 2 AC 465 that the right of a public authority landlord to enforce a claim for possession against an occupier whose right to occupy had ended would in most cases automatically supply the justification required by Article 8(2) ECHR and the courts would assume that domestic law struck the proper balance unless the contrary were shown. The House of Lords in *Huang* found the analogy unpersuasive: unlike the Immigration Rules, domestic housing policy had been a continuing subject of discussion and debate in Parliament over very many years, with the competing interests of landlords and tenants fully represented, and the outcome 'may truly be said to represent a considered democratic compromise.'

[63] Taggart, 'Proportionality', above n 20 at 460.

> importantly, provide some guidance to advisors and later courts in the process. In this way they will slowly but surely put signposts on the review rainbow or map. To give up on that task is, in my view an abdication of responsibility.

Shining through here is Mike's unswerving faith in the methodology of the common law, a belief in contextualism that never descends into treating cases as a welter of single instances, but which understands that, over time, guiding principles can emerge from decisions on the facts of particular cases that help decision-makers and courts to make decisions in later cases.[64] The quest to map the evolving common law of judicial review is undimmed, notwithstanding the lack of help from the judges.

Mike's account of due deference, however, purports to be confined to the rights side of the divide between rights and non-rights cases: deference is the complementary force that acts as a counter-weight to proportionality on the rights part of the rainbow. But there is nothing in Mike's account of deference that ties it to rights cases. On the contrary, here we have the seeds of a general doctrine of deference that can apply equally across the whole of administrative law: to interpretations of statute by administrative decision-makers, to the exercise of discretions and to decisions about what procedures are required in order to be fair.

Conclusion

This chapter has argued that the cumulative effect of Mike's key insights about public law is more far-reaching than Mike himself has been prepared to acknowledge in his writings. Mike has been driven to defend a bifurcated public law by his concern that, outside of rights review, proportionality collapses too easily into review for correctness and that the idea of 'due deference' is not sufficiently constraining to prevent that collapse. So he seeks to confine both proportionality and due deference to rights cases because he is concerned that due deference is too weak to constrain the judges.

There are powerful arguments against the bifurcation of public law into rights and non-rights cases, which would be a seriously retrograde step. The key to avoiding that step is to be found in Mike's own work on the interrelationship and constitutional nature of reason-giving, justification, proportionality and due deference. It has been argued that to avoid bifurcation we must seek to enshrine a

[64] Mike has always deplored the common judicial ploy of claiming that there are few if any guiding principles in public law, only decisions on the facts of particular cases in particular contexts: see, eg, Lord Cooke's comment that '[T]he subject [of administrative law] does not lend itself well to elaboration of principles. Statutory interpretation and the judicial attitude of mind are basically, in most instances, the governing factors. The crunch cases are not decided by textbook principles; they are exercises in line-drawing', cited in Taggart, 'The Contribution of Lord Cooke', above n 32 at 202, footnote 76. For an attempt to distil some principles from the case law see R Clayton, 'Principles for Judicial Deference' [2006] *Judicial Review* 109.

constitutional requirement to give reasons, to understand proportionality as a flexible methodology for ascertaining whether adequate justification for interference with fundamental values has been made out, and to redouble our efforts both to explain why public law needs a concept of due deference and to provide an account of it capable of constraining judges without collapsing into a non-justiciability doctrine.

Here, then, is the project for the coming decades for those who have found inspiration in Mike's writings: to marshal his wide-ranging insights about public law into a coherent vision of a new, democratic constitutionalism of which administrative law is an integral part. It is far too early to say precisely how this new constitutionalism will look. But Mike's contributions to these debates have begun the important work of sketching out for us the contours. If Mike's instincts are right, it is likely to include a wide, modern catalogue of rights and substantive values considered fundamental today; a requirement that decisions or actions interfering with those values be publicly justified by reasoned elaboration; a structured, transparent and context-sensitive methodology for assessing the adequacy of that justification; and a more worked out concept of due deference in which democratic considerations have an explicit role to play. That would be a legacy wholly out of keeping with the modesty of the man, but entirely justified by the ambition of his scholarship.

7

'You Say You Want a Revolution': Bills of Rights in the Age of Human Rights

GRANT HUSCROFT* AND PAUL RISHWORTH

I The Birth of the New Zealand Bill of Rights Act 1990: Tugging on Superman's Cape?

OVER THE YEARS we have admired Mike Taggart's penchant for choosing quirky titles for his articles. The enigmatic 'Tugging on Superman's Cape: Lessons from Experience with the New Zealand Bill of Rights Act 1990'[1] is one of his best. But what does it mean? In the Jim Croce song, whence the opening phrase comes, it is part of some sage advice about a certain 'pool shootin' son-of-a-gun' named Big Jim Walker. Just as one should not 'tug on Superman's cape', 'spit into the wind', or 'pull the mask off the old Lone Ranger', the song suggests it equally unwise to 'mess around with Jim'. As it happens, in the second verse a gentleman named Slim arrives from Alabama and beats Big Jim in a bar room brawl. The song's final refrain, then, is that 'you don't mess around with Slim'.[2]

This is a mystery for us all to ponder, but we have decided that Superman is the New Zealand Parliament with its supreme law-making power, and that the brave tugs on Parliament's cape are being made by the New Zealand Bill of Rights Act

* Thanks to Bradley Allan, Janet McLean, and David Dyzenhaus for their helpful comments and suggestions, and to Carolyn McKenna, James Green and Danielle Kelly, who provided outstanding research and editorial assistance.

[1] M Taggart, 'Tugging on Superman's Cape: Lessons from Experience with the New Zealand Bill of Rights Act 1990' [1998] *Public Law* 266, earlier version published in J Beatson, C Forsyth, and I Hare (eds), *Constitutional Reform in the United Kingdom: Practice and Principles* (Hart Publishing, Oxford, 1998) [Taggart, 'Superman's Cape'].

[2] J Croce, 'You Don't Mess Around with Jim', from the album *You Don't Mess Around with Jim* (1972).

1990 (NZBORA). Will Parliament's supremacy be defeated, perhaps by some sort of reinvented and invigorated NZBORA? And if this occurs, might we then come to fear the NZBORA itself? Or is mere 'tugging' enough, so that a sort of equilibrium emerges? Perhaps the town is indeed big enough for the both of them – parliamentary supremacy and a statutory bill of rights – and neither need be feared.

We are not without clues. In 2007 Mike made clear that he 'did not support judges being given (or taking) the power to invalidate statutes for failure to adhere to written or unwritten fundamental values',[3] a view he had no difficulty in reconciling with his view that the common law serves as a legitimate repository of values, which judges can bring to bear in interpreting statutes and judicially reviewing decisions. This led him to say that he was happy with the NZBORA (as an embodiment of some but not necessarily all of those values), and opposed 'to strengthening' it by entrenchment.[4] He was happy, then, with a parliamentary superman restrained by judicial (and judicious) cape-tugging.[5]

Our aim in this chapter is to give our own views on this topic, but it behooves us first to explain our own title.[6]

Written constitutions and bills of rights have, in many countries, emerged from revolutions, or otherwise at the birth of nations. New Zealand's unwritten constitution, in contrast, has developed peacefully, without a grand plan in place since its birth. It has something of an 'accidental' character. It is susceptible to changes wrought by law and practice, and some of these might be said to have the character of a 'quiet revolution'. Something like this has been happening in the field of human rights. The NZBORA was born in unpropitious circumstances – largely unloved by the profession, the citizenry, and even within the Labour Party that promoted it[7] – yet its stature has risen with the tide of international human rights consciousness. This tide has brought human rights into the New Zealand legal system through other pathways as well – as international treaty rights, as

[3] M Taggart, '"Dialogue" as Inter-Branch Communication' in C Geiringer & D Knight (eds) *Seeing the World Whole: Essays in Honour of Sir Kenneth Keith* (Wellington, Victoria University Press, 2008) 340 at 340 [Taggart, 'Dialogue'].

[4] Taggart, 'Dialogue', ibid.

[5] A sartorial metaphor to similar effect appears elsewhere: writing in 1992 with Janet McLean and one of the present authors, Mike likened the NZBORA in the field of administrative law to a 'loose-fitting methodological straitjacket which, while it can never completely tie the hands of the judges, does provide a significant restraint.' (McLean et al, 'Impact of the NZBORA' below n 17 at 97).

[6] It is the first line of the Beatles song 'Revolution', Lennon and McCartney (*The Beatles* [White Album] 1968).

[7] P Rishworth, 'The Birth and Rebirth of the Bill of Rights' in G Huscroft and P Rishworth (eds) *Rights and Freedoms: The New Zealand Bill of Rights Act 1990 and the Human Rights Act 1993* (Wellington, Brookers, 1995) 1 [Rishworth, 'Birth and Rebirth']. Then Minister of Health, the Hon Michael Bassett, has written of the proposal for a Bill of Rights: 'Few people demanded it and nobody else in Cabinet was an enthusiast. But it was a bee that had lodged firmly in [Minister of Justice Geoffrey] Palmer's bonnet.'(*Working with David: Inside the Lange Cabinet* (Auckland, Hodder Moa, 2008) at 199). Then, referring to the NZBORA subsequently enacted in 1990, Bassett writes: 'Against almost universal opposition from caucus because of earlier bad publicity, [Palmer] would insist on introducing and passing a truncated version of his earlier Bill of Rights' (ibid at 514).

fundamental common law rights, and in a renaissance of Maori rights in the Treaty of Waitangi. All of these things have tugged at Parliament's supremacy, mediated through doctrines surrounding judicial review and statutory interpretation, and Mike Taggart has been one of the most astute observers and interpreters of this phenomenon.

In the new constitutional settlement that has resulted the NZBORA is likely here to stay, even though it could be repealed by a simple parliamentary majority. It has a 'practical sanctity', to use a phrase of the late Lord Cooke. But some think that more should be done, and that the NZBORA should be strengthened to confer a judicial power to invalidate statutes. Like Mike, however, we oppose entrenchment, or constitutionalisation, of the NZBORA. In our view, constitutionalisation would only marginally 'strengthen' the protection of rights, but would do so at the cost of undermining New Zealand's constitutional order fundamentally. It would, indeed, be revolutionary. The decision not to pass a supreme law bill of rights was the right one in 1990, and it is the right one today. It has allowed New Zealand's human rights culture to continue to develop from the ground up, rather than be imposed by judges from the top-down.

We begin with an examination of the way in which the age of human rights has influenced public law within the existing context of parliamentary supremacy in New Zealand. With Mike, we believe that a proper understanding of the nature and extent of rights-protection provided by the system we have is critical to evaluating calls for fundamental change to that system. In the second part of the chapter we discuss some of the difficulties inherent in any proposal to adopt a supreme law bill of rights.

The Age of Human Rights

It is somewhat misleading to speak of an 'age of human rights', given that protecting rights and obligations is an ancient concern of the law. But the types of rights with which law is concerned, and the ways in which that concern is expressed, have changed over time and especially in the last 20 years. Indeed, as we shall see, a thesis of Mike Taggart and his co-authors David Dyzenhaus and Murray Hunt is that some of the events we are about to discuss are explicable as 'judicial updating of the set of common law values to which the administrative state has long been subjected by courts'.[8] In any event, for our purposes some starting point is necessary so we begin with the early 1990s. By that time the

[8] D Dyzenhaus, M Hunt, M Taggart, 'The Principle of Legality in Administrative Law: Internationalisation as Constitutionalisation' (2001) 1 *Oxford University Commonwealth Law Journal* 5 at 7 [Dyzenhaus et al, 'Principle of Legality'].

evocative phrase 'human rights' was heard around the world, although it dates back, of course, to at least the Universal Declaration of Human Rights in 1948.[9]

New Zealand adopted the NZBORA in 1990, a statutory bill of rights that affirms a number of civil and political rights and freedoms while preserving parliamentary sovereignty – specifically, by prohibiting courts from invalidating legislation on the basis of inconsistency with the Act.[10] The NZBORA was a retreat from the proposal to adopt a supreme law bill of rights.[11] Strong opposition to the establishment of judicial power to invalidate legislation had led to a watering down of the proposal and ultimately to passage of the NZBORA in ordinary statute form, but there is no suggestion in the brief Report of the Justice and Law Reform Committee on the White Paper that the implications of a statutory bill of rights were truly understood.[12] In particular, the textual adjustments made in the course of altering the draft 'supreme law' bill of rights to a statutory bill of rights were to lead to continuing confusion.[13]

The NZBORA was not greeted with any great interest or enthusiasm despite its high-sounding words, and there was a risk that it might become a dead letter – a victim of the indifference that is thought to have consigned the statutory Canadian Bill of Rights 1960 to irrelevance.[14] In its early years the NZBORA perplexed both bench and bar. The judiciary was not confident in its democratic legitimacy, and the bar saw little scope for its relevance beyond the field of criminal law. As a result, early cases saw it operating mainly as a constraint on police power, leading to case law concerning the right of detained persons to see a lawyer, to be free from arbitrary detention and unreasonable searches, and so on.[15] But as the international age of human rights began to envelop it, the

[9] Interestingly, New Zealand's first human rights legislation was the Human Rights Commission Act 1977, a title reflecting the body that the Act established. It was not until the revision in the 1990s that led to the Human Rights Act 1993 that the Act's title referred to the idea of rights themselves.

[10] See generally, P Rishworth, G Huscroft, S Optican and R Mahoney, *The New Zealand Bill of Rights* (Melbourne, Oxford University Press 2003) [Rishworth et al, *The New Zealand Bill of Rights*].

[11] *A Bill of Rights for New Zealand* (1985) AJHR A6 [*White Paper*]. The Minister of Justice and mover of the Bill of Rights proposal, Sir Geoffrey Palmer, has since portrayed himself as a prophet without honour. New Zealanders were, he wrote in 1992, 'amongst the most constitutionally underdeveloped people in the developed world.' See G Palmer, *Constitution in Crisis: Reforming our Political System* (Dunedin, John McIndoe, 1992) [Palmer, *Constitution in Crisis*]. Mike Taggart, who had then recently returned to New Zealand after lecturing in Canada, organised a major seminar held in August 1985 on the *White Paper*: see *A Bill of Rights for New Zealand* (Legal Research Foundation Seminar, Auckland, 16 August 1985).

[12] Justice and Law Reform Committee, *Final report of the Justice and Law Reform Committee on a White Paper on a Bill of Rights for New Zealand* (1988) I8C AJHR.

[13] We refer here to the 'section 4, 5 and 6 imbroglio'; see the account in Rishworth et al, *The New Zealand Bill of Rights*, above n 10 ch 4. Subsequent to that account, the same issues emerged in *R v Hansen* [2007] 3 NZLR 1 (SC).

[14] There are other explanations for the perceived failure of the Canadian Bill of Rights, which applied only to matters under federal jurisdiction. See P Hogg, *Constitutional Law of Canada* (Scarborough, Thomson-Carswell, 5th ed, 2007) ch 35 [Hogg, *Constitutional Law of Canada*] and W Tarnopolsky, *The Canadian Bill of Rights* (Toronto, McClelland & Stewart, 2nd ed, 1975).

[15] See, eg, *Ministry of Transport v Noort* [1992] 3 NZLR 260 (CA).

NZBORA came to be invested with greater significance and wider application.[16] Indeed, it became the model for other jurisdictions seeking to combine the affirmation of human rights with a continuing commitment to parliamentary supremacy.

The Bill of Rights and Administrative Law – McLean, Rishworth & Taggart Revisited

Shortly following passage of the NZBORA, Mike Taggart joined with Janet McLean and Paul Rishworth[17] ('MRT') to explore its potential impact on administrative law – a minority interest at the time. Their thesis was that the various rights in the Act operated so as to restrict the lawful scope of discretionary power. It was as though every statute that conferred ostensibly broad discretionary power included the implicit qualification 'but not so as to breach rights in the Bill of Rights'. The concept of 'breaching rights' meant imposing limitations that could not be 'demonstrably justified' as 'reasonable' in a 'free and democratic society' – the proportionality requirement that section 5 of the NZBORA established. MRT illustrated this proposition with five case studies of particular types of discretionary power, and described this approach as being logically prior to the doctrines that administrative law supplied for controlling discretion. The NZBORA was, after all, a catalogue of things that should *not* happen – there should be no discrimination, no denial of natural justice, no infringement of freedom of association, freedom of expression, and so on – all subject, of course, to the ability of the state to justify reasonable limits on the protected rights and freedoms. If decision-makers respected these boundaries then the NZBORA was satisfied, but administrative law might supply additional constraints – for example, through the concepts of relevant, irrelevant, and perhaps even mandatory considerations.

MRT recognised that the pivotal question became: what counted as inconsistency with the NZBORA?, and that this question involved the requirement of reasons, long a focus of Mike Taggart's scholarship. The state had to explain *why* rights were limited in particular cases, and courts had to assess those reasons. In turn, the duty to assess those reasons led to questions about the nature and extent of deference that was required. There was scope for deference at key steps of the justificatory process: in accepting, perhaps, the decision-maker's primary determination that there was a problem to be addressed of sufficient importance to justify impairing a right or freedom, or that the means by which the objective was accomplished were proportionate.

16 Rishworth, 'Birth and Rebirth', above n 7.

17 J McLean, P Rishworth, and M Taggart, 'The Impact of the New Zealand Bill of Rights Act 1990 on Administrative Law' in *Essays on the New Zealand Bill of Rights Act 1990* (Auckland, Legal Research Foundation, 1992) 62 [McLean et al, 'Impact of the NZBORA'].

These are matters to which we shall return, but for the moment it is enough to record that a bill of rights, almost by definition, denotes a set of general – and thus vaguely worded – baseline standards below which a state should not descend whether through enacted law[18] or actions. Identifying that baseline is first and foremost a question for elected representatives and administrative officials, but in contested cases may become a legal question for judges. The way in which the baseline is expressed is significant: rights may only be limited in ways considered justifiable in 'a free and democratic society'. The NZBORA does not make observation of the baseline a condition for the *validity* of legislation – indeed, section 4 makes it clear that inconsistent enactments remained legally valid and must be applied. But the justificatory standard in section 5 is clearly part of a package of provisions (along with the requirement in section 6 to prefer consistent statutory meanings and the Attorney-General's legislation-vetting role under section 7) that seeks to ensure general respect for the baseline by Parliament, Government, and bodies performing public functions. Implicit in the trilogy of sections 4, 5, and 6 is this proposition: judges may on occasion hold that legislation falls below the baseline and is therefore 'inconsistent' with the NZBORA. That seems inescapable. After all, a prior finding of inconsistency is a necessary step when obeying the injunction in section 6 to prefer consistent rather than inconsistent meanings when that 'can' be done. And any reliance on section 4, whereunder an unavoidably inconsistent enactment must be applied despite its inconsistency, also assumes a prior judicial finding of that inconsistency. Therein lay the germ of the idea of declarations of inconsistency (or incompatibility, as the UK was to put it in the Human Rights Act 1998).[19]

MRT did not envisage a rapid growth of administrative law cases involving the NZBORA, and it took a while for their thesis to be exemplified in judicial decisions. In a judicial review case about a primary school's conduct in relation to a child, Justice DAR Williams advocated a light-handed judicial approach, emphasising that 'issues of local educational administration [were] best left for resolution through the individuality of local communities'. Of the MRT article, he said:[20]

[18] And this includes the common law made by judges: see P Rishworth 'Taking Human Rights into the Private Sphere' in D Oliver and J Fedtke, *Human Rights and the Private Sphere: A Comparative Study* (London, Cavendish, 2006); S Gardbaum, 'The "Horizontal Effect" of Constitutional Rights' (2003) 102 *Michigan Law Review* 387.

[19] Rishworth et al, *The New Zealand Bill of Rights*, above n 10 at 833–35.

[20] *Maddever v Umawera School Board of Trustees* [1993] 2 NZLR 478 at 508. The case before Williams J lacked merit and cried out for dismissal, and for the reasons he gave – that no statutory power had actually been exercised in relation to the child concerned (whose parents had removed him from the school). So there was nothing to review. MRT would have agreed entirely with Williams J. In cases that involve termination or suspension of students' rights to be at a school, courts have been concerned to assess very carefully the process adopted by schools. It is conceivable that more deference might be shown in cases involving the validity of school rules that impact upon protected rights, such as school uniforms on freedom of expression. No cases of this type have occurred in the NZBORA era; cf *R (on the application of Begum) v Head Teacher and Governor of Denbigh High School* [2007] 1 AC 100 (UKHL).

> The concept of a more restrained judicial role may be unattractive to those who appear to consider that the robust expansion of judicial review is, per se, desirable: see, eg, [MRT] arguing, inter alia, that because of the New Zealand Bill of Rights Act 1990 there should be 'less scope for judicial deference to the decision-maker's own judgment as to the reasonableness of the infringement in a particular case' and that 'vague assertions of deference or non-justiciability have now to survive the transparent particularization in weighing which section 5 [of the Bill of Rights] requires'.

But in a minor case in 1996, only reported much later, a High Court judge accepted the proposition that delegated legislation must be consistent with the NZBORA.[21] Then, in 2001, a major statutory interpretation case about regulation-making powers exemplified the argument in a straightforward way. *Drew v Attorney-General*[22] concerned a provision in prison regulations that purported to prohibit legal representation in prisoners' disciplinary hearings. Mr Drew argued that his particular case was complex and demanded legal representation. Under established common law principles of natural justice, a tribunal hearing such a case ought to have been at liberty to allow legal representation if persuaded that it were required to ensure fairness. But the regulations ruled out representation in every case, even when natural justice required it. Attention then turned to the empowering legislation: did it really authorise the making of regulations that wholly excluded this aspect of natural justice? The Court of Appeal held that it did not, and that the offending clause in the regulations was ultra vires.

The Court of Appeal was somewhat coy about ascribing this outcome to the NZBORA, preferring to ground its decision on the common law right to natural justice. But the Court recognised that this right is affirmed by section 27(1) of the NZBORA, so *Drew* was and is seen as an illustration of the discretion-reducing and rights-respecting impact of the Act. The Court's reticence was likely a residual effect of the lack of a clear consensus about the NZBORA and its legitimate scope. But in a range of cases throughout the second half of the 1990s, it became clear that rights-infringing applications of ostensibly broad discretionary powers were precluded.[23] Finally, in *Cropp v A Judicial Authority* the proposition was stated categorically by the Supreme Court of New Zealand:[24]

> Subordinate legislation involving a relevant guaranteed right or freedom will be invalid when the empowering provision, read in accordance with section 6 of the Bill of Rights, does not authorise its making.

It was, of course, of great significance that throughout the late 1990s and early 2000s an identically structured argument was being made, and successfully, in English cases based upon 'fundamental rights' in the common law. Those cases

[21] *Collector of Customs v Kilburn Car Sales Ltd* [2004] NZAR 500 (HC). The judge did not consider that the example in front of him involved inconsistency.

[22] [2002] 1 NZLR 58 (CA).

[23] Rishworth et al, *The New Zealand Bill of Rights*, above n 10 at 158–60.

[24] [2008] NZSC 46 at para 25.

rested on the idea of the 'principle of legality'.[25] The commonality of that idea with rights enshrined in a document entitled 'Bill of Rights' seemed obvious. In a 2000 case Chief Justice Elias put the matter this way: 'This principle of legality, recognised by the common law, has been expressly enacted by section 6 of the New Zealand Bill of Rights Act 1990.'[26] As Mike Taggart noted, "[the principle of legality] is sections 5 and 6 of the [NZBORA] writ large".[27]

A major 2005 case in the immigration context, *Zaoui v Attorney-General*,[28] demonstrated the extent to which this basic proposition had infiltrated New Zealand law. The statutory power in issue read:

> **72 Persons threatening national security**—Where the Minister certifies that the continued presence in New Zealand of any person named in the certificate constitutes a threat to national security, the Governor-General may, by Order in Council, order the deportation from New Zealand of that person.

Against that, the combined weight of sections 8 and 9 of the Bill of Rights (rights to life, and against disproportionately severe treatment or punishment) was held to qualify the Minister's power to deport persons who might be at risk of torture – even, said the Court, in respect of persons judged a security risk to New Zealand and whose deportation would otherwise be justified under article 33.2 of the Refugee Convention. Again, the word 'may' was read as though it were followed with the words 'but not so as to breach rights in the Bill of Rights'. And those rights were themselves a window through which the jurisprudence attaching to their international analogues became relevant. The Supreme Court put it this way:[29]

> As directed by section 6 of the Bill of Rights, section 72 is to be given a meaning, if it can be, consistent with the rights and freedoms contained in it, including the right not to be arbitrarily deprived of life and not to be subjected to torture. Those rights in turn are to be interpreted and the powers conferred by section 72 are to be exercised, if the wording will permit, so as to be in accordance with international law, both customary and treaty based.

The notion of rights-respecting qualifications has also operated in other contexts, notably where criminal punishment is contingent on the interpretation of vague statutory provisions. This is seen as the routine application of section 6 of the NZBORA. In the high-water mark, *Police v Hopkinson*,[30] France J interpreted the

[25] Eg, *R* v *Lord Chancellor, ex parte Witham* [1998] QB 575; *Pierson v Secretary of State for the Home Department* [1998] AC 539; *R v Secretary of State for the Home Department ex parte Simms and O'Brien* [2000] 2 AC 115 [*Simms*].

[26] *Ngati Apa Ki Te Waipounamu Trust v R* [2000] 2 NZLR 659 at 712 (CA).

[27] 'Proportionality, Deference, *Wednesbury*' [2008] *New Zealand Law Review* 423 at 431. [Taggart, 'Proportionality]. See also Rishworth et al, *The New Zealand Bill of Rights*, above n 10 at 123–24.

[28] [2006] 1 NZLR 289 (SC).

[29] Ibid at para [90].

[30] [2004] 3 NZLR 704 (HC).

prohibition on destroying a New Zealand flag 'with the intention of dishonouring it'[31] so narrowly as to render it all but unenforceable, in order to protect flag burning as an example of freedom of expression.[32] This approach appears to meet its limits only when the plain words of an enactment specifically preclude ameliorating interpretations. An example of this 'brick wall' – a plain inconsistent meaning – was seen in *R v Hansen*,[33] where four of the five judges of the Supreme Court held that a 'reverse onus' in the Misuse of Drugs Act 1975 had to be applied (because it was plainly specified) despite their conclusion that it breached the presumption of innocence in section 25(c) of the NZBORA.[34] But cases of that ilk are decidedly rare.

Rights in Unincorporated Treaties

The international human rights renaissance was, by the early 1990s, manifesting itself in a different context. A series of immigration cases in New Zealand involved rights claims based on the Convention on the Rights of the Child (CRC), a ratified but unincorporated convention.[35] One particular argument centred on a child's right in article 3 to have his or her 'best interests' treated as a 'primary consideration' in immigration decisions affecting a parent. Strong dicta in the *Tavita* case suggested that the rights in CRC were a mandatory consideration, and this proposition was readily internalised in subsequent official policy and practice. Still, the existence of children was not seen by officials as a free pass around immigration controls, and subsequent cases involved the question whether the best interests of children were given proper weight in cases about parents' deportation.

[31] Section 11 of the Flags, Emblems, and Names Protection Act 1981 No 47 (as at 01 October 2008), Public Act provides as follows: Offences involving New Zealand Flag—(1) Every person commits an offence against this Act who,— (b) In or within view of any public place, uses, displays, destroys, or damages the New Zealand Flag in any manner with the intention of dishonouring it.

[32] France J read 'dishonour' as requiring vilification, which she held was not made out in the context of a man who, at an anti-war protest in front of the New Zealand Parliament, destroyed a New Zealand flag (he had been flying upside down) by setting it on fire.

[33] [2007] 3 NZLR 1 (SC).

[34] The fifth judge, Blanchard J, regarded the limitation on the right to be presumed innocent as being 'reasonable'. Interestingly, *Hansen* involved an explicit difference of opinion with not one but two other national supreme courts, the Supreme Court of Canada (which, with Blanchard J, would likely have held there to be no breach as implied by *R v Oakes* [1986] 1 SCR 103) and the House of Lords (which would likely have found the statute capable of a rights-protecting interpretation, as exemplified in *R v Lambert* [2002] 2 AC 545). On the use of foreign authority by New Zealand courts, see J Allan, G Huscroft, and N Lynch, 'The Citation of Overseas Authority in Rights Litigation in New Zealand: How Much Bark? How Much Bite?' (2007) 11 *Otago Law Review* 433.

[35] *Tavita v Minister of Immigration* [1994] 2 NZLR 257 (CA); *Puli'uvea v Removal Review Authority* [1996] 3 NZLR 538 (CA); *Rajan v Minister of Immigration* [1996] 3 NZLR 543 (CA); and *Zaoui v Attorney-General (No 2)* [2006] 1 NZLR 289 (SC) [*Zaoui*]. See also C Geiringer, '*Tavita* and All That: Confronting the Confusion Surrounding Unincorporated Treaties and Administrative Law' (2004) 21 *New Zealand Universities Law Review* 66; '*Zaoui* revisited' [2005] *New Zealand Law Journal* 285.

The CRC provides that the child's interests must be 'a primary consideration', albeit that the combination of the indefinite article and the word 'primary' are arguably oxymoronic. New Zealand courts proved reluctant to assess whether an acceptable degree of weight had been given by statutory decision-makers to an affected child's interests. At one level this reluctance may be explicable as concern about illegitimately incorporating the CRC 'by the back door'.[36] At another level, that seems less likely – the 'best interests' of an affected child hardly seems an alien value, one that can operate internationally but not domestically unless legislated into effect. After all, these international values reflect wide agreement amongst the countries of the world and New Zealand is assuredly in the mainstream. One suspects, therefore, that the real issue in these cases is the intractable nature of the problem presented by state sovereignty and the movement of peoples in the modern world. In most of these cases the applicant's best or only argument against deportation has been the existence of New Zealand-born children. The courts have so far been unwilling to displace the assessment of officials as to how these children's interests weigh against (a) the unlawful presence of the parent and (b) New Zealand's interest in maintaining a robust immigration policy that does not send the message 'get here somehow, and have a child'. Certainly, no New Zealand case has involved children being regarded by officials as a *negative* factor in the way that prompted the Supreme Court of Canada to invalidate the Minister's decision in *Baker v Canada (Minister of Citizenship and Immigration)*.[37]

So immigration cases involving the CRC are likely a special category. In any event, this area of uncertainty about the impact of unincorporated treaties in New Zealand is minor when compared to general acceptance of the ideas associated with 'the principle of legality' and the impact of rights in the NZBORA. Other effects of international treaties are worth noting too: when a majority of the New Zealand Court of Appeal developed the common law so as to create a right against unreasonable invasion of privacy, the existence of the right to privacy in the International Covenant on Civil and Political Rights (ICCPR) was an explicit part of the reasoning for two of the judges. (For the third judge, the right to privacy was implicit in the NZBORA, and properly taken into account for that reason).[38] In these ways, then, the international human rights renaissance of the 1990s is undoubtedly influencing New Zealand law.

[36] See Dyzenhaus et al 'Principle of Legality', above n 8 at 10.

[37] [1999] 2 SCR 817.

[38] See *Hosking v Runting* [2003] 3 NZLR 385 (CA). The two majority judges referred to are Gault and Blanchard JJ, the third Tipping J. The remaining two judges did not agree with the development of the tort). See also *Sellers v Maritime Safety Inspector* [1999] 2 NZLR 44 (CA) (statutory provision that created an offence read-down to preserve consistency with the international law of the sea).

Domestic Treaty Rights – A Uniquely New Zealand Enterprise

A different category of unincorporated treaty rights is especially significant in New Zealand – Maori rights under the Treaty of Waitangi. These are unique to the New Zealand landscape of human rights and similarly rose in prominence from the late 1980s to the present time. Judicial reckoning with those rights has had a similar trajectory to that of human rights generally.

The Treaty was the basis for New Zealand's colonisation in 1840. It has always been unincorporated, in the sense that no domestic law makes its provisions a direct source of legal rights – not, at least, in any wholesale sense. This probably reflects the perception that, in its English version, the rights in the Treaty (to continued possession by Maori of their property as long as they wished to retain it, and to equal citizenship) were secured by ordinary operation of English law. Enacting a general affirmation to replicate what happens anyway would not have seemed necessary. But the Treaty is in two languages, and the Maori version is capable of being read more expansively – as an affirmation of a continuing measure of Maori autonomy and influence in the new legal order that the Treaty made possible. And, linguistic details aside, the very idea of a Treaty with the indigenous peoples, if not the very idea of there being indigenous peoples in the nation (treaty or no treaty), implies a need to reckon with their rights as indigenous peoples. In modern times, general rights to ownership of property fail to capture this sense of what the Treaty and Maori indigeneity might require. Suffice to say that a combination of these factors now gives Treaty rights significant political traction, usually leading to political judgments as to what the Treaty requires in particular fields of policy and endeavour and with legislation being enacted to incorporate those judgments. The late 1980s were a starting point: legislation began to refer to 'the principles of the Treaty', albeit in discrete fields. The first example was section 9 of the State-owned Enterprises Act 1986 (SOE):

> Nothing in this Act shall permit the Crown to act in a manner that is inconsistent with the principles of the Treaty of Waitangi.

In the most famous of the 'Treaty cases' that ensued, the 1987 *Lands Case*, the Court of Appeal applied section 9 for the first time.[39] The SOE Act contained a statutory power for Ministers to transfer Crown land to the new 'state-owned enterprises'. The Court held that section 9 precluded the use of that power unless the land transfers included a mechanism enabling a particular parcel of land to later be recovered, should it be needed by the Crown to satisfy Maori claims for its return on account of injustice in the Crown's acquisition of that land from original Maori owners. A transfer without such protection would indeed be

[39] *New Zealand Maori Council v Attorney-General* [1987] 1 NZLR 641 (CA). See the discussion in PG McHugh's contribution to this volume.

inconsistent with the 'principles of the Treaty'. These principles, ruled the Court, included a requirement of good faith by Crown toward Maori as its 'Treaty partner', and 'redress' for past breaches.

This decision ascribed considerable weight to the interpretive principle in section 9 because the SOE Act had actually dealt with the issue of land subject to Maori claims – it provided a claw-back mechanism for the Crown to recover land, but only land subject to Maori claims as at the commencement date of the SOE Act. By applying section 9 so as, effectively, to require a similar protective arrangement even for future claims, the Court extended the legislature's express protection. This was 'human rights' style adjudication, the importance of the general rights-protecting provision in section 9 prevailing over the Crown's unsuccessful *expressio unius* argument for a restrictive interpretation.

More Treaty cases followed. The Court of Appeal went furthest in the *Whale Watching case*, reading a statutory power to grant whale-watching permits to tourism operators as subject to a requirement to consider the 'principles of the Treaty' even though there was no explicit requirement in the legislation.[40] Indeed, the Court went further and ascribed considerable weight to the Treaty principles in that context, commenting that a decision appropriately taking Treaty principles into account would likely give some protection to the established Maori whale-watching operation by protecting it from competition during its establishment phase.

Standing back, then, it was no surprise that government lawyers became cautious about recommending the inclusion of Treaty clauses in legislation. The post-1990s trend was away from statutory references to 'Treaty principles' in the abstract, and towards legislative provision for detailed outcomes representing a political judgment as to what the Treaty actually requires in the relevant field.[41] So, for example, in the environmental field there are rights for Maori to be consulted, and special provisions that require Maori interests to be respected; in the health field there are Maori seats on statutory health boards and legislated requirements to consider Maori health needs; in education there are Maori language immersion schools. In these ways, Treaty 'principles' (which, as declared by courts, always had a distinctly 'process' character – being rights to good faith, consultation, and so on) have worked their way into the detail of New Zealand law.

Left unresolved is whether the requirement of Treaty-consistency in Crown actions might be judicially imposed even without statutory incorporation. But this question becomes much less important when political agreements lead to specific legislative provision for Maori interests in key fields, and administrative

[40] *Ngai Tahu Maori Trust Board v Director General of Conservation* [1995] 3 NZLR 553 (CA). (There was in fact a 'Treaty clause' in a related piece of legislation administered by the same Government department.)

[41] MSR Palmer, 'The Treaty of Waitangi in Legislation' [2001] *New Zealand Law Journal* 207.

decisions are made within that legislative framework. The locus of Treaty application is mainly outside the courts.

Broad Treaty principles may still be relevant to resolving ambiguities or restricting the scope of discretionary power.[42] But that just serves to emphasise a background understanding that these principles are operating in political discourse.[43] And the rights conferred by article 27 of the ICCPR (the right of a cultural or linguistic minority to enjoy its culture and language), themselves affirmed by section 20 of the NZBORA, are operating as well.[44] To this extent, then, the impact of Treaty rights in New Zealand has been subsumed within the rubric of human rights law.

The Legitimacy of Judicial Reckoning with Human Rights

In 2001, Mike Taggart, along with David Dyzenhaus and Murray Hunt ('DHT'), essayed an analysis of these phenomena – the principle of legality and common law rights, the rise of international law rights, and the discretion-restricting impact of bills or charters of rights. They, like others, were concerned with the provenance and legitimacy of these developments, but found support for them in 'the traditional role of the common law as the repository of all the values considered to be fundamental in contemporary society'.[45] They argued that the principle of legality was 'a particular conception of democratic legal culture, the culture of justification, in which decision-makers are obliged to justify their decisions by showing either how the decisions conform to those values, or that they are justifiable departures from those values'.[46] For DHT, an explanation for these developments (and also a principle that should guide their future development) was the requirement that administrative decision-makers provide reasons. The impact of rights documents (and the new harder-edged common law rights) was to require justificatory reasons for their limitation. Courts assessing the consistency of decisions with rights were involved in assessing the validity of those reasons. This is the 'culture of justification', and so long as judges are directing their attention to the process of justification (has it been made out, etc) they are respecting their role as judges and not acting as primary decision-makers.

42 *Tainui Maori Trust Board v Attorney General* [1989] 2 NZLR 513 at 518–9 ('… the Court should be slow to ascribe to Parliament an intention to permit conduct inconsistent with the principles of the Treaty').

43 See generally, P McHugh, 'Treaty Principles: Constitutional Relations inside a Conservative Jurisprudence' (2008) 39 *Victoria University of Wellington Law Review* 39.

44 See Rishworth et al, *The New Zealand Bill of Rights*, above n 10 ch 15. One of the five case studies in McLean et al, 'Impact of the NZBORA', above n 17 (discussed in the text above) concerned section 20 of the Bill of Rights.

45 Dyzenhaus et al, 'Principle of Legality', above n 8 at 32.

46 Ibid at 6.

Of special interest in the DHT explanation is the notion that heightened judicial scrutiny and inquiry is explicable as an updating of the values of the common law, beyond a liberty and property-based conception such as underpinned cases like *Bradford Corporation v Pickles*.[47]

No doubt this is simply putting the DHT point a different way, but it seems to us that the impact of rights, whether in bills of rights, international treaties, or as common law rights, can also be attributed to a major shift in orientation: that the right, rather than the power, is the 'starting point'. The *Simms* case[48] makes this explicit. By commencing with a detailed inquiry into the rights of prisoners to communicate with journalists (and recognising also the legitimate state interests in restricting that communication), the result is a balanced and measured conception of the scope of the right. Then, turning to the statutory power, one is better equipped to see if the legitimate scope of the right might be fully accommodated within the legitimate scope of the power. The point is that discretionary powers may certainly be used to limit rights reasonably. When used unreasonably, they are most likely to be beyond the power (although there remains the possibility that Parliament may have made it clear that it intends the application that a court believes to be unreasonable).

Plainly, judicial method in determining the reasonableness of limits placed on rights by administrative decision-makers then becomes very important. In MRT, and again in DHT, the message was that the NZBORA (and related developments overseas premised on the principle of legality) imposed a judicial method – a 'loose-fitting methodological straitjacket'.[49] The point was that restraint on official power depended ultimately on judicial vigour in evaluating the effect of official decisions on protected rights. The requirement of justification in section 5 of NZBORA and its analogues should oust 'vague assertions [that is, by judges] of deference'.[50] The NZBORA required a shift in judicial approach when reckoning with administrative action affecting rights. This is what we now speak of as 'proportionality'. In 2008 Mike, lamenting the despair expressed by some who see only uncontrolled and unpredictable judicial discretion in judicial review cases, wrote: 'It is hoped and expected that proportionality would herald a more transparent, systematic, rigorous, evidence-and-fact-based and principled process.'[51]

But this was in the cause of protecting rights against administrative action taken under statutory (or indeed even non-statutory) powers. The rights-protecting capability of the common law, even in the invigorated form enforced

[47] *Bradford v Pickles* [1895] AC 587, and see M Taggart, *Private Property and Abuse of Rights in Victorian England: The Story of Edward Pickles and the Bradford Water Supply* (Oxford, Oxford University Press, 2002).

[48] Above n 25.

[49] McLean et al 'Impact of the NZBORA', above n 17 at 97.

[50] Dyzenhaus et al, 'Principle of Legality', above n 8 at 20.

[51] Taggart 'Proportionality', above n 27 at 459.

by judges as 'the principle of legality', did not address the supremacy of Parliament itself. New Zealand law has not embraced the idea championed by Lord Cooke in a series of obiter dicta,[52] and in the academic context by TRS Allan,[53] that common law rights can overcome legislation. The NZBORA and legislation that incorporates the protection of the Treaty of Waitangi or its principles are also subject to parliamentary sovereignty.[54]

This preservation of parliamentary sovereignty concerns some, and it is sometimes argued that the protection of rights in New Zealand is tenuous in the absence of a supreme law bill of rights – a bill of rights immunised against amendment or repeal, save through some form of super-majoritarian process, that empowers the courts to invalidate legislation. We turn to this argument, and Mike Taggart's view, in Part II.

II The Future of Rights Protection in New Zealand

Much has changed in the years since the NZBORA was passed and many lessons have been learned. Despite its humble origins, the Act has established a distinctly New Zealand approach to the protection of human rights, an approach that has been emulated in the Commonwealth. The Human Rights Act 1998 (UK), the Charter of Human Rights and Responsibilities Act 2006 (Victoria), and the Human Rights Act 2004 (ACT) are all statutory bills of rights that deny judges the power to invalidate legislation. The Canadian Charter of Rights and Freedoms – the supreme law bill of rights model that New Zealand rejected – has set Canadian constitutional law on a distinctly different course.

Consider this statistic: In the first 24 years of the Charter, some 89 laws were invalidated by the Supreme Court of Canada on the basis of that court's decision that they were inconsistent with the Charter.[55] The doyen of Canadian constitutional law scholars, Professor Peter Hogg, has characterised this as 'activism':[56]

[52] Lord Cooke asserted in *Taylor v New Zealand Poultry Board* [1984] 1 NZLR 394 at 398 (CA) that '[s]ome common law rights presumably lie so deep that even Parliament could not override them'. The development of this point in subsequent cases is traced (and criticised) in M Kirby, 'Lord Cooke and Fundamental Rights' in P Rishworth (ed), *The Struggle for Simplicity in the Law: Essays for Lord Cooke of Thorndon*, (Wellington, Butterworths, 1997) 331.

[53] See, eg, TRS Allan, *Constitutional Justice: A Liberal Theory of the Rule of Law* (Oxford, Oxford University Press, 2001) and 'Constitutional Justice and the Concept of Law' in G Huscroft (ed), *Expounding the Constitution: Essays in Constitutional Theory* (New York, Cambridge University Press, 2008).

[54] See generally, J Goldsworthy, *The Sovereignty of Parliament: History and Philosophy* (Oxford, Clarendon Press, 1999). See also J Goldsworthy, 'Unwritten Constitutional Principles in G Huscroft (ed), *Expounding the Constitution*, ibid at 277; 'Is Parliament Sovereign? Recent Challenges to the Doctrine of Parliamentary Sovereignty' (2005) 3 *New Zealand Journal of Public and International Law* 7; and 'Homogenizing Constitutions' (2003) 23 *Oxford Journal of Legal Studies* 483 (reviewing TRS Allan, ibid).

[55] This number is taken from PW Hogg and AA Bushell, 'The *Charter* Dialogue between Courts and Legislatures (Or Perhaps the Charter of Rights isn't Such a Bad Thing After All)' (1997) 35

> Canada is a tolerant, sophisticated, liberal society with a flourishing democracy. For so many of its laws to be found in conflict with the Charter guarantees can only be explained by activism on the part of the Supreme Court of Canada.

'Activism' is a loaded term in constitutional law discourse, but whatever Hogg means by the term,[57] this is a surprisingly large number of laws to have been invalidated.

Judicial power to invalidate legislation is the most significant difference between the Charter and the NZBORA, and has brought Canadian constitutional law much closer to American law than most Canadians are prepared to acknowledge. The power to invalidate is often rationalised by characterising the interaction of courts and legislatures as 'dialogue', a point to which we will return later. Dialogue theory is contestable, but there is no doubt that in Canada, as in the United States, fundamental issues of public policy invariably end up before the highest courts, and that those courts play an important if not determinative role in their ultimate resolution. The Supreme Court of Canada has addressed the constitutionality of legislation regulating access to abortion (unconstitutional[58]); prohibiting assisted suicide (constitutional[59]); allowing extradition to face capital crimes (constitutional,[60] later unconstitutional[61]); prohibiting hate speech (constitutional[62]); and limiting collective bargaining rights (constitutional,[63] and later unconstitutional[64]); as well as common law limiting marriage to opposite-sex couples (refused to answer[65]) and a host of other controversial issues under the Charter – all issues that in New Zealand would be resolved by Parliament. The

Osgoode Hall Law Journal 75 [Hogg and Bushell, 'The Charter Dialogue'], which covers the period 1982–1997, and PW Hogg, AA Bushell Thornton, and WK Wright, '*Charter* Dialogue Revisited – Or "Much Ado About Metaphors"' 45 *Osgoode Hall Law Journal* (2007) 1 [Hogg, '*Charter* Dialogue Revisited'], which covers the period 1997–2007.

56 PW Hogg, 'Canada: From Privy Council to Supreme Court,' in J Goldsworthy (ed), *Interpreting Constitutions: A Comparative Study* (New York, Oxford University Press, 2006) 88. Hogg made the activism comment based on a total of 83 federal and provincial laws that had been invalidated from 1982–2002.

57 Hogg is not known as a critic of the Charter. His 'dialogue theory', discussed in the text below, is aimed at justifying the practice of judicial review under the Charter, as the subtitle to his famous article on dialogue theory ('Or, Perhaps the Charter of Rights isn't Such a Bad Thing After All') suggests; above n 55.

58 *R v Morgentaler* [1988] 1 SCR 30.

59 *Rodriguez v British Columbia (Attorney General)* [1993] 3 SCR 519.

60 *Kindler v Canada (Minister of Justice)* [1991] 2 SCR 779; *Reference Re Ng Extradition (Can)* [1991] 2 SCR 858.

61 *United States of America v Burns* [2001] 1 SCR 283.

62 *R v Keegstra* [1990] 3 SCR 697.

63 *Reference Re Public Service Employee Relations Act (Alta)* [1987] 1 SCR 313; *RWDSU v Saskatchewan* [1987] 1 SCR 460; *PSAC v Canada* [1987] 1 SCR 424; *Professional Institute of the Public Service of Canada v Northwest Territories (Commissioner)* [1990] 2 SCR 367.

64 *Health Services and Support – Facilities Subsector Bargaining Association v British Columbia* [2007] 2 SCR 391.

65 *Reference re Same-Sex Marriage* [2004] 3 SCR 698. See G Huscroft, 'Political Litigation and the Role of the Court' (2006), 34 *Supreme Court Law Review* 35.

adoption of a supreme law bill of rights would limit Parliament's power to legislate in regard to all of these matters and more.

Is this what New Zealand wants? Is this what it needs?

New Zealand's Experience without a Supreme Law Bill of Rights

The *White Paper* downplayed the consequences of a supreme law bill of rights, insisting that judicial review would be concerned with process rather than substance:

> [W]ith a very few quite basic exceptions the Bill of Rights would not control matters of substance;[66]
>
> For the most part [the Bill of Rights] would not control the substance of the law and of the policy which would continue to be elaborated in, and administered by, present and future parliaments and governments.[67]

For good measure, in his introduction to the *White Paper* then Minister of Justice Geoffrey Palmer acknowledged that the judicial power to invalidate legislation would be an 'important change', but insisted that 'too much should not be made of it. Courts will only infrequently declare provisions in Acts of Parliament contrary to the Bill of Rights.'[68] It is as though the consequences of constitutionalisation were simply not understood.[69]

These sorts of assurances could not be taken seriously today, and would not be made in any event. It is well understood that a superior law bill of rights would

[66] *White Paper*, above n 11 at para 4.11. This categorical statement was followed by a question-begging qualification: 'It is another matter if [policies] are pursued beyond necessity and beyond their proper importance at the expense of individual rights and freedoms…'. Concepts like 'necessity' and 'proper importance' are anything but self-applying.

[67] *White Paper*, above n 11 at para 4.14. Remarkably, the *White Paper* described freedom of speech, assembly and association as fundamental *procedural* rights, adding that these rights were in a substantive sense 'value free'. The *White Paper* described freedom from torture, discrimination, and cruel and unusual punishment as fundamental substantive rights, adding '[t]hese are freedoms about which there is no real dispute (although their exact extent might of course be argued).' As in para 4.11 (discussed ibid) the qualification undermines the point being made.

[68] *White Paper*, above n 11 at 6. See also, Palmer, *Constitution in* Crisis, above n 11 at 70: In the New Zealand context the argument is that it is both safe and appropriate to give the courts in New Zealand power to measure law, of the type discussed in the examples above, against the standards of an entrenched Bill of Rights. To do so is not empowering the judges to legislate. It is asking them to apply the law. It is so similar to what they do now in applying legislation that it amounts only to a moderate increase in judicial power.

[69] Plainly, the leading proponents of the Bill of Rights were influenced by John Hart Ely's process-based justification for judicial review. See Rishworth, 'Birth and Rebirth', above n 7 at 13–14, and Taggart, 'Tugging on Superman's Cape', above n 1 at 268. See also KJ Keith, 'A Bill of Rights for New Zealand? Judicial Review Versus Democracy' (1985) 11 *New Zealand Universities Law Review* 307. The *White Paper's* faith in the courts was not complete, however; the power of the courts to interfere in social policy was apprehended in regard to equality, and as a result the *White Paper* proposed to omit a general right to equality. See the discussion in G Huscroft, 'Rights, Bills of Rights, and The Role of Courts and Legislatures' in G Huscroft and P Rishworth (eds), *Litigating Rights: Perspectives from Domestic and International Law* (Oxford, Hart, 2002) 3.

involve New Zealand courts in determining the legality of legislation based on its substance, and Canadian experience shows how unpredictable the results may be.

How should arguments for the adoption of a supreme law bill of rights in New Zealand be evaluated? In our view, any argument about altering the balance of power between Parliament and the judiciary must take into account New Zealand's pre-existing political premises. New Zealand is not a constitutional blank slate. It has a vibrant democratic order: the rule of law is well established; there are free and fair elections; honest police and fair trials; and civil liberties are in general well respected. Things are not perfect, of course, but in a relative sense they are very good. Judged against any democratic country in the world, including those countries that have supreme law bills of rights – countries like Canada and the United States – New Zealand fares very well indeed. Its largely unwritten constitution has served it well.

Consider the ways in which some of the leading moral issues of the day have been dealt with by the New Zealand Parliament, in the absence of a supreme law bill of rights. Parliament enacted legislation decriminalising and regulating abortion in 1977 after a Royal Commission and a Parliamentary debate, and attained a result not too different from that which the US Supreme Court ordered in *Roe v Wade*[70] – but without the rancor that case has engendered.

Parliament decriminalised homosexual sex in 1986, roughly in step with the rest of the western world but interestingly in the same year in which the US Supreme Court ruled that the equal protection guarantee in the 14th Amendment did not protect a right to homosexual practices.[71] Discrimination based on sexual orientation was prohibited in 1993. In contrast, sexual orientation discrimination was not prohibited in all Canadian jurisdictions until the Supreme Court of Canada read the prohibition into the Charter in 1995,[72] and it took several years for the prohibition to be fully reflected in Canadian legislation.

Indigenous rights have developed in a manner that is broadly consistent with the jurisprudence generated by article 27 of the ICCPR. So, for example, when New Zealand courts have had the chance to articulate the principles of the Treaty of Waitangi they have done so in terms of process. Maori tribes have been recognised as having a right to a substantial measure of consultation, while the ultimate power of government belongs to the Crown.[73]

[70] 410 US 113 (1973). The Supreme Court of Canada invalidated Canada's abortion law early in the life of the Charter, leaving a legislative vacuum that has never been filled. See *R v Morgentaler* [1988] 1 SCR 30.

[71] *Bowers v Hardwick* 478 US 186 (1986). The criminalisation of homosexual activity survived until *Bowers* was overruled in *Lawrence v Texas* 539 US 558 (2003).

[72] *Egan v Canada* [1995] 2 SCR 513.

[73] So, for example, when the Sealords Fisheries Settlement was challenged by, amongst others, the Chatham Islands Maori on the basis that they were going to lose their very valuable historic fishing rights, affirmed by the Treaty, and have them replaced by the rather uncertain prospect of sharing in the pool of fishing quota that the settlement would produce, they took their case to the UN Human Rights Committee claiming that the Sealords settlement removed their right (in article 27 of ICCPR) to enjoy their culture. The HRC, relying on its jurisprudence generated in relation to the Sami people

Many other examples could be given, but enough has been said to make the point that New Zealand's history of reckoning with rights is, in terms of its processes, a legitimate one. Responsibility for rights is allocated throughout the branches of government. Some things are done by legislation because they must be, or can be. Others are done by the courts through the common law. But on any fair reading of history, New Zealand's record on human rights is impressive. Certainly, it cannot be said the protection of rights has suffered because the courts have lacked the power a supreme law bill of rights would have provided. The argument fails not only because there are few examples of rights denials – as opposed to disagreements at the margins about the approaches that Parliament has taken in limiting rights – but also because there can be no guarantees as to how things would have turned out had a supreme law bill of rights been in force in any event.[74]

This is the context in which proposals for the adoption of a supreme law bill of rights must be assessed. New Zealand is not South Africa, whose constitutional bill of rights was designed to empower the judiciary to change things – in many cases dramatically – in order to establish a rule of law culture. The *White Paper* proceeded on the basis that passage of a supreme law bill of rights in New Zealand was simply a matter of *affirming* rights to which New Zealand was already committed, and sought to make a virtue out of New Zealand's constitutional order, arguing that good times were the best time to undertake constitutional reform. No doubt similar arguments would be made today.

But change to New Zealand's constitutional order would come at a cost to New Zealand's successful political culture. The problem is as old as the practice of judicial review itself. Writing at the turn of the 20th century in the United States, constitutional scholar James Bradley Thayer warned:[75]

> The tendency of a common and easy resort to this great function [judicial review], now lamentably too common, is to dwarf the political capacity of the people, and to deaden its sense of moral responsibility. It is no light thing to do that.

This is, in our view, one of the main risks of adopting a supreme law bill of rights: it diminishes the likelihood of political engagement, and the possibility of settlement, of moral issues that are important to the community.[75] The consequences of this are apparent in Canada. The Supreme Court of Canada often attempts to justify its decisions on the basis that Canadian legislatures have refused to act, but there is a chicken-and-egg problem here. The Court's decisions

of Scandinavia and the indigenous peoples of Canada, rejected the complaint, holding that the degree of consultation had been adequate in the circumstances. See *Mahuika* v *New Zealand* (2001) 8 IHRR 372; CCPR/C/70/D/547/1993.

[74] Cf Palmer, *Constitution in Crisis*, above n 11 at 65, insisting that particular legislation would have been invalidated under a supreme law bill of rights.

[75] The constitutionalisation of rights may also distort political discourse. See B Miller, 'Justification and Rights Limitations' in Huscroft (ed), *Expounding the Constitution: Essays in Constitutional Theory* (New York, Cambridge University Press, 2008) 93.

create incentives and disincentives to political action. If, at the end of the day, legislation achieved at great political cost may be invalidated by a court, it is easy to see why legislators might prefer to leave matters to the court in the first place. More troubling, governments might prefer to leave some matters to the courts because the courts are thought likely to deliver outcomes that they could not obtain through the normal political processes. The executive, in other words, may connive to circumvent the legislature when it suits.

Opening a can of worms?

To this point we have argued that New Zealand has a successful constitutional order that would be undermined by grafting a supreme law bill of rights onto it. But there is more at stake in any argument about adopting a supreme law bill of rights than this, for it is not a matter of simply repealing the limitation on judicial power under section 4 of the NZBORA and adding an entrenchment provision.

The more difficult it is to amend a bill of rights – the more deeply entrenched a bill of rights is to be – the more important it is for the various factions to ensure that their concerns are addressed before they give their consent, since it will be much more difficult to amend the bill of rights once it is entrenched and, as a political matter, there will be scant leverage available to secure amendments in any event. As a result, many parties with conflicting goals would have to be accommodated if the broad-based consensus required for the adoption of a supreme law bill of rights were to be achieved. How difficult would this be?

It is easy to forget that the NZBORA was passed in ordinary statute form following the government's inability to obtain the support required to pass a constitutional bill of rights. It is easy to forget, too, that the NZBORA is a Labour Party bill of rights. Its passage did not reflect a consensus in Parliament, still less amongst the general population. On the contrary, the NZBORA was passed on a party vote in a majority government-dominated Parliament, operating under an electoral system that has since been rejected. Many did not get what they wanted when that Act passed, and they are sure to be heard from if a proposal for a supreme law bill of rights is on the table. Demands will be raised for the protection of additional rights and freedoms. There will also be demands to amend some rights and perhaps to delete others. In short, there is every reason to expect that the contents of a supreme law bill of rights would be contested.

Consider an obvious example – property rights. It is reasonable to suppose that property rights would have been included in the NZBORA had that Act been the product of a National rather than Labour government. It was omitted, however, and no less than four attempts have been made to amend the NZBORA to include the protection of property rights in some form or another. The question is: why would anyone who favours the protection of property rights consent to the passage to a supreme law bill of rights that excludes them? Why agree to privilege the protection of some rights while making it more difficult to achieve similar protection for property rights in future? Or consider the anti-discrimination guarantee in section 19 of the NZBORA. Why would anyone who favours a broad equality guarantee accept a narrow anti-discrimination provision with a closed list of prohibited grounds?

In fact, demands for the inclusion of number of additional rights are likely to be made by political parties, citizens, the Human Rights Commission, academics, and others involved in the political process. Once constitutional arrangements are opened up there is no end to the demands that might be made. Some will argue for the inclusion of a right to privacy, others for a right to dignity, both of which have precedents internationally. Others will argue that a civil and political bill of rights is inadequate, and that economic and social rights – for example, rights to housing, education, healthcare, social welfare benefits, and so on – must be included. These were omitted from the NZBORA deliberately,[76] but that that decision would certainly be revisited. Then, too, there are Treaty rights to consider, environmental rights and other 'third generation' rights, and more. If a supreme law bill of rights is to be passed political deals will have to be made, and assuming a consensus could be reached the final product may look considerably different from the NZBORA.

As if all of this were not enough, if the judiciary is to be empowered to make final and binding decisions on the legality of legislation that deals with divisive moral questions, a different problem arises. Is it possible to achieve agreement on the terms of a supreme law bill of rights when the sorts of issues that are bound to arise in litigation are known in advance? There are really only two options. One is to leave things to chance, finessing disagreement[77] about particular rights disputes by agreeing to the adoption of rights at a high level of generality, knowing that those rights will be relevant to resolving the particular disputes, and hoping that things will go your way. On this approach, judicial review will result in winners and losers. The other option is for the various parties to advocate the drafting of rights in a manner conducive to outcomes they favour – or at least, in a manner that does not preclude the outcomes they favour. On this second approach, the parties seek to determine winners and losers in advance. But if either side in a particular dispute insists on getting its way at drafting time, it is difficult to see how the consensus required to adopt a supreme law bill of rights could be achieved.

[76] Palmer, *Contribution in Crisis*, above n 11 at 57.

[77] This phrase is borrowed from Jeremy Waldron. See J Waldron, 'Some Models of Dialogue' in G Huscroft and I Brodie (eds), *Constitutionalism in the Charter Era* (Toronto, LexisNexis, 2004) 12 [Waldron, 'Some Models'].

Can Parliamentary Sovereignty be Preserved in a Supreme Law Bill of Rights?

It might be thought that the difficulties canvassed above would be mitigated, if not avoided, if a supreme law bill of rights did not entail the finality of judicial decisions – if there were, in other words, checks on the courts' power to invalidate legislation. Certainly, the stakes are highest in a constitutional order in which the decisions of the courts in interpreting a bill of rights enjoy de jure finality. In such a system, the only way in which to overcome a judicial decision is by successful invocation of the amending formula, and this is designed to be very difficult to achieve.[78]

In theory, however, it is possible to preserve parliamentary sovereignty to a greater or lesser extent, even in the context of a supreme law bill of rights, by empowering Parliament to legislate regardless of the protected rights. The Canadian Charter is the model for this approach. It includes the following provision:

> 33(1) Parliament or the legislature of a province may expressly declare in an Act of Parliament or of the legislature, as the case may be, that the Act or a provision thereof shall operate notwithstanding a provision included in section 2 or sections 7 to 15 of this Charter.

In essence, the 'notwithstanding clause', as it is known in Canada, allows legislation to be enacted regardless of most, but not all, Charter rights, for five-year renewable terms. Such legislation may be passed prior to a judicial decision interpreting the Charter or subsequent to it, and in either case is immune from judicial review under the Charter.[79]

The inclusion of the notwithstanding clause in the Charter seems surprising, yet it was key to the decision to pass the Charter. Its inclusion was demanded by the provinces, who were leery of ceding too much power to the courts and insisted on a means of dealing with aberrant judicial decisions.[80] The clause has been the focus of much rhetorical heat; one former prime minister has declared that it renders the Charter 'not worth the paper it was written on',[81] and another

[78] The *White Paper*, above n 11, proposed a requirement of 75 per cent support of all the members of Parliament for an amendment, or a majority of votes cast in referendum. This is a lower threshold for amendment than in Canada or the United States, where cumbersome procedures are required given the federal structure of these countries. Still, even without federalism or an upper house, the difficulty of obtaining an amendment under such requirements should not be underestimated, especially in an MMP environment in which the support of several political parties would be required.

[79] The notwithstanding clause cannot be invoked with retrospective effect. See *Ford v Quebec (Attorney General)* [1988] 2 SCR 712.

[80] H Leeson, 'Section 33, The Notwithstanding Clause: A Paper Tiger?' in P Howe and P Russell (eds) *Judicial Power and Canadian Democracy* (Montreal, McGill-Queen's University Press, 2001) 297.

[81] The Rt Hon Brian Mulroney has described the decision to include the notwithstanding clause as '[a] surrender of rights ... total and abject'. See *House of Commons Debates,* Vol. 1 (6 April 1989) at 153 (Right Hon. Brian Mulroney), quoted in Leeson, ibid at 314.

announced his plan to amend the Charter to remove the clause in the midst of an election campaign[82] – even though it has never been invoked by the federal Parliament. Indeed, the clause has not been used to any consequence outside the province of Québec,[83] which for a number of reasons is a special case; Québec never agreed to the adoption of the Constitution that now binds it. The notwithstanding clause has fallen into desuetude in most provinces as well as federally, and in the result Canada's constitutional order is best described as one of de facto judicial supremacy.[84]

How did this come about? The answer lies in the fact that the notwithstanding clause is commonly referred to in Canada as the 'Charter override'.[85] It is perceived, in other words, as means of legislating despite Charter rights, and the popularity of those rights – and of the Charter itself – renders this politically impossible.[86]

It wasn't supposed to be like this, of course; the notwithstanding clause was designed to function as a check on judicial power – a check on the *interpreted* Charter rather than the Charter itself. After all, the notwithstanding clause is *part of* the Charter, rather than external to it; its invocation can hardly be inconsistent with the Charter. It was intended to allow legislatures to disagree with judicial decisions interpreting the Charter – to ensure, in other words, that legislatures had a means to address Charter decisions they considered erroneous, short of invoking the constitutional amendment procedure.

The language of a notwithstanding clause can be modified, but we doubt that modification would make such a clause any more usable. Invocation of any provision that allows the legislature to prevail over the courts is likely to be perceived as a raw exercise of political power, rather than a reflection of good faith disagreement about the interpretation and application of rights, and illegitimate on that account.

Not only are such clauses likely to be unusable, but their inclusion in a bill of rights may exacerbate the very problem they are supposed to address. That is so because the availability of a notwithstanding clause may relieve the judiciary of the responsibility for its decisions – thus leading to more adventurous interpretations of the bill of rights. Some advocate such interpretations in Canada, urging

[82] The Rt Hon Paul Martin, campaigning in the 2006 federal election, made the surprise announcement during a televised leaders' debate. He was at that time perceived to be losing the election, and went on to be defeated.

[83] See generally Hogg, *Constitutional Law of Canada*, above n 14, ch 39.8.

[84] G Huscroft, 'Rationalizing Judicial Supremacy: The Mischief of Dialogue Theory' in J Kelly and C Manfredi (eds) *Contested Constitutionalism: Reflections on the Charter of Rights and Freedoms* (Vancouver, University of British Columbia Press, 2009) [Huscroft, 'Rationalizing'].

[85] See, eg, Hogg, *Constitutional Law of Canada*, above n 14, whose usage of the term has likely helped popularise it.

[86] Waldron, 'Some Models', above n 77. Cf J Goldsworthy, 'Judicial Review, Legislative Override, and Democracy' 38 *Wake Forest Law Review* 451 (2003).

the judiciary to over-enforce Charter rights on the basis that if the judiciary goes too far, its decisions can be reversed by the invocation of the notwithstanding clause.[87]

When it comes to supreme law bills of rights, you cannot have your cake and eat it too. Judicial power to invalidate legislation changes the constitutional order fundamentally, and it is better to address whether that is desirable than to attempt to mitigate the change by purporting to preserve parliamentary sovereignty.

The Balance of Power Between Parliament and the Courts

'Dialogue theory' is often invoked as an answer to concerns about judicial power under a supreme law bill of rights such as the Canadian Charter. As conceived by Peter Hogg and Alison Bushell in a 1997 article,[88] dialogue theory posits that judicial interpretation of the Charter is less important than is commonly supposed, because it is usually possible for the relevant legislature to pass new legislation following a decision of the Supreme Court of Canada to invalidate a law. This is so because reasonable limits may be created on rights; some rights are subject to definitional limitations; and ultimately Canadian legislatures can (in theory) invoke the notwithstanding clause to ensure that its view prevails.

Dialogue theory is problematic for a number of reasons, as many have pointed out,[89] and it is remarkable that it has been so influential in defending judicial power. It fails to take into account the impact of judicial decisions on the political order – something not amenable to the empirical analysis on which the theory is based – and is misleading in that it does not consider the nature and quality of replacement legislation that is passed following a judicial invalidation. Hogg et al count as 'dialogue' a legislative decision repealing a law the Court has invalidated, as well as legislation that simply implements the Court's prescriptive agenda.

In truth, there is little room for meaningful dialogue so long as judges have the power to invalidate legislation. The premises of dialogue theory give this away. Hogg et al insist on judicial interpretive supremacy.[90] Once the Court has determined the meaning of a Charter provision, they consider that it is the legislature's duty to legislate accordingly. There is no room for disagreement

[87] Kent Roach puts the point this way: 'The fact that their decisions under the Charter can be revised or reversed by the legislature suggests that judges can afford to err on the side of more robust approaches to judicial review.' See 'Dialogic Judicial Review and its Critics,' in Huscroft and Brodie, *Constitutionalism in the Charter Era*, above n 77 at 71–72.

[88] Hogg and Bushell, 'The Charter Dialogue', above n 55.

[89] See, eg, C Manfredi and J Kelly, 'Six Degrees of Dialogue: A Response to Hogg and Bushell' (1999) 37 *Osgoode Hall Law Journal* 513; G Huscroft 'Constitutionalism from the Top Down (2007) 45 *Osgoode Hall Law Journal* 91; A Petter, 'Taking Dialogue Theory Much Too Seriously (Or Perhaps Charter Dialogue Isn't Such a Good Thing After All' (2007) 45 *Osgoode Hall Law Journal* 147; and Huscroft, 'Rationalizing', above n 85.

[90] Hogg, 'Charter Dialogue Revisited' above n 55 at 30–38.

when it comes to meaning; the Constitution is assumed to mean whatever a majority of the Supreme Court says that it does.[91]

There is no reason to dignify this by calling it a 'dialogue'. Nor is this a matter of 'much ado about metaphors', as Hogg et al have suggested. Dialogue theory ignores the impact of judicial decisions on the political process while exaggerating the ability of the political branch of government to respond to judicial decisions. In a world of reasonable disagreement about the interpretation and application of rights and freedoms, the ability to invalidate legislation places judges at the pinnacle of a country's constitution, and changes the constitutional and political order fundamentally. Dialogue theory is, at best, a rationalisation of this state of affairs rather than an argument in support of it.

If a true dialogue about rights is possible, it is possible in a system of weak judicial review, as for example in New Zealand under the NZBORA. The most a New Zealand court can do when faced with a statute that is inconsistent with the NZBORA is to issue a declaration of incompatibility.[92] If the inconsistency is to be addressed Parliament must be convinced to act, and in deciding whether or not to do so it may form its own view on the question of inconsistency, a view that differs from the court's.

We have no illusions that Parliament will often disagree with judicial interpretations of the NZBORA. The same considerations that make it difficult to invoke the notwithstanding clause in Canada make it difficult for the New Zealand Parliament to resist the force of judicial declaration of inconsistency. But disagreement is in our view more likely to occur in a system of weak judicial review than in a system of strong judicial review, in which the courts have the power to invalidate legislation. Whereas New Zealand legislators must be convinced of the correctness of a court's interpretation of the NZBORA in order to be persuaded to legislate to give effect to it – or at least, be persuaded that it is not worth fighting with the court about it – Canadian legislators must be convinced of the incorrectness of a judicial decision interpreting the Charter, and even then can do no more than to suspend its impact temporarily by invoking the notwithstanding clause.

[91] This brings to mind US Supreme Court Chief Justice Hughes' aphorism: 'We are under a Constitution, but the Constitution is what the judges say it is.' Hughes, Speech before the Elmira Chamber of Commerce, May 3, 1907, in *Addresses and Papers of Charles Evans Hughes, Governor of New York, 1906–1908* (New York, GP Putnam & Sons, 1908) 133 at 139. Hughes's remark is widely misunderstood, and is often cited erroneously as authority for the proposition that Hughes rejected. See the discussion in G Huscroft, '"Thank God We're Here": Judicial Exclusivity in Charter Interpretation and Its Consequences' (2004) 25 *Supreme Court Law Review* (2d) 241 at 249–52.

[92] See Rishworth et al, *The New Zealand Bill of Rights*, above n 10 at 833–38. The declaration jurisdiction is not set out in the NZBORA, as it is under the UK Human Rights Act, but was announced by the New Zealand Court of Appeal in *Moonen v Film and Literature Board of Review* [2000] 2 NZLR 9.

To Constitutionalise, or not to Constitutionalise? That is the Question

Mike Taggart resolved any doubt about his view on bills of rights in a paper he did at a conference honouring one of the architects of the NZBORA, Sir Kenneth Keith. Replying to a paper by Peter Hogg, he wrote in his inimitable style:

> Let me raise my cloven hoof at the outset. I do not support judges being given (or taking) the power to invalidate statutes for failure to adhere to written or unwritten fundamental values. That makes me old-fashioned, I know. ...In short, I am happy with our present bill of rights, the New Zealand Bill of Rights Act 1990 (the Bill of Rights Act). I concede it is a 'weak form' of protecting fundamental rights, but I am opposed, for all the familiar reasons, to strengthening the Bill of Rights Act by 'entrenching' it (a term that seems to have gone out of fashion) or by inserting a 'notwithstanding clause' of the Canadian Charter variety.

Like Taggart, we see no reason to empower New Zealand judges to invalidate legislation, and it goes without saying that we would strongly oppose any purported judicial decision to assume such power. So we oppose the adoption of a supreme law bill of rights. But we cannot conclude without addressing the additional point Mike raised. Is it inconsistent to oppose a supreme law bill of rights whilst accepting that rights are properly brought to bear on the interpretation of legislation and state action on the basis that they are considered 'fundamental'?

Mike did not think so and nor do we. But we would not underestimate the degree to which contentious issues about judicial power and authority arise under the 'common law constitution'. Questions about the 'fundamentality' of common law rights are inevitable, and so too are questions about the integrity of proportionality analysis. And so we should not be surprised to find, in time, some of the consequences that attend the adoption of a supreme law bill of rights: the increasing use of courts to advance political causes and the politicisation of judicial appointments.[93] After all, the stakes are in many cases no less high under a common law/statutory rights regime than under a supreme law bill of rights.

The difference between the two regimes might come down in the end to the 'clear statement' rule, whereunder a clear statement precludes 'saving constructions' under the NZBORA. There already seems to be scope for disagreement about what counts as 'clear' – recall the *Pora* case.[94] In these circumstances the

[93] See P Rishworth, 'Human Rights and the Reconstruction of the Moral High Ground' in R Bigwood (ed) *Public Interest Litigation: New Zealand Experience in International Perspective* (Wellington, LexisNexis NZ, 2006) 115.

[94] In *R v Pora* [2001] 2 NZLR 37 (CA) six judges of the Court of Appeal divided equally over whether which of two conflicting provisions in the Criminal Justice Act 1985 prevailed. The first was a general prohibition on retrospective penalisation for offenders, 'notwithstanding any enactment or rule of law to the contrary'; the second was a subsequently enacted provision in the same Act that increased the minimum no-parole period for murderers as from the date of its enactment 'even if the offence concerned was committed before that date'. Three judges held that the later, specific, provision

parliamentary cape is well and truly tugged by the system we have. There seems little reason to change the system to impose explicit judicial supremacy. The cases that a supreme law bill of rights would reach, beyond those reached already under the current system, will be those in which Parliament has explicitly enacted unreasonable limitations on rights. But the Parliamentary record does not support the view that this is a real problem that must be addressed, and the cost to New Zealand's political culture of establishing judicial supremacy would be great.

The recent controversy over reform of campaign financing legislation in New Zealand affords a good illustration of what is at stake. The Electoral Finance Bill proposed the establishment of limits on electoral advertising by third parties, not only in support of or opposition to a political party but also in regard to any position with which a party is associated. The Attorney General concluded that the bill constituted a justified limitation on the freedom of expression, but a spirited debate took place in the community about the bill. Everyone from the Business Roundtable to the Human Rights Commission, the New Zealand Law Society, academics, the media and the public were involved, in addition to politicians from all of the political parties. Many insisted that the bill was inconsistent with the NZBORA and lamented the inability of the courts to intervene.[95] A supreme law bill of rights, it was said, would have allowed the courts to overturn the legislation that was passed subsequently.

To be sure, passage of the Electoral Finance Act is not one of Parliament's finest moments. Ideally, electoral legislation would be regarded as a non-partisan enterprise. But the problems with the Electoral Finance Act have nothing to do with the absence of a supreme law bill of rights. As we have argued, there is no guarantee that any particular results will obtain under a supreme law bill of rights. All that is certain is that the ultimate decision about legislation would be made by the court, rather than the people. Perhaps a New Zealand court would have overturned the legislation if it had the power; but there is no guarantee that a judicial decision would be better than one reached by the people in any event. In Canada, the constitutionality of similar electoral legislation was challenged under the Charter, and was upheld several years later by a majority of the

prevailed over the earlier, general, prohibition of retrospectivity. The other three held the retrospective increase in the minimum non-parole period to be of no effect because of its inconsistency with the earlier, general, prohibition. But another pathway to avoid the effect of the new minimum was also available, and these six judges, along with the seventh, decided the case on that basis. For an interesting discussion of the case see J Waldron, 'Retroactive Law: How Dodgy was Duynhoven?' (2004) 10 *Otago Law Review* 631 (discussing the *Pora* case but also another example of legislation, in that case retroactive rather than retrospective).

95 An application for judicial review of the Attorney General's apparent decision *not* to report that the Bill was inconsistent with NZBORA failed in *Boscawen v Attorney- General (No 2)* [2008] NZAR 468. The High Court struck out the claim as incapable of success on the ground that the Attorney General's actions or omissions under section 7 are a 'proceeding' in Parliament and therefore immune from review by operation of parliamentary privilege, as well as under general principles of comity. An appeal is pending.

Supreme Court of Canada.[96] The matter was removed from the political arena while it was before the courts, and the Supreme Court's decision has had the effect, as many judicial decisions in Canada do, of stifling political discussion. In New Zealand, by contrast, the matter remains alive politically; the government that supported passage of the bill has been defeated, and the next government may amend or repeal the legislation if it chooses. All in all, we think this a much better outcome.

Conclusion

In the Beatles song to which our own title alludes, the suggestion 'you say you'll change the constitution' draws the riposte 'you better free your mind instead'. The revolution is supposed to happen inside all of us, and it is not about institutions. True, that is a little romantic, but we think there is a valid point there. To the extent that any new constitution and supreme law bill of rights would reflect the rights and freedoms that a majority agrees to be most important – as it assuredly would — why are we not content to let things work themselves out through the ordinary political process? Why, in other words, do we need a supreme law bill of rights, really?

The standard answer is that we cannot trust ourselves, or those who come later, to faithfully respect the standards to which we have agreed. This strikes us a sad conclusion to reach, and not a conclusion justified by the facts about New Zealand, nor even by the facts about what has really been accomplished, over the long term, by countries with supreme law bills of rights. If the concern is that inconsistent laws might pass unnoticed, then this is something dealt with by section 7 and the parliamentary scrutiny process – a process that may be improved. If the concern is that bad laws may be enacted, the ameliorating principle of legality, replicated in section 6, can be invoked to ensure respect for rights in the interpretation process.

To establish a judicial power of invalidation would do more than simply address those cases that slip through these protective nets. It would change the very fundamentals of New Zealand constitutionalism, and we see no reason to do so. The NZBORA represents a different approach to the protection of rights, an approach that is not court-centred. That others are drawing inspiration from this approach ought to give us the confidence we need to continue on our present course.

[96] *Harper v Canada (Attorney General)* [2004] 1 SCR 827.

8

Why the History of English Administrative Law is not Written

MARTIN LOUGHLIN

Introduction

IN HIS INAUGURAL Lecture at Cambridge in 1888, FW Maitland suggested that one reason why the history of English law had not been written was because of the insularity of the traditional method of legal practice. '[A]n isolated system cannot explain itself', he noted, 'still less explain its history'.[1] But, important though this factor was, insularity was a secondary phenomenon, operating primarily to reinforce the prevailing treatment of history in what he called the 'legal mind'. The legal mind, Maitland claimed, thrives on a productive misreading of history; the past must be continuously attuned to the needs of the present. Consequently, not only is the past often depicted anachronistically, but the novelty of the present must also be denied. In such a situation, Maitland argued, the professions of lawyer and historian must remain fundamentally at odds.

Maitland delivered his lecture during the critical period that gave birth to modern English legal scholarship. Since the 1880s much work has been undertaken—not least by Maitland himself—to address these difficulties in the writing of legal history.[2] It might nevertheless be noted that many of Maitland's contemporaries were concerned not merely to rework but to abandon altogether the historical method in legal thought. In 1885, for example, A V Dicey began his textbook on *The Law of the Constitution* by rejecting a historical approach. Noting, with tongue firmly in cheek, that 'it were far better, as things now stand,

[1] FW Maitland, 'Why the History of English law is not Written' in his *Collected Papers* HAL Fisher (ed.) (Cambridge, Cambridge University Press, 1911) vol.1, 480–97 at 489 [Maitland, 'Why the History'].

[2] See only JH Baker, 'Why the History of English Law has not been Finished' (2000) 59 *Cambridge Law Journal* 62 [Baker, 'Why the History'].

to be charged with heresy, than to fall under the suspicion of lacking historical-mindedness', Dicey claimed that the historical method led either to 'simple antiquarianism' or to the veneration of a constitution which, having no creator, could not be fully comprehended. In the hands of the common lawyers, he elaborated, it even led to 'the illusion … that modern constitutional freedom has been established by an astounding method of retrogressive progress; that every step towards civilisation has been a step backwards towards the simple wisdom of our uncultured ancestors'.[3] In its place, Dicey proposed a modern analytical method: instead of 'religious enthusiasm' or 'fervent self-complacency' towards the constitution, scholars must dispassionately explain its workings by uncovering the rules of the constitution, arranging them in order, explaining their meaning and exhibiting their logical connection.[4]

Maitland and Dicey evidently shared a conviction in the need to rid English legal scholarship of its more romantic aspects, and each apparently recognised the distortions effected by what might be called the 'common law habit of thinking', the belief in the immemorial and ideal character of customary legal practices.[5] But did the common aim of seeking to place scholarship on a more scientific footing lead to consensus over appropriate methods and values? Hardly, and on the subject of administrative law their views could scarcely be more different. This essay considers these divergences. It suggests that the differences between Maitland and Dicey on the question of administrative law form the polarities around which the controversies that have since dogged the subject have revolved and that these controversies continue to permeate discussion of administrative law today. It also argues that unless these divergences are openly acknowledged and set in an appropriate framework, it will be impossible to write a scholarly account of the history of administrative law.

This modern history is the important task to which Mike Taggart has recently been devoting his considerable research energies.[6] This essay seeks to contribute to that larger enterprise only by undertaking a modest, ground-clearing task. It considers the reasons why the idea of administrative law has been anathema to the English constitutional tradition, and assesses these claims in the light of historical evidence. But I also argue that many of the problems in twentieth century administrative law scholarship have arisen because of what might be

[3] A V Dicey, *Introduction to the Study of the Law of the Constitution* (London, Macmillan, 8th ed, 1915) 14, 17 [Dicey, *Law of the Constitution*].

[4] Ibid at 3–4, 31.

[5] On which habit see JGA Pocock, *The Ancient Constitution and the Feudal Law* (Cambridge, Cambridge University Press, 1957) ch 2 [Pocock, *The Ancient Constitution*].

[6] See, eg, M Taggart, 'Prolegomenon to an Intellectual History of Administrative Law in the Twentieth Century: The Case of John Willis and Canadian Administrative Law' (2005) 43 *Osgoode Hall Law Journal* 223; M Taggart, 'From "Parliamentary Powers" to Privatization: the chequered history of delegated legislation in the twentieth century' (2005) 55 *University of Toronto Law Journal* 575.

called the Diceyan inheritance. Dicey's approach to the subject has prevailed—the analytical has triumphed over the historical—and this has generated particular problems.

Many of these problems track back to a single source: notwithstanding the veneer of scientific objectivity in his analytical method and his criticisms of Whig belief in 'retrospective progress', Dicey's rule-based frame was erected on precisely the same set of values as those incorporated in the common law mind-set. These values led Dicey to link the rise of administrative law directly to the decline of the constitution, to skew the history of the subject, and thus to engage with administrative law in a highly politicised manner. The challenges we face in writing the history of administrative law do not in the main flow from the huge labours entailed 'in disinterring enough of the evidence to write the history' from the 'thousands of miles of abbreviated Latin' etched on the skins of over a million sheep.[7] Nor does it this labour generally require 'a strong arm, a flexible neck and back, an immunity to dust and soot, a working knowledge of Victorian knots, an ability to speed-read abbreviated Latin (if possible upside down)…'.[8] The difficulties we face flow from the fact that the history of English administrative law can be written only once those ideologically charged elements that have permeated discussions from its earliest moments have been unravelled and the subject itself placed on a more scholarly foundation.

FW Maitland and AV Dicey

In his *Constitutional History*, which was based on lectures delivered in 1887–88, Maitland warned students against taking too narrow a view of the categories of law. There are, he argued, 'vast departments of law' lying outside the traditional boundaries of crime, property, torts and contracts and 'that part of constitutional law which is concerned with king and parliament'. Most of these departments, he suggested, may be called administrative law: 'for the most part they are statutory and of recent creation, the work of the last fifty years: but their importance is very great'.[9]

Maitland went on to offer illustrations: 'if one takes up any business or employment, if one begins to build a house or thinks to open a lodging house, or keep a trading-ship or be a baker or a chimney sweep, straightaway one comes into contact with a mass of statutory rules, and if one keeps all the rules expressly laid down by statute still one is not safe, one may come across the rules, orders and regulations which some Secretary of State or central board has been empowered to make or the bye-laws of a municipal borough or of a local sanitary

[7] Baker, 'Why the History', above n 2 at 66, 70.

[8] Ibid at 72–73.

[9] FW Maitland, *The Constitutional History of England* (Cambridge, Cambridge University Press, 1908) 505 [Maitland, *The Constitutional History*].

authority'.[10] Since these statutory powers are limited in scope, there is, he recognised, extensive judicial oversight. 'If you take up a modern volume of the reports of the Queen's Bench division', Maitland noted, 'you will find that about half the cases reported have to do with rules of administrative law'.[11] His overall message was forthright: 'do not neglect their existence in your general conception of what English law is'. If you do, 'you will frame a false and antiquated notion of our constitution', since 'to leave them out of the picture is to make the picture a partial one-sided obsolete sketch'.[12]

Maitland's dispassionate, empirically orientated approach to the growth of administrative law in the English system bears direct comparison with Dicey's. Embracing Maitland's argument that the history of a subject cannot be understood in isolation, Dicey had devoted a section, and in later editions an entire chapter, of the *Law of the Constitution* (1885) to a comparison between 'the rule of law' and 'a scheme of administrative law … known to Frenchmen as *droit administratif*'.[13] But for Dicey the purpose of the comparison was anything but subtle; its objective was solely to highlight the virtues of the English practice and the deficiencies of the French system.

Dicey argued that the French expression had no proper English equivalent since 'the words "administrative law", which are its most natural rendering, are unknown to English judges and counsel' and the concept 'rests on ideas foreign to the fundamental assumptions of our English common law'.[14] He argued that modern *droit administratif* received its form from Bonaparte, who 'fused together what was strongest in the despotic traditions of the monarchy [i.e. the *Ancien Régime*] with what was strongest in the equally despotic creed of Jacobinism' and that it had developed along similar lines ever since.[15] At the heart of the French system lay the Council of State whose function 'in so far as they acted judicially (for they fulfilled many duties that were not judicial) was to determine questions of administrative law'.[16] This system, he argued, removed the ordinary courts from considering matters of administrative law, led to sterile jurisdictional disputes, protected government officials from legal challenge, and bore the hallmarks of the prerogative claims of the Tudors and Stuarts that were defeated in the mid-seventeenth century English revolution. Dicey recognised the point made by Maitland that the powers of government during the nineteenth century had increased. But he vehemently rejected the claim that the existence of these powers—being subject to supervision by the ordinary courts—could change the character of English law or alter our understanding of the nature of the constitution.

[10] Ibid.
[11] Ibid.
[12] Ibid at 506.
[13] Dicey, *Law of Constitution*, above n 3 at 324–25.
[14] Ibid at 326, 324–25.
[15] Ibid at 331–32.
[16] Ibid at 336.

In undertaking this comparative task, it is generally acknowledged that 'he distorted *droit administratif* beyond recognition'.[17] Given Dicey's specific and skewed understanding of the nature of administrative law, it is not surprising that, in response to an inquiry from Joseph Berthélemy of the University of Paris, he is reported to have said that 'in England we know nothing of administrative law, and wish to know nothing about it'.[18] In later life, however, Dicey's supreme confidence in the virtues of the British constitution started to falter. 'Where shall we now find the ardent believers in the constitution of England?' he asked—rhetorically—in 1905. 'If they exist at all', he suggested, 'they belong in spirit to the past'.[19] The main reason for Dicey's late pessimism was his belief that the spirit of liberalism was deeply embedded in the character of the British constitution, and this liberal spirit was becoming stifled under the weight of collectivist political beliefs. For Dicey, this nascent collectivism was the true source of an emerging administrative law.

Dicey's argument leads not only to an understanding of administrative law as a twentieth century creation but also one that, from the moment of its birth, was riddled with political controversy. Dicey argued that these collectivist political beliefs, variously known as 'new liberalism', progressivism or social democracy,[20] stood in opposition to classical liberalism. Underpinning these collectivist beliefs were the convictions that humans were intrinsically social creatures and that 'real' freedom could not be realised without collective action on a significant scale. And in order to realise these beliefs, administrative government, organised through a system of administrative law, was required.

We thus find Dicey in 1915, in the last edition of his classic work on the *Law of the Constitution*, complaining that recently the rule of law has suffered a 'marked decline' and arguing that this is occurring because 'the law of England is being "officialised" . . . by statutes passed under the influence of socialistic ideas'.[21] Dicey noted that since the turn of the century there has been 'a very noticeable though comparatively slight approximation towards one another of what might be called the official law of England and the *droit administratif* of France'.[22] This rapid growth of administrative law—'the invasion of the rule of law by imposing

[17] RA Cosgrove, *The Rule of Law: Albert Venn Dicey, Victorian Jurist* (London, Macmillan, 1980) 94 [Cosgrove, *Rule of Law*]; cf FH Lawson, 'Dicey Revisited' (1959) 7 *Political Studies* 109 (Pt I), 207 (Pt II).

[18] Cited in WA Robson, 'Administrative Law' in M Ginsberg (ed) *Law and Opinion in England in the Twentieth Century* (London, Stevens, 1959) 193.

[19] AV Dicey, *Lectures on the Relation between Law and Public Opinion in England during the Nineteenth Century* (London, Macmillan, 1905) 440 [Dicey, *Law and Public Opinion*].

[20] See JA Hobson, *The Crisis of Liberalism: New Issues of Democracy* (London, PS King, 1909); JT Kloppenberg, *Uncertain Victory: Social Democracy and Progressivism in European and American Thought 1870–1920* (New York, Oxford University Press, 1986). On its influence in public law thought in the United Kingdom see M Loughlin 'The Functionalist Style in Public Law' (2005) 55 *University of Toronto Law Journal* 361.

[21] Dicey, *Law of Constitution*, above n 3 at xxxviii, xliv.

[22] Ibid at xliii.

judicial functions upon officials'—was, he suggested, due 'to the whole current of legislative opinion in favour of extending the sphere of the State's authority'.[23] Unless these be treated as the ill-considered ramblings of an old man[24]—Dicey was then aged 79—it is but a short trek from here to the claims of the 'new despotism', 'administrative lawlessness', 'bureaucracy triumphant' and so on.[25]

These highly ideological claims about the nature, purpose and constitutional implications of the development of administrative law dominated discussion in the early decades of the twentieth century and have cast a long shadow over the subject. They have ensured that the subject of administrative law has remained mired in political controversy. Only by placing these claims in perspective and by returning to Maitland's empirically-orientated investigations, it is suggested, will we be able to make progress in producing a scholarly account of the history of the discipline. But in order to be able to do this, it is necessary to carry out two preliminary exercises: first, to return to ancient history and assess the general constitutional basis of Dicey's claim that the English know nothing of administrative law, and secondly to reconsider his argument about the nineteenth-century developments. These are examined in turn.[26]

Whig Fundamentalism

The reason why the concept of administrative law has never become embedded in the British system lies deeply buried in English constitutional history. One significant factor is the importance given to institutional continuity within the common law habit of thinking. The fact that the outlines of our main institutions of government can be traced to a dim and distant past has given rise to a peculiar trope in English constitutional history: the apparent need to claim that progress is measured against the yardstick of antiquity. This claim, which as we have seen was ridiculed by Dicey, came to prominence during the constitutional conflicts of the seventeenth-century, when the common lawyers devised the myth of the ancient constitution. They asserted that there existed an ancient, Anglo-Saxon constitution based on principles of liberty and democracy and which continued in existence as the source of our 'fundamental laws'.[27] At that time, the argument was used primarily to assert the privileges of Parliament and the common law courts against the prerogative claims of the Crown. But the ideas lingered on to

[23] Ibid at xxxix.

[24] See Lawson, 'Dicey Revisited' at 109.

[25] See Lord Hewart of Bury, *The New Despotism* (London, Benn, 1929) [Hewart, *New Despotism*]; C K Allen, *Bureaucracy Triumphant* (London, Oxford University Press, 1931).

[26] The following sections draw on the arguments made in ch 1 of M Loughlin, *Legality and Locality: The Role of Law in Central-Local Government Relations* (Oxford, Clarendon Press, 1996) [Loughlin, *Legality and Locality*].

[27] See Pocock, *The Ancient Constitution*, above n 5 esp ch 2; JW Gough, *Fundamental Law in English Constitutional History* (Oxford, Clarendon Press, 1955).

form a grand tradition of constitutional history which flourished in the nineteenth century,[28] and which has become known as the 'Whig interpretation of history'.[29]

A key tenet of this body of thought is that local self-government lies at the centre of the historic constitution. Under the ancient constitution, so it was claimed, exclusive responsibility for the management of local affairs, including that of taxation, rested with the *gemote* (moot or meeting) of all the freemen of the township. The *gemote* provided the foundation of the entire governmental structure, since the heads of the *gemotes* (the *reeves*) met collectively in the *witenagemote* (great council), and it is from this council that the modern parliament emerged. The structure of governmental authority thus rested on the will of the people expressed through their local communities. Neither the king nor his government had the power to make law or levy taxes without first obtaining the consent of the nation in parliament.

Within this mode of thought, English constitutional history is seen as the history of the struggle to ensure that these ancient local liberties—the fundamental laws—are not usurped by the central authority. The traditional Whig view was that the Norman Conquest was simply a disturbance, rather than a breach, in constitutional continuity. They argued, further, that the historic outcomes of post-Conquest struggles are reflected in such key documents as the Magna Carta (1215), the Petition of Right (1628) and the Bill of Rights (1689); these, the Whigs claimed, asserted no new political principles but simply required the better observance of the ancient fundamental laws and sought the redress of grievances which had arisen as a consequence of their neglect. In this narrative, England became 'pre-eminently the country of local government',[30] and the existence of this tradition of local government prohibited the formation of a singular notion of administration and ensured that no system of administrative law could be created.

Parliament and Local Government

There is little doubt that the comparatively unusual pattern of English constitutional development—even without the Whig embellishments—had a major influence over the shape of administrative arrangements. These arrangements can most succinctly be highlighted by way of contrast with continental practices. By the end of the eighteenth century it had been widely recognised throughout continental Europe that responsibility for the internal administration of the

[28] The leading figures were Stubbs, Freeman, Macaulay and Hallam: see JW Burrow, *A Liberal Descent. Victorian Historians and the English Past* (Cambridge, Cambridge University Press, 1981).

[29] See H Butterfield, *The Whig Interpretation of History* (London, Bell, 1931); H Butterfield, *The Englishman and His History* (Cambridge, Cambridge University Press, 1944).

[30] E Jenks, *An Outline of English Local Government* (London, Methuen, 5th ed, 1921) 9.

country was that of the ruler. That is, as the functions of governing increased, a distinction emerged between judgment and the execution of a judgment. From this differentiation, two discrete activities came to be identified: the rule of judicature and the rule of administration. This 'rule of administration' is close to what Dicey understood by administrative law. This concept of administrative law was founded on the power of the sovereign to issue ordinances: since administration was acknowledged to be the peculiar domain of the sovereign, these orders were treated as being his law and this body of orders—administrative law—came to form a distinct system, equivalent to the laws of the land. This idea of administrative law thus emerged in part because of the existence of a formal separation of powers,[31] with the central authority acquiring responsibility to control and regulate the activities of administrative agencies.

As Dicey noted, this continental practice was to be contrasted with the English experience. Although England has, at least since the Norman Conquest, always been *ruled* from the centre, the central authority has not generally sought to *administer* from the centre. While there have been periods, such as the Henrician Reformation or the Stuart dynasty, when attempts were made to introduce administrative law in the continental sense, the idea that administration is the special preserve of the sovereign, and that disputes concerning administrative issues should be resolved by separate courts in accordance with special principles, has never been accepted. This achievement was primarily a consequence of the efforts of Parliament to keep the Crown in check. But after the seventeenth century upheavals, the parliamentary system was bolstered by claims that the common law formed an undivided system of law. One consequence was that in the English system no clear distinction could be drawn between public law and private law (or between administrative law and common law). Since the administration remained subordinated to the ordinary law, the principle of the rule of law in the English system came to represent the rule of judicature.[32]

Two particular implications of this tradition of the rule of law throw into relief the question of administrative law. The first is that it is because of the tradition of local government that there has never emerged in England a hierarchical and undifferentiated concept of administration. Local institutions have evolved not as creatures of the central authority, but as representations of historic communities within a structure of national laws to which both the Crown and the localities are equally bound. The central government thus possessed no inherent superior jurisdiction over local institutions. It is in this sense that the English inheritance is claimed as a tradition of local government rather than a system of local administration.

The second, equally important, implication of the rule of law tradition concerns the central role of Parliament. The common law, as an undivided

31 See Dicey, *Law of Constitution*, above note 3 at 333–34.

32 Ibid ch 4; E Barker, 'The Rule of Law' (1914) *Political Quarterly* 117.

system of national laws, could not be altered by the Crown alone; the Crown could act only with the consent of the people expressed in Parliament. This principle of Parliamentary sovereignty is thus entwined with the idea of the unity of law.[33] There being few significant prerogative powers in the domestic sphere, the Crown-in-Parliament, as a supreme legislature, came to exercise absolute authority over internal administration. The Act of Parliament thus became the form through which was framed, not only all new laws, but also all the ordinances which regulate the conduct of administrative activity. One consequence is that, for the exercise of their legal powers, administrative institutions became answerable not to the central authority, but to the courts and to Parliament. In the English tradition, then, the relationships between the centre and the administration of local areas were not primarily worked out through arrangements between central government and institutions of local administration, but through a network of relationships between local government, central government, Parliament and the courts.

The Rule of Judicature

Within the English tradition, the Act of Parliament became the formal method by which the will of the central authority was expressed to all administrative institutions. The central government thus needed to secure the approval of a Parliament composed essentially of the representatives of local communities. The House of Commons, as its name implies, was a body consisting of representatives of the ancient local communities who were (and still are) referred to as such in Parliamentary proceedings (and although peers attended Parliament in their own right, they too took—and take—local titles). Parliament provided the localities with a forum within which their interests and grievances could be brought to the attention of central government.

Until the end of the eighteenth century, the Crown and Parliament had generally left local institutions free to deal with their administrative responsibilities. But when new needs made themselves felt through the demand for new services, the centre inevitably became involved. These demands took the form of petitions from local bodies seeking new powers to act. By retaining control over this process, Parliament was able to assume a jurisdiction that in continental states had become the preserve of the central authority under administrative law. This was achieved primarily through the private Bill procedure, in which Bills were generally presented on the petition of local bodies and were deliberated upon mainly by the representatives of the localities concerned. In the evolution of parliamentary practice it gradually came to be recognised that two different

[33] See Dicey, *Law of the Constitution*, above n 3, ch 13 (eg, at 402: 'the sovereignty of Parliament ... favours the supremacy of the law, whilst the predominance of rigid legality throughout our institutions evokes the exercise, and thus increases the authority, of Parliamentary sovereignty').

activities were being carried out under the general form of an Act: legislating both for the common interests of the country (public general legislation) and legislating for particular administrative requirements (private or local Acts). Through the development of this latter instrument,[34] Parliament became the intermediary between the central authority and those local or functional authorities undertaking administrative tasks.

This direct Parliamentary control over administrative powers provided a mechanism for central regulation that was compatible with this liberal constitutional spirit. Control through a Parliament in which the localities were represented bolstered the tradition of local self-government and since Parliament assumed an essentially judicial mode of inquiry through the private Bill procedure, this practice of 'the High Court of Parliament' could also be claimed to express the principle of the rule of law.

The principle of the rule of law in the English system is thus founded on the rule of judicature. It means, in essence, that every exercise of public power must be have a lawful source of authority and that, having no system of administrative law, the sole judge of legality is the ordinary courts applying the ordinary (*sc.* common) law. There have been occasions, especially under the Tudors and Stuarts, when attempts were made to fashion a special administrative jurisdiction. Under Henry VIII, for example, proclamations and royal warrants were issued direct to the Justices of the Peace, thus bringing them directly under the authority of the Crown; and under the Stuarts the Star Chamber, a committee of the Privy Council, threatened to develop into a supreme administrative authority.[35] But such measures led to fundamental constitutional conflicts in the seventeenth century, and after the Restoration in 1660 no further attempt was made to develop a separate administrative jurisdiction.

By the eighteenth century, then, the courts had emerged as important agencies for the control of administrative action. This control was executed mainly through the use of the prerogative writs which enabled the actions of administrative officers to be brought to judicial attention.[36] And the fact that most of the work of local administration during this period was carried out by Justices of the Peace who were also judicial officers, reinforced the conviction that administration was based on law.

[34] See OC Williams, *The Historical Development of Private Bill Procedure and Standing Orders in the House of Commons* (London, HMSO, 1948); S Lambert, *Bills and Acts: Legislative Procedure in Eighteenth-Century England* (Cambridge, Cambridge University Press, 1971).

[35] See, eg, Maitland, *The Constitutional History*, above n 9 at 261–64.

[36] EG Henderson, *Foundations of English Administrative Law: Certiorari and Mandamus in the Seventeenth Century* (Cambridge, Mass. Harvard University Press, 1963).

Gneist and Local Self-Government

With the institutionalisation of the doctrine of parliamentary sovereignty in the eighteenth century, the belief in the idea of law as a body of ancient custom to which all were bound was severely eroded. How then could sovereignty and liberty be reconciled? Since English commentators focused solely on practical questions, the task of discovering the mainspring of the English system was left to foreign observers, of whom Montesquieu became the most feted.

Fearing that European monarchical traditions might come to be replaced by various forms of despotic rule, Montesquieu went in search of an alternative model. He claimed to have discovered it in the English system which, being based on the mechanism of the separation of powers, enabled a reconciliation to be achieved between royal integrity, aristocratic wisdom and popular sentiment.[37] Montesquieu's claim that a balancing mechanism within English constitutional arrangements had operated to preserve liberty in the face of change was happily adopted by the British scholars of the period.[38] But the big gap in his analysis concerned the question of how, in practice, the country was actually governed. It took another foreign scholar to supply the answer.

The revolutionary crises of 1848 had shaken all the constitutions of Western Europe, leaving only the British constitution unaffected. How had this been achieved? Surely it was because of the liberalism of our institutions, which had ensured harmony between the monarchical, aristocratic and democratic elements? Rudolf Gneist was not convinced since if the constitution was actually based on the separation of powers, then Britain might have been especially prone to conflict. Gneist investigated beyond the facade of the constitutional arrangements and discovered that the real basis of English government was to be found not in separation but in unity. England, Gneist contended, was governed from top to bottom by a class of wealthy landowners, who performed unpaid personal service not only as members of the Lords and Commons but also as Justices of the Peace who administered the counties. Beneath the apparent divisions there existed a deep unity, which Gneist referred to as 'self-government'.[39]

The 'real practical basis' of the English constitution was to be found not in a system of rights but in a network of duties: 'It is not the rights of Parliament and the forms of parliamentary government that have founded England's greatness, but . . . the personal co-operation of all, from the lower classes in the social scale

[37] Montesquieu, *The Spirit of the Laws* [1748] Bk11, ch 6.

[38] See MJC Vile, *Constitutionalism and the Separation of Powers* (Oxford, Clarendon Press, 1967) ch 3; JN Shklar, *Montesquieu* (Oxford, Oxford University Press, 1987) 112: 'Montesquieu in effect wrote out the English constitution, and Blackstone in copying it gave that version a semi-official standing'.

[39] Gneist's writings on this subject are contained primarily in *Self-Government: Communalverfassung und Verwaltungsgerichte in England* (Berlin, Springer, 3rd edn, 1871) and *Englische Verfassungsgeschichte* (Berlin, Springer, 1882); Eng trans. *The History of the English Constitution* PA Ashworth trans (London, Clowes, 1886).

upwards, in the daily duties of the State'.[40] Within this network, the Justices of the Peace performed a critical role. Being entrusted with the combined tasks of administration and justice free from active control by the central authority, the Justices constituted the principal organs of self-government. These 'simple, sober and earnest' institutions, though they are 'far removed from the fantastic pictures once disseminated . . . by the author of the *Esprit des Lois*', are 'firm and durable, and in the hour of danger and trial . . . they display the energy and greatness of character of a proud free nation'.[41] Gneist believed that 'it is only the transformation and moderation which class contrasts receive from this local self-government, that produces those moderate political parties, which are capable of conducting a parliamentary government after the English fashion'.[42]

Gneist's portrayal of the system of self-government was based not only on personal service and an aristocratic principle, but also on a sense of cohesion between sovereign rights and local government. He did not root his scheme in some romantic-historical idea of Teutonic folk-freedom, with governmental authority being constructed from the locality upwards. He argued that the English state was highly centralised and that 'England has to thank the Norman kings for an absolute government which enabled her to develop a consciousness of unity and strength at a time when all the great nations of the Continent were disintegrated by feudalism'.[43] It was precisely because England had centralised early and that no serious challengers existed to the sovereign authority of the central state that it was able to concede so much liberty to the organs of local government. But the autonomy of the Justices of the Peace was purely administrative and it was limited by the legislative power of Parliament and (in theory at least) policed by the common law courts.

Though Gneist had identified a major weakness in Montesquieu's constitutionalist edifice, his own interpretation of the tradition of self-government was scarcely immune from criticism. In particular, the structure of eighteenth century government, which Gneist had designated as self-government, was more accurately identified by Redlich as 'a form of government in which all authority was monopolised by certain social and economic interests, and employed by them to their own advantage'.[44] One of the main aspects of aristocratic 'self-government' Redlich noted, was its 'subordination of efficiency to the maintenance of class rule'.[45] The conclusion we are driving towards is that the lack of a formal regime of administrative law was in large part a consequence of the high degree of

[40] Gneist, *History of the English Constitution*, ibid at 438.
[41] Ibid at 438–39.
[42] Ibid at 387.
[43] J Redlich & FW Hirst, *Local Government in England* (London, Macmillan, 1903), vol 2, 395 [Redlich & Hirst, *Local Government*].
[44] Ibid at 402.
[45] Ibid at 409.

cohesion within the governing class.[46] The Justices of the Peace as the agencies of local administration, the parliamentarians that checked the policies of the central state, and the judges who managed 'the rule of judicature' had all been educated in a common tradition of rule. This shared culture of the governing class contributed greatly to the operation of a regime in which, although there was a significant amount of administration, there was no need for anything resembling a system of administrative law.

Utilitarianism and the Industrial Revolution

During the eighteenth century both the Crown and Parliament left matters of internal administration in the hands of the local authorities: there were few subjects of an administrative character which were beyond their remit, and there were few restraints on the manner in which they were exercised.[47] But these administrative arrangements were haphazard, forming a complex mosaic of parochial, manorial, borough and county institutions, originating in a jumble of local customs, common law, royal charters and Acts of Parliament and inextricably entangled with one another in accordance with local needs and circumstances.[48] There was certainly no recognisable system and it was not surprising to discover that these eighteenth-century arrangements were singularly ill-equipped to respond to the challenges presented by the economic and social changes of the Industrial Revolution. Industrialisation was the crucible in which the modern administrative practices were forged.

The coming of the Industrial Revolution had a particularly powerful impact on the urban areas. As a result of increased trade, growth in population and the rapid conversion of rural communities into urban centres, the social structures that underpinned the traditional administrative arrangements disintegrated. The impact of urbanisation often meant that the governmental challenge was greatest in the areas in which local administrative arrangements were weakest.[49] The transformation of the physical environment in these growing urban centres

[46] On the common law tradition generally, see Baker, 'Why the History', above note 2 at 79–80: 'Trying to glean law from the year books is like trying to learn the rules of chess or cricket merely by watching video-recorded highlights of matches. The reader soon senses that contemporaries must have known something he does not, some common understanding to enable them to appreciate the moves. There must have been a body of presuppositions and ground rules which do not appear in the books themselves, except in oblique glimpses'.

[47] See WS Holdsworth, *History of English Law* (London, Methuen, 1938) vol. 10, 160–62 for an inventory of powers and duties of the Justices of the Peace.

[48] See B Keith-Lucas, *The Unreformed Local Government System* (London, Croom Helm, 1980).

[49] Describing the situation in Manchester in 1835, eg, Tocqueville commented that 'everything in the exterior appearance of the city attests the individual powers of man; nothing the directing powers of society': A de Tocqueville, *Journeys to England and Ireland*, G Lawrence & KP Mayer trans (London, Faber & Faber, 1958) 105.

created major problems of housing, sanitation, crime and environmental pollution for which the traditional arrangements were hopelessly deficient. New arrangements were required to deal with these new challenges.

The initial response was the establishment, under local Acts, of special bodies, such as sewer commissions, improvement commissions, turnpike trusts and, under public Acts, of the factory inspectorate and the railways commission to take on the governmental challenge in the industrial era. At this stage it seemed likely that although the ancient local institutions would continue to represent the locality in a ceremonial sense, special administrative bodies would be established to undertake the utilitarian functions of domestic government. And since the latter would remain dependent on the central authority, a regime of administrative law would be formed.

As it materialised, the position became more complicated. Eventually the industrialists and merchants of the towns and cities, who had found themselves excluded from the institutions of local government, began to demand the reform of these local institutions under the banner of 'equal privileges for all of equal station'. Once these reforms were instituted local government was restored to a central role in the provision of public services. Thereafter, the practices of administrative government expressed a tension between respect for the ancient local institutions and the establishment of single-purpose special bodies, between respect for local autonomy and the promotion of (centrally-controlled) uniformity and efficiency.

If the driving force of administrative reform was industrialisation, then its philosophical underpinning was that of Bentham's utilitarianism.[50] Bentham had sought to devise a science of politics from immutable laws of human nature: in his formulation, the principle of utility was translated from the sphere of individual self-interest to that of public action through the principle of the greatest happiness of the greatest number.[51] Utility was the benchmark against which all laws and institutions were to be assessed; any appeal to preserve local custom and common law on the ground that it embodied traditional wisdom handed down by our ancestors was rejected as simple superstition. Armed with this philosophy Bentham devised a plethora of schemes for social reform, most of which required major administrative reform. These reform proposals, which related to such fields as schools, prisons, local administration, and reform of the poor law, followed a common organisational pattern: Bentham's philosophy amounted to a sustained assault on the influence of the aristocratic principle in government.

[50] The precise influence of Benthamism on administrative reform has, however, become one of the major controversies of nineteenth century history. For a concise introduction to the debate see AJ Taylor, *Laissez-faire and State Intervention in Nineteenth-Century Britain* (London, Macmillan, 1972).

[51] See D Roberts, 'Jeremy Bentham and the Victorian Administrative State' (1959) 2:3 *Victorian Studies* 193.

Bentham based his administrative reforms on the principles of hierarchy, centralisation and the establishment of a set of rewards and punishments that would ensure effective and responsible public service.[52] He planned, in effect, to subject public administration to the discipline of commercial principles by, for example, putting out to competitive tender tasks such as the execution of public works or the management of prisons and then ensuring that the work was properly undertaken by subjecting contractors to surveillance through inspection. Benthamism in general was a highly centralist philosophy. As Halévy recognised: 'The State, as conceived by Bentham, is a machine so well constructed that every individual, taken individually, cannot for one instant escape from the control of all the individuals taken collectively'.[53] Since the necessity was to secure the greatest happiness of the greatest number, no local authority could be given autonomous powers in respect of its locality; there could be no sphere of public administration in which the central authority could not interfere.

Bentham's reform proposals, which had a major impact on both local and central administrative actors, were invariably centralising and rationalising. They sought to establish clear lines of authority for administrative action, with a supervisory power being vested in central government departments, and public service provision being placed on a clear statutory foundation. Such structures would lead not only to the formation of a singular framework of administrative government but also, with central departments displacing courts as the primary agencies of supervision, to the formation of a system of administrative law.

Dawn of the Modern Era of Local Government

The Reform Act of 1832 marked the great turning point in the modernisation of the system of government. In extending the franchise to just over 5 per cent of the population, the Act was scarcely a democratic measure: it marked a transition precisely because, being a compromise measure which was devoid of principle, it paved the way for the gradual democratisation of Parliament. The reformed Parliament immediately turned its attention to the archaic arrangements of local government, which by 1832 had fallen into decay. After appointing a Royal Commission in 1833 to inquire into the existing state of the municipal corporations, reform soon followed. The Municipal Corporations Act 1835 restored municipal corporations as governmental institutions by separating the functions of justice from those of administration and by establishing the corporations as

[52] See NL Rosenblum, *Bentham's Theory of the Modern State* (Cambridge, Mass, Harvard University Press, 1978) ch 6.

[53] E Halévy, *The Growth of Philosophic Radicalism* M Morris trans. (London, Faber & Gwyer, 1928) 432.

representative councils elected by the local ratepayers. The Municipal Corporations Act of 1835 ushered in the modern era of local government.[54]

The importance of the 1835 Act is to be found in two of its basic features. First, the Act was a measure of sweeping simplicity which, by imposing uniform constitutions on the boroughs, established the juristic concept of the municipal corporation.[55] Secondly, by imposing on the town council the general duty of 'the good rule and government of the Borough', it reversed the tendency to split off function after function to special authorities. The Act thus restored the principle that a general authority should assume responsibility for the administrative needs of local areas. This process of municipalisation was gradually extended to the other institutions of local government during the nineteenth century,[56] and consequently it became possible during the twentieth century to generalise the rules relating to the constitutions of all local authorities.[57] While the Webbs had detected 'the pure milk of Benthamism'[58] in the 1835 Act principles, the nineteenth century arrangements remained rather complicated, and these complicated arrangements remained more or less intact until the reforms to local government of the 1970s.

The influence of Benthamism over local government reform is more powerful, however, once the focus shifts from structure to functions. From this perspective, the critical moment which opened the new era was not the 1835 Act, but the Poor Law Amendment Act enacted in 1834. By the 1830s, the financial burden of poor relief, which was administered by 15,000 parishes and which 'affected everybody, pleased few, and was understood by nobody',[59] was becoming unbearable. A Royal Commission, on which Bentham's disciples were heavily represented, was established and it produced the report that led to the formulation of the 1834 Act.

The administrative arrangements established by the poor law reforms were radical. Rather than working within the historic boundaries of local government, the administrative map was redrawn and new units were created. Rather than

[54] See, eg, WI Jennings, 'The Municipal Revolution' in HJ Laski, WI Jennings, and WA Robson (eds), *A Century of Municipal Progress* (London, Allen & Unwin, 1935) ch 3.

[55] See further Redlich & Hirst, *Local Government*, above n 43, vol 1, 112: 'the constitutions of towns differed one from another in accordance with their charters of incorporation, which had been acquired at times and under conditions so various. . . . No statute had ever defined a municipal corporation. In 1833 you could hardly have found two municipal corporations of the same species; and there was no genus, or none known to the Jurist.'

[56] The Local Government Act 1888 created elected county councils to undertake the governmental functions previously assigned to the Justices in Quarter Sessions and the Local Government Act 1894 replaced the ancient system of parish government by vestries with urban and rural district councils established. See B Keith-Lucas, *The English Local Government Franchise: A Short History* (Oxford, Blackwell, 1952).

[57] Local Government Act 1933.

[58] S & B Webb, *English Local Government* (London, Cass, 1963) vol 4, 755 [Webb, *Local Government*].

[59] SE Finer, *The Life and Times of Sir Edwin Chadwick* (London, Methuen, 1952); FH Lawson, 'Dicey Revisited' (1959) 7 *Political Studies* 109 (Pt I), 207 (Pt II) 42.

permitting local discretion, a relatively uniform system of local administration was instituted. And in order to realise the objectives of this national system, a Central Board was established and vested with extensive powers to promulgate rules and orders to be followed by local agents. By establishing central administrative supervision of local administration of poor relief, the first steps towards establishing a modern system of administrative law had been taken.[60]

The tensions between the principle of autonomy (underpinning the 1835 Act) and that efficiency (underpinning the 1834 Act) highlight the stresses in the shaping of nineteenth-century administrative reform. The municipalisation movement was based mainly on the principle of self-government, particularly as there was no effective method of directing a council to exercise its powers and even the enforcement of duties required judicial proceedings to be instigated. But the councils possessed few powers and these could be extended only by Act of Parliament. Initially this was left mainly to local initiative through the promotion of private Bills,[61] and then to the framing permissive legislation, that is, public general legislation that left local authorities free to adopt the powers conferred.[62] However, eventually the model of public general legislation, which generally empowered, or occasionally required, authorities to undertake particular tasks was utilised.[63] And with this last development, the principles relating to poor law administration—especially that of central department supervision—came to play a more prominent role.[64]

Although the reconstitution of local government was designed to restore the principle of self-government, the need to respond efficiently to the material problems flowing from demographic, social and economic change provided a critical impetus for central action. The poor law reforms thus became the harbinger of centralisation; they provided the model that was to be emulated in

[60] By focusing on political aims rather than administrative means, the 1834 Act was, for Dicey, simply another step in the promotion of individual liberty. He thus noted only that the statute saved 'the property of hardworking men from destruction by putting an end to the monstrous system under which laggards who would not toil for their own support lived at the expense of their industrious neighbours': Dicey, *Law & Opinion*, above n 19 at 202.

[61] See, eg, D Fraser, *Power and Authority in the Victorian City* (Oxford, Blackwell, 1979), which shows the manner in which the corporations of Liverpool, Leeds and Birmingham built up their powers through local Acts.

[62] See, eg, Local Government Act 1858; on which see J Prest, *Liberty and Locality: Parliament, Permissive Legislation, and Ratepayers' Democracies in the Nineteenth Century* (Oxford, Clarendon Press, 1990).

[63] This impetus came about mainly through the public health movement and then later through educational reform: see WC Lubenow, *The Politics of Government Growth: Early Victorian Attitudes Toward State Intervention 1833–1848* (Newton Abbott, David & Charles, 1971), ch 3 (public health); Redlich and Hirst, *Local Government*, above n 43, vol.1, 134–73 (development of a sanitary code); vol.2, 224–36 (organisation of education).

[64] See Finer *Life and Times* 88: 'the administrative proposals of the [Poor Law] Report are worthy of the highest praise. They have proved the source of nearly all the important developments in English local government, viz. central supervision, central inspection, central audit, a professional local government service controlled by local elective bodies, and the adjustment of areas to administrative exigencies.'

the field of public health from the 1840s and education after the 1870s.[65] Thereafter, matters of local administration would remain bound up with central government concerns.

Boards, Commissions, Inspections

During the eighteenth century, local institutions operated independently of central government. The Justices of the Peace 'enjoyed, in their regulations, an almost complete and unshackled autonomy' and the municipal corporations 'regarded their corporate property . . . as well as their exemptions and privileges as outside any jurisdiction other than their own'.[66] These administrative institutions derived their authority from the law and could be confined and checked only by the superior courts of law. There was no active supervision by central government: in 1815 the Home Secretary was assisted by two under-secretaries and eighteen clerks,[67] and with an establishment of only twenty the Home Office simply did not possess the administrative capacity to undertake active supervision of local administration. As a consequence of the nineteenth-century reforms, however, central government began to replace the courts as the primary agency for regulating local administration.

The Poor Law Commission established under the 1834 Act was the first central department of state created for the purpose of regulating and controlling local administration. In 1871, this Commission merged with the Public Health Department of the Privy Council and the Local Act Branch of the Home Office to form the Local Government Board. The Local Government Board continued in that form until, in response to functional reorganisation, it was in 1919 reconstituted as the Ministry of Health. This department, together with the Home Office, which retained responsibility for the police, and the Board of Education which was established in 1899 from two committees of the Privy Council, were the main central departments which acquired general powers of supervision over domestic administrative matters.

Although various statutes established an administrative relationship between the central department and local authorities, this relationship was not a simple one of superior and inferior. Local authorities became bound to the central department by many administrative ties but the Board possessed no general right to issue administrative commands that compelled obedience. Rather than being indicative of strong directive leadership from the centre, the Board became

[65] Dicey expressed more concern about these types of measures, though again this concern was directed to the substance rather than method: see, eg Dicey, *Law & Opinion*, above n 19 at 276–78, noting that after 1891 'elementary education became what is called free' and '[t]his last change completely harmonises with the ideas of collectivism'.

[66] S & B Webb, *Local Government* above n 58, vol 4, 352.

[67] See Redlich & Hirst, *Local Government*, above n 43, vol 2, 238 (n 1).

known for its pragmatism and conservatism.[68] The mosaic of controls, particularly as exercised, respected the independent authority of local government.

Nevertheless, during this period central departments took over important powers from both Parliament and the courts. The Board, for example, acquired certain powers over private Bill legislation which traditionally had been exercised by Parliament alone.[69] While streamlining central business, this marked a shift in power from the legislature to the executive.[70] An illustration of the assumption of judicial powers was the acquisition by the Board of the powers of a tribunal of appeal for parties aggrieved by the auditor's decisions on surcharge or disallowance of expenditure. These powers included the power to remit surcharge or disallowance, even if the decision were unlawfully made, in cases in which it was considered 'fair and equitable' so to do.[71] What the pattern of controls indicated was not so much the establishment of directive control by the centre, so much as the construction of a system of administrative law.

With the acquisition of these supervisory powers, petitions for extensions to local powers came to be channelled through central departments; local authorities thus began to lose their channel of direct access to Parliament. In one sense, Parliament became, for the first time, a true legislative body having responsibility for laying down general rules of social conduct and, with this more formal division of powers, leaving to departments of state the task of addressing questions of administration. But the range of powers conferred on Ministers became extensive and included powers to issue rules, regulations and orders; to approve the bye-laws, plans and schemes of local authorities; to determine various appeals against local authority decisions; to intervene in default of action

[68] C Bellamy, *Administering Central-Local Relations 1871–1919: The Local Government Board in its Fiscal and Cultural Context* (Manchester, Manchester University Press, 1988) 233.

[69] As a result of the growing burden on Parliament in dealing with private Bills, the process was streamlined through the use of the technique of the provisional order. This technique required the local authority to petition the Minister rather than Parliament and this resulted in the Minister holding an inquiry rather than a Parliamentary committee being established. If ministerial approval were obtained the order was made, though it did not become valid until confirmed by Parliament. Provisional orders could be made under many Acts, including the Tramways Act 1870, the Gas and Water Works Facilities Act 1873, the Public Health Act 1875 and the Local Government Act 1888. These statutes conferred powers to make orders in relation to such matters as the compulsory acquisition of land, the supply of gas, the alteration of local authority boundaries and the amendment of local Acts.

[70] A further example of this shift is to be found in the use of Royal Commissions of Inquiry, which since the beginning of the nineteenth century were used to investigate pressing problems of social and economic life and which were the source of almost all of the century's administrative reforms. Redlich & Hirst, *Local Government*, above n 43, vol 2, 320, estimated that over 150 Royal Commissions were established between 1832 and 1844 and that they provided a key vehicle through which 'Bentham's demand for the application of scientific principles to legislation and government' could be realised.

[71] Poor Law Audit Act 1848, s.4. Under the Local Authorities Expenses Act 1887 these powers were extended to permit the Board to sanctioning expenditure which would otherwise be unlawful. In the year 1888–89 the Poor Law authorities made 1,130 applications to the Board to sanction expenditure and approval was granted in all but 29 cases: Redlich & Hirst, *Local Government*, above n 43, vol 2, 274 (n 2).

by local authorities; to exercise certain controls over local officers; and to inspect, inquire and obtain reports. In addition to these administrative controls, there existed a range of financial powers concerning grant-aid and borrowing controls that could be used to enhance the authority of these administrative mechanisms.

The characteristic technique of this structure of central supervision was that of inspection. The Home Secretary's supervision of police was, for example, rooted in inspection; each police authority was required to produce an annual report to the inspectors who were obliged 'to visit and inquire into the state and the efficiency of the police for every county and borough' and to 'report generally on such matters' to the Secretary of State.[72] Inspection, the technique invented and promoted by Bentham, was the foundation of central supervision not only in relation to the police, but was also applied to the poor law, public health, education and, through audit, to the system of local finance and expenditure. Inspection, concluded Redlich, is a characteristically English invention, since 'it is designed to obtain the advantages of efficiency without the incubus of bureaucracy'.[73]

In practice, the centre's supervisory powers were not used for the purpose of giving strategic policy direction; they were mainly used to ensure the provision of basic minimum standards of service and were deployed because local complaints were being brought to the attention of the central departments. Whatever their original purpose, these supervisory powers were in practice used mainly for the quasi-judicial purpose of ensuring the fair treatment of the various local interests affected by the exercise of local authority powers. That is, the powers were used to resolve local disputes through administrative processes according to standards that emerged through practice. To the extent that the jurisdiction of the courts was more or less ousted, a relatively closed system of administrative law was constructed. The system of central controls that emerged was thus much more in the nature of an emerging system of administrative law than one that sought to guide the development of public service provision.

Courts, *Ultra Vires* and the Emergence of Administrative Law

What impact had this emerging system of administrative law on the role of the courts? One direct impact of the nineteenth-century changes reforms was to enhance the degree of formalisation in the mechanisms of judicial control. This came about mainly because of the formulation during the nineteenth century of the *ultra vires* doctrine and its application to public authorities. This doctrine was developed by the courts in relation to disputes in the mid-nineteenth century

[72] County and Borough Police Act 1856, section 15.
[73] Redlich & Hirst, *Local Government*, above n 43, vol 2, 251.

concerning the trading powers of railway companies established under statutory powers, where it was held that 'a statutory corporation, created by Act of Parliament for a particular purpose, is limited, as to all its powers, by the purposes of its incorporation as defined in that Act'.[74] As a result of the 'statutorification' of local government, this doctrine also came to be applied to local authorities.[75]

Although its application to elected local authorities was criticised, given the degree of controversy during the latter half of the nineteenth century over the issue of municipal trading,[76] the application of the *ultra vires* doctrine to local government activities was only to be expected. But recognising that an overly-strict application of the doctrine could frustrate the ability of public authorities to undertake the tasks entrusted by Parliament, the judiciary tried to adopt a flexible approach, holding that 'whatever may fairly be regarded as incidental to or consequential upon those things which the Legislature has authorised, ought not (unless expressly prohibited) to be held to be *ultra vires*.'[77]

Thereafter, to the extent that the courts created a general supervisory jurisdiction over public authorities during the latter half of the nineteenth century, this was achieved mainly through the development of the prerogative writs.[78] They did so by extending the use of prerogative remedies, which had been designed to control the actions of courts of inferior jurisdiction, to the quasi-judicial functions of administrative authorities. They were set on course by Brett LJ who in 1882 stated that 'whenever the Legislature entrusts to any body of persons other than the superior Courts the power of imposing an obligation upon individuals, the Courts ought to exercise as widely as they can the power of controlling those bodies of persons, if those persons admittedly attempt to exercise powers beyond the powers given to them by Act of Parliament'.[79] Since then the courts have adapted the writs to keep public authorities within the boundaries of their powers.

But this was neither a simple nor a linear process. When the exercise of these powers was subject to official review in the early 1930s, it was accepted that the maintenance of the jurisdiction was essential, though it was also felt that the existing procedures were 'too expensive and in certain respects archaic, cumbrous and too inelastic'.[80] This refrain continued to be expressed throughout the mid-twentieth century, though it was not until 1977 that the procedures were

[74] *Ashbury Railway Carriage & Iron Co.Ltd v Riche* (1875) L. 7 H. 653, 693 (per Lord Selborne).

[75] See, eg, *Attorney-General v Newcastle-upon-Tyne* (1889) 23 QBD 492.

[76] See Dicey, *Law & Opinion*, above n 19 at 283–87; H Finer, *Municipal Trading: A Study in Public Administration* (London, Allen & Unwin, 1941).

[77] *Attorney-General v Great Eastern Railway Co. Ltd* (1880) 5 App Cas 473, 478.

[78] Jennings notes that Brice on *Ultra Vires*, the standard work which was written in 1877, did not even mention the jurisdiction of the prerogative writs, whereas its successor in 1930 (Street on *Ultra Vires*) discusses the question at considerable length: Jennings, 'Central Control' in Laski, Jennings and Robson (eds), *A Century* 417 at 422.

[79] *R v Local Government Board* (1882) 10 QBD 309, 321.

[80] *Report of the Committee on Ministers' Powers* Cmd4060 (London, 1932), 99.

streamlined through the introduction of a single 'application for judicial review'. But the fact is that judicial review through the prerogative writs was often of marginal importance because of a general tendency from the early decades of the twentieth century to insert in statutes conferring powers on public authorities the power to appeal decisions on questions of law to the High Court.

Some scholars have offered highly critical conclusions about the general impact of judicial supervision of decisions of public authorities, especially concerning questions of policy.[81] As a result of his studies of judicial decisions concerning local authorities in the early twentieth century, for example, Jennings drew as its general point 'the frequency with which the Courts manage to interpret—no doubt correctly in law—in such a way as to obstruct efficient administration'.[82] 'It is a remarkable fact', he continued, 'that so often a decision of a court acts as a spanner in the middle of delicate machinery'.[83] But this type of criticism should not deflect from the basic fact that from the late-nineteenth century the judiciary readily acquiesced in the emergence of this informal and relatively closed system of administrative law.

Consider, for example, the case of *Pasmore v Oswaldtwistle UDC*[84] in which the plaintiff mill-owner, having unsuccessfully petitioned the authority to bring the sewers up to standard, sought an order of mandamus requiring the authority to discharge its statutory duty under the Public Health Act 1875. In finding for the authority, the House of Lords held that the plaintiff should have used the statutory default procedure provided for in the Act. It held that where statute created the obligation and provided a remedy, the general rule is that it could not be enforced in any other manner: 'the particular jurisdiction to call upon the whole district to reform their mode of dealing with sewage and drainage should not be in the hands, and should not be open to litigation, of any particular individual, but should be committed to a Government department'.[85] Decisions of this type provided ready acknowledgement of the fact that the ordinary courts simply did not possess the capacity to reach an adequate resolution of these administrative issues.[86] The matter was better left to administrative channels of appeal. Through the establishment of these central mechanisms of supervision, a non-juridified system of administrative law emerged. Judicial supervision of

[81] For representative accounts see: HJ Laski, 'Judicial Review of Social Policy in England' (1926) 39 *Harvard Law Review* 832; WI Jennings, 'The Courts and Administrative Law—the Experience of English Housing Legislation' (1936) 49 *Harvard Law Review* 426; JAG Griffith, 'Judges in Politics' (1968) 3 *Government & Opposition*. 485; P McAuslan, 'Administrative Law, Collective Consumption and Judicial Policy' (1983) *46 Modern Law Review* 1.

[82] WI Jennings, *Local Government in the Modern Constitution* (London, Knight, 1931) 3.

[83] Ibid.

[84] [1898] AC 387.

[85] Ibid at 395 (per Lord Halsbury).

[86] For examples of such acquiescence see *Board of Education v Rice* [1911] AC 179 and *Local Government Board v Arlidge* [1915] AC 120. See WJL Ambrose, 'The New Judiciary' (1910) 26 *Law Quarterly Review* 203.

public authorities, a basic characteristic of the old regime, had been replaced by the administrative supervision of central departments.

Dicey had feared that if the use of administrative tribunals was extended and regularised, particularly if judicial review were excluded, Britain would rapidly develop an independent and more formalised system of administrative law. Late in life, he acknowledged that recent legislation, as interpreted by the judiciary, appeared to be introducing into English law 'a body of administrative law resembling in spirit, though certainly by no means identical with the administrative law (*droit administratif*) . . . of France'.[87] This is precisely the trend that Maitland had been identifying 30 years earlier. But in the decade or so after the First World War, the topic became highly politicised, with (on the one hand) the disciples of Dicey defending a rigid normativism that led logically to the abolition of administrative government,[88] and (on the other) the detached empiricism of Maitland being superseded by an explicit advocacy of the need to modernise the emerging administrative state by adopting a formal system of administrative law in the French sense.[89]

Conclusion

Twentieth century developments—the primary focus of Mike Taggart's important historical work—will not here be examined. My claim, however, is that the predominant approach to the subject in the twentieth century (though certainly not Taggart's) has absorbed far too much of Dicey's method and underlying values. Since Dicey bolstered his views with a poor comparative understanding and weak historical research, it is not surprising that his influence has contributed greatly to a polarisation of scholarly views and has helped to ensure that so much of the academic writing on administrative law would remain mired in

[87] AV Dicey, 'The Development of Administrative Law in England' (1915) 31 *Law Quarterly Review* 148 (commenting on the *Rice* and *Arlidge* cases).

[88] See in particular, Hewart, *New Despotism*, above n 25 at 14. The 'new' despotism Hewart was referring to (in contrast with the old despotism of the Stuart prerogative claims of the seventeenth century) was the positing of the central government departments 'above the Sovereignty of Parliament and beyond the jurisdiction of the Courts'.

[89] See in particular WA Robson, *Justice and Administrative Law: A Study of the British Constitution* (London, Macmillan, 1928), which argued that 'whether or not we have a "government according to law and by means of law" there is in fact at the present time in England a very considerable body of administrative law' (at 31). And by the time of the second edition (London, Stevens, 1947, at 30), Robson was arguing that 'no modern student of law or political science has today the slightest doubt that there exists in England a vast body of administrative law. … English administrative law is, indeed, so extensive that the problem is not to discover it but rather to master its widespread ramifications and reduce it to some kind of order and coherence'.

political contention. Writing the history of the subject in such circumstances is almost impossible, not least because there is no agreement on what *is* the subject.[90]

In this essay, I have sought first to identify the core of sense in Dicey's claim that England knows nothing of administrative law. What we find is that this claim lies less on the constitutional principle of 'the rule of law' than on the central importance of parliament in the British system of government (and the manner in which these parliamentary arrangements bolstered respect for a tradition of local government). But, as I have indicated, these two features of the constitutional inheritance—parliamentary controls and local autonomy—could hardly survive the impetus for modernisation driven by industrialisation: traditional local governmental arrangements because they were haphazard, inefficient and thoroughly anti-democratic, and parliamentary arrangements largely because the volume of business together with the need for expertise and continuous oversight of administrative action required that a clearer differentiation between parliamentary and governmental functions be made.

Dicey almost entirely ignored these critical aspects of the British system of government in his study of constitutional law,[91] he overlooked the extent to which the formative period of modern administrative law is to be found in the early nineteenth-century,[92] he underplayed the degree to which the common law courts acquiesced in the emergence of this body of law, and by giving a skewed interpretation of Benthamite liberalism he failed to acknowledge the degree to which the administrative law he despised was a direct consequence of the political philosophy he espoused.[93] Although Bentham's rationalism and modernism was thoroughly antithetical to the common law habit of thinking, Dicey

[90] Harry Arthurs made this point succinctly, if polemically, when he explained that for most lawyers 'administrative law is not the law *of* the administration; it is the law directed *against* the administration, the law by which reviewing judges ensure that the administration does not overreach': HW Arthurs, *'Without the Law': Administrative Justice and Legal Pluralism in Nineteenth-Century England* (Toronto, University of Toronto Press, 1985) 6 [Arthurs, *Without the Law*]. Arthurs' distinction, of course, replicates the differences between Maitland and Dicey's conceptions of the subject.

[91] Cf the many radical works of Joshua Toulmin Smith in the mid-nineteenth century: see, eg, JT Smith, *Government by commissions illegal and pernicious* (London, Sweet, 1849); *Local self-government un-mystified* (London, Stanford, 1857); and *Local self-government and centralization* (London, Sweet, 1858).

[92] Arthurs, *Without the Law*, above n 90 at129: 'If we were to ask ourselves when administrative law emerged, we would have to see when its distinctive characteristics …became identifiable: "The problem is … to indicate the period when such administrative tools as delegated legislation, administrative tribunals, inspection, and exchequer grants, came into general use. That period was the 1830s"'; (citing H Parris, *Constitutional Bureaucracy: The Development of British Central Administration since the Eighteenth* Century (London, Allen & Unwin, 1969) 190). See also Cosgrove, *Rule of Law*, above n 17 at 93: 'The most remarkable aspect of Dicey's concern with administrative law was the almost invincible ignorance he displayed about the evolution of domestic administrative jurisdiction during his own lifetime'.

[93] See Dicey, *Law & Opinion*, above n 19, Lecture 6, esp 175: 'Benthamism was … little else than the logical and systematic development of those individual rights, and especially of that individual

treated it as a form of classical liberalism in tune with common law values; treating it as an extension and logical development of the common law, he did not seem to realise that Bentham's method led directly to the construction of a system of administrative law. And although Dicey may have been correct in his assumption that administrative law eroded the foundations of the post-1688 constitutional settlement, this observation simply pushes back discussion to the more basic questions. How does a historic, evolutionary constitution acquire normative status? Can such immanent normativity retain its authority in the light of social, economic and cultural change? By what methods is a scholar able to outline constitutional requirements? And '[i]s it possible that so-called "constitutional law" is in reality a cross between history and custom which does not properly deserve the name of law at all?'[94]

Dicey and Maitland may have been among the first generation of scholars to address these questions, but their divergent answers continue to set the frame for contemporary thinking about administrative law. Notwithstanding his adoption of a scientific idiom, it is evident that Dicey drew his normative values from the professional classes of mid-Victorian society: that is, his understanding of both the common law and the constitution was refracted through the values of classical liberalism. Why, it must be asked, should these political values be accorded an almost entrenched constitutional status? And such questions should not only to be asked of Dicey; they must also be addressed to all scholars who claim to have discovered the fundamental values on which the British constitution rests. Today, for example, many analogous constitutional claims are being made in the name of the separation of powers or of certain immanent values of the common law. Whatever their authority, it is doubtful that they can be said to rest on history. 'It is curious', noted Maitland, 'that some political theorists should have seen their favourite ideal, a complete separation of administration from judicature, realised in England; in England of all places in the world, where the two have for ages been inextricably blended.[95] The mistake, he explained, 'comes of looking just at the surface and the showy parts of the constitution'.[96]

Maitland, by contrast, had promoted a rigorous, empirically grounded historical approach to the subject. But, asked Dicey, surely this leads to 'simple antiquarianism'? Maitland's response, as expressed in a letter to Dicey in 1896, is as follows: 'The only direct utility of legal history…lies in the lesson that each generation has an enormous power of shaping its own law. I don't think that the study of legal history would make men fatalists; I doubt it would make them conservatives. I am sure that it would free them from superstitions and teach

freedom which has always been dear to the common law of England. … [Benthamism] is heavily indebted to Coke, and utilitarianism has inherited some of its most valuable ideas from Puritanism'.

[94] Dicey, *Law of Constitution*, above note 3 at 21.

[95] FW Maitland, 'The Shallows and Silences of Real Life' in his *Collected Papers*, above n 1, vol 1, 477–78.

[96] Ibid at 478.

them that they have free hands.'[97] Here we find the core claim of Maitland's empirically-orientated treatment of the subject. But if today this teaches us only that 'the constitution is…what happens',[98] then it may not be surprising to find that the subject—both constitutional and administrative law—remains wrapped up with partisan political values.

These differences between Maitland and Dicey remain with us. For Dicey and his disciples 'administrative law' is treated as the 'law' that emanates from the executive; it therefore focuses on the rule-making and adjudicatory powers acquired by government. By invoking the principle of parliamentary sovereignty but, more especially, the doctrines of the separation of powers and the rule of law, his disciples claim that the very existence of such powers raises major constitutional questions. For these normativists, 'real' administrative law is converted into the method by which the administrative powers acquired by government are to be subjected to supervision by the common law courts. From Maitland's perspective, however, the subject of administrative law emerged in a different, and altogether broader, frame. From an empirical perspective, it is the body of law establishing, organising and regulating public administration. Thus viewed, it is a vast subject encompassing the establishment and jurisdiction of public authorities, the law relating to the civil service and other public officials, relations between central department and local authorities, between Ministers and public corporations and boards, the duties and liabilities of public authorities, judicial review of administrative action, as well as the organisation of administrative tribunals and the rule-making powers of government.

We now get some sense of why the history of administrative law is not written. For the fact of the matter is that even today administrative lawyers are unlikely to agree on the boundaries of the subject, the methods for examining it, and the values that inform it. Treated empirically, the history of administrative law becomes almost coterminous with the history of modern government and increasingly—now that Benthamism has finally triumphed in government—the subject appears to possess few yardsticks other than economy, efficiency, and effectiveness.[99] Treated normatively, we find today the insinuation of liberal values in the guise of what is now called 'common law constitutionalism', a movement that returns us back to the old tensions between law and history. As Maitland astutely put it, the 'process by which old principles and old phrases are charged with a new content, is from the lawyers point of view an evolution of the true intent and meaning of the old law', whereas 'from the historian's point of

[97] Cited in CHS Fifoot, *Frederic William Maitland: A Life* (Cambridge, Mass, Harvard University Press, 1971), 143.

[98] JAG Griffith, 'The Political Constitution' (1979) 42 *Modern Law Review* 1 at 19.

[99] For the argument about the triumph of Benthamism, see Loughlin, *Legality & Locality*, above n 26 at 72–77 and, more generally, CD Foster and FJ Plowden, *The State under Stress* (Buckingham, Open University Press, 1996).

view it is almost of necessity a process of perversion and misunderstanding'.[100] Finding the vantage point from which a history of the subject can be written remains as elusive as ever.

[100] Maitland, 'Why the History', above n 1 at 491.

9

Mike Taggart and Australian Exceptionalism

SIR ANTHONY MASON

I AM AN unabashed admirer of Mike Taggart and of his outstanding contribution to our understanding of administrative law, while not always agreeing with him. I have always enjoyed his combative commentary and all the more so when it is directed at judicial targets other than myself.

Broadly, I agree with Mike in his use of the expression "Australian exceptionalism" to describe Australian judicial review of administrative action when it is compared with judicial review in other common law jurisdictions. I also agree with his view that Australian judicial review of administrative action is unsatisfactory by reason of the narrow scope accorded to "*Wednesbury* unreasonableness". But it seems to me that Mike does not appreciate how deep-seated are some of the considerations that led to the present state of Australian administrative law and that Australian exceptionalism can be explained partly, though not wholly, by Australia's non-adoption of a charter of rights and the attitudes that underlie that non-adoption.

For present purposes the relevant features of Australian exceptionalism in administrative law jurisprudence are a heavy emphasis on a strict constitutional separation of powers; a restricted conception of judicial power; a rejection of the concept of judicial deference; the restriction of review to jurisdictional error rather than errors of law;[1] a strong scepticism about the utility of the concept of legitimate expectations except in limited situations relating to procedural fairness; the absence of any intensified standard of review beyond "*Wednesbury* unreasonableness" (including a rejection of the concept of proportionality); and a narrow view of "*Wednesbury* unreasonableness".

In addition to these features, which are identified by Mike, the point should be made that, although Australian administrative law, in common with that of other

[1] With the qualification that relief for error of law on the face of the record is available: see *Craig v South Australia* (1995) 184 CLR 163.

jurisdictions, is based on the principle that judicial review does not extend to merits review, Australian courts are more energetic than others in fencing off merits review. The concern that the use of the concept of proportionality will shade off into merits review, or something like it, has resulted in the rejection of proportionality as an element in judicial review. This was a concern initially expressed in England only to be later discarded.

Because the considerations that underpin the Australian minimalist conception of judicial review are largely doctrinal and, to some extent, attitudinal rather than functional, they are vulnerable to criticism from a comparative perspective of the kind that Mike has made. And most of the features of Australian administrative law already identified have a doctrinal and, to some extent, an attitudinal basis. I employ the expression "attitudinal basis" to signify the judicial perspective that there exists, or should exist, a relationship of mutual respect between the courts and the other arms of government. This perspective entails that the courts will avoid, so far as it is legitimately possible to do so, trespassing upon administrative decision-making, thereby generating public controversy leading to criticism of the courts and possible loss of respect for, and public confidence in, the courts. It was probably such an attitude of mind that lay behind Sir Owen Dixon's conception of judicial power and his opposition to the vesting in a federal court of jurisdiction in industrial arbitration, a jurisdiction the exercise of which would plunge the federal courts into the turbulent and controversial world of industrial relations.[2] A possible reflection of the same attitude of mind was the belief that the courts are better insulated from public controversy if the law maintains an aura of mystique.

I do not suggest that this attitude of mind is confined to judges. Far from it. It is an attitude that may well be shared by the Australian legal community or a large section of it and perhaps by the wider community. In essence, it conceives of judges as appearing to have a limited role. And it may stem from a very strong adherence to majoritarian democracy that would help to explain Australia's unwillingness so far to adopt a charter of rights. In this respect, it is significant that the major argument against even a statutory Charter advanced by the commentators is the transfer of power from elected politicians to unelected judges. It is no accident that there have been many Australian supporters of Dicey's doctrine of parliamentary sovereignty notwithstanding the limits set by the Australian Constitution to the powers of the Australian legislatures.

Of the considerations that characterise Australian exceptionalism, first and foremost is the rigid separation of federal judicial power that, in turn, has led to the adoption of a narrow conception of judicial power.[3] Although there is now an

[2] See *R v Kirby; Ex parte Boilermakers' Society of Australia* (1956) 94 CLR 254 [*Kirby*].

[3] See M Groves, 'Judicial Review of Administrative Action in the High Court of Australia' (2008) 33 *Queen's Law Journal* 327.

accumulation of authority to support that rigid separation and the narrow scope of federal judicial power, there are some inherent problems in each of the two elements.

Thus, in relation to judicial power, it has been said that 'if the ultimate decision may be determined not merely by the application of legal principles to ascertained facts but by considerations of policy also, then the determination does not proceed from an exercise of judicial power.'[4] The dichotomy between legal standards and policy is by no means precise, and the High Court has in the past been willing to discern the existence of ascertained and ascertainable standards from words of general import and even from general discretions conferred upon a court in circumstances where criteria can be articulated. But it is clear that federal judicial power does not extend to matters of policy.[5]

There is also the principle that federal judicial power is not engaged unless the case is one that calls for an immediate right, duty, or liability to be established by the determination of the court.[6] So a curial declaration that will produce no foreseeable consequences for the parties does not fall within the exercise of federal judicial power.[7] On this basis it is suggested that if a federal charter of rights were enacted conferring power on a court to make a declaration of incompatibility (as made under the *Human Rights Act 1998* (UK)), the making of such a declaration might well fall outside the exercise of federal judicial power.[8] In this area, there is certainly a case for recognising that the making of such a declaration, being related and incidental to the central issue of statutory interpretation, is within judicial power, even on a narrow view of the power.

Despite reservations expressed many years ago by Barwick CJ and myself in *R v Joske; Ex parte Shop Distributive & Allied Employees' Association*[9] about the decision in the *Boilermakers Case*[10] and academic criticism[11] of that case, the decision still stands as authority for the proposition that non-judicial power that is not incidental to the exercise of judicial power cannot be vested in a federal court. The High Court and the Privy Council rejected the more attractive and less stringent proposition that powers incompatible with the exercise of federal judicial power cannot be vested in federal court.

In sketching the framework that influences the shape and scope of federal judicial review, the starting point is necessarily the Constitution. The role of the courts under the Constitution is to declare and enforce the law and, in so doing,

[4] *Precision Data Holdings Ltd v Wills* (1991) 173 CLR 167 at 189.

[5] *Ibid*; LR Zines, *The High Court and the Constitution* (Annandale, Federation Press, 5th ed, 2008) 249–55 [Zines *The High Court*].

[6] *Bass v Permanent Trustee Company Ltd* (1999) 198 CLR 334.

[7] *Ainsworth v Criminal Justice Commission* (1992) 175 CLR 564 at 582.

[8] See J Stellios, 'State/Territory Human Rights Legislation in a Federal Judicial System' (2008) 19 *Public Law Review* 52.

[9] (1976) 135 CLR 194.

[10] *Kirby*, above n 2; affd by the Privy Council sub nom *Attorney-General (Cth) v R; Ex parte Boilermakers' Society of Australia* (1957) 95 CLR 529.

[11] LR Zines, *The High Court*, above n 5 at 295–99.

to determine the limits of the power conferred by statute upon administrative decision-makers. To say this is simply to recognise that one of the assumptions on which the Constitution is based is the rule of law. Because there is a constitutional separation of powers, the High Court has a strongly arguable basis for its conclusion that the *making* of executive (including administrative discretionary) decisions is not a matter for the judicial arm of government.[12]

But it does not follow from the separation of powers that administrative discretionary decisions are unreviewable by the judicial arm of government when authority to review them is conferred by statute. On any view of the separation of powers, executive acts and decisions (including administrative discretionary decisions) are susceptible of judicial review. In principle, such decisions should be reviewable on any basis that lends itself to the exercise of judicial power. On the High Court's conception of judicial power, merits review of many administrative decisions, though not all, would fail this test.

Be this as it may, there is no reason why the separation of powers should preclude the Parliament from authorising a court, on judicial review, to correct an error of law, whether going to jurisdiction or not. The High Court's decision in *Craig v South Australia*,[13] limiting judicial review to jurisdictional errors does not rest on the Constitution; its stance rests on the common law.

Apart from constitutional limitations on power, in the nature of things it is the statute, interpreted in the light of the common law, that marks out the limits of the power it confers. In ascertaining those limits it is relevant to look to the grounds of review established by the common law. Review for jurisdictional error is the traditional basis for judicial review of administrative decisions. Elsewhere, notably in England, there has been a shift to error of law as a basis for review, largely as a result of the difficulty of distinguishing between jurisdictional error and error of law. Ironically, the English conception of error of law now extends to include material errors of fact giving rise to unfairness, where the true facts or the evidence were uncontentious or objectively verifiable.[14] The complexities inherent in this development replace the old uncertainties associated with the distinction between jurisdictional and non-jurisdictional errors of law. The position taken by the High Court is consistent with the common law and one suspects that it is unlikely to change in the near future.

On the other hand, there is no compelling reason, leaving aside common law history, for attributing to the statute conferring power on the decision-maker authority to make a decision that is erroneous in point of law so long as it does not amount to a jurisdictional error. Indeed, it is artificial to impute to the statute

[12] *Enfield City v Development Assessment Committee* (2000) 199 CLR 135 [*Enfield*]; and see *Minister for Immigration & Multicultural Affairs; Ex parte Lam* (2003) 214 CLR 1 (where constitutional objections to the doctrine of substantive legitimate expectations were raised).

[13] [1995] 184 CLR 163.

[14] *E v Secretary of State for the Home Department* [2004] QB 1044 at 1071.

the grant of any authority to make errors of law. Why not imply, as the English courts have done, an intention that the decision is to be made in accordance with law?

Although the High Court has rejected the concept of deference, in particular, the *Chevron*[15] doctrine, the Court made it clear that, in appropriate cases, weight will be given to the findings and opinions of administrative tribunals and decision-makers, especially in areas of special expertise.[16] In this respect, the Australian position scarcely merits the description "exceptional".

It is not surprising that Australia has not intensified the grounds of review beyond *Wednesbury* unreasonableness. Intensification of review elsewhere usually has been a consequence of entrenched or statutory protection of human rights, a development that has not taken place in Australia. Unlike the United Kingdom, Australia has not been called upon to react to the imposition of external standards, such as those arising from the *European Convention on Human Rights and Fundamental Freedoms* and membership of the European Union. The principle of legality—the rule of construction applying to statutes trenching upon human rights or common law "rights"—has, however, been recognised.[17] This recognition could well lead to some intensification of review, though at present this seems unlikely.

What is surprising is that *Wednesbury* unreasonableness as an independent ground of review seems almost to have sunk without trace in the area of federal judicial review. There is very little evidence of its application. Resistance to it is associated with opposition to merits review, perhaps because it is thought that, like proportionality, it can shade too readily into merits review.

Mark Aronson is correct in pointing out that, accepting the "lunacy" version of *Wednesbury*, federal judicial review is inadequate in failing to provide a remedy where something has obviously gone wrong.[18] The example he gives is that of the decision-maker who fails to give genuine consideration to the case. For my part, I do not understand how the concept of *Wednesbury* unreasonableness can be so narrow as to exclude such a case. Indeed, I would favour a development that recognises irrationality or unreasonableness as such (including gross distortion of the individual values of the relevant factors to be taken into account) as a ground of review. In the area of judicial review the functional importance of making available adequate remedies should prevail over doctrinal considerations and apprehensions that judges may go too far. Appellate courts exist to correct errors of that kind.

[15] *Chevron USA Inc v Natural Resources Defense Council, Inc*, 467 U.S. 837 (1984).

[16] *Enfield* , above n 12 at 154–55.

[17] *Coco v The Queen* (1994) 179 CLR 427 at 437; *Electrolux Home Products v AWU* (2004) 221 CLR 309 at 328–29.

[18] M Aronson, 'Process, Quality, and Variable Standards: Responding to an *Agent Provocateur*', in this volume.

By way of concluding comment I should refer to the suggestion sometimes made that the federal system of administrative law combining tribunal merits review, which was set up in 1975,[19] with the statutory system of judicial review[20] has perhaps had a constraining effect on judicial development of the common law of judicial review in Australia. Although the existence of recourse to merits review in the Administrative Appeals Tribunal may have diminished the prospects of expanding the scope of judicial review, I am not at all persuaded that this is so or that current problems in the area of federal judicial review can be legitimately traced back to the Kerr Committee (of which I was a member) which recommended the reforms of the 1970s. So I decline to end this piece with an apology. Instead I shall repeat my tribute to Mike Taggart.

[19] *Administrative Appeals Tribunal Act 1975* (Cth).
[20] *Administrative Decisions (Judicial Review) Act 1977* (Cth).

10

Public Function Tests: Bringing Back the State?

JANET MCLEAN*

Introduction

TO WHOM DO the values of public law apply? In recent years there have been various attempts to answer this question by the application of 'public function' style tests that ask: 'is this body, function or act inherently "public"'? We ought not to be surprised that the results have been inconsistent and controversial. At the heart of these disputes is a clash of views about the nature and basis of the state and the place of the common law within it.

'Public function' type tests, in their various case law and statutory incarnations, seem to have achieved the greatest currency in the United Kingdom where they now inform (at least in part) the scope of judicial review,[1] the law of state immunity,[2] freedom of information jurisdiction,[3] aspects of European Union law,[4] and the scope of the application of the Human Rights Act 1998.[5] Why this reliance on the notion of 'public function'? And more perplexingly, why the proliferation of public function type tests, at the very time when the post-war consensus about the proper role of government is being revisited?

On one reading of the recent history, the widespread restructuring of government in much of the common law world signified the victory of an ideology that denied the very existence of inherently 'public functions'. Under the public choice

* Thanks to Alan Page and the editors for their helpful comments

[1] *R v Panel on Mergers and Take-Overs, ex parte Datafin plc* [1987] QB 815 (CA) [*Datafin*].

[2] State Immunity Act 1976 (UK) section 3(3) distinguishes commercial transactions from exercises of sovereign authority.

[3] Under section 5(2)(a) of the Freedom of Information (Scotland) Act 2002, for example, Scottish Ministers can make a designation order for organisations that appear to exercise functions of a public nature or provide, under contract made with a Scottish public authority, any service whose provision is a function of that authority.

[4] For example, rules about state aid and environmental information reporting.

[5] Section 6 Human Rights Act (UK).

theories that have driven restructuring, all human activity could be reduced to an aggregation of private preferences. Against this background is it possible to regard 'public function' type legal tests as the potential site of resistance to such theories and ideology? What should a 'green light' style judge make of the statutorily imposed versions of such tests? Should she support a government's choice of private law modes of governance and leave these within the regulation of private law? Should she see her role as part of the regulatory armoury of the core state and seek to correct regulatory and market failure? Should she view the public function tests as a legislative mandate to 're-unify' the state in an aggregate form and as a license to aid the proliferation and enforcement of public law norms (however sporadic and peripheral judicial review case law may be)? What legal resources are available to judges with which to deal with such questions? The red and green light metaphor no longer assists[6] and traditional statutory interpretation is unlikely to help. How is this juridification process[7] to understand, and perhaps even to 'resuscitate', the modern state?

In this chapter I take as my starting point the public function tests contained in the Human Rights Act 1998 UK ('HR Act') and, to the extent to which it provided a model, the New Zealand Bill of Rights Act 1990 ('NZBOR' Act), and assess them against the political context of privatisation. The tests apply human rights norms to all core public authorities and extend these norms into the private sphere in cases where private bodies are performing acts that involve public functions. The UK provisions were introduced against the background of the increasing involvement of the private sector in the delivery of public services and there is some evidence to suggest that they were intended as a salve to privatisation and its associated practise of contracting out, or at least as a response to the bewildering new range of forms government now assumes. That being so, there is potential for a public function approach to serve as a legal mechanism for spreading public law norms into the private sector (in Jody Freeman's terms).[8]

Legislative intention cannot by itself, however, ultimately determine the matter. What resources do administrative lawyers have at their disposal to perform such a task? The statutory tests appear wrongly to assume that we had a clear view of what was a public function immediately *prior* to privatisation. The common law has long allowed the core state sometimes to pursue a 'private life' depending on the function being performed and the source of power being used.

[6] C Harlow and R Rawlings, *Law and Administration* (London, Butterworths, 2nd edn, 1997) esp chapters 2 and 3. Broadly speaking, red light theorists have traditionally been categorised as favouring judicial control of the executive and as formalists, and green light theorists as tending to favour political processes and as functionalists. Red lighters no longer tend to be formalists; political processes have been put at arms-length from policy delivery. See further M Taggart, 'Reinvented Government, Traffic Lights, and the Convergence of Public and Private Law: Review of Harlow and Rawlings' [1999] *Public Law* 124.

[7] By juridification I mean the process of bringing legal rules and judicial scrutiny to bear on matters that were formerly regarded as properly within the political sphere.

[8] J Freeman, 'The Private Role in Public Governance' (2000) 75 *New York University Law Review* 543; 'The Contracting State' (2000) 28 *Florida State University Law Review* 155.

The substance of what is a 'public function' or rather its converse a 'commercial function' has changed with political and economic fashion. Where a *legal* distinction between public and private functions has been maintained, this has mainly been for the purpose of extending private law rather than public law norms. Moreover, the common law has never restricted the obligation to observe at least some human rights on the basis of 'function'. Given this common law background, it is unclear how 'public function' as a concept can help us to determine when a private entity should be subject to human rights norms. It may introduce a new procedural hurdle in its wake.

This paper argues that the public function approach provides a lens through which to measure the extent to which privatisation has provoked a 'crisis' or challenge to administrative law and its traditional modes of thought and methodology.[9] It has the potential to force us to confront questions that administrative lawyers have avoided throughout the twentieth century. I seek to place the idea of public function within this wider context of the common law's difficulties with, and ambivalence to, the notion of the state and its obsession with sovereignty and ask whether we have the intellectual resources to meet the challenges brought by the new forms of governance associated with privatisation. If prior to privatisation we could not agree about what was a public function—even when the state itself was performing the activity—how are we now to determine when a private entity is doing something public?

A Link Between Public Function Tests and Privatisation?

It is possible to identify a direct link between the statutory adoption of public function type tests and privatisation policies and to view public function tests as a deliberately chosen potential counterweight to such policies or at least as a judicial means to regulate 'government' as constituted in its new post-privatisation forms. The clearest evidence can be found in the UK White Paper that preceded the HR Act 1998. It explains that the definition of what constitutes a public authority is in deliberately wide terms and includes within its scope:[10]

> to the extent that they are exercising public functions, companies responsible for areas of activity which were previously within the public sector, such as privatised utilities.

There is a sense, here, of preserving the judgments made prior to the reforms about what should be regarded as 'public' and as subject to human rights norms. As we shall see this is potentially problematic even when the test is taken to refer to the immediate historical past.

[9] As I write this we are entering a new phase of nationalisation of banks sparked by the credit crisis. I do not attempt to look ahead to how administrative law is likely to adjust to these new developments.

[10] *Rights Brought Home: The Human Rights Bill* CM 3782 24 October 1997 at para 2.2. See also the speeches by the Home Secretary, HC Deb, 16 February 1998, col 773; 17 June 1998, cols 409–10.

The earlier text on which much of the UK HR Act was modelled (including its application provisions)[11] is the NZBOR Act. The White Paper commentary to the New Zealand Bill of Rights proposal links 'public function' much less directly to privatisation and understandably so given its timing. The White Paper was published in 1985, the year after the fourth Labour Government came into power and it furthered a promise in Labour's election manifesto to put a proposal for a bill of rights to the people. The same manifesto made *no* mention of the momentous economic reforms that were to come during the Labour Government's time in power, but it is hard to imagine that those future reforms would not also have been in the minds of at least some of the framers of the Bill proposal as it emerged post-election. The State-Owned Enterprises Act 1986 which provided the mechanism by which to corporatise and thence privatise various parts of the state sector would be passed in just the following year. Because of this timing, ascertaining the relationship between the economic reforms and the New Zealand proposal for a bill of rights is harder to do.

It is possible to argue a case that the liberal and state-limiting values the Bill of Rights espoused and the values that spawned economic liberalisation shared a great deal in common.[12] At the time, however, there did not appear to be any broad political commitment within the Labour Cabinet or caucus to the Bill of Rights as part of the wider package of economic reform. Rather the Bill of Rights was presented to the public as a distinct constitutional reform driven by the personal commitment of the then Minister of Justice and Deputy Prime Minister Geoffrey Palmer, a dynamic and determined US trained lawyer-academic turned politician.[13]

The White Paper itself describes New Zealand as no longer a nineteenth century state 'limited in its functions'[14] but as a:[15]

> large intrusive State which regulates the economy and provides extensive welfare services, which undertakes extensive public works and provides education, which is heavily involved in health services and in subsidising or supporting a great range of private activity… .

[11] The proposed section 2 (eventually enacted as section 3) stated):
This Bill of Rights guarantees the rights and freedoms contained in it against acts done
(a) by the legislative, executive, or judicial branches of the government of New Zealand; or
(b) in the performance of any *public function*, power or duty conferred or imposed on any person or body by or pursuant to law (emphasis added).

[12] R Hirschl, 'The Political Origins of the New Constitutionalism' (2004) 11 *Indiana Journal of Global Legal Studies* 71 at 105.

[13] P Rishworth, 'The Birth and Rebirth of the Bill of Rights' in G Huscroft & P Rishworth (eds) *Rights and Freedoms* (Wellington, Brookers, 1995) at 12.

[14] *A Bill of Rights for New Zealand* (1985) AJHR A6 at 29 [*White Paper*].

[15] Ibid at 30.

Although some of the Bill's supporters may have shared a sense with the economic reformers of 'the state as the problem', there is no hint here that the 'massive and growing role of the State'[16] the White Paper describes is about to be brought to an end (or even to a pause).

The White Paper goes on to explain that under the public function test, the Bill of Rights:[17]

> will apply to bodies which are essentially private in nature, but in which have been vested certain public functions. Examples would include the New Zealand Law Society and other professional bodies which exercise statutory public disciplinary powers over their members in the public interest.

There is a connection here to the statutory reforms that had extended the availability of review to sporting and disciplinary bodies around that time, but the example does not indicate that privatisation and contracted-out services were directly in mind.[18]

The public function test, as formulated in the New Zealand proposal, appears to have had its intellectual origins, instead, in the US state action doctrine. The commentary refers exclusively to US case law defining which bodies are covered by the US Bill of Rights. The list includes the judges applying the common law (*New York Times v Sullivan*,[19] enforcement by a court of the common law of defamation); the exercise of other forms of judicial power (*Shelly v Kraemer*,[20] the issue by a court of an injunction to enforce a racially restrictive covenant to which only private individuals are parties); racially discriminatory practices of a private company town (*Marsh v Alabama*[21]); and the discriminatory practices of a private company that provides a basic service such as electricity (*Jackson v Metro Edison*[22]). The White Paper suggests that what these examples have in common is that 'the action can be seen as having a public character in some substantive sense even though the actor is not a public body.'[23]

Mention of the *Jackson Edison* case is the most direct indication that public utilities—soon to be corporatised and then privatised—were considered potentially to be covered by the Bill of Rights provisions. These examples go even further. However much we might be prepared to concede that the common law *already* contains anti-discrimination principles these cases contemplate a much more robust rights-protecting common law than we would usually recognise.

[16] Ibid at 30.

[17] Ibid at 46–47.

[18] The reforms were prompted by the reports of the Public and Administrative Law Reform Committee: see Sir R Cooke, 'The Public and Administrative Law Reform Committee: The Early Years' (1988) 13 *New Zealand University Law Review* 150; J Farmer, 'The Work of the Public and Administrative Law Reform Committee' (1988) 13 *New Zealand University Law Review* 155.

[19] 376 US 254 (1964).

[20] 334 US 1 (1948).

[21] 326 US 501(1946).

[22] 419 US 345 (1974).

[23] *White Paper*, above n 14 at 70.

They envisage human rights constraints on matters usually thought of as within the private sphere.[24] The proposal seems to offer a 'level playing field' of regulation between public and private spheres but, in contradistinction to the ideology that was growing in dominance at the time, a level-playing field that would be based on public rather than private law norms.

In terms of this narrow exposition of the legislative history then, it is possible to mount an argument that public function tests were 'intended' to fill a regulatory gap left by privatisation policies (at least where human rights were concerned). Given the timing, the case is stronger in relation to the United Kingdom than New Zealand. Of course, that cannot be the end of the matter. Parliament speaks with a forked tongue. At the same time Parliament was passing legislation (and executive government was taking executive action) restructuring, privatising, and contracting out various matters. Moreover, all of these changes took place at a time when the background norms of public choice theory and institutional economics, also originating out of the US, had achieved a certain currency in governmental circles.[25]

Public choice theory provided the justification for economic liberalisation, contracting out and privatisation. Its technical programme of reform did not overtly appear to threaten administrative lawyers' values. Indeed public choice theorists spoke a similar language of institutional reform and raised administrative law issues about transparency, accountability and instrument choice.[26] Power would be decentralized and put at arms' length from elected officials. Legislation associated with command and control methods of regulation would be replaced by contractual methods of governance. Publicly owned assets would be divested to corporations. Direct control would be taken away from politicians. Self-regulation would be preferred.

The normative underpinnings of public choice theory present a challenge to values at the very heart of the public law project. Its bleak critique is that every one acts in his or her individual self-interest, hence politicians and bureaucrats are incapable of representing the 'public interest'. Indeed, if such a thing exists, the 'public interest' is merely the aggregation of individual preferences and is most reliably expressed in the market.[27] Public choice theorists would not acknowledge there is anything distinct about public morality (and hence public

[24] See the discrimination and 'right to exclude' cases in which Mike Taggart has been particularly interested such as *Wood v Leadbitter* (1845) 13 M & W 838; 153 ER 351; *Constantine v Imperial Hotel* [1944] 1 KB 693; *Forbes v New South Wales Trotting Club Ltd* (1979) 143 CLR 242 (HCA).

[25] D Osborne and T Gaebler, *Reinventing Government: How the Entrepreneurial Spirit is Transforming the Public Sector* (Reading Mass, Addison-Wesley Publishing Co, 1992); P McAuslan 'Public Law and Public Choice' (1988) 51 *Modern Law Review* 681.

[26] JL Mashaw, *Greed Chaos and Governance: Using Public Choice to Improve Public Law* (New Haven, Yale University Press, 1997).

[27] I have put this crudely: scholars broadly within the public choice tradition have questioned whether democratic choice and consumer choice should be treated as equivalents within public choice theory.

law)—there are only private preferences. If any norms were to be proliferated within the new structures they would be private law rather than public law norms.

However favourably one is inclined to read the legislative history,[28] given these diverse background ideologies, a search for the statutory intention alone cannot resolve the issue of how judges and officials ought to operate the public function test. In any event, we cannot assess what the public function tests ask of judges and officials until we have a sense of what was the position prior to privatisation.

Novel Questions

When the public function tests enacted in section 6 of the HR Act 1998 are examined within the broader context of British administrative law, we will begin to appreciate just how novel and potentially far-reaching they are.[29] Section 6 makes it unlawful for a 'public authority' to act incompatibly with human rights (subsection (1)) and defines a public authority as 'any person certain of whose functions are functions of a public nature' (subsection 3(b)). It also applies the same prohibition to 'any body which is not a public authority but certain of whose functions are of a public nature, save in respect of a particular act if the nature of that act is private' (subsection (5).[30] These formulations are hardly straightforward and have been elaborated in the case law. Effectively they: (1) oblige all of the core parts of government to comply with human rights in all their activities; and (2) subject some bodies who are not otherwise public authorities to observe rights when they are exercising public functions.[31] These are separate but related matters and both are striking in their own ways. I shall consider them in turn.

[28] See Lord Bingham (dissenting) in *YL v Birmingham City Council* [2007] UKHL 27 at para 20 [*YL*].

[29] The test contained in the New Zealand Bill of Rights Act 1990 section 3 differs in its formulation but the basic approach is the same.

[30] I am borrowing from Lord Bingham's formulation in *YL*, above n 28 at para 3.

[31] See *Aston Cantlow v Wallbank* [2004] 1 AC 546 where a distinction was made between core public authorities which must always act compatibly with the Human Rights Convention and hybrid public authorities to which a functional test applies (see Lord Nicholls at paras 7–12 and Lord Hope at paras 35–38 and especially at 38 where he decides that the functional test does not apply to core public authorities); Baroness Hale in *YL*, above n 28 at para 37. See further D Oliver, 'Public Authorities and Public Functions Under the Human Rights Act' [2000] *Public Law* 476 and 'Functions of a Public Nature under the Human Rights Act [2004] *Public Law* 329; P Cane, 'Church, State, and Human Rights: Are Parish Councils Public Authorities' (2004) 120 *Law Quarterly Review* 41–48.

a) *All* Activities of Public Authorities Subjected to Human Rights Norms

In this first respect, Canada, New Zealand and the UK have each taken the same approach: *everything* done by *core* government is subject to (legislatively protected) human rights constraints.[32] This represents an important break with other parts of public law as it stood at the time the instruments were adopted. Up until that time, functional type tests had been applied to the 'core state' in order to identify the zone of the state's private or commercial life where public law norms or immunities would not enter.

One of the earliest examples of attempts to make a distinction in British law between the commercial and trading activities of the state and its 'sovereign functions' can be found in relation to the East India Company.[33] In 1839 the Company was described by Tindal CJ as having two-fold powers by Charter and statute 'to carry on trade as merchants, and (subject only to the prerogative of the Crown...) power to acquire and retain and govern a territory, to raise and maintain armed forces by sea and land, and to make peace or war with the native powers of India.'[34] He was echoing a discussion that appeared earlier in the Committee debates on the Regulating Bill 1773. Lord North who was promoting the Bill and its measures to increase ministerial control of the Company emphasised 'that military and civil commands should be separate from the commercial'.[35] We get a sense from the proceedings that there was something new and experimental in Lord North's proposed distinction. Contemporaries on the other side of the debate, such as Laurence Sulivan, argued that no such line could or should be drawn. He refused to make a distinction between 'commands' and 'commercial' activities, arguing that 'executive authority' was indispensable to the Company for the exercise of its commercial activities. The native population, he said, would 'never part with their money but by compulsion'.[36] While the passage of the Bill did go some way to achieving North's objectives,[37] (significantly it declared all the Company's extensive property acquisitions to belong to the Crown) the controversy about whether the Crown's sovereign and trading powers

[32] Their Lordships in *Aston Cantlow* above use the expression 'core public authorities'.

[33] By contrast the French Companies had never been as distinct from or independent of the state as the English and Dutch—perhaps reflecting their respective views of the state. French companies were described by Grewe as the 'artificial products of a clearly conceived political will of [the] State' and as lacking in the individualistic spirit of enterprise of the English and Dutch: WG Grewe, *The Epochs of International Law* (Berlin, Walter De Gruyter, trans Michael Byers, 2001) at 301.

[34] Per Tindal CJ in *Gibson v East India Company* (1839) 5 Bing NC 262.

[35] HV Bowen, *Revenue and Reform: The Indian Problem in British Politics 1757–1773*, (Cambridge, CUP, 1991) at 179. Debate of 2 June 1773.

[36] Ibid.

[37] This was the first of a series of Acts that foretold the Company's eventual dissolution. It was followed by the 1784 India Act, the 1833 Act which put an end to the Company's trading, and eventually the 1958 Government of India Act which transferred the government of India from the Company to the Crown and the army to the service of Her Majesty.

should be separated continued into the early nineteenth century.[38] By mid-nineteenth century the distinction had been accepted both politically and legally. The courts demonstrated an increasing willingness to treat trading and sovereign functions differently—sometimes treating the actions of the company as the exercise of delegated political powers or acts of state[39] and sometimes treating the company as a private contractor or owner.[40] The reason for making the distinction was important: an act of state attracted immunity or, in some cases, *parens patriae* jurisdiction over individuals dying intestate.

British legislation and case law in the later nineteenth and early twentieth centuries appears to reflect a slight shift in attitudes toward the distinction between public or sovereign and commercial functions. This may have been the consequence of a steady increase in collectivist policies and legislation from the middle of the nineteenth century.[41] The Public Authorities Protection Act 1893 UK, for example, signalled a certain blurring of the understanding of the distinction between sovereign and commercial powers. It extended immunity to 'a municipal corporation (or other public body) as a trader, provided it does not trade for profit'. The controversy was focused on what 'for profit' meant. Although 'for profit' trading enterprises were clearly excluded from the immunity even when public utilities were claiming to be acting in the interests of the public,[42] it was less clear what approach should be taken to activities operated in a commercial manner but whose profits were applied to the reduction of rates.[43] Some kind of 'nature of the power' test was also contemplated by the statute.[44] To attract immunity under the Act, the impugned activity performed by the public authority was not required to be undertaken in pursuance of a statutory

[38] James Mill was an important proponent of such a separation: R Harris, *Industrializing English Law: Entrepreneurship and Business Organisation 1720–1844* (Cambridge, Cambridge University Press, 2000) at 205–6.

[39] *Doss v Secretary of State for India in Council* (1875) 19 Eq 509; *Nabob of the Carnatic v East India Co* (1793) 2 Ves Jun 56; *Secretary of State for India v Kamachee Boye Sahaba* [1859] 7 Moore's Indian Appeals 476, 19 ER 388 (PC); [1869] 13 Moore 22 15 ER 9. See also the argument in *Attorney-General v Brodie* [1846] 4 Moore's Indian Appeals 190, 18 ER 671 about whether the Crown or the East India Company could exercise *parens patriae* power in India.

[40] *Moodalay v East India Co* (1785) 1 Bro Ch C 469; *Government of Bengal v Mussamat Shurruffutoonissa* [1860] 8 Moore's Indian Appeals 225, 19ER 516; *Gridhari Lall Roy v Bengal Government* [1868] 12 Moore's Indian Appeals 448, 20 ER 408.

[41] The 'welfare state' as a label was commonly applied only from 1940 but in fact welfare reforms and the expansion of state activities in Britain began long before: D Fraser, *The Evolution of the British Welfare State* (London, Palgrave Macmillan, 3rd edn, 2002). This was after a period of laissez-faire that did not exist to the same extent in New Zealand or Canada.

[42] *Attorney-General v Company of Proprietors of Margate Pier and Harbour* [1900] 1 Ch 749.

[43] *The Ydun* [1899] P 236 at 240; *Parker v London City Council* [1904] 2 KB 501; *Lyles v Southend Corporation* [1905] 2 KB 1.

[44] CS Emden, 'The Scope of the Public Authorities Protection Act 1893' (1923) 39 *Law Quarterly Review* 341 at 349–54.

authority, but it was required to be imposed 'from without' rather than self-imposed. The Courts apparently accepted this legislative reform 'with hesitation.'[45]

Another example of shifting attitudes to whether a functional distinction between governmental and commercial activities could be made can be found in the law of state immunity. From 1880 the English common law operated an absolute doctrine of state immunity. All activities of government would be immune from legal process in foreign courts. Britain resisted pressure for a more restricted form of state immunity until the mid-twentieth century when the distinction between trading and governmental purposes began to reassert itself—a development that can be traced to the US law and practice surrounding sovereign immunity (and no doubt a reaction to the increasing involvement of foreign governments in commercial activities).[46] A foreign state's procedural immunity from suit came to be restricted to its governmental and not its commercial activities.[47] These tests followed the form rather than the substance or purpose of the transaction[48]: even if such dealings were in pursuance of public purposes they were treated as having a private character.[49]

A similar approach began to be taken around the same time in relation to public corporations that administered nationalised industries. For the purpose of determining whether a privilege applies, a statutory presumption operated that a commercial corporation acts on its own behalf and not as an agent of the Crown even when it is controlled by a government department.[50]

Such examples involve the question of whether state immunities or privileges should apply to commercial functions. The functional distinction is used here to restrict the availability of immunities and privileges in order to proliferate *private* law rather than public law norms. The cases should cause us pause to reflect on the thinness of our public law norms until relatively recently. Importantly, the reason why the state is allowed to engage in activities to which private law norms apply is not in order to preserve the state's 'autonomy' but rather to limit its autonomy, to ensure it does not gain an unfair advantage over private companies and in some cases to enhance its efficiency. What about the different question (closer to our case) of whether public law norms, such as administrative law remedies, should be extended into the private sphere—and where the private party's autonomy *is* presumably at stake?

[45] Ibid at 346. See also the interesting discussion about whether the Act was intended to give immunity to natural persons or corporations at 342–43.

[46] For a full discussion see H Fox, *The Law of State Immunity*, (Oxford, Oxford University Press, 2002) at 128ff [Fox, *State Immunity*]. *Rahimtoola v Nizam* [1958] AC 379 (upholding the absolute rule); *The Philippine Admiral* [1977] AC 373 (PC) (restrictive); *Trendtex Trading v Central Bank of Nigeria* [1977] QB 529 (CA). The State Immunity Act 1976 also effected a change to the absolute rule.

[47] *Trendtex Trading v Central Bank of Nigeria* [1977] QB 529 (CA).

[48] Section 3(1) State Immunity Act 1976 (UK).

[49] Fox, *State Immunity*, above n 46 at 198.

[50] *Tamlin v Hannaford* [1950] 1 KB 18.

Judicial review cases have never *directly* asked the question whether the decision or decision-maker was essentially 'public' or 'commercial'. Rather the question was framed in terms of whether the disciplines and remedies of judicial review should apply to a particular decision and decision-maker. In the first part of the twentieth century, at least, the legal tests associated with judicial review were suffused with questions about whether a decision-maker had a 'duty to act judicially' or had a 'statutory source of power'.[51] In the case of the latter, contractual and prerogative sources of power were not regarded as reviewable. Such tests may have provided a partial proxy for 'publicness' but did not, and were never intended to, determine the scope of what was 'public'. Indeed, judicial review tended to treat some matters going to the very heart of what was 'public' as unreviewable and/or non-justiciable.

Important turning points occurred in *R v Criminal Injuries Compensation Board ex parte Lain*[52] and *R v Panel on Mergers and Take-Overs, ex parte Datafin plc.*[53] The first appeared to signal that the source of the power (in this case the prerogative) would no longer necessarily be decisive. The second finessed the traditional source of power test by adding a public function element. In *Datafin* Lloyd LJ suggested that at one extreme are those cases involving statutory power, which *are* reviewable, and at the other extreme are those cases involving contractual sources of power, which *are not.* But:[54]

> in between these extremes is an area in which it is helpful to look not just at the source of the power but at the nature of the power. If the body is exercising public law functions, or if the exercise of its functions have public law consequences, then that may… be sufficient to bring the body within the reach of judicial review.

There are two important things to note about this case for our purposes. The first is that source of power still matters. According to Lord Lloyd's formulation, core public authorities exercising 'purely' contractual powers remain unreviewable. To this day the law remains unsettled as to the reach of administrative law remedies when governments are engaged in commercial contractual undertakings.[55] A zone of private life still seems to be preserved for the state in administrative

[51] Atkin dictum in *R v Electricity Commissioners, ex parte London Electricity Joint Committee Co* [1924] 1 KB 171 (CA). See further D Mullan, *Administrative Law* (Toronto, Emond Montgomery, 5th edn, 2003) at 1095.

[52] [1967] 2 QB 864 (CA).

[53] *Datafin*, above n 1.

[54] Ibid at 847 per Lloyd LJ.

[55] See, eg, *Shell Canada Products v Vancouver (City)* [1994] 1 SCR 231; *Mercury Energy Ltd v Electricity Corporation of New Zealand* [1994] 1 WLR 521 (PC); *Lab Test Auckland v Diagnostic Med Lab* [2008] NZCA 385. Of course the courts have traditionally been more prepared to intervene in domestic tribunal type cases notwithstanding that the source of power was contractual—see further D Mullan, 'Administrative Law at the Margins' in M Taggart, *The Province of Administrative Law* (Oxford, Hart, 1997) at 134, and in cases which are not 'purely contractual' eg, *Phipps v Royal Australian College of Surgeons* [1999] 3 NZLR 1 (CA); cf *Petrocorp Exploration Ltd v Minister of Energy* [1991] 1 NZLR 1 (CA) 641 (PC).

law—based, if not strictly on a distinction between commercial and governmental functions, then at least on the contractual source of power under which such commercial functions are undertaken. The second is that this case effectively extended at least *some* of the remedies of judicial review to a private or quasi-private body—based on the public nature of the function that it was performing.[56] It was the first case to do that. We shall return to this in a moment.

At the time of the enactment of the public function tests in the HR Act and NZBOR Act, the concept of public function had largely been used to delimit the extent to which the government enjoyed immunity in certain of its activities. It was not the function but the source of power that determined whether administrative norms applied to particular activities of core government. The tests as stated in the 1990 and 1998 Acts heralded a significant change in approach: the core parts of government are no longer entitled to a 'private life' (at least where human rights are concerned) regardless of whether they are contracting or engaged in commercial dealings. That is a significant move on a question about which the common law has historically waxed and waned for more than 150 years. It is a question about which administrative law remains uncertain.

Although Canada has rejected the use of a public function formulation for the purpose of spreading human rights norms to the private sector, it too has taken the approach that the core parts of the state are restricted by the Canadian Charter of Rights and Freedoms [the Charter] in all of their activities—whether commercial or governmental. To get a sense of the extent to which this signals a sea change compare the statement of Lloyd LJ in *Datafin* with the approach of La Forest J, in a 1997 case responding to the argument that the Charter should not apply to government when it engages in activities that are 'private, commercial, contractual or non public in nature':[57]

> We no longer expect the government to be simply a lawmaker in the traditional sense; we expect government to stimulate and preserve the community's economic and social welfare. In such circumstances, government activities which are in form "commercial" or "private" transactions are in reality expressions of government policy, be it in the support of a particular region or industry or the enhancement of Canada's overall international competitiveness. In this context, one has to ask: why should our concern that government conform to the principles set out in the Charter not extend to these aspects of its contemporary mandate? To say that the Charter is only concerned with government as law maker is to interpret our Constitution in light of an understanding of government that was long outdated even before the Charter was enacted.

We ought to pause here. This represents an important moment for public law. A government cannot choose to be treated in law as a private person by the choice of contract as its preferred legal instrument (at least where human rights are concerned). In another case La Forest J puts the point even more directly: 'To

[56] *Mercury Energy Ltd v Electricity Corporation of New Zealand* [1994] 1 WLR 521 (PC).

[57] *Eldridge v British Columbia* (1997) 3 SCR 624 at para 40, per La Forest J.

permit government to pursue policies violating Charter rights by means of contracts and agreements with other persons or bodies cannot be tolerated.'[58] Public law norms administered by judges, and not the executive state itself, should decide how the government is legally manifested in any particular transaction. It is law that defines the state rather than the other way around. We are a long way from an Austinian conception of the state as merely coercive power here.

There is a possibility that this 'moment' may also have a flow-on effect on the scope and application of administrative law remedies more generally. Certainly cases involving the government in its contractual dealings seem to be arising more frequently.[59] But the challenge for administrative law is perhaps greater than for human rights norms: administrative law grounds of review were initially designed for judicial decisions and then extended to administrative decisions. Can they actually work in a commercial setting? Leaving aside ideological commitments, are they (to use current management speak) fit for the purpose of containing commercial power?[60] Preliminary indications from the courts are that in situations where commercial decisions are subject to administrative law norms then only *some* of the grounds of review will apply—a mix and match approach will be taken.[61] Human rights norms, by contrast, have a more universal flavour and raise different issues. Indeed, certain human rights (such as to be free from unlawful imprisonment, trespass and so on) have always applied to public and private actors alike without reference to a public/private distinction of any kind.

b) Private Bodies Performing Public Functions

If prior to the Human Rights Act we have not treated everything done by the government as a public function, we are on very shaky ground indeed in attempting to use a public function analysis to extend public law norms to private bodies. It would be so much easier to extend human rights to the private sector under such a test if prior to privatisation everything done by the government had been considered public. Such a conception has never been a fixed part of the common lawyer's mental framework. There have long existed more refined common law doctrines that impose disciplines on commercial undertakings such as the concept of common callings and 'businesses affected with a public interest'.[62] Significantly, these older doctrines are not premised on a functional analysis that looks backwards to what government used to do.

[58] La Forest J in *Douglas/Kwantlen Faculty Assn v Douglas College* [1990] 3 SCR 570 at 585.

[59] See above n 55.

[60] M Aronson, 'A Public Lawyer's Responses to Privatisation and Outsourcing' in M Taggart (ed), *The Province of Administrative Law* (Oxford, Hart, 1997) 40.

[61] See above n 55.

[62] M Taggart, 'Public Utilities and Public Law' in PA Joseph, *Essays on the Constitution* (Wellington, Brookers, 1995) at 214.

Unsurprisingly, the courts have found the tests in section 6 very difficult to operate in practice and judges seem to have divided along fairly predictable lines. A recent case to reach the House of Lords has explicitly addressed privatisation practices (broadly construed). It is a case involving the contracting out by a local authority of elderly residential care services to a private for profit care home (pursuant to a statutory obligation to make provision for care in a mixed economy). I do not wish to consider *YL v Birmingham City Council* in any great detail here except to outline the kinds of problems that the analysis has raised in general terms.[63]

The dissenting judges, Baroness Hale and Lord Bingham, start where this paper started—with the political context and background to the public function test.[64] They focus on the subject matter of what has been contracted for and consider whether the government historically assumed such a function. They take the view that the state has accepted a welfare responsibility for the elderly for over 60 years, and continues to do so by providing funds for those who cannot pay.[65] They see section 6 as providing a means by which public law continues to operate despite privatisation and contracting out, and as a regulatory counterweight, and additional safeguard, against such policies. Public law norms trump the private law form of the transaction.

The majority of the House of Lords find that a private care home operating as a commercial entity for profit, without direct public funding[66] or special statutory powers, is not a private body exercising a public function for the purposes of section 6. The judges resort to familiar forms of common law and judicial review analysis.[67] They all place emphasis on the contractual source of the home's obligation to deliver care.[68] Lord Scott's analysis is particularly striking. In answer to the question of how it could be that the functions of a local authority in operating its own care homes could unquestionably be of a public nature while the operation of the same functions by a privately owned care home could not, he resorts to a source of power test. The local authority carries out its tasks

[63] [2007] UKHL 27 [YL]. See further S Palmer, 'Public, Private and the Human Rights Act 1998: An Ideological Divide' (2007) 66(3) *Cambridge Law Journal* 559; M Elliott, '"Public" and "Private" defining the Scope of the Human Rights Act' (2007) 66(3) *Cambridge Law Journal* 485; A Williams '*YL v Birmingham City Council:* Contracting Out and "Functions of a Public Nature"' (2008) 4 *European Human Rights Law Review* 524; J Landau, 'Functional Public Authorities After *YL*' [2007] *Public Law* 630 and for earlier commentary see R Drabble, 'Public Authorities and the Human Rights Act' (2006) 11 *Judicial Review* 38; H Quane, 'The Strasbourg Jurisprudence and the Meaning of a "Public Authority" Under the Human Rights Act' [2006] *Public Law* 106; P Craig, 'Contracting Out, the Human Rights Act, and the Scope of Judicial Review' (2002) 118 *Law Quarterly Review* 551.

[64] Baroness Hale quotes the same passage from the UK White Paper above n 10 (*YL* above n 63 at para 54).

[65] Lord Bingham, above n 63 at para 20.

[66] Some of the patients, including the claimant, received funding as an individual subsidy—a matter the dissenting judges, Lord Bingham and Baroness Hale, emphasised.

[67] Lord Neuberger regarded it as relevant that a private care home would not be susceptible to judicial review, above n 63 at para 160.

[68] Lord Neuberger, above n 63 at para 133.

pursuant to statutory powers and duties (that are, therefore, imposed by public law), and the private care home carries out its tasks pursuant to powers and duties imposed by tort and contract (making it private).[69] Of the majority judges Lord Mance at times gets closer to attempting to define the substance of what is a public function: actual provision of care is not a public function but the arranging for such provision *is* inherently public.[70]

For the majority there is already a sufficient regulatory scheme in place—both provided by the state in its general regulation of care homes and by contract law. Indeed, for Lord Mance, the extensive general regulatory system already in place is indicative of the private nature of the enterprise.[71] The contracts, between the local authority and the care home and between the care home and the resident, each impose an obligation on the care home to observe Convention rights. This might have been interpreted as an indication that the state wished to delegate its Convention obligations to the care home and to enlist the courts via the public function test in section 6 Human Rights Act as an additional mechanism for the enforcement of such obligations. The majority did not consider that approach—contracts would be governed by contract law causes of action. There would be no mixing of public and private law. They should be kept procedurally distinct even when they both address the issue of human rights.

Finally, all of the judges struggle with the methodology here, which seems to force a determination of the status of the function *a priori* without reference directly to the rights at stake. This leads to 'all or nothing' determinations of whether a function is public or private—the kind of determination that, in my view, is uncongenial to the common law way of thinking. The majority, for example, is concerned that if a care home is found to be performing a public function here then its managers and nurses would be considered a public authority for all other purposes.[72] Conversely, Baroness Hale, in the dissent, is concerned that if a care home is not found to be exercising a public function here then it will not be considered to be doing so when it is detaining particularly vulnerable patients receiving treatment for psychiatric orders, or feeding and toileting patients at the same time.[73] A search for 'public function' in the abstract is not something that common lawyers are used to: it is the legal rights and obligations that a person or body enjoys that determines the moral contours of legal persons and not the other way around.[74] The US public function cases, listed in the New Zealand Bill of Rights White Paper, do not go about the business of determining function in that way. All but two of the cases listed, involve the

[69] Above n 63 at para 29. For Lord Neuberger the existence of a statutory power is not necessarily determinative of whether the function is public but is a very powerful factor (para 167).

[70] Above n 63 at para 115.

[71] Above n 63 at para 116. See also Lord Scott at para 32.

[72] Above n 63 at para 30 per Lord Scott.

[73] Ibid at para 69.

[74] HLA Hart, 'Definition and Theory in Jurisprudence: An Inaugural Lecture Delivered Before the University of Oxford on 30 May 1953' (Oxford, Clarendon Press, 1953).

fourteenth amendment equality provisions and concern the extent to which racial discrimination provisions apply in the private sphere.[75] Starting with the rights themselves may lead to a much more fruitful analysis.

We common lawyers have never faced the question of what is a public function or indeed, of what is the state, as an abstract matter, and we have scant resources with which to do so. We are locked into old habits of mind that may not work as well in modern contexts into which continental approaches to the state are increasingly intruding. In the next section I explore how, even at the point of nationalisation in the twentieth century, administrative lawyers avoided the issues surrounding the functions of the state and conducted their discourse instead within the contours of parliamentary sovereignty.

A Crisis Posed by Privatisation?

In a sense the chickens may only now be coming home to roost as far as the common law is concerned. French administrative lawyers confronted the question of whether the state was able to enjoy a private life in the early twentieth century at the stage at which the state first began to expand its functions. That is not to say that the French necessarily have all the answers in relation to issues of contracting out, but they begin with a more settled notion of what 'public functions' may comprise.[76] In France it was nationalisation that provoked a crisis about the theory, functions, and rationale for the state. Duguit felt compelled to reinterpret the nature of the state to accommodate these new functions. He argued that the state could engage in commercial activities but in so doing it should be regarded as the 'the provider of a public service, regulated by public law' rather than as a private person governed by private law.[77] He added:[78]

> The concept of public service was, therefore, instrumental in articulating the need for the socialization of the state with the maintenance of its authority and of the specificity of public law.

Cecile Laborde suggests that in Britain, during the same period, there was no need to embark 'upon a basic rethinking of the *nature* of the state'.[79] The

[75] For extremely helpful analyses see S Gardbaum, 'The Horizontal Effect of Constitutional Rights' (2003) 102 *Michigan Law Review* 387, and P Rishworth, 'New Zealand Taking Human Rights into The Private Sphere' in D Oliver and J Fedtke (eds) *Human Rights in the Private Sphere: A Comparative Study* (London, Routledge-Cavendish, 2007) at 312 ff.

[76] See, eg, J-B Auby, 'Comparative Approaches to the Rise of Contract in the Public Sphere' [2007] *Public Law* 40.

[77] C Laborde, 'The Concept of the State in British and French Political Thought' (2000) 48 *Political Studies* 540 at 546 [Laborde, 'Concept of the State']. I am grateful to Mike Taggart for this reference.

[78] Ibid.

[79] Ibid at 553.

extension of state functions in the early twentieth century did not create anything like the crisis in Britain as it had in France because:[80]

> in the absence of a single discursive idiom about "the state", legal and institutional questions tended to be kept distinct from enquiries about the moral and social functions of the state. Furthermore, in the absence of a strong distinction between the state and society, the blurring of the frontier between public and private brought about by state intervention was hardly seen as a threat to the specificity of the state, in the way it was for Duguit and his contemporaries.

How exactly was the nationalisation debate transacted in Britain and what might that reveal about the intellectual resources that were and are available to administrative and common lawyers?

a) Nationalisation

Laborde is no doubt correct to suggest that in Britain there was an absence of a 'single discursive idiom' that combined legal discussions about the state with discussions about its proper moral and social aspects during this time. Austinian positivism and its separation of morals and law had a pervasive influence in that respect. (Exactly why this is so, given the unpopularity of Austin during his lifetime and the important work of the British idealists and pluralists, is a question for another time.) That is not to deny, however, that in Britain there *was* a dominant discursive idiom in which the debates about statehood were transacted (also imposed by way of Austinian positivism). Issues about statehood were collapsed into a single but restrictive language of parliamentary sovereignty. The Idealist TH Green had predicted that the Austinian emphasis on sovereignty would overwhelm any prior discussion of the moral and political claims to 'statehood' on which that sovereignty was based.[81] Mark Francis suggests that his prediction was borne out: the sovereignty question was to become 'the graveyard of political philosophy' in British political thought.[82]

The contemporary political and legal commentary tends to confirm that the processes of nationalisation and expansion of state functions did not spark equivalent 'legal' crises in Britain or in the wider Commonwealth to those provoked in France. The arguments that did take place were conducted, as Green had predicted, within the rubric of Parliamentary sovereignty. Remarkably, even Sydney and Beatrice Webb's *A Constitution for the Socialist Commonwealth of Great Britain* (1920)[83] was infected by the sovereignty question. Anticipating that

[80] Ibid.

[81] TH Green *Lectures on the Theory of Political Obligation*, (London, Longmans Green, reprinted 1941) first delivered in 1879 and published after his death in 1882 at 136–37. Green himself has been criticised for his obsession with coercion.

[82] M Francis, 'The Nineteenth Century Theory of Sovereignty and Thomas Hobbes' (1980) *History of Political Thought* 517 at 531.

[83] London, Longmans, 1920; new edition Cambridge, Cambridge University Press, 1975.

if all power including industrial power, were to be ultimately vested in Parliament (as they advocated) there would be a potential threat to individual rights, they proposed that there ought to be two Parliaments—one political and the other social.[84] Much later (1949), Tawney the left-wing historian would somewhat ruefully reflect on his belief in sovereignty: 'The evil legacy of suspicion left by capitalism … cannot be wound up by the sections of an Act of Parliament.'[85]

As Mike Taggart's work has shown, in the first half of the twentieth century, constitutional and administrative lawyers from both the left and right, believed unwaveringly in Parliamentary sovereignty.[86] Though Lord Hewart would suggest that the dominance of the executive in Parliament, the concomitant expanding power of bureaucrats, and the growth in the use of regulatory powers, was a manipulation or *misuse* of sovereignty, he did not contest its central tenets. Lawyers on the left such as John Willis may have railed against Hewart's formalism but Willis '[l]ike Hewart, but for very different reasons, [ ] was uncritical of Parliamentary sovereignty.'[87] After all, parliamentary sovereignty (and the delegated legislation it authorised) would become the vehicle for effecting his preferred policies—the growth of the administrative state and (importantly for our purposes) the spread of state functions. Left and Right would argue about the detail in established and shared terms. Should Ministerial responsibility apply to statutory corporations?[88] Is parliamentary control of delegated legislation to be preferred to judicial control? Should statutory presumptions operate to protect the individual against collectivist legislation (and, if so, is that on Parliament's behalf or against Parliament's intention)? The use of legislation, including legislation conferring broad powers to the bureaucracy, advisory boards and tribunals, as the legal means to give effect to collectivist ends, would ultimately win the day.

Parliamentary legislation would also be the focus of novel concerns and modes of analysis by which the new administrative lawyers would differentiate themselves from the constitutional lawyers of the nineteenth century. They would be interested in 'institutions' in ways in which Anson and AV Dicey of the previous century never were.[89] Legislation, viewed as a means by which to attack the

[84] Ibid, discussed in R Kelf-Cohen, *Twenty Years of Nationalisation* (Edinburgh, Macmillan St Martin's Press, 1969) at 20–25 [Kelf-Cohen, *Twenty Years*].

[85] Quoted in R Kelf-Cohen, ibid at 13, from an essay 'Social Democracy in Britain, R Hinden (ed) *The Radical Tradition* (London, Allen & Unwin, 1964) 163.

[86] M Taggart, 'From 'Parliamentary Powers' to Privatization: The Chequered History of Delegated Legislation in the Twentieth Century' (2005) 55 *University of Toronto Law Journal* 575.

[87] J Willis, *Parliamentary Powers of English Government Departments*, 2nd ed (London, Pitman, 1957) at 584.

[88] The Haldane Committee on the Machinery of Government 1918 (A Committee of Inquiry on the Post Office Cmd 4149/1932 H M Stationery Office) reported against the institution of a system of administrative boards saying that: 'there should be no omission of the ordinary responsibility to Parliament of all state undertakings' (as reported by WA Robson in, 'The Progress of Socialization in England' (1932–1933) 11 *Foreign Affairs* 501 at 503 [Robson, 'Progress of Socialization'].

[89] Although Laborde is correct to suggest that for the most part 'legal and institutional questions tended to be kept distinct from the moral and social functions of the state' (Laborde, 'Concept of the

laissez-faire tenets of the common law, would be the life spark of the new administrative law project for such leading figures as J Willis, W I Jennings, WA Robson, J G Griffith and H Street.[90] It was statute and not the common law that would save us all—and that meant not only contemporary legislation, but legislation that had been enacted in the previous century for public health and housing and had been systematically ignored by both public and private teachers and scholars of the law.[91] The debates about nationalisation illustrate some of these broader phenomena.

Nationalisation (sometimes called socialisation) took place in several stages and was not solely the post World War Two (Labour Party) phenomenon it is often now thought to be. Indeed, public ownership of industry in the United Kingdom began with municipalities in the late nineteenth century (giving rise to the immunity provisions in the Public Authorities Act 1893). Gas and Water supply was always owned by local authorities and electricity was publicly owned relatively early.[92] The two World Wars saw the state take extensive powers over economic life and the establishment of the early examples of public corporations. There was a marked degree of continuity in the structure and rationale for the boards established to distribute food, munitions, and other supplies during and between the wars and those established to run the newly nationalised industries post World War Two.[93] The 'socialisation' movement was particularly active between the wars.[94] Even by 1933, Robson suggested that 'All the old simple and clear-cut lines between private ownership and public provision seem useless as a guide'.[95] A more practical working out of the Webbs' proposal during that time

State', above n 77 at 553), even an interest in institutions was a relatively new development for the common lawyer. See WI Jennings, WA Robson, ECS Wade, 'Administrative Law and the Teaching of Public Law' [1938] *Journal of the Society of Public Teachers of Law* 10 at 10 [Jennings, Robson and Wade, 'Administrative Law'].

[90] See for example J Willis, 'Three Approaches to Administrative Law: The Judicial, The Conceptual, and The Functional' 1 *University of Toronto Law Journal* 53 (1935–1936) at 60; WI Jennings, 'Administrative Law and Administrative Jurisdiction' 20 *Journal of Comparative Legislation and International Law* (1938) 99 at 111–31 which discusses at length the legislative framework governing sewers and public health and how the judges made a 'mook o' that' (at 131); Jennings, Robson and Wade, 'Administrative law', above n 89 at 11, about the slowness of public law teachers to respond to the important legislative changes of the late nineteenth century eg, the Public Health Acts 1865 and Housing Acts 1867 and how these had altered the common law; and JG Griffith and H Street, *Principles of Administrative Law* (London, Pitman, 1957) esp ch 1.

[91] WI Jennings, WA Robson and ECS Wade, ibid.

[92] The Electricity Act 1882 (UK) declared that electricity franchises would revert to local authorities after an initial period of 21 years. See further, R Kelf-Cohen, *Twenty Years,* above n 84 at 17.

[93] See, for example, JC Hanson, 'The Wartime Crown Companies of Canada' (1950–51) 4 *University of New Brunswick Law Journal* 24. The Canadian Crown Companies were modelled on the UK companies (at 25) and served as a 'buffer between the cabinet and entrepreneurs' (at 26).

[94] Robson, 'Progress of Socialization', above n 88 at 509. WA Robson describes the situation in 1933 thus: 'At the present time England quite clearly stands between capitalism and socialism' and rather than using the term 'nationalization of the means of production' refers to the 'socialization of the means of production' (ibid at 502).

[95] Ibid at 509.

was that the regulation of publicly controlled services would be separated from the general machinery of Parliamentary responsibility of the traditional kind. Hence Robson contrasts the 'old' nationalised industries such as the Post Office to which ministerial responsibility still attached with the 'new' forms of 'socialised' industries such as the BBC which was 'conducted by a public corporation acting as trustees for the national interest' and which enjoyed considerable independence from the traditional 'British Constitutional system'.[96] This included independence from Parliamentary control in its day-to day management, self-contained finance, and separate terms of pay, promotion, and recruitment.[97] Robson claims that these were attempts institutionally to 'divorce the administration of economic functions from the ordinary political or 'police power' activities of government.'[98] Later commentators, writing in 1944, however, would regard the form taken by these semi-autonomous public boards in the inter-war years, as 'due more to accident' than design rather than as a prototype for the independent boards that were to come.[99] Only later would commentators attempt to explain the different categories of boards, their organisation and their levels of independence from Parliament.[100] It would be fair to say that nationalisation was a creeping phenomenon, and its implementation a rich blend of ideology and pragmatism.[101]

It was indeed the institutional framework on which the lawyers focused in relation to nationalisation. But the debate was framed narrowly. The issues ranged between whether there should be public ownership or some degree of public control—and not over whether public ownership should be chosen over normal private enterprise.[102] The idea of public function or public service played a very limited role in the debate. Indeed, what is most striking to a modern eye is that the arguments for nationalisation near the beginning of the twentieth century were almost exactly the same as the arguments for corporatisation and privatisation near its end. The discussions about the governance of nationalised industries by statutory boards raised issues about the need for industry as compared with civil service expertise, how best to achieve efficiency, how to hold bodies financially accountable while freeing them from the strictures of the Treasury,[103] and how to hold them politically accountable without politicians

[96] Ibid at 502, 507.

[97] Ibid at 507.

[98] Ibid at 511.

[99] HRG Greaves, 'Public Service Boards' 7 *Modern Law Review* 25 (1943–1944) at 25 quoting TH O'Brian.

[100] W Friedmann, 'The New Public Corporations and the Law' (1947) 10 *Modern Law Review* 233 (Part I); 377 (Part II) [Friedmann, 'New Public Corporations'].

[101] The source of that ideology was the Fabian Society formed in 1883–84. Its members Sydney and Beatrice Webb worked tirelessly for the cause of public ownership.

[102] DN Chester, *The Nationalisation of British Industry 1945–51* (London, Trinity Press, 1975) at 20 [Chester, *Nationalisation*].

[103] J McEldowney, 'Nationalization and Privatization' in R Blackburn (ed) *Constitutional Studies: Contemporary Issues and Controversies* (London, Mansell, 1992) at 42–64 [McEldowney, 'Nationalization and Privatization'].

interfering with their day to day running.[104] Friedmann's work is the best attempt to categorise the different levels of autonomy they enjoyed. He distinguishes between public corporations 'designed to run an industry or public utility according to economic and commercial principles but in the public interest' and social service corporations 'designed to carry out a particular social service on behalf of the Government'[105] and categorises the detailed variations in Ministerial involvement, financial oversight, appointment practices and so on.

Then as later, bold claims, without any supporting evidence, would be made in the debates about how a change of ownership would promote greater efficiency, reduce production costs and make commodities cheaper for the public and would also inject much needed capital investment. The only element that was present in the nationalisation debates and not as prominent in the debates about privatisation was the issue of the need for coordination—especially in relation to the railways, and in the Bank of England's need for a close relationship with the Treasury.[106] Significantly, in contrast to our time, the forms of governance and accountability or even control chosen for the various industries were never used explicitly as indicia that the functions were themselves more or less public (even as the forms differed for commercial as opposed to social service enterprises).[107] The form of governance itself did not determine the 'public nature of activity'. The public importance of such activities was simply the unarticulated starting point. Expressions such as 'the public interest' and the pursuit of 'public policy' were used.[108]

This sense of shared public interest, not requiring articulation or justification, almost certainly can be attributed to the collective experience of two World Wars and the solidarity that experience had engendered. Discussions about which accountability regimes to apply to the boards created to run the newly nationalised industries took as their uncontested starting point that such activities affected the public interest, and then proceeded to consider how much ministers should be able to interfere or hold such boards to account. The question of 'what is a public function', if it had been asked at all, had been answered by politics. The legal focus was on how best to deliver goods and services not whether there was something public about what such corporations were trying to do. At least where

[104] JES Fawcett, 'Legal Aspects of State Trading' 25 *British Year Book of International Law* 34 (1948); HRG Greaves, 'Public Service Boards' 7 *Modern Law Review* 25 (1943–44), WA Robson; 'The Progess of Socialization in England' 11 *Foreign Affairs* 501 (1932–33); J Carlisle Hanson, 'The Wartime Crown Companies of Canada' 4 *University of New Brunswick Law Journal* 24 (1950–51); Friedmann, '] New Public Corporations', above n 100 at 377; J McEldowney, 'Nationalization and Privatization' above n 103 at 42–64.

[105] W Friedmann, 'New Public Corporations', above n 100 Part I at 237.

[106] Chester, *Nationalisation*, above n 102 at 16.

[107] The only place I have found 'public function' referred to is W Friedmann, 'New Public Corporations', above n 100 Part II at 379, where he suggests that the public function of statutory corporations for commercial purposes overshadows its private form—but this is in the context of his suggestion that they equally should not be legally identified with the Government.

[108] W Friedmann, ibid, Part I at 237.

public corporations were concerned, the question about whether judicial control would be preferred to political control did not even make it onto the political agenda.[109]

British nationalisation processes did not create a crisis for public law thinking and neither did they provoke debate in the abstract about the nature of public functions. In typical fashion the debate revolved around the proper role for Parliament and pragmatic utilitarian concerns about which particular institutional forms 'would work' best.

b) And Privatisation?

Of course in some respects privatisation processes have raised the same questions as nationalisation about the proper scope for parliamentary intervention and oversight, sub-delegation, how to make bodies accountable, the proper extent of executive power, and parliamentary versus judicial forms of accountability. As deregulation has given way to a new era of re-regulation, it is still the case that the choice is between public ownership and public regulation and not between public and private ownership. It is now commonly thought that regulation imposed by statute or statutory instrument may often better ownership as a form of control.

Some matters, however, are harder now to analyse through the familiar prisms of public law. While contractual powers may be authorised and even regulated by statute, the details of regulation by contract and relating to the contracting out of functions, circumvent many of the hard won *ex ante* parliamentary controls which were the response of earlier lawyers to delegation and subdelegation. Statutorily imposed public function tests are particularly novel in that they seem to suggest an *ex post* regulatory role for the courts: Parliament could even be regarded as having abdicated the question of principle of what should be regulated as 'public' to the courts—making this a question not of politics but of law—a reversal of the position under nationalisation. Parliament at once has authorised the disaggregation of the state through privatisation and contracting out and some kind of *ex post* re-aggregation of the state through statutory tests of public function. *That* conflict cannot be resolved by resort to notions of parliamentary sovereignty. Neither can it be resolved through a resort to formalism—the public function tests seem to suggest that form should not be decisive. An act can be 'public' notwithstanding the source and origins of the power, and authority of the decision-maker or actor. That seems to be predicated on an assumption that there is something inherent as a matter of substance rather than form in the notion of the 'public': something we never decided at the point at which the state expanded its functions.

[109] AC Page, 'Public Law and Economic Policy; The UK Experience' (1982) 9 *Journal of Law and Society* 225 at 246.

Conclusion

Nationalisation did not create a crisis in public law thinking. Indeed, it may have been part of the making of it in the common law tradition. Nationalisation, and the related expansion of state functions, spawned a new, creative and exciting period of administrative law in contradistinction to constitutional law and its unhelpful formalist obsession with separation of powers, and to the common law and its laissez-faire norms. Privatisation, at the end of the century, by contrast, has a much stronger claim to have given rise to a crisis for common law administrative lawyers and scholars—if perhaps, given recent events, a relatively temporary one. Mike Taggart's work has made a leading contribution to exploring the challenges it has posed for traditional administrative law. The role and nature of the state has become an issue for administrative lawyers in a way that it has not before.

Public function tests encapsulate important aspects of that challenge. Judicial decisions are increasingly split or inconclusive and there is a welter of scholarship about the public and private distinction as judges and academics take to their political corners. It may be an exaggeration (and un-Anglo-Saxon) to say that the public lawyers are facing a crisis about how to approach the question of how to conceive of the state—but there is at least a discernible angst—not least because that now seems to have become *their* task. There is a way forward that has the potential to provide a more fruitful analysis and to reflect habits of the common law mind. That is to begin not with concepts of statehood and its functions but rather with the rights themselves —thence can the common law state be defined.

11

A History of the Modern Jurisprudence of Aboriginal Rights – Some Observations on the Journey So Far

P G MCHUGH

IN THE LATE 1970s and early 80s a group of scholars began encouraging national courts of Canada, then Australasia, to recognize the common law basis of tribal claims to the ownership of lands traditionally used and occupied by them. Until then the courts had mostly regarded the Crown's dealings with the tribes and their land as non-justiciable and at its discretion as a form of 'political trust'. The Australian fiction of *terra nullius* was then the extreme formulation of that hands-off position. Whatever rights tribes held *qua* tribes came from statute.[1] In all those loyalist jurisdictions this was the received position institutionalized throughout the branches of national government and the embedded position that the aboriginal title argument challenged.

At that time common-law aboriginal title was primarily an academic enterprise, mostly the effort of a small group of lawyers led by Brian Slattery followed by those connected to him and the College of Law at the University of Saskatchewan, namely Kent McNeil and myself joined by Richard Bartlett in the early 1990s. The exception was the historian Henry Reynolds, whose attention was on Australia and where, eventually, his professional situation as historian-advocate rather than lawyer was to get him into stormy conditions we lawyers never struck.

[1] For example M Hickford in 'John Salmond and Native Title in New Zealand: Developing a Crown Theory on the Treaty of Waitangi, 1910–1920' (2007) 38 *Victoria University of Wellington Law Review* 853.

By the mid-1990s – and especially after Australia's breakthrough case *Mabo No 2* (1992)[2] – common-law aboriginal title had become a frequent subject of academic comment.

To be sure, during the 1980s there were other legal scholars concerned with the plight of tribal peoples. These tended either to focus on the question of how the legislative power might be used beneficently to assist tribes cope in a modern capitalist economy and polity,[3] or else they were tribal sovereigntists of a radical CLS outlook, some of them indigenous scholars or others with close association to them. That scholarship accepted that the courts' refusal to get involved in Crown-tribe relations was embedded and irreversible, the sovereigntists using that as a platform for more radical arguments sometimes of a separatist character. Indeed, these self-styled radicals were the fiercest critics of the common-law exhortation when it appeared. They were scornful of its moderating aspect and dubbed some of its advocates 'organic intellectuals' of white colonialist hegemonic dominance.[4] The criticism was that the argument for common-law aboriginal title failed to take into account the inherently exploitative and dispossessory role of law in the colonialist setting and that its objectionable foundational premise was the exclusive sovereignty of the Crown.

One also sensed the radical lawyers resented the trespass of what was essentially conciliatory legal scholarship onto a patch they had staked in association with the land-rights militants of the early 1970s. They saw their association with the tribes as a strategic alliance in support of a radical agenda. Tribes, of course, are not single purpose entities but a variegated group composed of all ages, dispositions, and beliefs, knitted together by kinship and custom. During the 1990s some radicals deserted the tribes as they turned from oppressed victims in need of counsel and succour into wannabe capitalists and showed they were as faction-prone as most other associations of human beings (the left wing most exemplarily). 'Tribal capitalism' was acquiring pejorative overtones.

During the 1980s common-law aboriginal title was an idea whose proverbial time had come. It invoked principles of constitutional and property law that were familiar and persuasive, without reliance upon legislative processes that did not

[2] *Mabo v Queensland* [No. 2] (1992) 175 CLR 1 (HCA).

[3] The classic example is the article by K Lysyk 'The Unique Constitutional Position of the Canadian Indian' (1967) 45 *Canadian Bar Review* 513, which first appeared as a commissioned first part of a chapter in the Hawthorn Report (H B Hawthorn (ed) *A Survey of the Contemporary Indians of Canada: a report on Economic, Political, Educational Needs and Policies* (Ottawa, Queen's Printer, 1966) volume 1, chapter 12). The federal Government commissioned this research report from the University of British Columbia, where a kiwi anthropologist, Harry Hawthorn who had studied with Malinowski, oversaw the project. See the retrospective and comment of Alan Cairns (who wrote the second half of the chapter) that the Lysyk article concentrated almost entirely on the federal and provincial fields of legislative competence: 'Kenneth Lysyk, the Hawthorn Report, and "The Unique Constitutional Position of the Canadian Indian"' (2005) 38 *University of British Columbia Law Review* 275 at 277.

[4] See the account in P Havemann, '"The Pakeha Constitutional Revolution?" Five Perspectives on Maori Rights and Pakeha Duties' (1993) 1 *Waikato Law Review* 53.

seem interested in progressing beyond the recent trend towards ensuring the norm of non-discrimination applied to tribe members. The regimes legislated in the 1970s gave indigenous peoples equality as individual citizens outlawing discrimination on grounds of race but did not authorize or validate their 'aboriginal' position as first nations holding collective rights. Certainly there was a rose tint in the work of the leading aboriginal-title protagonists, myself most especially perhaps. It was a common-law idealism that made the radical wince, and that from this distance now seems somewhat naïve. Until that time the lead discipline for aboriginal studies had mostly been anthropology. By the early-mid 1980s it was clear that the lawyers were arriving. Ten years later, as a new century loomed, 'lawfare' dominated tribal affairs.

The aboriginal-title scholarship that was maturing during the 1980s into a distinct inter-jurisdictional corpus did not come from nowhere. It originated in Canada during the early 1970s. Early versions appeared in an influential chapter in the second edition of Cuming and Mickenberg's *Native Rights in Canada* (1971), and the powerful and pioneering advocacy of Thomas Berger taken up by the Supreme Court judgments in *Calder* (1972),[5] especially the dissent of Justice Hall.[6] Most take *Calder* as the key moment for its judicial reception in Canada along with the injunction in favour of the Cree Nation against the James Bay hydro project (1972). However, in *Calder* acceptance was obiter and no other major court case followed for several years until the rather under-fleshed first instance judgment in *Baker Lake* (1978).[7] Also, in those early cases the argument for legal recognition was raw and not in the taut engagement with the method of the common law brought by Slattery. The earliest version tended to draw compositely upon a mishmash of sources ranging through Spanish publicists of the sixteenth century, a reinvention of the nineteenth-century Marshall cases on Indian title and status, and African appeals to the Privy Council on tribal property. The argument from those sources was the simple proposition that at (common) law the property rights (*dominium*) of the tribes survived the Crown's acquisition of the territorial sovereignty (*imperium*) of their territory.

In his celebrated Oxford PhD dissertation (1979) Slattery presented the argument in scholarly common-law style, marshalling the authority meticulously. He explained the juridical basis of the principle of 'modified continuity' – the legal principle that the proprietary aboriginal title continued but was rendered inalienable other than to the Crown. He also set out the historical origin and legal basis of the Royal Proclamation (1763) as another, though independent, juridical foundation for the aboriginal title. His dissertation was 'published' by

[5] *Calder v Attorney General of British Columbia* [1973] SCR 313.

[6] And see the comment of K Lysyk, 'The Indian Title Question in Canada: An Appraisal in the Light of *Calder*' (1973), 51 *Canadian Bar Review* 450, who contributed a chapter to the Cuming and Mickenberg book.

[7] *Hamlet of Baker Lake v Minister of Indian Affairs* (1979) 107 DLR (3rd) 513 (FCTD). See also the dicta in *Mathias v Findlay* [1978] 4 WWR 653 per Berger J at 655. Justice Berger was a notable proponent of Indian rights, acting as counsel for the Nisga'a Nation in the *Calder* litigation.

the Native Law Centre at the University of Saskatchewan, where he was briefly Director of Research, and was already in considerable circulation and acclaim by the time I became his Masters student in 1980.

In Canada by the time of the Constitution Patriation Controversy (1981–82) the momentum of aboriginal title was growing, moved by the cumulative push of *Calder*, the James Bay injunction (and negotiations) and *Baker Lake*, Brian's dissertation, the *Guerin* litigation in Vancouver,[8] and the evident feeling spreading through the legal profession that this nascent 'doctrine', as it was being termed, held some (though still uncertain) traction. That, together with the enforcement of prairie treaty rights under the Natural Resource Agreements statutorily recognized under the Indian Act, gave substance to the political arguments of Indian representative organizations during the Controversy. These groups claimed that the patriation of the British North America Act 1867 with an entrenched Charter of Rights and Freedoms exposed their statutory and emergent common-law rights to the possibility of casual extinguishment. Prime Minister Trudeau's original package had not been drawn up with their consent or involvement and made no provision for those rights. Although the Indian organizations lost in the courts,[9] the spectre of their legal rights – however inchoate – and the claim that under his original package they were being rendered highly vulnerable were enough to convince the Prime Minister to include section 35 in the Canada Act, 1982, as a mollifying gesture. The wording, with its protection of '*existing* aboriginal and treaty rights' signalled the belief that those rights were not of a particularly extensive order. This was a political miscalculation on a par with the New Zealand Government's when it inserted section 9 into the State Enterprises Act 1986. Both these provisions subsequently gave the courts the platform for more interventionist legalism than the executive branch had contemplated at the time of concession.

Kent McNeil and I were essentially disciples of Brian Slattery, both of us following his example by completing Oxbridge PhDs and building upon his work. Kent constructed common-law aboriginal title in terms of the key proprietary concepts of possession and occupation and the book that followed[10] has rightly become a classic text frequently cited by Anglo-Commonwealth courts, as indeed was Brian's work. In 1980, as part of my Master's degree research, Brian suggested I try to 'make sense' of the New Zealand cases on Maori customary property rights. The result was a rather jejune essay published by the Native Law Centre in 1982, by which time I had commenced doctoral research in England. It was followed by the publication in 1984 of two papers written the year before as

[8] This culminated in *Guerin v The Queen* [1984] 2 SCR 335.

[9] *Manuel v Attorney General* [1982] 3 All ER 822 (CA); *R v Secretary of State for Foreign and Commonwealth Affairs, Ex p Indian Association of Alberta* [1982] QB 89 (CA).

[10] K McNeil *Common Law Aboriginal Title* (Oxford, Clarendon Press, 1989).

Cambridge Research Fellowship audition-pieces.[11] My father, then Deputy Chief Judge of the Maori Land Court, copied those to Chief Judge Ed Durie at a time when the reform of the Fisheries Act 1908 was in the offing. At one stage it seemed likely that the 1908 statute's recognition in section 77(2) of 'Maori fishing rights' would not be replicated in the new Act. It was a provision that had anyway been narrowly limited to statutory rights expressly conferred on Maori, of which there were virtually none.[12] However, having seen my papers in draft form, Chief Judge Durie sought – and obtained – the continuance of a version of the old section, which appeared as section 88(2) of the Maori Fisheries Act 1983. This provision echoed – one suspects deliberately – the wording of Canada's section 35 in exempting '*existing* Maori fishing rights' from statutory regulation. The evident belief (and, again, miscalculation) was that this exemption was limited in the way that the courts had already been describing: The possibility of common-law rights did not surface publicly until 1984 and they were soon used in defence to a prosecution under the new Act. In the *Te Weehi* case (1986), Justice Williamson quashed the conviction of a Maori exercising customary fishing rights on the basis of unextinguished common-law rights that did not amount to a claim to exclusive ownership (non-territorial rights).[13]

By 1986, then, the common-law argument was also running in New Zealand where it had found quick acceptance.[14] To some extent its contemporary scope was thought to be limited because of the comprehensive transmutation of the original native title into Maori freehold land. Further, legislation since the early twentieth century had made that title unenforceable against the Crown – a negation of property rights the newly-received doctrine was now vilifying as unconstitutional. At the time it was thought that any residual native title rights were limited to vestigial fisheries around the coastline, and, soon after, that these rights were covered in the Maori fisheries settlement of September 1992 (the 'Sealords Deal').[15] This meant that the historical claims processes under 'Treaty

[11] 'Aboriginal title in New Zealand courts' (1984) 2 *University of Canterbury Law Review* 235; 'The legal status of Maori fishing rights in tidal water' (1984) 14 *Victoria University of Wellington Law Review* 247. And also 'Maori Fishing Rights and the North American Indian' (1985) 6 *Otago Law Review* 62.

[12] *Waipapakura v Hempton* (1914) 33 NZLR 1065; *Inspector of Fisheries v Ihaia Weepu* [1956] NZLR 920; *Keepa and Wiki v Inspector of Fisheries* [1965] NZLR 322. For a history of the law affecting Maori fisheries see Waitangi Tribunal *Report of the Waitangi Tribunal on the Muriwhenua Fishing Claim* (Wai.22, 1988), chapter 6.2.

[13] *Te Weehi v Regional Fisheries Officer*, [1986] 1 NZLR 680.

[14] See the historical account in D V Williams 'Customary rights and Crown claims: *Calder* and other Canadian contributions to the revival of the doctrine of aboriginal title in Aotearoa New Zealand', A paper prepared for 'Let Right Be Done: *Calder*, Aboriginal Rights and the Treaty Process: Looking Forward, Looking Back' November 2003, University of Victoria, BC (online at <http://www.law.uvic.ca/calder/Papers/David%20Williams.pdf)> Also dicta in the Court of Appeal: *Te Runanga O Muriwhenua v Attorney General* [1990] 2 NZLR 641 and *Te Runanga o Te Ika Whenua Society v Attorney-General* [1994] 2 NZLR 20.

[15] By the Deed of Settlement the Crown agreed to fund Maori into a 50/50 joint venture with Brierley Investments Ltd to bid for Sealord Products Ltd (New Zealand's biggest fishing company) holding 27% of the New Zealand quota resource. 20% of the new species quota was also promised as

principles' dominated the direction of the New Zealand jurisprudence. For Maori, issues of land loss pressed more insistently than those surrounding land retention. This right to pursue historical claims was incorporated into two key statutes passed by the Fourth Labour Government[16] that soon spilled into court and enabled the Court of Appeal to prioritize historical claims settlement processes as matters of national (and constitutional) importance in a series of *Maori Council* cases (1987–91).[17] The common law argument thus receded in prominence until it resurfaced with a vengeance in the foreshore and seabed controversy (2003–5).

By the beginning of the 1990s, Australia was the remaining major loyalist jurisdiction where common-law title had not been recognised, although by then the *Mabo* litigation was in train. For many of us, it was not a question of if but when that judicial step would occur. The surprise, often outrage, that *Mabo No 2* ignited in Australia was remarkable: had not the Australian legal community noticed the Canadian and New Zealand pattern and seen it coming? Nonetheless, the ferocity of its reception – its sheer momentousness – almost instantaneously gave birth to a popular and scholarly literature that quickly surpassed the other jurisdictions in breadth, intensity and fury.

The Commonwealth responded with the passage of the Native Title Act 1993, which attempted controversially to house the inchoate common-law right inside a statutory process that enabled interim use of the land and established a judicial mechanism for ascertainment of title. An antipodean pattern was set by which major court decisions on native title, perceived as pro-tribal and potentially (too) far-reaching, resulted in legislation designed to contain that reach. This recurred twice, and on both later occasions perhaps more combustibly, after the High Court of Australia's *Wik* decision (1996)[18] and the foreshore and seabed case *Ngati Apa* (2003) in the New Zealand Court of Appeal.[19] On those occasions the legislation brought formal international attention to both countries, scrutiny that rankled the executive branch, particularly the Howard Government in Australia. As these legislative regimes were being imposed, tribal representatives and their supporters invoked the rule of law. They argued that their resort to the courts was

well as greater representation of Maori on statutory bodies on fisheries management. The Maori Fisheries Commission was to be restructured and named the Treaty of Waitangi Fisheries Commission, making it more accountable to Maori and giving it more input to fisheries management. The settlement was legislated as Treaty of Waitangi (Fisheries Claims) Settlement Act 1992.

[16] Treaty of Waitangi Amendment Act 1985 extending jurisdiction of Tribunal to consider historical claims; State Enterprises Act 1986 section 9.

[17] For an account of the impact of these cases, including the role of the late Sir Robin Cooke, see PG McHugh '"Treaty Principles": Constitutional Relations Inside a Conservative Jurisprudence' (2008) 38 *Victoria University of Wellington Law Review* 39.

[18] The Native Title Amendment Act 1998 (Cth) was based upon Prime Minister Howard's so-called 'Ten Point Plan', which, in turn, was ostensibly in response to *Wik Peoples v State of Queensland* [1996] HCA 40, although it is believed that the case provided the excuse and the changes were anyway in the pipeline.

[19] The Foreshore and Seabed Act 2004 (NZ) passed in the aftermath of *Ngati Apa v Attorney-General* [2002] 2 NZLR 661 (HC); [2003] 3 NZLR 643 (CA).

being short-circuited, or at least statutorily abridged, in a manner that pared their rights to the least rather than the most generous that might have ensued through court-led development. This argument was difficult to rebut; although the caution of courts in all three jurisdictions during the final years of last century and early in the new suggested they would not continue to demonstrate the boldness and sensitivity to tribes' claims that the breakthrough cases had seemed to promise a decade earlier. However, that later judicial retrenchment was not an expectation at the time the antipodean governments decided to legislate over the important court judgments. In this, there was more than a whiff of executive wariness, if not distrust, of the judicial branch.

Canada never embarked upon a course of pouring the common-law aboriginal title into a statutory regime. It did not expedite the process of legal articulation by erecting statutory mechanisms of title ascertainment. By 1985 the federal government had (finally) set a comprehensive claims policy and there were numerous negotiating tables. The key judgments after *Guerin* (1981)[20] were *Sparrow* (1990),[21] the so-called *Van Der Peet* trilogy (1996),[22] and *Delgamuukw*[23](1997). Canadian jurisprudence drew a distinction between aboriginal *title* and *rights*. The former represented entitlement to an exclusive title whereas aboriginal rights signified distinct stand-alone rights (possibly in bundles) not amounting to exclusive ownership. The Supreme Court of Canada issued separate tests for title and rights, tying itself into ever more complex knots, and avoiding key juridical concepts accepted as core Down Under (in particular, a continuity test acknowledging that aboriginal title protected extant rights rather than exhumed them as they were centuries ago at the time of Crown sovereignty). Academic commentators tracked this erratic pattern with frustration yet cleaved to a distinctly Canadian form of rights-fetishism, urging the Court back in the 'right' (that is, pro-aboriginal) direction. For them it was all a matter of good rights-design and the hope remained that the Court would eventually get it right. Lately that disposition, a child surely of the Charter culture, has begun to ease off. Brian Slattery is now describing the common-law spectrum as generative, meaning that rights-design is an ongoing generative project accomplished by a combination of court decision and negotiation between government and tribe.[24] The realization is that the courts cannot be expected to form those rights entirely by themselves and through the haphazard and often fact-specific iterative course of litigation.

Of course, the judges probably did not expect that such a heavy onus of doctrinal development would be placed upon them institutionally and in such concentrated circumstances, with all the expectations and dashed hopes that later

[20] *Guerin v The Queen* [1984] 2 SCR 335.

[21] *R v Sparrow* [1990] 1 SCR 1075.

[22] *R v Van Der Peet* [1996] 2 SCR 507; *R* v *Smokehouse* [1996] 2 SCR 672 and *R* v *Gladstone* [1996] 2 SCR 723.

[23] *Delgamuukw v British Columbia* [1997] 3 SCR 1010.

[24] B Slattery 'The Generative Structure of Aboriginal Rights' (2007) 38 *Supreme Court Law Review* (2d) 595; 'Aboriginal Rights and the Honour of the Crown' (2005) 29 *Supreme Court Law Review* 433.

came from their performance of this task. They faced it squarely, though not always consistently, nor, as the tone of many judgments made plain, patiently. The breakthrough cases had been intended to give the tribes new leverage in their dealings with governments and the judicial hope – often expressed quite overtly – had been that the claims would be resolved by negotiation and settlement rather than litigation. Commentators spoke of these claims as 'polycentric' and inherently unsuited to the zero-sum resolution of the adversarial process.[25] Nonetheless, whilst the commencement of negotiated and agreement-led settlements and the formation of very considerable bureaucratic structures to run them was certainly an outcome of the breakthrough cases, resort to judicial process had now become a tactic (as well as a gamble) in government-tribe relations.

The structures and formats for government-to-tribe dialogue, designed as they were to facilitate eventual settlement, compounded ongoing and deep, fundamental issues in those relations even as the rhetoric of 'new beginnings' blasted from the early 1990s on. These structures might be statutory (as housed in Australia's Native Title Act in particular the Indigenous Land Use Agreement or New Zealand's Foreshore and Seabed Act) or extra-statutory (New Zealand's historical-claims settlement processes, Canada's comprehensive- and specific-claims resolution machineries). Yet all re-inscribed the tribes' historical experience of the Crown as formless, as a row of changing faces difficult to pin down. To them the Crown was a mysterious officialdom whose political commitment to agreement, movement even in that direction, was difficult to gauge much less trust. Frequently that be-suited bureaucracy of the Crown was itself under-incentivised internally in terms of careers stuck on the treadmill of aboriginal claims. These officials' negotiated to sketchy remits and held limited capacity to sway (much less commit) ministers worried by the electoral impact of concessions to the tribes. If anything for the tribes, the evident sincerity and integrity of those officials and their personal commitment towards fair agreements aggravated rather than ameliorated the Crown's semblance of slipperiness.[26] An upward ratcheting of antagonism was a consequence that the common-law scholarship of the 1980s had not contemplated.

Nonetheless, that scholarship had aimed for the resurgence (or, in Australia, the commencement) of a political relationship between the Crown and tribes. The breakthrough judgments rightly regarded themselves as setting that stage. Whilst it was never thought that the courts' involvement would stop with those cases, academic attention never contemplated the path of future doctrinal development. The emphasis had been upon establishing the basic common-law principle of 'modified continuity.' The scholarship indicated that the articulation

[25] E Colvin, *The Resolution of Indian Claims* (Saskatchewan, The Native Law Centre, 1981).

[26] See, for example, J McLean, 'Crown Him With Many Crowns: The Crown and the Treaty of Waitangi' (2008) 5 *New Zealand Journal of Public and International Law* 35.

of that continuity would have to incorporate the tribes' customary law but did not travel into the detail much beyond that. And it was in the detail that the devil was later shown to lurk.

Legal scholarship on aboriginal peoples' rights was, then, in a formative phase by the mid-1980s. The two basic approaches were either radical or concentrated upon the common law. The breakthrough cases transformed and enlarged the scholarship, bringing law into dramatic prominence, but now also spreading across a range of disciplines. Tribes were now entering the rights-place and the scholarship broadened encompassing much more than the specifically legal. By the early 1990s several distinct pathways were appearing, all of which crisscrossed one another.

One specifically legal pathway of development has been identified already. This was the judicial amplification of the common law aboriginal-title property rights. More and more, this left behind the features of public-interest litigation to become more evidently the proprietary paradigm it had always declared itself to be. In all jurisdictions, academic commentary on this became commonplace, its tone at the end of the century largely disillusioned as the courts struck a note of caution, if not conservatism. In Australia and New Zealand the housing of the common-law rights inside statutory mechanisms augmented that process of judicial articulation. And, of course, governments and tribes began negotiating and settling rather than awaiting or relying upon the bench. Contract (confirmed by legislation) thus defined the respective rights as much as courtroom.

Another important path opened from the supposition that the enjoyment of legally cognisable rights supposed a competent rights-holder. As tribes faced the prospect of major asset revestment, governments insisted not unreasonably that if these assets were formally to be in tribal ownership, there should be in place effective rights-management and governance regimes. It was one thing for the legal system to allow representative actions on behalf of the tribe as a collectivity of changing membership united by kinship and custom and for the Crown to enter into negotiations with such a fluid body (though mandating became a more pressing issue in the new century). It was another to expect that amorphous legal being to hold and manage valuable assets from the public weal. Tribal governance became an issue of the 1990s and after. Constitution-building gripped the tribes and upwrenched their politics. Tribes, if they were not to be left behind in the division of the new riches, were required to leave the compass of the purely customary for the brave new world of textual constitutionalism. Custom was supplanted by codes of leadership, membership, financial reporting, voting rights and the like. In all tribes this process caused friction both internally and in their relations with governments (especially when template regimes were imposed or threatened[27]). As this happened, and following the longstanding lead

[27] In Canada, the First Nations Governance Bill 2002 [died on the Order Paper 2003], much like New Zealand's short-lived Runanaga Iwi Act 1990 [repealed 1991], established template though interim corporate forms for tribes yet to reach settlement. In Australia the Native Title Act established

of the Harvard Project in the United States, tribal governance became a new area of academic interest,[28] particularly in Australia where the orientation of the literature has always held a more practical character (and the politics a more impelling momentum) than the rights-fetishism of the Canadian.

Though these areas of legalism lay downstream from the breakthrough judgments, much of the elaboration occurred through processes outside the courtroom. Comprehensive land-claims settlements and governance involved matters that the adversarial process itself could not address directly other than as vague over-spilling from the fact-specific setting of the case at bar. If there are rights, there must be rights-bearers, the identification of whom will necessitate administrative structures, perhaps presided over by the state or perhaps from within the group itself. In determining who's in and who's out, these processes will themselves be subject to potential court review, certainly procedurally and maybe substantively. And once you are forming a better idea of the composition of the rights-bearing group there will be issues refining the nature of the right(s) they hold, this occurring usually at first by means of bureaucratic initiative in the absence of court guidance that later may confirm or unseat that essential anticipation (or second-guessing). And there will the relativities of the group right *inter se* and with other rights-bearers (such as gender, environment, municipalities). Downstream such questions awaited.

The legalism that pervaded aboriginal affairs from the mid-1990s might be expected from application of a proprietary paradigm with asset-management issues, be the ownership derived from common-law aboriginal title, historic claims settlement (New Zealand) or on-reserve gaming operations (the United States). Another focused on the development of international law, a distinct and increasingly important orbit of post-breakthrough legalism not considered here. The juridical habilitation of the tribes in North America and Australasia gave impetus to the claims of indigenous peoples at international law, emboldening tribal representatives from those jurisdictions to push – successfully after a decade – for United Nations acknowledgement. Prompted by the emergent municipal and international jurisprudences and spurred by the settler states' evident willingness (as activated by the courts) to recognize a distinct corpus of 'aboriginal rights', there appeared a wider literature and broader fields of scholarly enquiry. I turn to that now.

* * *

requirements of a Prescribed Body Corporate (PBC). New Zealand's FSA likewise establishes governance entity requirements as a prerequisite to conferral of either territorial or non-territorial coastline rights under the Act. These imposed governance requirements have been most unpopular and certainly in Australia their operation has been problematic.

[28] See now the important dissertation by K Gover, 'Constitutionalizing Tribalism: States, Tribes and Membership Governance in Australia, Canada, New Zealand and the United States' (JSD Dissertation, NYU, 2007).

The issue of tribal self-government had always been at the heart of aboriginal sovereigntist literature of the 1980s and after. The proprietary paradigm of the common law that had argued successfully for tribal *dominium*, seemed to rule out, as the sovereigntists emphasised, any residual *imperium*. The common-law aboriginal title was juridically founded on the arrival of feudal tenure with Crown sovereignty, burdening that with the tribes' *dominium*. As Australia's Prime Minister John Howard often remarked during the 1990s, self-management, the consequence of *dominium*, was not the same as self-government. By the late 1980s the Diceyan notion of absolute indivisible Crown sovereignty was under siege in all common law jurisdictions as an outdated, if not obsolete, Victorian construction of the state's constitutional authority. Influential scholars, like McNeil, had intellectual sympathy with the tribes' claims to residual sovereign status. With recognition of the tribal *dominium* achieved, there was a push to extend the common law towards an *imperium* as well. No common-law court made that step.[29] Provision for aboriginal self-government was left to the policy agenda of the executive branch and argumentation to the aboriginal and academic worlds.

Nonetheless, after the breakthrough judgments, and as international law began developing norms during the 1990s,[30] the tribes' claims to self-determination became the central thread of the set they described as 'aboriginal'. This right, they insisted, was not a new one, although they and their supporters argued that it was becoming recognized more forcefully by the developing state of legal art. They presented the right as ancient and inherent, stemming from the continuance of tribal organization under customary law rather than any benediction of municipal or international law. For the tribes it was the foundation right and embodied in the adjective 'aboriginal'.

This question of tribal self-government pressed more as national polities accommodated and became habituated to aboriginal claims, and the 'right' was put at the heart of those claims. The insistence upon aboriginal self-government

[29] See J Levy, describing this as a step too far for the common law: 'land rights grounded in the self-government model … look more like political territory rather than like private property' ('Three Modes of Incorporating Indigenous Law', in Kymlicka and Norman (eds) *Citizenship in Diverse Societies: Theory and Practice* (Oxford, Oxford University Press, 2000) 172. Also C Pateman and CW Mills, *Contract and Domination* (Cambridge, Polity Press, 2007) at 74–76. Most notably the Canadian Supreme Court has yet to uphold self-government as an inherent right protected under section 35 of the Constitution Act, 1982, although the vast weight of the academic literature is affirmative. It is discussed in S Tierney *Accommodating Cultural Diversity* (Aldershot, Ashgate, 2007) at 103–5. Kent McNeill insists that notwithstanding the absence of Supreme Court endorsement it is clear the right exists in law: 'The Inherent Right of Self-Government" Emerging Directions for Legal Research' (A research report prepared for the First Nations Governance Centre, November 2004). Online at <http://fngovernance.org/pdf/KentMcNeillInherent0105.pdf> This Canadian literature is, of course, exhortative, replicating the 1980s style.

[30] I do not discuss international law in this essay, which became an important dimension of the aboriginal rights legalism in the 1990s. On its percolation to grassroots and mixture into the 1990s local legalism see GA Sarfati, 'International Norm Diffusion in the Pimicikamak Cree Nation: A Model of Legal Mediation' (2007) 48 *Harvard International Law Journal* 441.

went to the very nature of liberal democratic practice in settings of cultural pluralism. In New Zealand, this widening of the discourse onto the national stage was captured brilliantly in Andrew Sharp's *Justice and the Maori* (1992). Other important scholars now entered – or in some cases (such as J G A Pocock and Alan Cairns) returned to – this broad field, like Will Kymlicka, Jeremy Waldron, Charles Taylor, Iris Marion Young and James Tully. Much had already been written of multiculturalism in liberal democratic theory and practice, but it was re-energised by the judicial legitimation of aboriginal claims. That literature now focused upon theoretical explanations or assessments of rights that were being received and articulated inside (common law) legal systems as adjectivally 'aboriginal' and that went beyond universalised minority norms of non-discrimination. That literature entered a 'second wave' where the level of abstraction was noticeably scaled down.[31] One writer, for example, claimed that first-wave multicultural theory demonstrated a tendency to over-generalize from particular but unexamined cases, pursuing a universal theory of cultural rights or nationalism.[32] Kymlicka's *Multicultural Citizenship* (1995) was emblematic and influential. He argued famously that immigrant ethnic groups made different claims for accommodation than those of indigenous peoples equipped with 'aboriginal' rights.[33] More recently he has seriously doubted the exportability of those arguments to the differently situated minorities of Eastern and Central Europe.[34] If that doubt reflects the juridical specificity of aboriginal rights anchored in a common-law milieu – a distinct legal accommodation peculiar to the North American and Australasian settings – then it accentuates the issues of historiography I am about to discuss. Historiography is a domain where context is paramount.

Political philosophy, jurisprudence, and historiography responded to and ruminated upon the breakthrough legalism. The direction of 'second-wave' enquiry panned in from multiculturalism's 1970s universalism and engaged the more distinguishing themes of the new legalism: Could tribal groups hold distinct 'aboriginal' rights in liberal democratic states where suppositions of a culturally undifferentiated citizenship had usually applied? Beyond a blanket norm of non-discrimination, what might those rights be and could they be accommodated consistent with the rights of others? What, if any, was the philosophical justification for them? How had the memory that the state and

[31] JT Levy, 'Contextualism, Constitutionalism, and Modus Vivendi Approaches', forthcoming in A Laden and D Owen (eds) *Political Theory and Cultural Pluralism: New Directions* (Cambridge, Cambridge University Press).

[32] J Spinner-Halev, 'The Universal Pretensions of Cultural Rights Arguments' (2001) 4(2) *Critical Review of International Social and Political Philosophy* 1.

[33] W Kymlicka, *Multicultural Citizenship: A Liberal Theory of Minority Rights* (Oxford, Oxford University Press, 1995).

[34] W Kymlicka, 'Multiculturalism and Minority Rights: West and East' (2002) 4 *Journal of Ethnopolitics and Minority Issues in Europe* 1; 'Western Political Theory and Ethnic Relations in Eastern Europe,' in W Kymlicka and M Opalski (eds) *Can Liberal Pluralism be Exported? Western Political Theory and Ethnic Relations in Eastern Europe* (Oxford, Oxford University Press, 2002).

ethnic tribal nation conserved and narrated of themselves as law-bound polities evolved over time in the light of the prospect and, perhaps, achievement of such accommodations, including the settlement of claims?

Only at the fringes did this vast literature take seriously any secessionist element to those claims.[35] Rather, the overriding intellectual concern was with the philosophical justification (or otherwise) for the state's formal accommodation of aboriginal rights inside its constitutional space. This was an essentially philosophical line of enquiry. One might distinguish that from the historiographical one, which concerned itself less with an explanation for contemporary and distinct aboriginal rights than with examination of the manner in which the past was being used in the construction (and justifications) for those rights. I will return to that distinction between the philosophical and historiographical dimensions of the literature as each entail quite different exercises. In my own venturing beyond those topics that I have already described as specifically legal, my goal has not been philosophical in character or aspiration. I have not addressed the theoretical justifications for aboriginal rights in terms of liberal democratic theories of the state, nationhood, citizenship, contract or the like. My subject has been the history and politics of historiography.

The germ was planted by a comment after my PhD dissertation defence in January 1987. 'Well, you've convinced me,' the internal examiner said, 'but I am not sure that it happened.' The penny took a little while to drop. When it did, I realized that what was working as an argument for rights arising from common-law aboriginal title in the present-day New Zealand legal system was not necessarily a depiction of actual historical experience. My attention turned to the relative spheres of 'law' and 'history'. The common-law doctrine I was espousing was an effective legal argument enabling courts to protect remnant traditional property rights (in my submission around the New Zealand coastline). However, it suggested also that this law was the 'true' set of common-law principles that colonialist legal systems could have – and should have – applied but spurned in favour of a 'false' one that gave the Crown an unbridled discretion, enabling it to ride roughshod and unlawfully over the tribes' property rights. The question was whether an argument that carried conviction in contemporary legal terms also represented historical truth? Had Crown officials and colonial courts actively ignored and shunned the legal principles that late-twentieth century common-lawyers (Slattery, McNeil and McHugh) and one historian (Henry Reynolds) insisted were staring them in the face?

I first signalled this new direction in a presentation to the Auckland Law School in December 1993 when Michael Taggart was Dean.[36] It was a time when

[35] B Slattery, 'The Paradoxes of National Self-Determination' (1994) 32 *Osgoode Hall Law Journal* 703; J Levy 'Indigenous self-government' in S Macedo and A Buchanan (eds) *Nomos XLV: Secession and Self-Determination* (New York, New York University Press, 2003) 120.

[36] The presentation, dedicated to the retiring Professor FM 'Jock' Brookfield, was eventually published as 'The Historiography of New Zealand's Constitutional History' in PA Joseph (ed) *Essays*

we were both becoming more drawn into the legal past. For myself this 'turn' involved a closer examination and historicisation of common-law method and law/history became the theme of most of my work for the next ten years, culminating in the collection edited with Andrew Sharp entitled *Histories Power and Loss* (2002). Rightly, that turn has been associated with the intellectual influence of (non-legal) scholars with a strong Cambridge connection, notably Professors J G A Pocock, whose essay anchored the collection, and Quentin Skinner. It has recently become the subject of comment and critique[37] to the extent that those ruminations upon historiography have been described as the foundation of a 'New Zealand school' of legal history. Auckland, as well as Cambridge, has influenced that turn, so it is appropriate to consider it here. This approach is sometimes known, perhaps misleadingly, for this suggests an underlying agenda, as 'Cambridge contextualism'. As a style it has implications for the writing of histories of public law in common-law contexts other than the somewhat specialized setting of antipodean examinations of the constitutional situation of the tribes. I have often stressed that in conversation with Michael (not always soberly) and it is an approach that fellow-contributor Martin Loughlin has grasped and been demonstrating for some while.

Meanwhile, during the 1990s there formed what has now become a considerable literature on the historiographical dimensions of aboriginal rights. Its ambit has been wide. Indeed, the many facets have been debated with considerable ferocity in a range of venues and before a variety of audiences: on *marae* and in long-houses, before tribunals and courts, in academic periodicals and the popular press. The past and the manner of its report have become something upon which many have opinions, including those who insist upon its irrelevance. As aboriginal issues have magnified in national prominence and the most important consequence of the tribes' new leverage has become clear – significant asset (re)vestment – the past has become an evidently political place. Or rather, politics have poured into an array of pasts – tribal, inter-tribal, pan-tribal, colonial, imperial, legal (to name the obvious) – where the same ostensible set of facts have generated different histories. Frequently these pasts have spilled rather messily from specific audiences into the prone, glaring and judgemental light of public opinion where they have informed – or misinformed – intense political argumentation.

on the Constitution (Wellington, Brookers, 1995) 344. The essay described the Whig pattern of New Zealand constitutional historiography and so bewildered the editor he described it as 'polemical.'

[37] M Walters, 'Histories of Colonialism, Legality and Aboriginality' (2007) 57 *University of Toronto Law Journal* 819; I Hunter, "Natural Law, Historiography, and Aboriginal Sovereignty' (2007) 11 *Legal History* 137 [Hunter, 'Natural Law']; M Finnane, 'The tides of customary law' [2006] ANZLH-E journal (online at http://www.anzlhsejournal.auckland.ac.nz/pdfs_2006/Keynote_1_Finnane.pdf); M Hickford, '"Decidedly the Most Interesting Savages on the Globe": An Approach to the Intellectual History of Maori Property Rights, 1837–53' (2006) 27 *History of Political Thought* 122 and 'Strands from the Afterlife of Confiscation: Property Rights, Constitutional Histories and the Political Incorporation of Maori, 1910–40' (publication forthcoming) and D Ward '"A Means and Measure of Civilisation": Colonial Authorities and Indigenous Law in Australasia' (2003) 1 *History Compass* 1.

In the vast literature of aboriginal rights, there are several areas where historiographical issues have arisen, making the way in which the past is used and recounted a matter of debate.

One zone has been inside aboriginal culture relating to the narratives the tribes recount to their own members, and perhaps to a wider audience, as they portray themselves as enduring polities exercising ancient rights over territory. As those accounts have adjusted to the claims culture of the common-law settler state there has been an inevitable change in their public as well as tribal presentation (not to say the fraught inter-tribal borders of overlapping claims). Another zone has concerned the use of traditional evidence before common-law courts and state tribunals using (and privileging) essentially western standards of proof and authenticity. Essentially intimate telling of a bygone tribal past became testimony for external, adversarial, and, often, hostile fora with their own institutional tests of veracity. Unsurprisingly, many groups soon realised that presentation was all. Occasionally, signs of adaptability in tribal historiographies have been pilloried in order to undermine the credibility of what they tell and might obtain. It is as though other – that is to say, western – styles of history themselves have never adjusted to the ear of their audience and the stage on which they are recounted. No style of history can emerge unscathed from tests of authenticity that are not its own. A political community's way of believing their history is their own, not one they can expect others to share. As with any other past, the ways in which the tribal ones are told are never static or unchanging. Historiography, as an entirely human activity, lives in time. Indeed, its change reflects the vitality and dynamism of that (or any) culture.

The above paragraph describes issues arising from the generation of history by and within tribal polities. They concern processes inside tribal culture that I have never been qualified to discuss, other than to comment, as above, that change in tribal historiography is as natural as it is in western forms of narrative. Indeed, reading Judith Binney's reverential and monumental history of the prophet Te Kooti *Redemption Songs* (1995) one is struck by the sheer sophistication and fluidity of those Maori narratives and their capacity constantly to reconfigure and take mosaic and localized forms in complex settings of nativised Christianity, pan-tribalism, and colonialism.[38] Rather, my concern has been with that part of the historiographical sphere where the settler state is considering its own past. How has the settler state recounted its own legal past and to what purpose? The key question has been quintessentially Pocockian: What is (and has been) the role of historical memory in the constitutional imagination transplanted into the loyalist settlement colonies with their common law legal systems, particularly in the encounter with the indigenous tribal peoples?

[38] J Binney *Redemption Songs: A Life of Te Kooti Arikirangi Te Turuki* (Auckland, Bridget Williams Books, 1995).

Australia's so-called 'History Wars' have been the most dramatic manifestation of that set of concerns revolving around the settler state's account and contemporary use of its past. When the aboriginal title argument emanated from sources professionally identifying themselves as lawyers, little controversy ensued. The Saskatchewan firm of Slattery (senior partner), McNeil and McHugh presented aboriginal title as a legal argument, an exhortation addressed primarily to the legal community seeking judicial recognition of extant property rights. However, when Henry Reynolds narrated aboriginal title as an historical truth occluded conspiratorially by *terra nullius* he was unable to invoke the professional mantle of the common-lawyer. Somehow there was a difference between the advocate as historian, which was more permissible, than the historian as advocate. The moralising inherent in the aboriginal title argument was less detectable – or, rather, more impregnable – dressed in the format of legal argumentation.[39] However, in Henry Reynolds' work there was no such professional insulation. His historiography became more exposed and combustible in the aftermath of *Mabo No 2* (1992). Prime Minister Howard joined those who scorned the 'black arm-band' approach to white Australia's history.

We are back at the intersection of 'law' and 'history' as distinct practices. The former sets out to solve problems in the present using the past instrumentally to those ends; the latter attempts explanation of problems addressed by actors in a past that interests us now. These are two modes of thought where the past has a contemporary resonance and, as the unpicking of Henry Reynold's work has shown, they are apt to intertwine. In both zones presentism may occur – that is to say, the past may be viewed through the agenda of the present. Presentism has been a necessary, enduring, and archetypal property of common-law thought with its practical attitude towards the past. In the aboriginal-title argument of the 1980s that inherent property blended with a redemptive historiography of the moral nation.[40] Like the seventeenth-century ancient constitution in its time, it offered the Australian polity at the end of the twentieth century a purging route away from an intolerable present impatient with the sovereign helm. It fell back on the timeless wisdom of the common law.

The History Wars were an episode in the ongoing history of Anglo settler states' construction and intellectual accommodation – or otherwise – of the tribes. As I became interested in constructing a panoramic legal history of that encounter the Cambridge pathway seemed clear. It was not enough to track the emergence of doctrine through the positive sources inhabited by legal principle, such as cases, statutes, proclamations, and law officers' opinions. One had to historicise the common law as a language of thought, recognising that at any

[39] For an early and vigorous depiction of the aboriginal-title argument in explicit moralising terms see FM Brookfield, 'The New Zealand constitution: the search for legitimacy' in I H Kawharu (ed) *Waitangi: Maori and Pakeha: Perspectives on the Treaty of Waitangi* (Auckland, Oxford University Press, 1989).

[40] Hunter, 'Natural Law', above n 37.

given moment its encounter with the tribes could only be articulated inside its own range of expressive possibilities as held at that time. For example, invocation of the pattern of royal instrumentation (such as charters erecting colonies or proprietary provinces for the New World) to explain legal conceptualization of the colonial enterprise and its relation to the tribes itself depended upon seeing that royal activity as reflecting an early-modern view of law. A modern territorialized notion of *imperium* would see these charters as conclusive of an absolute Crown *imperium*, yet the authority they constitute is not expressed in such terms. Indeed, they become contradictory if one attempts to construe them in that manner. That pattern repeats itself throughout the seventeenth century, and such inscription itself is emblematic of an idea of legality that is not a latter-day and positivist one of law emanating from sovereign command: The charters inhabit that pattern, each is not freshly constituting so much as reflecting a view of the nature of Crown authority. One had to heed how law was being articulated as much as retrieve its normative content.

The outcome in *Aboriginal Societies and the Common Law* (2004) was a highly schematic division of the history of common law thought and practice into two distinct phases. These were not intended as a rigid bifurcation of the history of common-law thought into classical and modern eras, a stark and unsubtle 'before' and 'after' historiography, so much as a Cambridge-like notification that the language of legal thought was always experiencing change and this awareness had to be woven through any historical report of its encounter with tribal peoples. The shape of my argument was broad. I believed that during the transitional nineteenth century an earlier 'jurisdictional' approach[41] became superseded by a more thoroughgoing territorialized conception of settler state *imperium* over the tribes and with it a more deliberative use of law in the management of relations (land particularly). By the end of the nineteenth century, legislative regimes had largely replaced, or, in Canada, codified, the management of those affairs by executive discretion. The common law went from being a language of governance and expression of an immanent and integrated world order identifiable by reason, particularly (though not exclusively) that of the lawyer, to being a positive and professionalized construction of statute and precedent. Benthamite positivism saw legislation as the state's purposive instrument for social engineering and policy, a new phenomenon that the statutory encompassment of tribal affairs in the North American and Australasian jurisdictions illustrated powerfully. Likewise, formalism allowed courts to believe in the separation of legal reasoning from normative considerations. By the beginning of the twentieth century the term 'common law' itself described both a language of

[41] See the excellent work of L Ford and D Ward, capturing in detail the legalism of the first half of the nineteenth century when concepts of jurisdiction and sovereignty – ie, the manner in which Crown *imperium* was articulated –were resolving into the modern territorialized and absolute form.

thought and, within that language, the judge-made sector of law (that, in turn, branched into common-law proper and equity) that had increasingly moored itself to the doctrine of precedent.

I did not portray positivism as representing an enduring philosophical explanation of law's provenance and practice, any more than I am about to see Dworkin and his ilk in that light. Positivism was an historical phenomenon that heavily influenced the format of legalism in a particular era with a momentum that has lasted into the present.[42]

It is usual to associate the professionalisation of legal thought, practice and education in the late-nineteenth century with the rise of the legislating Parliamentary state, concomitant legal formalism and the disengagement of law from morality. This is the so-called Separation Thesis, law being seen as inhabiting a separate sphere to morality. This has been a central conception of the positivist tradition and the source of argument amongst legal theorists inside and outside that tradition, particularly in the past fifty years and especially as it applies to judge-made law.[43] Certainly the raw Separation Thesis has traction as an unsophisticated explanation of how a good section of the legal community has regarded the nature of adjudication over the past century, or at least so much as they have ever thought about it in the duration of their professional lifetimes. Some have thought and still think it a good description of what it is judges do (or should be doing). Yet strong and implanted as the Separation Thesis may have been and remain in the consciousness (and education) of many ordinary common-lawyers, there has been a strong counter-tradition that refuses to regard adjudication as a neutral and descriptive activity.

Ronald Dworkin has been most prominent amongst the post-War Anglo-American jurists who have rejected the Thesis and its image of legality as a morally neutral activity. Consider his statement:[44]

> Changes in society's expectations of law and judges were well under way, however, even in the 1930s when they wrote[[45]] and with accelerating velocity in the decades that

[42] See WJ Waluchow, 'The Many Faces of Positivism' (1998) 48 *University of Toronto Law Journal* 387, especially at 391, where positivism is considered as a philosophical rather than a momentarily influential theory of legalism: "Just what is it to be a legal positivist? … Is commitment to legal positivism commitment to a *conceptual* thesis, a *factual* or descriptive thesis, a *moral* thesis, an *interpretive* thesis, a *methodological* thesis, or some combination of these? Put another way, in arguing for or against legal positivism, is one engaged in conceptual clarification, theoretical explanation, normative moral philosophy, definitional stipulation, or something else?"

[43] D Dyzenhaus, 'The Genealogy of Legal Positivism' (2004) 24 *Oxford Journal of Legal Studies* 39.

[44] R Dworkin, 'Hart's Postscript and the Character of Political Philosophy' (2004) 24 *Oxford Journal of Legal Studies* 1 at 34.

[45] The reference is to the 'progressives' of the American Supreme Court in a series of cases in the first quarter of the twentieth century using the 'muscular rhetoric' of positivism to "save law … from reactionary morality." Oliver Wendell Holmes' famous dissent is quoted *Southern Pacific Co v Jensen* 244 US 205 at 222 (1917): 'The common law is not a brooding omnipresence in the sky, but the articulate voice of some sovereign or quasi sovereign that can be identified; although some decisions with which I have disagreed seem to me to have forgotten the fact.'

> followed, that made positivism's general conception of legality steadily more implausible and self-defeating. Elaborate statutory schemes became increasingly important sources of law, but these schemes were not – could not be – detailed codes. They were more and more constructed of general statements of principle and policy that needed to be elaborated in concrete administrative and judicial decisions; if judges had continued to say that law stopped where explicit sovereign direction ran out, they would have had constantly to declare … that legality was either irrelevant to or compromised in their judgments.

In this passage, Dworkin might be seen as making the historical argument that late-nineteenth century positivism was eclipsed by the early-twentieth century rise of the legislating administrative state. However, he does not mean that. Rather, he makes the philosophical argument that positivism has never sufficed, not even momentarily, as an explanation of legality, especially in the practice of adjudication. He has created the imposing superhuman figure of Hercules to explain what it is that judges do and have always done. In building Hercules, it has been argued that Dworkin has (unwittingly) ensured continuity between the inherent moral properties of classical common law thought and its modern, secularized form.[46] In short, despite the positivists' declaration otherwise and their belle-epoch moment in the sun, there are those who believe common-law adjudication has always remained an inherently moralistic activity.

For Dworkin, then, truth about what is just (or moral or legal) arises through a process of reflection that oscillates between consideration of beliefs or convictions about particular examples or paradigm cases of justice (or morality or legality) and a general theoretical structure that shows those beliefs to constitute a unified and justifiable body of conviction. Particular beliefs and general theory rock back-and-forth[47] in a process of continual refinement that works towards a form of 'reflective equilibrium'.[48] Hercules is Dworkin's almighty jurist. He is the superhuman composite of all judicial activity. Panoramically and minutely he surveys the legal terrain, using its diversity to construct a comprehensive theory of political morality that is coherent and unified.[49]

Mark Walters sees a pervasive bleakness in my book *Aboriginal Societies and the Common Law* about the use and presence of law in the management of relations

[46] M Walters, 'Legal Humanism and Law-as-Integrity' (2008) 67 *Cambridge Law Journal* 352, arguing that Dworkin has eliminated the 'natural law sting' [Walters, 'Legal Humanism'].

[47] The description used by J Waldron, 'Do Judges Reason Morally?' in G Huscroft (ed) *Expounding the Constitution: Essays in Constitutional Theory* (New York, Cambridge University Press, 2008) 38 at 51 [Waldron, 'Do Judges Reason Morally?'].

[48] A concept associated with J Rawls, *A Theory of Justice* (Cambridge, Harvard University Press, 1979) at 579. A responsible moral agent aims for this state. Moral justification rests on how the set of general moral norms to which we subscribe "fits in with and organizes our considered judgments in reflective equilibrium."

[49] See Walters, 'Legal Humanism', above n 46 at 33–35. There are deeper issues about invocation of 'morality', of course, as Waldron explains in 'Do Judges Reason Morally?', above n 47. Suffice it here that the term as used in the Dworkinian sense does not mean the subjective impression of each judge but a set of institutional practices and culturally-constructed norms.

with the tribes over the past century. He detects a view of law from the late-nineteenth century onwards that is too negative, nihilistic even. The book describes sites of perpetual contestation where the settler state's hard-won physical domination is articulated through legal instrumentalism (legislation especially) on high pitted against resistant aboriginal agency on the ground. He has posited an alternative Herculean narrative of that legalism where law embodies a political morality and is seen as more than an oppressive instrument of settler state prediction and control of relations with the tribes. There are, he suggests, positive as well as negative elements in the history of that legalism. It is hard to controvert that observation and I would never attempt to do so. However, is Hercules ever-present in the history of common-law legalism's encounter with the tribes? My view of the plausibility of his presence depends upon whether one sees Dworkin (and his counter-positivist camp) as expressing valid, historically-enduring (and durable) truths or as framing a philosophical theory of justice and adjudication for its own – that is, our – time.

First, and although he did not identify it as such, one dimension of the legalism described in my book and that Walters specifically intended (I believe) to cast in a Dworkinian light was the judge-made body of law activated by the breakthrough cases. At least in that sphere of legal activity (in which he, like me, has been professionally involved), and for all the occasional aberrations and wayward moments, Walters suggests that there has been (and presumably still is) overall a constant purifying of the common law as it 'works itself clean', tending (imperfectly, perhaps, like all human enterprise) towards 'reflective equilibrium.' He is too charitable, however, to indict me explicitly in terms of an evident failure to follow my own historiographical strictures when it comes to my historical account of the post-breakthrough case law. Certainly in *Aboriginal Societies and the Common Law* I historicised the format of the post-1980s legalism including the judge-made sector, noting that initial court-led rights-recognition had progressed onto second-generation doctrinal issues of rights-management (tribal governance) and –integration. However, I made scant attempt to historicise the nature of common law thought and theory-talk in this contemporary era in order to give what I have represented elsewhere and in opening the book as nearest a 'true' – that is, a Cambridge – historical account. In short, my contemporary history of aboriginal rights was entirely doctrinal. My strong insistence upon seeing the common law as a dynamic system of thought and language of possibilities did not travel into my own narrative of the late-twentieth century by way of an attempted assessment or even acknowledgement of the impact upon judicial law-making of contemporaneous theories of justice and/or adjudication. As Walters indicates, Dworkin, a late-twentieth century jurist whose influence one cannot deny or overlook (even if one has difficulty gauging its actual extent), was left out.

The breakthrough aboriginal title cases are particularly amenable to a Dworkinian analysis. Much of the literature they spawned made the link between law and political morality in a Dworkin-like manner often without invoking the *eminence grise* himself. In these cases, even the later retrenching ones paring down the potential reach of tribal *dominium*, there is evidently an underlying judicial approach to the adjudicative role that transcends the formalistic. The courts' implicit self-depiction is incapable of formulation in late-nineteenth century terms, because so much of those modern-day judgments – the vocabulary, conceptualising, proceduralism, results – display exactly what courts of the previous century were not doing (for all the late-twentieth century aboriginal title argumentation that they could and should have done so). If Dworkin and his ilk are vital for any explanation of the nature of adjudication in common law thought and method of the 1980s and after, as, say, Austin or Dicey in the late-nineteenth, and as manifest in the aboriginal-rights case-law, then their omission from *Aboriginal Societies and the Common Law* cannot be defended in terms of the historiography I have set myself. That much of Walters' critique has traction. *Mea culpa.*

Hercules lives rather than travels in time. That holds for him, no less or more than for Hobbes' *Leviathan.* Yet, Walters suggests that Hercules, or the ongoing systemic effort to construct law in the morally-integrated manner that he personifies, might (not, should) be seen as omnipresent in the common law (as a language of thought) throughout its encounter with tribal peoples. It is an essentially idealistic prayer by a common-law seminarian, offered as an antidote to the pessimistic, hellbound view that he sees my book (and that of Peter Russell) taking of the past century's legalism. The fear, perhaps, is that unless one injects the Herculean spirit, there is a risk that the whole legal enterprise degenerates into cynical gamesmanship and downward-spiralling. That is, we are to take at face value Dworkin's claim to be setting out an enduring philosophical truth about the nature of common-law adjudication and this should be woven thematically into the whole historical narrative.

One might contrast that with Quentin Skinner's insistence upon the necessarily local and specific nature of any political or philosophical argument:[50]

> [A]ny statement is inescapably the embodiment of a particular intention on a particular occasion, addressed to the solution of a particular problem, and is thus specific to its context in a way that it can only be naïve to try to transcend . . . there are no perennial questions in philosophy. There are only individual answers to individual questions, and potentially as many different questions as there are questioners.

Dworkin's 'law-as-integrity' theory is a philosophical argument about the conjunction of law and morality written in the last half of the twentieth century. That setting is the context of his argument, despite any claim to render a theory that transcends it. Historians of political thought would not be surprised by the appearance and seeming influence of a body of work giving a theoretical justification for intensified judicial law-making at an historical period when that

[50] Skinner, 'Meaning and Understanding', *Visions*, i. 88.

was actually becoming (or felt to become) a more pronounced feature of legal activity. It is not an historical account of the weakening grip of positivist thought on legal and adjudicative practice through that century. To the extent that he describes that occurrence, as in one possible reading of the passage quoted earlier, it is not to make an historical argument but to exemplify his belief in the timelessness of his theory and its inevitable manifestation even in the short period when legal positivism was seemingly ascendant. Dworkin has admitted that the legal method that his theory best describes 'is in fact the traditional common law method'.[51] Does not his own style of argument, invoking the timeless and ahistorical to explain – and endorse – judicial activity in his own time, yet outside of it, itself display key characteristics of that method? Simply because Dworkin is not interested in his own historicity and purports to operate oblivious to it, does not mean his work can escape it. His 'eternal truths' inhabit a local and specific late-twentieth century context of inquiry – including philosophising – over the nature of (intensified and intensifying public sphere) adjudication. This is to apply a Cambridge approach to Dworkin's theorising and to see it as historically situated activity.

By turning attention towards the necessarily parochial nature of ideas, and further insisting that individuals cannot transcend their context through abstract argument, Quentin Skinner has been accused of leaving the history of ideas with merely 'the dustiest antiquarian interest'.[52] Dworkin, then, is a present-day relic, just as Hobbes is that of the seventeenth century. Certainly a moral scepticism is central to this way of seeing the past. Skinner has been described as 'openly dismissive of any attempt to "fix" normative language, and by extension, rejects the possibility of any past attempt to do so.'[53] There is not and cannot be, he claims, any stable 'language of morals', nor should we seek one. Ethical concepts, including our idea of legality, are to be regarded 'less as statements about the world than as tools and weapons of ideological debate'.[54] Ultimately, it has been said, there is a moral core to this. It is not free-falling relativism, so much as gaining instruction from the awareness that this historical consciousness – a sense of one's own mortality – gives. The claim "is that by learning from the past, we can learn the contingency of our own values, and further, that realising this truth of relativism is important."[55]

[51] Quoted by Walters in 'Legal Humanism', above n 46 at 353.

[52] Skinner, 'Introduction' in *Visions*, i, 5. See R Lamb 'Quentin Skinner's "Post-Modern" History of Ideas' (2004) 89:3 *History of Political Thought* 424 [Lamb, 'Quentin Skinner's Post-Modern History']. And Skinner's own theorising about the writing of history and its denunciation of grand narratives is itself susceptible to his own contextualist positioning. It has been argued that his work comes in the face of the decline of Whig interpretations of history, for which his Republicanism offers a substitute source of legitimacy in the wake of the collapse of the British Empire and of the loss of social and intellectual influence of Christianity (not least in the Faculty of History, Cambridge University): E Perreau-Saussine 'Quentin Skinner in Context' (2007) 69 *The Review of Politics* 106.

[53] Lamb, 'Quentin Skinner's Post-Modern History', ibid at 429.

[54] Skinner, *Visions*, i, 177.

[55] Lamb, 'Quentin Skinner's Post-Modern History', above n 52 at 430.

Of course, we can today buy into a Dworkin-like philosophical explanation of what it is judges are doing, or argue over it, and agree that subscription, or contestation, embodies a sincere and committed (because fiercely debated) commitment to a deeper public and political morality for our time. Unless it is to degenerate into cynical legal manipulation, our commitment to justice may lead some of us into pronouncements of faith that there is a morality inside present-day adjudication that is ultimately and enduringly truthful. Or, it may spread that political morality more evenly across our democratic institutions and be wary of pronouncements that judges reason with moral supremacy.[56] This is not to diminish the contemporary importance of Dworkin and the activity he represents, or the afterlife that such work may acquire. Indeed, it is to emphasize its contemporary profundity and to see that it might have some persuasive and forward momentum through time. But any contemporary faithfulness does not guarantee that future generations will likewise accept his report of adjudication as they are encountering it themselves. What may persuade philosophically today will not necessarily and always convince. Future historians will set out to understand what we thought and how we acted upon it, and future philosophers will produce their own understanding of that activity as they experience it in their own time. In doing so they may construct a new set of eternal verities, or even retool ours to let Hercules live on.

Therefore, legal philosophy and legal historiography represent two different pursuits, not least in the literature of aboriginal rights. There are undoubtedly gaps in my use and account of both in *Aboriginal Societies and the Common Law*, not least in the largely doctrinal account of the modern history of aboriginal rights. But one must not collapse the two.

* * *

I have succumbed to the contemporary fixation with adjudication despite an earlier remark that the common-law enterprise encompasses more than this activity. So much of the scholarly attention today is on adjudication without concerning itself with the deeper-rooted spread and manifestations of legalism. Judges have become immersed in the cult of celebrity, a development abetted less by their own complicity – though that is not entirely absent – than by the academy (and its recent subjection to performance-based modes of assessment), the proliferation of legal periodicals, and the wider, media-led obsession with the famous and influential. Rights-fetishism is a form of legal determinism and prestidigitation convinced that if the courts get it right, everything (or mostly everything) else magically follows.

What, it may be asked, has Hercules' movement of the national constitutional plates achieved for the tribes? He may stand behind the politicians' backs, pressing them on to settlement of claims that once the executive dismissed almost

[56] J Waldron, 'Do Judges Reason Morally?', above n 47 at 38.

nonchalantly. Certainly there have been numerous claims resolutions that have empowered some tribal groups politically and economically. These settlements have helped more generally in the emergence of an (admittedly still small) indigenous middle class. And yet, even whilst acknowledging that his sphere is only a part of the legalism that engulfs tribes today, over twenty years of Herculean endeavour has not dramatically improved the overall lot of tribal peoples. Indeed, in Australia their condition may have worsened. The labours of Hercules continue not in that hopeful new dawn of the 1980s but in the cold, pragmatic light of the new century. Are the contemporary jurisprudences of aboriginal rights working themselves clean? Or bleaching? Indigenising? Are Anglo settler states hosting forms of legalism that later generations will denigrate as readily as we now condemn those before us, supposing ourselves on higher legal and moral ground? Hercules today will never have the authority he will be commanding tomorrow where surely he stands looking backwards at us with an admonishing eye. Our pasts are not maps, but it certainly helps to see them that way.

12

'Because I Said So!' Is That Ever Good Enough?—Findings and Reasons in Canadian Administrative Law

DAVID MULLAN

Introduction

FOR OVER TWENTY-five years from the time he was an LL.M. student at the Harvard Law School, Mike Taggart has pondered the role of findings and reasons as core values of judicial and administrative processes. In 1981, he won the Legal Research Foundation's Prize for the best article published on New Zealand law in 1980 for his article in the *New Zealand Universities Law Review*, 'Should Administrative Tribunals Be Required to State Findings of Fact?'[1] His answer to his title was a ringing affirmative. That was also true of 'Should Canadian Judges Be Legally Required to Give Reasoned Decisions in Civil Cases?', an article that appeared in the *University of Toronto Law Journal* in 1983.[2] Three years later, he made it clear not only that he believed that administrative tribunals should be under a duty to support their decisions by stating findings of fact, but also that the common law should impose a duty on tribunals to provide reasons for their decisions. This came in '*Osmond* in the High Court of Australia: Opportunity Lost',[3] as a response to the decision of the High Court of Australia in *Public Service Board of New South Wales v Osmond*,[4] rejecting the creation of a common law duty on the part of tribunals to provide reasons and defaulting to the legislature for the imposition of that requirement. A further twenty-one years

[1] (1980) 9 *New Zealand Universities Law Review* 162.
[2] (1983) 33 *University of Toronto Law Journal* 1.
[3] In M Taggart (ed), *Judicial Review of Administrative Action in the 1980s–Problems and Prospects* (Auckland, Oxford/Legal Research Foundation, 1986) 53 [Taggart, *Problems and Prospects*].
[4] (1986) 159 CLR 656.

on, in 2007, in partnership with David Dyzenhaus, he authored 'Reasoned Decisions and Legal Theory', a chapter in *Common Law Theory*,[5] a volume in the Cambridge Studies in Philosophy and Law series. Here, as the title indicated, the authors located the duty to provide reasons within a particular theory of the common law.

The objective of this paper is neither to summarise nor to take issue with Mike Taggart's outstanding contribution to our understanding of the justifications for and theoretical foundations of a requirement on the part of courts (both civil and criminal) and administrative tribunals to generally provide the factual foundations of and the reasons for their decisions. His arguments are compelling. Indeed, as recently as October 2, 2008, the Supreme Court of Canada cited favourably his 1983 University of Toronto Law Journal article in *R v REM*,[6] a case involving the content of the duty to give reasons in criminal cases.

I have two missions. First, I will explore the way in which the Supreme Court of Canada has incorporated a common law duty on the part of statutory authorities to provide reasons into the structure and theory of Canadian judicial review law. To the extent that the Court, in the course of this evolution, has relied on the work of David Dyzenhaus, Mike Taggart's long-time collaborator, it has obvious connections with Mike's own contributions. Secondly, I will consider the extent of the reach of the common law duty to give reasons in Canadian law, both as an independent issue but also as one that bears upon the claim of the Supreme Court of Canada that it has developed a comprehensive or overarching theory of judicial review of administrative action, one that is applicable in all contexts.

The Duty to Provide Reasons and Judicial Review

Among the justifications for the imposition of a duty on statutory authorities to support their decisions with reasons (including factual findings) is the facilitation of what in Canada is a constitutionally guaranteed right of access to judicial review for those affected by administrative action, at least on jurisdictional grounds.[7] Writing more generally, Dyzenhaus and Taggart express it in the following terms:[8]

> The judicial statement of findings and reasons also enables the losing litigant (with legal assistance in most cases) to determine whether good grounds exist for an appeal. Unexplained decisions both encourage appeals and make it difficult, even impossible,

[5] D Dyzenhaus and M Taggart, 'Reasoned Decisions and Legal Theory' in D Edlin (ed), *Common Law Theory* (New York, Cambridge University Press, 2007) 134 [Dyzenhaus and Taggart, 'Reasoned Decisions'].

[6] 2008 SCC 51 at para 11 (McLachlin CJ).

[7] *Crevier v Québec (Attorney General)* [1981] 2 SCR 220 and *MacMillan Bloedel Ltd v Simpson* [1995] 4 SCR 725.

[8] Dyzenhaus and Taggart, 'Reasoned Decisions', above n 5 at 148.

for the appellate court to determine whether the lower court erred. Where there is no appeal provided by statute, an unreasoned judgment in most cases similarly stymies judicial review.

In *Baker v Canada (Minister of Citizenship and Immigration)*,[9] in which the Supreme Court of Canada recognised for the first time a common law duty to provide reasons, L'Heureux-Dubé J expressed the same idea succinctly in the particular context of judicial review of administrative action: 'Reasons…are invaluable if a decision is to be appealed, questioned or considered on judicial review.'[10]

However, it is by no means obvious how precisely reasons are 'invaluable' in the facilitation of judicial review. Certainly, in the absence of reasons, the focus of the court in any judicial review or statutory appeal will have to be on the result reached and the record (if any) filed in support of that decision. It will then become the task of the court to, in effect, reconstruct the possible factual findings and reasoning processes that led the statutory authority under review to reach the conclusion that it did, and to make a judgement on whether there is a sufficient justification in any of those possible reconstructions for the outcome under review or statutory appeal. Not only can this be a speculative and time-consuming process, but it also involves the courts stepping into the shoes of the statutory decision-maker in a way that potentially undermines the autonomy and legislatively designated authority of that decision-maker. This is particularly so when the reviewing court approaches this task on the assumption that it is engaged in correctness, rather than some form of deferential review. Where adequate and honest reasons exist, speculation is removed or minimised, the process becomes less time-consuming, and the reviewing court can, even within a correctness standard, benefit from the reflections (and often expertise) of the decision-maker under review or appeal. The parties, too, have a much clearer basis on which to advance their competing contentions as to the validity or correctness of the decision under attack.

Nonetheless, when reasons are provided, their role in the conduct of judicial review is not straightforward, particularly where, as in Canada, reviewing courts accept that, at least on occasion, they ought to accord some degree of deference to the decision on appeal or under review.

There are at least two ways in which this might be played out. The first is to treat the existence (and quality) of reasons as an independent basis for according deference. This is the substance of the position taken by Dyzenhaus in his

[9] [1999] 2 SCR 817 [*Baker*].
[10] Ibid at para 39.

influential paper, 'The Politics of Deference: Judicial Review and Democracy.'[11] In advocating 'deference as respect' in contrast to 'deference as submission', Dyzenhaus states that courts[12]

> have to take the tribunal's reasoning seriously because what they are primarily concerned to do is to find any reasons that best justify any decision, *whether legislative, administrative or judicial*....

It might well be true that a court would come to a different conclusion as to statutory meaning than the one the tribunal reached had the tribunal not given a reasoned decision, but the context is different just by virtue of that decision. The issue for the court is not then what decision it might have reached had the tribunal not pronounced, but whether the reasons offered by the tribunal justify its decision.

In contrast, an alternative way of proceeding is to establish a standard of review by reference to other criteria and, then, if deference is indicated, to conduct deferential review in the light of and with presumptive sympathy for the reasons that the decision-maker has provided. Indeed, this is how L'Heureux-Dubé J in *Baker* articulated the role of the decision-maker's reasons in the actual conduct of review. The mere fact that the decision-maker had offered reasons did not justify automatic deference; that had to be determined on the basis of independent or separate criteria. However, once the Court had determined that those independent criteria indicated the need for judicial deference and, in particular, deference in the form of 'unreasonableness' or 'unreasonableness *simpliciter*' review, any evaluation of the decision or reasons by reference to that standard had to pay homage to the reasons provided. It was in this context that L'Heureux-Dubé J cited Dyzenhaus approvingly (though probably misleadingly):[13]

Professor Dyzenhaus has articulated the concept of "deference as respect" as follows:

> Deference as respect requires not submission but a respectful attention to the reasons offered *or which could be offered* in support of a decision.

Let me for the moment park the significance of the language to which I have added emphasis in the two extracts from Dyzenhaus's paper and move on to the most significant subsequent development in the theory of Canadian judicial review of administrative action, a development where, once again, Dyzenhaus is treated as having addressed the issue of how to approach unreasonableness review when reasons are given, as opposed to reasons providing an independent justification for restraint or deference irrespective of the context.

[11] D Dyzenhaus, 'The Politics of Deference: Judicial Review and Democracy' in M Taggart (ed), *The Province of Administrative Law* (Oxford, Hart, 1997) 279 [Dyzenhaus, 'Politics of Deference'].

[12] Ibid at 303 [emphasis added].

[13] *Baker*, above n 9 at para 65, citing Dyzenhaus, 'Politics of Deference', above n 11 at 286.

When the Supreme Court decided *Baker*, it accepted that there were three possible standards of review: correctness, unreasonableness (or unreasonableness *simpliciter*), and patent unreasonableness. For reasons that need not detain us in this context, in *Dunsmuir v New Brunswick*[14] the Court decided to eliminate the patent unreasonableness standard, leaving only one deferential standard, that of unreasonableness. Here, once again, the Court cites Dyzenhaus approvingly,[15] but also, once again, in the context of how to approach the task of discerning whether a decision is unreasonable, not for the purposes of determining whether the reviewing court should or should not defer. This is clear from the following sentence that follows the repetition of the same extract from Dyzenhaus that the majority deployed in *Baker*: 'Deference in the context of the reasonableness standard therefore implies that courts will give due consideration to the determinations of decision makers.'[16]

Indeed, the majority judgment goes on to elaborate the criteria for identifying whether any deference in the form of unreasonableness review is merited.[17] The identified criteria for this standard of review analysis correspond to those used under the former 'pragmatic and functional' test for identifying which of three standards applied. In other words, the question whether there is any requirement of judicial deference remains independent of whether the decision-maker has or has not provided reasons for the decision under attack. The reasons become relevant only when the court has determined that a deferential standard of review is appropriate.

I will return later to the issue whether the choice between the 'true' Dyzenhaus approach or the Dyzenhaus approach as interpreted by the Court makes any difference, and, if so, which is to be preferred. Of more immediate concern, however, is the way in which the Court translates its endorsement of Dyzenhaus into an approach to unreasonableness review. In fact, the majority had already indicated its methodology before quoting the extract from Dyzenhaus:[18]

> Tribunals have a margin of appreciation within the range of acceptable and rational solutions. A court conducting a review for reasonableness inquires into the qualities that make a decision reasonable, referring *both* to the process of articulating the reasons *and* to outcomes. In judicial review, reasonableness is concerned *mostly* with the existence of justification, transparency and intelligibility within the decision-making process. But it is also concerned with whether the *decision* falls within a range of possible, acceptable outcomes that are defensible in respect of the facts and the law.

This ambiguous statement admits of a number of possibilities. It might mean any or some, but not all, of the following:

14 [2008] 1 SCR 190.
15 Ibid at para 48.
16 Ibid at para 49.
17 Ibid at paras 51–71.
18 Ibid at para 47 [emphasis added].

1. To meet the test of reasonableness, not only must the decision-maker's reasons pass the test of reasonableness but overall the outcome or result must be a reasonable one;
2. Where a decision is not supported by any reasons, inadequate reasons, or reasons that do not pass the reasonableness threshold, the decision can still withstand scrutiny if, on the whole of the material before the reviewing or appellate court, the outcome or decision is reasonable;
3. Reasonableness review involves not just an assessment of the reasons but also the outcome, and it is by reference to both of these in tandem that the court determines whether a decision meets the reasonableness standard; and/or (though less likely)
4. A decision will pass the reasonableness test if either the reasoning process *or* the outcome (or result) is reasonable.

This menu of possible interpretations is not just a theoretical construct. It has important practical implications for the conduct of judicial review. Two items at least (1 and 3) require the reviewing or appellate court to make an independent assessment of the actual outcome or result reached. In the other two (2 and 4), that assessment may be necessary depending on the court's review of the reasons provided. Indeed, the Court's reference to the reasonableness of the outcome or result hearkens back to traditional common law theory as identified by Dyzenhaus and Taggart in 'Reasoned Decisions and Legal Theory':[19]

> The authority of the judgment, strictly speaking, comes from the fact of the decision by the judge, rather than from the reasons… And, finally, an appeal is lodged against the result or formal judgment (the most canonical feature of the common law judgment) and not from the reasons (if any) given by the judge. This recognizes that the reasoning may be wrong but the result correct nonetheless. Hence, the emphasis on reaching a result – on resolving the dispute at hand by authoritative decision – rather than on reasoned elaboration is deeply engrained in the common law.

It is also worth noting that leaving open the possibility of constructing a defence of the decision taken on a basis other than contemporaneous reasons is seemingly not inconsistent with the Court's quotation from Dyzenhaus, a quotation that refers not just to the reasons that have been provided but also those 'which could be offered in support of a decision.'[20]

In such a world, the conduct of review or appeal will be influenced by various procedural considerations such as the entitlement of parties, irrespective of the existence or content of reasons, to construct an account of the merits of the dispute that is at odds with the result reached and any reasons provided. Moreover, assuming an entitlement to develop other theories of the merits of the decision taken, there is then the further question whether such theories must be based on or confined to the record properly before the reviewing or appellate

[19] Dyzenhaus and Taggart, 'Reasoned Decisions', above n 5 at 140.
[20] Dyzenhaus, 'Politics of Deference', above n 11.

court or could be supplemented by additional information not on the formal record. Alternative 2 also countenances the possibility that a failure to provide reasons or adequate reasons does not necessarily lead to judicial review, provided the outcome can be established as reasonable either independently of or in tandem with any reasons that the decision-maker has provided.

Although it remains to be seen how the Supreme Court of Canada clarifies and elaborates on this troubling part of its judgment in *Dunsmuir*, three specific comments are warranted:

The greater room the courts allow for reconstruction of the merits of the case on judicial review or statutory appeal, the more complicated the process of judicial review will become and the closer it will be to an appeal *de novo*;

As an obvious corollary of the first comment, the closer any judicial review or limited appeal proceedings come to being an appeal *de novo*, the greater will be the intrusion on the decision-making autonomy of the designated statutory authority;

The supplementation of the record that takes place in some cases when a decision is challenged on the basis that it involves a deprivation of rights and freedoms guaranteed by the *Canadian Charter of Rights and Freedoms* makes it clear that the spectre of what in effect are re-hearings has a basis in reality, albeit restricted to rare cases.[21]

More generally and more importantly in terms of the objectives of this paper, although the duty to give reasons implicates procedural fairness objectives by providing some measure of assurance that the participants in any decision-making process have actually been heard, in the sense of being listened to, it also serves other ends. Whether viewed from the perspective of Dyzenhaus or Dyzenhaus as read by the Supreme Court of Canada, as with the traditional judicial review record this duty now forms an important instrumental requirement of the effective conduct of judicial review. In the words of Mary Liston, herself drawing on other work by Dyzenhaus and Fox-Decent,[22] the duty to give reasons is 'a substantive instantiation of the rule of law.'[23] By requiring decision-makers to justify their outcomes, it constitutes a concrete manifestation of values inherent in the rule of law and provides a basis for the effective conduct of judicial review and statutory appeals, processes that are not only elements in an overall scheme of procedural fairness but also substantive components of the rule of law. As such, the duty to provide reasons serves as both a ground of, and essential evidential component of or reference point for the conduct of at least some species of substantive review.

[21] *Multani v Commission scolaire Marguerite-Bourgeoys* [2006] 1 SCR 256.

[22] 'Rethinking the Process/Substance Distinction: *Baker v Canada*' (2001) 51 *University of Toronto Law Journal* 193 at 238–42.

[23] M Liston, '"Alert, Alive and Sensitive": *Baker*, the Duty to Give Reasons, and the Ethos of Justification in Canadian Public Law' in D Dyzenhaus (ed), *The Unity of Public Law* (Oxford, Hart, 2004) 113 at 138 [Liston, 'Alert, Alive and Sensitive'].

The Reach of the Duty to Give Reasons

In the second part of this paper, I want to take up the question left hanging by the last sentence in the previous section. Is the duty to give reasons a universal requirement for statutory and prerogative decision-making in Canada, or are there situations to which the duty does not adhere? To what extent does the recent judgment of the Supreme Court of Canada in *Dunsmuir* affect this situation? Finally, if the duty to give reasons is not all pervasive, does it mean there are serious gaps in the commitment of current Canadian judicial review principles to the rule of law and, at a practical level, instances where the courts must conduct judicial review without the benefit or expectation of reasons for the decision under challenge?

Mike Taggart's 1980 article is, on its face, restricted to tribunals and whether they should have an obligation to state findings of fact. His comparative database consists in large measure of statutory instruments and court precedents in the United States, the United Kingdom, and Canada that impose reasons obligations on tribunals and agencies, not all statutory and prerogative authorities. Although in his attack on *Osmond* he talks in terms of the obligation of 'administrative decision-makers' to provide reasons for their decisions,[24] his emphasis is clearly on statutory decision-makers that adjudicate and that are subject to the requirements of procedural fairness. The 2007 Dyzenhaus/Taggart paper is also located in the context of adjudication whether in the courts of criminal or civil jurisdiction or administrative tribunals and agencies. However, towards the end of this paper, the authors raise the issue of a more broadly based concept of the duty to give reasons.[25]

Dyzenhaus and Taggart describe the traditional antagonism of the common law to imposing reasons requirements on adjudicative bodies as influenced by the command conception of authority and, in particular, the version articulated by Hobbes in *Leviathan*: 'Hobbes tells us that we obey a command not because the commander gives us reasons to justify the command but because the command comes from the commander.'[26] They contrast this with what they describe as the main thrust of common law tradition, a conception of law's authority as 'reason-based'.[27] Eventually, this forces the authors to face up to the question whether any exemption for certain categories of statutory and prerogative authority from the common law duty to provide reasons undermines the legitimacy of those decision-makers in terms of a reason-based (as opposed to command) theory of law. Their response is a qualified recognition that the

[24] Taggart, *Problems and Prospects*, above n 3 at 53.
[25] Dyzenhaus and Taggart, 'Reasoned Decisions', above n 5 at 166–67.
[26] Ibid at 152.
[27] Ibid.

command theory of the authority of law may still have a place in a legal system where the default position is one in which public decision-making requires reasons:

> Not only is it the case that generally speaking the validity of statutes is best understood in accordance with the command conception, but even the exercise of legal authority by those charged with implementing the statute might on occasion be better understood in terms of the command rather than the reason-based conception. It might, for example, be simply inappropriate to require written reasons for all official decisions, especially for the category of decisions that neither affect an important individual interest nor are based largely on legal considerations.[28]

Ultimately, they conclude that probably the best way of rationalising the situation is to treat the command and reason-based conceptions as two ends of a spectrum with the command conception end of that spectrum as 'not to be approached too closely without compelling reasons.'[29]

That leaves dangling the very real question of what, in a reason-based legal world, might constitute the 'compelling reasons' for excluding certain decision-makers from the duty to give reasons for their decision or actions. In saying this, I am not intending to be critical of Dyzenhaus and Taggart. This was a no more than a sidebar to their paper. It is, however, an informative sidebar, nonetheless, particularly in the light of Dyzenhaus's assertion in 'The Politics of Deference' that courts have to take the reasons for decision of statutory authorities seriously 'whether legislative, administrative or judicial.'[30] The requirement to take reasons seriously is not predicated on a requirement that all legislative, administrative, and judicial bodies provide reasons for their decisions.

Once again, however, that does not assist in identifying the situations where there should be no requirement of reasons. In so far as the duty to provide reasons is treated as creating a right in those to whom procedural fairness is owed, it might be argued that the existence of the duty is subject to the same threshold requirements as attend the duty to act fairly.[31] In other words, those who perform legislative functions or are engaged in decision-making with polycentric characteristics and dependent on broadly based conceptions of public policy are subject to neither the duty to act fairly nor the duty to give reasons.[32] Thus, even though the formal decision-maker in *Baker* was a Minister of the Crown and even though the substantive claim in that case involved a seemingly open discretion to permit non-citizens to remain in Canada on humanitarian and compassionate grounds, the fact remains that the context was one in which the government had conceded that the duty to act fairly was

[28] Ibid at 166.
[29] Ibid.
[30] Dyzenhaus, 'Politics of Deference', above n 11.
[31] RW Macaulay and JHL Sprague, 3 *Practice and Procedure Before Administrative Tribunals* (Thomson/Carswell, serial) proceed on this basis at 22.3(b)(i).
[32] *Knight v Indian Head School Division No 19* [1990] 1 SCR 653.

triggered. Albeit that Baker was a 'mere applicant', that concession was presumably wise given the individuated nature of the determination in question and its serious personal impact on both Baker and her Canadian-born children.

Nonetheless, writing for the majority in *Baker*, L'Heureux-Dubé J insisted that there was no 'rigid dichotomy' between discretionary and non-discretionary decisions.[33] More significantly, it was in the context of reviewing the substantive determination that she made reference to Dyzenhaus's theory about the need for 'respectful attention to the reasons offered.'[34] Although this does not in any sense amount to a recognition that all discretionary decision-making is subject to a duty to provide reasons, the reference was made in the context of developing a general theory of how to conduct unreasonableness review of discretionary decision-making.

Does this suggest that L'Heureux-Dubé J conceived of a duty to give reasons extending beyond the realm of those decision-makers subject to the requirements of procedural fairness? Almost certainly not! First, in the domain of decision-makers obliged to accord procedural fairness, her acceptance of the duty to give reasons was qualified. Even within this group, the obligation was triggered only 'in certain circumstances.'[35] Secondly, in the context of developing the methodology of reasonableness review, L'Heureux-Dubé J included the whole of the quote from Dyzenhaus in which he referred not just to the reasons provided but 'the reasons ...which could be offered in support of a decision.'[36] Although Dyzenhaus does not explain what he meant by suggesting that deference as respect might have traction with respect to reasons that could be—but were not—used to justify a decision, its recognition by L'Heureux-Dubé J speaks to two possibilities. First, it could be referring to an ability to provide explanations for decisions in the context of judicial review proceedings when there has been a failure to meet a legal obligation to give contemporaneous reasons (as discussed in the previous section of this paper). Secondly, and more importantly in this context, it might also imply there are certain decision-makers and species of discretionary power that do not attract a legal duty to provide contemporaneous reasons but where, on occasion, 'justification' after the event might be a permissible and necessary response to an application for judicial review.

In fact, when we move from the abstract to the actual functioning of discretionary decision-making, the reality of the second scenario becomes apparent. As indicated by *Black v Chrétien*,[37] Canadian law recognises that certain exercises of discretion particularly under residual prerogative powers are not even judicially reviewable. The Prime Minister was under no legal obligation to Conrad Black in advising the Queen on the conferral of honours. More generally, Canadian law

[33] *Baker*, above n 9 at para 54.
[34] Ibid at para 65.
[35] Ibid at para 43.
[36] Ibid at para 65.
[37] (2001) 54 OR (3d) 215 (CA).

still does not conceive of government allocation of various forms of largesse, such as grants, subsidies, and scholarships as attracting a duty of procedural fairness, let alone a duty to give reasons.[38] The same is true of many aspects of the commercial operations of government, such as the award of contracts after a call for tenders and the award of franchises.[39] Indeed, there are certain legitimate forms of 'decision-making' that are simply incompatible with the provision of reasons, such as allocations by ballot or lottery (as in the instance of selective compulsory military service).

In addition, the Supreme Court itself has been very reluctant to probe the motivations or reasons for decisions made by collectivities. Thus, in the context of an attempt to review an Order in Council on the basis of an improper purpose or bad faith in *Thorne's Hardware Ltd v Canada*,[40] Dickson J (as he then was) stated: '[T]he government's reasons for expanding the harbour are in the end unknown. Governments do not publish reasons for their decisions; governments may be moved by any number of political, economic, social or partisan considerations.'[41] The Court's position is that the same holds for 'legislative' bodies that make decisions by voting. This is clear from *Consortium Developments (Clearwater) Ltd v Sarnia (City)*,[42] involving an attempt to probe members of a city council on their motivations for voting for the appointment of a commission of inquiry. According to Binnie J, delivering the judgment of the Court: The motives of a legislative body consisting of numerous persons are 'unknowable' except by what it enacts.[43]

It is against this background that it becomes necessary to assess the impact of *Dunsmuir*.[44] Even though the issues in *Dunsmuir* arose out of the decision of an adjudicative tribunal, Bastarache and LeBel JJ, in their joint majority judgment, professed to be developing a template that would 'address first and foremost the structure and characteristics of the system of judicial review as a whole.'[45] In fact, Binnie J, in a separate judgment concurring in the result, questioned how the majority could legitimately deal with the system of judicial review as a whole

[38] *Webb v Ontario Housing Corporation* (1978) 93 DLR (3d) 187 (Ont. CA). In reference to access to Ontario government subsidized housing, MacKinnon ACJO stated (at para 21): The determination to grant her this benefit was made when she was accepted as a tenant. That decision was one which, in my view, could be made by OHC without any intervention of a rule or principle of procedural "fairness."

[39] RA Macdonald and D Lametti, 'Reasons for Decision in Administrative Law' (1990) 3 *Canadian Journal of Administrative Law and Practice* 123 at 161. Indeed, this article provides a sophisticated and functional analysis of the utility and feasibility of reasons requirements across a broad spectrum of government decision-making.

[40] [1983] 1 SCR 106.

[41] Ibid at 112.

[42] [1998] 3 SCR 3.

[43] Ibid at para 45.

[44] Above n 14.

[45] Ibid at para 33.

where their database was almost entirely adjudicative tribunals.[46] Nevertheless, it is on the majority's own terms that the impact of the judgment on the duty to provide reasons must be assessed.

As described above, at least in situations where the deferential unreasonableness standard of review is applicable, the majority directs reviewing courts to concentrate on the 'existence of justification, transparency and intelligibility within the decision-making process.'[47] That edict only makes sense in situations where the decision-maker under review has provided reasons for decision. That, of course, raises the question whether implicit in the Court's reasoning is acceptance of the proposition that the duty to give reasons is now all-pervasive. However, it would be surprising if the Court, in the wake of *Baker*'s qualified acceptance of the duty to provide reasons, would take that kind of controversial step in such an indirect manner. Given that, the more likely explanation of the judgment's impact on decision-makers that do not have to and do not provide reasons for their decisions rests in the Court's alternative version of what can constitute a reasonable decision: one that 'falls within a range of possible, acceptable outcomes which are defensible in respect of the law and the facts.'[48] This is the terrain that almost certainly is occupied by a wide range of discretionary decisions for which there are no explicit reasons. How wide that range is probably still remains to be settled. There is also the question that I will return to later whether, if a decision-maker within that range voluntarily undertakes to provide reasons for a decision, that decision-maker attracts automatically a level of deference generally accorded to other decisions resulting from a process that has the hallmarks of 'justification, transparency and intelligibility.'

Among Canadian writers on the duty to give reasons in an administrative law setting, Mary Liston comes closest to advocacy of a legal duty to provide reasons not bounded by the situations to which procedural fairness attaches. At the level of positive law, she accepts that there is 'not yet a general duty imposed on all statutory and prerogative authorities in Canada.'[49] However, she goes on to state, in the context of discretionary Ministerial decision-making: '[I]f public officials keep their cogitations private and do not provide any evidence of reasoning, the duty to give reasons can be no more than a sham.'[50] This suggests that Liston indeed favours a broadening of the duty to provide reasons beyond the current scope of procedural fairness obligations. Later, she sees the duty to provide reasons as a requirement that 'complements' democratic involvement in the political process.[51] In this context, she makes the following claim:[52]

[46] Ibid at para 121.
[47] Ibid at para 47.
[48] Ibid.
[49] Liston, 'Alert, Alive and Sensitive' above n 23 at 124.
[50] Ibid at 132.
[51] Ibid at 141.
[52] Ibid.

> The procedural protection afforded by the duty to give reasons accords with a view of democracy that is participatory and therefore respects individual agency by facilitating the exercise of moral responsibility and by providing fair procedures that treat the individual as a whole person thereby respecting human dignity.

Where can this lead but a more generalised duty to give reasons than was specified in *Baker* itself? Does this not imply that statutory authorities should be obliged to support even broadly based policy choices made under statutory and prerogative powers with reasons?

There does, however, appear to be a problem with the political process analogy or parallel on which this argument stands. Participation in political processes and the Canadian version of democracy does not demand of government contemporaneous justification through reasons for various forms of political choice and, in particular, the introduction and passage of legislation. Operating at its best, our democracy provides procedural opportunities for participation in the formulation and making of those political choices, not just in the form of the ballot box but also through lobbying and access to parliamentary committees as well as a process of advance justification in the form of policy papers and the like. For the most part though, the final political choice, whether it is in the form of legislation, primary or subordinate, or broadly based policy initiatives, is not supported by anything resembling formal reasons. After the event accountability is the accepted surrogate.

Indeed, earlier in her paper, Liston stopped short of the precipice of requiring reasons of all statutory and prerogative authorities by continuing to define access to that entitlement in terms of the 'exercise of public power that affects individual rights',[53] though leaving open what qualify, for these purposes, as individual rights (as opposed to 'collective interests'?).

In terms of Dyzenhaus and Taggart in 'Reasoned Decisions and Legal Theory' and, indeed, Liston's own benchmarks, this raises again the question: how far short of a generalised duty of reasons for the exercise of statutory and prerogative authority can the courts stop? When do they incur the criticism of veering too far in the direction of a command theory of law and away from a conception of the rule of law of which the provision of reasons is a central feature or, putting it another way, from a 'legal culture of justification', borrowing again from Dyzenhaus[54] who in his turn was borrowing from Etienne Mureinik?[55]

[53] Ibid at 140.

[54] Dyzenhaus, 'Politics of Deference' above n 11 at 302.

[55] 'Emerging from Emergency: Human Rights in South Africa' (1994) 92 *Michigan Law Review* 1977. Indeed, for Dyzenhaus, the legal culture of justification forms an essential component of his version of the rule of law. See also, Liston, 'Alert, Alive and Sensitive', above n 23 at 139 and Dyzenhaus and Taggart, 'Reasoned Decisions', above n 5 at 159, in discussing Bentham's rejection of the common law: And that tells us something about the pull of justification that seems to be part of the idea of rule through law. The pull is to more than a claim that decisions by those with legal authority should be justified by reasons as well as justifiable; the pull goes to the claim that reasons that justify should be legal reasons—that is, reasons which rely on the resources made available by law.

In my view, this is not a question that can be answered satisfactorily in isolation. The response has to be rooted in a sense of what other devices are available and, in fact, used for shoring up the rule of law against the perpetuation of a command theory of law.

As noted already, in the world of parliamentary politics and legislation the command theory, as it attaches to legislative edict, is tempered in various ways and not just through sporadic general accountability to the populace in the form of elections. In the contexts of both primary and subordinate legislation and, indeed, broad policy making initiatives taken under legislative grants of power, 'pre-decisional' checks come in the form of policy papers, lobbying, parliamentary debates, and question periods, and, more effectively in some systems, through hearings by parliamentary committees. Legislatively, in the United States and Québec and by 'soft law'[56] at the federal level in Canada, notice and comment opportunities provide a vehicle not only for participatory opportunities but also checks on the legality of policy initiatives and proposals. It is also the case that, in many situations, the distribution of government largesse takes place under strictly regulated specifications, with the criteria for applications serving as an indication of the reasons why or why not an application may be successful. This is even more so in the case of government requests for proposals with the parameters of the bidding process clearly defined and the courts, on the basis of principles that transcend public law, policing the fairness of the tendering process and its outcomes and paying particular attention to the legality of accepting non-compliant bids.[57] Indeed, legality is the direct focus of the work of parliamentary committees scrutinising proposed subordinate legislation and, since the advent of the *Canadian Charter of Rights and Freedoms*, the various devices that are in place for certification that pending legislation, both primary and subordinate, is in conformity with the *Charter*.

It also has to be recognised that courts do not have a monopoly on the business of requiring legal justification. The public institutions of most jurisdictions in Canada include other methods for requiring justification from public officials, not just in terms of policy and sound administration but also legality: Ombudsman, Auditor General, Coroner, and situation specific public inquiries. Moreover, the powers of compulsion exercised by these institutions often far outreach those possessed by the courts when it comes to effective access to high public officials and Ministers of the Crown and their reasons (including legal justifications) for particular initiatives, actions, and decisions.

[56] The federal Canadian equivalent of American notice and comment requirements, the prepublication of proposed regulations accompanied by a Regulatory Impact Analysis Statement with opportunities for constituency input, was the result not of primary legislation or regulation or Order in Council but a series of administrative initiatives in the 1980's.

[57] As in *MJB Enterprises Ltd v Defence Construction (1951) Ltd* [1999] 1 SCR 619, though cf *Double N Earthmovers Ltd v Edmonton (City)* [2007] 1 SCR 116.

Within the purview of the courts, the absence of a formal duty to provide reasons does not necessarily mean that judges will remain neutral in the face of a failure to provide reasons or adequate reasons. Liston is acutely aware of this point, which she makes effectively by reference to two Canadian decisions:[58] *Mount Sinai Hospital Center v Québec (Minister of Health and Social Services)*[59] and *Lalonde v Ontario (Commission de restructuration des services de santé)*.[60]

In the first, in his concurring judgment, Binnie J, supported by McLachlin CJ, examined the record of decision-making of various Ministers over the years. In the light of that record, he concluded that there was no basis for allowing the current Minister to resist judicial review, on the basis of policy and fiscal considerations, of his decision to deny a licence that had earlier been promised to the Hospital in return for certain modifications to its mission. From the record built in the context of the judicial review application, even absent formal reasons, Binnie J was able to construct an account of what had happened that permitted judicial review even by reference to the then most deferential standard: that of patent unreasonableness. From the record, as opposed to the reasons, the two judges concluded in effect that there was no room for deference as respect.

In much the same way, in *Lalonde*, an unexplained change in government policy led the Court of Appeal for Ontario to put the onus on the responsible commission (exercising delegated ministerial powers) to justify itself in the context of the judicial review proceedings.[61] And, justifications based on 'administrative convenience and vague funding concerns' simply did not suffice.[62]

Indeed, it is appropriate to see both these judgments as following the path that the House of Lords elaborated forty years ago in *Padfield v Minister of Agriculture Fisheries and Food*.[63] On the basis of the judicial review case built by the applicant, the Court could see no good reason for the exercise of Ministerial discretion that was the target of the proceedings and, in the absence of a reasoned justification from the Minister, the House of Lords presumed an abuse of discretion. Even earlier, in 1946, the Judicial Committee of the Privy Council, in the context of a Canadian taxpayer's appeal from the Minister of National Revenue, had adopted a similar stance in *Canada (Minister of National Revenue–MNR) v Wrights' Canadian Ropes*.[64] After holding that there was nothing in the Act that obliged the Minister to give reasons for his decision, Lord Greene MR, delivering the advice of the Judicial Committee, stated:

> But this does not necessarily mean that the Minister by keeping silence can defeat the taxpayer's appeal. To hold otherwise would mean that the Minister could in every case,

[58] Liston, 'Alert, Alive and Sensitive', above n 23 at 131–32 and 134–35.
[59] [2001] 2 SCR 281.
[60] (2001) 56 OR (3d) 505 (CA).
[61] Ibid at para 166.
[62] Ibid at para 168.
[63] [1968] AC 997.
[64] [1947] AC 109.

> or, at least, the great majority of cases, render the right of appeal given by the statute completely nugatory. The court is, in their Lordships' opinion, always entitled to examine the facts which are shown by the evidence to have been before the Minister when he made his determination. If those facts are in the opinion of the court insufficient in law to support it, the determination cannot stand.[65]

It is also important to recognise the additional dimension that was present in *Lalonde* and that contributed to the burden of justification that the Court of Appeal in effect placed on the government. The interest at stake—the continued functioning of the sole francophone hospital facility in Ottawa—was one protected by an underlying principle of the Canadian Constitution, 'protection of minorities' as recognised by the Supreme Court of Canada in *Reference re Secession of Québec*.[66] This feeds into the more general point, adverted to earlier, that, in cases where an exercise of statutory or prerogative power impinges on a right or freedom guaranteed by the *Canadian Charter of Rights and Freedoms*, section 1 of the *Charter* imposes a formal burden of justification on the government. After the event reasons become a necessary component of any defence of the decision under attack. Indeed, the same is true of primary and subordinate legislation that *prima facie* violates the *Charter*.

This is not meant to suggest that the processes of judicial review will always prove an adequate surrogate for the absence of a duty to provide contemporaneous reasons for exercises of various forms of statutory and prerogative discretion. Thus, for instance, even in the context of a judicial review application that raises suspicions of impropriety, as in *Clearwater*, the Supreme Court's unwillingness to probe the reasons of a collectivity that operated on the basis of a vote leaves an obvious gap. More generally, it will not always be easy to provoke a reviewing court to take the position that, absent an answer from the government, there must have been an abuse of discretion. Proving or sufficiently raising the possibility within a deferential standard of review that there are no reasonable justifications for the decision taken encounters all the usual difficulties inherent in establishing a negative. Moreover, it is salutary to recall that had it not been for the shameless frankness in the witness box as to his motives, Maurice Duplessis would never have been responsible for the damages suffered by Frank Roncarelli in what is still Canada's most important case on the abuse of ministerial power.[67] Indeed, as Mary Liston points out,[68] there are disturbing echoes of this in Binnie J's judgment in *Mount Sinai Hospital*:[69]

> [I]f the successive Ministers had gone through the same cogitations and deliberations as they did between 1984 and 1991, but kept their thoughts to themselves, I think it unlikely the respondents would succeed in obtaining the order they seek.

65 Ibid at para 11.
66 [1998] 2 SCR 217.
67 *Roncarelli v Duplessis* [1959] 1 SCR 121.
68 Liston, 'Alert, Alive and Sensitive', above n 23 at 132.
69 *Mount Sinai*, above n 59 at para 4.

Part of the answer to this may be a modest extension in the reach of the duty to give reasons (assuming that the current law is not already at this point), and to treat it as applying to the statutory context not just in *Roncarelli* but also *Mount Sinai Hospital* and *Lalonde*, on the basis that these kinds of decision are sufficiently focused or individuated in terms of *Baker* and Mary Linton's sense of what constitute individual rights and interests. Of course, there is always the danger that this will lead to attempts to provide judgment-proof reasons, but this is always a possibility even with the decisions of the most adjudicative of tribunals.

This brings me back to Dyzenhaus's advocacy of reasons providing a free standing justification for deference as opposed to simply being an element in the process of conducting reasonableness review once the reviewing court has conducted a standard of review analysis and concluded that deference is owed. Admittedly, where the challenge is to the decision of a Minister of the Crown or a high public official, it is highly likely that a standard of review analysis is going to produce a deferential standard of review. Nonetheless, to provide automatic deference where there are reasons that, in the words of L'Heureux-Dubé J in *Baker*,[70] are 'alive, attentive and sensitive' to the interests at stake may provide an incentive, in at least some contexts, for these species of decision-makers and those acting on their behalf to provide justifications for their actions and decisions as a way of both staving off the possibility of judicial review and enhancing the 'legal culture of justification.'

Conclusion

Mike Taggart has insisted on the importance of factual findings and reasons as an element of both procedural fairness and wider conceptions of the rule of law, and, as such, providing an appropriate measure of control on the exercise of statutory and prerogative power. The influence of his advocacy has now extended well beyond the contexts in which he researched and wrote initially—courts of civil and criminal jurisdiction and adjudicative tribunals. In his work with David Dyzenhaus, Mike has also explored the potential reach of the legal requirement to provide reasons when viewed from the perspectives of the rule of law, a 'legal culture of justification', and democratic participatory values.

This paper is a modest attempt to further the discussion that this overarching vision of the role of reasons has generated. More particularly, it has made the argument that any attempt to extend the reach of the legal duty to provide reasons and the role of such a duty in a 'legal culture of justification' should at least pay heed to the varying ways in which legislative and administrative processes and other adjectival or instrumental features of the actual conduct of

[70] *Baker*, above n 9 at para 73.

judicial review and statutory appeals promote that same value. As such, they coalesce with and in some instances act as a surrogate for the existence of a broader duty to provide reasons. Whether that is adequate when coupled with a somewhat more expansive reach of the common law reasons requirement remains to be seen.

13

To Be or Not to Be: The Constitutional Relationship Between New Zealand and Australia

CHERYL SAUNDERS

A Touch of Taggart

THE PURPOSE OF this chapter is to explore the character of the relationship between New Zealand and Australia from a legal and constitutional perspective. At one level no difficulty appears. Since their respective historic decisions in the 1890s, it is clear that both Australia and New Zealand are distinct sovereign states one of which, Australia, takes a federal form.[1] At another level, however, the intricate network of arrangements of a governmental kind between the two countries makes it clear that this is no ordinary international relationship and that, in many respects, it has a domestic air.

Complex, multi-faceted relationships between jurisdictions are not a new phenomenon. Inevitably, however, they give rise to new types of public institutions and new forms of public decision-making that are not easily accommodated within traditional systems of legal and political accountability, developed in the context of a single, typically unitary, nation state. There is now an extensive literature, dealing largely although not exclusively with the distinctive case of the European Union, theorising these relationships as a guide to resolving the questions of public law to which they give rise. This paper applies these insights to the relationship between New Zealand and Australia.

The paper is written as a tribute to my friend and colleague Mike Taggart. It is also inspired by his work, in at least two ways. First, from the time of his

[1] The six Australian colonies became States in an Australian federation with effect from 1 January 1901: Commonwealth of Australia Constitution Act 1900 (Imp). New Zealand participated in early discussion of federation, but in the event decided not to join.

inaugural professorial lecture in 1990,[2] Mike Taggart has been curious about the impact of new forms of governmental decision-making on public law in common law systems. The focus of his interest has been corporatisation and privatisation, on which he is now a leading authority. My interest here is the different world of intergovernmentalism, in which decisions are made by bodies that draw their legitimacy from multiple jurisdictions, but the extent of the challenge to the principles and practices of public law is much the same.

The implications of intergovernmental relations for the accountability and transparency of public bodies is a relatively common concern in common law federations with parliamentary systems, to the point of attracting the label of 'executive federalism'. Australia is such a federation and to that extent, this paper covers familiar ground. It departs from the familiar, however, both by including New Zealand and by directing the inquiry principally to the relationship between the two countries, to which the federal character of Australia is a backdrop, although an important one. And herein lies the second link with Mike. Two decades ago, we jointly founded the first journal dedicated to the public law of Australia and New Zealand and we have collaborated as editors ever since. Our stewardship of the *Public Law Review* has had its dramatic moments, but the collegiality of our relationship and the intellectual satisfaction of working on the *Review* together have been constant pleasures, at least for me.

The paper falls into two parts. The first describes the legal relationship between Australia and New Zealand, both generally and by reference to a case study that highlights particular dimensions of its impact on public law: the Trans-Tasman Mutual Recognition Arrangements (TTMRA). The second part of the paper examines the character of the relationship between the two countries by reference to a spectrum of possibilities that extends from a federation at one end to a classically international relationship on the other. I hope that the analysis here provides some guide to the way in which future arrangements should be structured or at least to problems to avoid. The conclusion draws attention to some of the ironies of the present relationship between the two countries, in the light of their joint history.

The State Of Affairs

1. Breadth and Depth

Australia and New Zealand have always enjoyed a relationship that is closer than that between most sovereign states. The evidence lies most obviously in the consideration given by both sides to trans-Tasman federal union during the

[2] M Taggart, *Corporatisation, Privatisation and Public Law* (Occasional Paper, Auckland, Legal Research Foundation, 1990).

course of the 1890s,[3] which still is reflected in the terms of the Commonwealth of Australia Constitution Act 1900 (Imp),[4] even though nothing came of the idea. Even before the 1890s, however, there were dimensions of the relationship between the colonies of Australia and New Zealand that marked it as distinctive.[5] And even after the failure of the negotiations over federation signs of closeness remained, for reasons that are not hard to find: shared status as colonies within the British Empire and later, as Dominions in the British Commonwealth; a broadly similar European settler population; geographic distance from other centres of population and in particular from those to which the majority of the population felt the closest affinity; mutually familiar public institutions, including a shared monarch; and comparable social, economic and political standards.

The integration that has taken place over the last few decades of the 20th century, however, is something else again.[6] The immediate catalyst was globalisation, including the fallout from United Kingdom membership of the European Communities. The principal starting point was the creation of a free trade area under the Closer Economic Relations (CER) agreement in 1983,[7] although with hindsight this was seeded by earlier arrangements still, including NAFTA in 1966[8] and the trans-Tasman travel arrangements of 1973.[9] The CER Agreement was designed to progressively eliminate barriers to trade between the two countries

[3] J Quick and RR Garran, *The Annotated Constitution of the Australian Commonwealth* (1976 reprint, Sydney, Legal Books, 1901) 228; G Martin, *Australia New Zealand and Federation 1883–1901* (London, Menzies Centre for Australian Studies, 2001).

[4] Covering clause 6 lists New Zealand among the 'colonies … as for the time being are parts of the Commonwealth' in its definition of 'The States' for the purposes of the Constitution. The clause has the odd but probably insignificant effect that if New Zealand were now to join the federation, presumably using the procedure for the admission of new States in section 121, it would be the only new State to be recognised by name in the old Constitution. It is clear, however, that the clause now gives New Zealand no special legal status under the Constitution and no particular claim to statehood.

[5] EJ Tapp, 'New Zealand and Australian Federation' (1952) 5 *Historical Studies: Australia and New Zealand* 244, 245, describing early forms of attempted integration, including an inquiry into a customs union in 1868 [Tapp, 'Federation'].

[6] G Palmer, 'International Trade Blocs—New Zealand and Australia: Beyond CER' (1990) 1 *Public Law Review* 223, 226.

[7] The Australia New Zealand Closer Economic Relations Trade Agreement 1983. The origins and effect of CER are surveyed in Commonwealth of Australia, Department of Foreign Affairs and Trade, *Closer Economic Relations: Background Guide to the Australia New Zealand Relationship* (Canberra, Australian Government Publishing Service, 1997) [*Background Guide*]. With some hyperbole, but with his usual capacity to provoke thought, Justice Michael Kirby has described CER as an attempt to 'mollify' the 'deprivation' that was the result of New Zealand's decision not to join the federation, which placed it outside the freedom of 'trade, commerce and intercourse' guaranteed by section 92 of the Commonwealth Constitution: M Kirby, 'Australia & New Zealand—Past, Passing & to Come?' (Presentation at Knowledge Wave 2003: The Leadership Forum, 2003) <http://www.knowledgewave.org.nz/forum_2003/speeches/Kirby%20M.pdf> accessed 4 October 2008.

[8] New Zealand Australia Free Trade Agreement; *Background Guide*, above n 7 at 6.

[9] The current arrangements are summarised at New Zealand, Ministry of Foreign Affairs and Trade, 'Trans-Tasman Travel Arrangement (TTTA)' <http://www.mfat.govt.nz/Foreign-Relations/Australia/0-trans-tasman-travel.php> accessed 3 October 2008.

through a series of regular reviews.[10] In doing so, the types of trade included in the Agreement expanded beyond goods to include an increasingly wide range of services and anti-dumping sanctions were replaced by competition law, as a more appropriate mechanism for abuse of market power under the more integrated arrangements between the two countries.[11] More significantly still, for present purposes, steps began to be taken under the Agreement to deal with areas of regulation that affect trade indirectly, including quarantine and customs,[12] standards for goods and services,[13] government procurement,[14] and business law.[15] By 2004, 80 percent of New Zealand standards were aligned with those in Australia.[16] In 2006, the Standing Committee on Legal and Constitutional Affairs of the Australian House of Representatives noted that there were more than 80 agreements of various kinds between New Zealand and Australia dealing with trade and commerce, broadly conceived.[17]

In a significant extension, more ambitious formal goals were set for the Agreement in 2004, through a commitment by both governments to the creation of a Single Economic Market (SEM). This was directed not only to reducing the more obvious implications of borders but also to actively co-ordinating and streamlining the regulatory environment within which Trans-Tasman commercial activity occurs,[18] so as to eliminate 'significant discrimination in the markets of each country arising from differences in [their] policies and regulations'.[19] Developments under the SEM include co-ordination in banking supervision, involving reciprocal legislative change and co-operation between regulators;[20]

[10] In 1988, 1992, and 1995. Thereafter, reviews were held annually through meetings of the respective Ministers for Trade: *Background Guide* (n 7) 8.

[11] *Background Guide*, above n 7 at 18.

[12] Protocol on the Harmonisation of Quarantine Administrative Procedures and the subsequent Arrangement on Food Inspection Measures.

[13] Principally, through the Trans-Tasman Mutual Recognition Arrangement, from 1998, but also through a series of arrangements dealing specifically with food standards, on which Food Standards Australia and New Zealand is based.

[14] Australia New Zealand Government Procurement Agreement 1997.

[15] Memorandum of Understanding on Business Law Harmonisation 1988; Memorandum of Understanding on the Co-ordination of Business Law 2000.

[16] J Diplock, 'Trans Tasman Law Reform Potential' (Paper presented at the conference of Australasian Law Reform Agencies, 15 April 2004) (copy on file with the author) quoting Standards New Zealand.

[17] Standing Committee on Legal and Constitutional Affairs, 'Harmonisation of Legal Systems' House of Representatives (2006) 36 <http://www.aph.gov.au/house/committee/laca/harmonisation/report/fullreport.pdf> accessed 3 October 2008 [*Harmonisation 2006*].

[18] New Zealand, Ministry of Foreign Affairs and Trade, 'The Single Economic Market Agenda' (26 January 2007) <http://www.mfat.govt.nz/Foreign-Relations/Australia/2-SEM/0-work-programme.php> accessed 3 October 2008.

[19] *Harmonisation 2006*, above n 17 at 39, citing the Australian Productivity Commission.

[20] Commonwealth of Australia, 'Australian Government Response, Harmonisation of Legal Systems within Australia and between Australia and New Zealand' (2008) 6 <http://www.ag.gov.au/www/agd/agd.nsf/Page/LegalSystemandjustice_GovernmentResponse-HarmonisationoflegalSystems Report accessed 4 October 2008 [*Harmonisation Response, 2008*].

treaty on the Mutual Recognition of Securities Offerings 2006; an Agreement between the New Zealand Commerce Commission and the Australian Competition and Consumer Commission 2007 to facilitate closer co-operation, including joint meetings and exchange of information;[21] and a treaty on Court Proceedings and Regulatory Enforcement 2008. Other initiatives reported by Ministers to be under consideration in 2008 include projects on business names, standard business reporting, product safety and the sharing of resources for patent examinations.[22] With understandable caution, the joint ministerial statement agreed also to the 'importance of … officials maintaining close contact' in relation to the future compatibility of policies to deal with climate change.[23]

This catalogue of developments tells a story that already is familiar within Australia, that one thing is likely to lead to another in perfecting the free flow of trade. In the case of the relationship between New Zealand and Australia, however, both sensitivity about national sovereignty and the political reality of different constituencies with different attitudes and needs have put some brake on the breadth and depth of integration. There is no single tariff, in deference to the different competitive strengths of the two countries;[24] no signs of a single currency, despite occasional murmurings;[25] and no agreement to include telecommunications within the single market.[26] From this perspective, the focus of the relationship almost exclusively has been on questions of low rather than high politics.[27] Similarly, New Zealand in particular has been insistent that deepening the market by removing impediments to it does not necessarily involve harmonisation, if harmonisation is equated with uniformity. Other forms of co-ordination falling short of uniformity may sometimes be adequate to the purpose: mutual recognition of standards and processes;[28] reciprocal judicial and

[21] Cooperation Agreement between the Australian Competition and Consumer Commission and the Commerce Commission (2007) <http://www.comcom.govt.nz/TheCommission/InternationalAgreements/australia.aspx#792> accessed 4 October 2008.

[22] M Cullen and W Swan, 'Australia, NZ progress bilateral economic interest' (Press release: Joint media statement) (17 July 2008) <http://www.scoop.co.nz/stories/PA0807/S00321.htm> accessed 4 October 2008.

[23] Ibid.

[24] D Caygill, 'Comments on "The Constitutional and Political Implications of a Single Economic Market?"' (Comments at Whose Law is it Anyway?, 9 March 2007) (copy on file with the author).

[25] In *Harmonisation 2006*, above note 17, the Committee on Legal and Constitutional Affairs recommended that the governments pursue a common currency: at 35. The recommendation was rejected in the response of the Australian government, by reference to the stability of the Australian currency: *Harmonisation Response, 2008*, above n 20 at 5.

[26] *Harmonisation Response, 2008*, above n 20 at 9.

[27] This distinction is drawn by A von Bogdandy 'The European Union as a Supranational Federation: A Conceptual Attempt in the light of the Amsterdam Treaty' (2000) 6 *Columbia Law Journal* 27 at 33 [von Bogdandy 'Supranational Federation'].

[28] Trans-Tasman Mutual Recognition Arrangements; Mutual Recognition of Offer Documents: *Harmonisation 2006*, above n 17 at 40.

administrative procedures;[29] information exchange;[30] cross-appointments to tribunals and other bodies;[31] and joint policy development in various forms.[32]

The leverage offered by national sovereignty can be seen also in the form of many of the co-operative arrangements to which New Zealand is a party, even when uniformity is sought. This is particularly striking because, in many respects, New Zealand is the weaker partner in negotiating such arrangements with Australia. Particular initiatives may be more important to New Zealand than to Australia in economic terms, leading to an assumption on the part of the latter that, should the arrangement go ahead, New Zealand will adopt Australian standards. All arrangements are necessarily subject to the constraints of the Commonwealth Constitution; New Zealand has no comparable lever, however, lacking an entrenched Constitution of its own. In some cases, of which mutual recognition is an example, New Zealand becomes party to an arrangement that has been operating in Australia for some time and is expected to accept processes that are already in place. Even where this is not so, there is a tendency on the part of Australia to assume that the rich and complex range of techniques that have evolved over more than a century as the vehicle for co-operation within the Australian federation are suitable also when New Zealand is a partner. Nevertheless, in negotiating arrangements with Australia, New Zealand often manages to structure a position for itself that respects the obvious proprieties of nationhood, in contrast with the position of the Australian States, even when the arrangements otherwise take a somewhat federal form.

The involvement of New Zealand in the Australian ministerial council network illustrates both the extent to which New Zealand has been drawn into Australian intergovernmental arrangements and the difference that independent nationhood makes. New Zealand is listed as a member of 26 of the 34 Ministerial Councils in the current compendium of Commonwealth-State Ministerial Councils.[33] In the case of 15 Councils, New Zealand is a full member; in the others it is

[29] For example, co-operation between the New Zealand Reserve Bank and the Australian Prudential Regulatory Authority in carrying out their respective functions: Joint Standing Committee on Foreign Affairs Defence and Trade, 'Review of Australia-New Zealand Trade and Investment Relations' House of Representatives (2006) 15 <http://www.aph.gov.au/House/committee/jfadt/nz_cer/report/finalreport.pdf> accessed 3 October 2008 [*Trade and Investment,2006*]. Reciprocity between courts in service of process, taking evidence and recognition of judgments is an example of another kind: at 16.

[30] For example, the exchange of information between the Australian Competition and Consumer Commission and the New Zealand Commerce Commission: ibid at 6.

[31] For example, between the Australian Financial Reporting Council (FRC) and the New Zealand Accounting Standards Review Board (ASRB) in the interests of the co-ordination of accounting standards: Pete Hodgson, 'Trans-Tasman Accounting Body cross appointments' (16 March 2006) <http://www.beehive.govt.nz/node/22471> accessed viewed 3 October 2008.

[32] Trans-Tasman Accounting Standards Advisory Group; Trans-Tasman Council on Banking Supervision: *Harmonisation 2006*, above n 17 at 43–44.

[33] Council of Australian Governments, 'Commonwealth-State Ministerial Councils: A Compendium' (September 2007) < http://www.coag.gov.au/ministerial_councils/docs/compendium.doc> accessed 4 October 2008 [*Compendium*].

an observer or, in case of the Australian Procurement and Construction Council, an 'associate member'.[34] In any event, New Zealand has both membership and voting rights in any Council in which a question arises under the Trans-Tasman Mutual Recognition Arrangements, for purposes described in the next part. New Zealand is often a full member when the Australian Council of Local Government Associations (ALGA) has only observer status. In the case of the Corrective Services Ministers' conference, New Zealand is a full member while the Commonwealth has observer status. In several cases, the objectives of the Ministerial Council include governance outcomes in New Zealand.[35] The foreword to the *Compendium* identifies New Zealand and Papua New Guinea as the two 'regional' governments that might be invited to join Australian Councils; in fact, however, the contrast between the two is stark. PNG participates in only five Ministerial Councils and is listed as having full membership status only in one.[36] The *Harmonisation 2006* report recommended that New Zealand be offered full membership of all 'Australasian' Ministerial Councils,[37] although the recommendation was not accepted by the government.[38]

The details of the structure and operation of Ministerial Councils are not always clear from the *Compendium*. As a generalisation, however, Councils are usually, although not always, chaired by the Commonwealth; usually, although not always, have their secretariat provided by a Commonwealth department; usually take decisions by consensus but occasionally and increasingly use weighted majority voting; invariably are supported by a standing committee of officials from each participating jurisdiction; and occasionally share the costs of running the Council. At least where New Zealand is a full member, it can be assumed that it participates in these arrangements as well.

On the other hand, New Zealand is a member of an Australian Ministerial Council only by invitation. Many of the councils in which it is not involved have an exclusively Australian focus: the Ministerial Council for Commonwealth-State Financial Relations is an example for which the rationale is clear. Even where New Zealand is listed as a full member of a Council it occasionally is expressly precluded from participating in certain decisions, deemed to be of interest to Australian ministers only.[39] The *Compendium* states that membership of Councils by other parties, including New Zealand, 'should not intrude on the central

[34] Oddly, Tasmania is listed only as an observer on this Council: *Compendium*, above n 33 at 71.

[35] The Environment Protection and Heritage Council and the Local Government and Planning Ministers' Council; one goal of the latter is to 'enhance the effectiveness of local government and planning in Australia and New Zealand': *Compendium*, above n 33 at 60.

[36] Sport and Recreation Ministers' Council: *Compendium*, above n 33 at 76.

[37] *Harmonisation 2006*, above n 17 at 35.

[38] *Harmonisation Response, 2008*, above n 20 at 5, 6.

[39] New Zealand is a full member of the Environment Protection and Heritage Council, but not for National Environmental Protection Council (NEPC) matters; similarly it is a full member of the Ministerial Council for Consumer Affairs, but not on questions of credit, from which the Commonwealth also is excluded.

functions of the development and co-ordination of policy, problem-solving and joint action by jurisdictions within the Federation'.[40]

It may be presumed that in practice New Zealand Ministers are less engaged than representatives of Australian jurisdictions in many of the matters that come before the councils in which they have participation rights. It is not clear to what extent New Zealand subscribes to the statement in the foreword to the *Compendium* that 'Ministers carry the authority of their governments and those Ministers convened as a Ministerial Council may, where appropriate, determine to finality all matters in their field of concern'.[41] This statement has implications for the operation of cabinet government in Australian jurisdictions; its application in New Zealand merits further inquiry. Most significantly of all, relations between New Zealand and Australia also are developed in international fora, bilateral, regional and multilateral, in which heads of government, ministers or officials meet as representatives of two separate states.[42]

The remainder of this part examines more closely an example of an intergovernmental arrangement in which New Zealand has joined with Australian jurisdictions to deepen the Australasian market. The example chosen is mutual recognition: arguably the most developed of the integrative arrangements presently in operation between New Zealand and Australia. Mutual recognition has several advantages for present purposes. First, it illustrates many of the principal techniques presently in play in Trans-Tasman intergovernmental arrangements. Secondly, it serves to demonstrate both the extent to which Trans-Tasman arrangements have been assimilated to those for Australian intergovernmental arrangements, and the extent to which separate statehood makes a difference. To highlight these points, the case study deals separately with mutual recognition within Australia and with the Trans-Tasman Mutual Recognition Arrangements (TTMRA). Finally, because mutual recognition also provides a context within decisions can be made about regulatory standards that require harmonisation between the two countries it also provides an indication of where integration may lead and how it might get there. Arrangements for harmonisation of food standards already are in place. A proposal for the harmonisation of standards for therapeutic goods along highly integrated lines has been negotiated for some years but recently seems to have failed.

2. Mutual Recognition

Mutual recognition began as an arrangement between the Australian States and Territories in the early 1990s. It was one of many initiatives taken at that time to deepen Australian economic union by removing regulatory impediments to the

[40] *Compendium*, above n 33 at 6.
[41] Ibid (Foreword).
[42] Ibid at 30.

movement of goods and people and improving the processes of intergovernmental co-operation.[43] Unlike many other such initiatives, mutual recognition does not seek uniformity of regulation. Rather, it assumes that the regulatory regimes of all jurisdictions are, in most cases, sufficiently similar to be acceptable to each other. In that sense, it is a useful tool in a federation in which jurisdictions are distinct but also, by definition, have much in common with each other.[44] As developed in Australia, the mutual recognition principles provide that goods that can lawfully be sold in one jurisdiction can also be sold in other participating jurisdictions, even though they do not comply with their regulatory standards and that people who are registered to carry out an occupation in one jurisdiction can be registered to carry out an equivalent occupation in other participating jurisdictions without further assessment of their qualifications and experience.[45] The principles thus are directed to overcoming restrictions on the sale of goods and the registration of occupations. At least in their current form, they do not extend to restrictions on the use of goods or the licensing of businesses, although some consideration has been given to extending their scope in these directions.[46]

Application of the mutual recognition principles may qualify or directly contradict the laws of jurisdictions participating in the scheme. A device therefore is needed to ensure that, in the case of conflict, the mutual recognition principles will prevail. In the Australian context, this was provided by the enactment of legislation by the Commonwealth to require compliance with the mutual recognition principles,[47] which under section 109 of the Commonwealth Constitution prevails over inconsistent State law. Mutual recognition was a State initiative and a solution conferring additional power on the Commonwealth is not normally considered an attractive option. In the case of mutual recognition, however, the States retained some control over the Commonwealth legislation, which depended for its validity on action by the States themselves, authorising the Commonwealth to enact the Mutual Recognition Act 1992 in an agreed form, using the procedures under the reference power in section 51(xxxvii) of the Constitution. New South Wales and Queensland made the initial references on which the Commonwealth Act was based, leaving the other jurisdictions to adopt the Commonwealth Act, so as to give it operation throughout Australia. The references were phrased so as to restrict the power of the Commonwealth to amend the legislation without the consent of the participating States and

[43] C Saunders, 'Australian Economic Union' in Anne Mullins and Cheryl Saunders (eds), *Economic Union in Federal Systems* (Sydney, Federation Press, 1994).

[44] Mutual recognition also takes place in the European Union but in a somewhat different form, due in part to regulatory differences between jurisdictions: Australian Government, Productivity Commission, 'Evaluation of the Mutual Recognition Schemes' (Research Report) (2003) 303 <http://www.pc.gov.au/projects/study/mra/docs/finalreport> accessed 28 September 2008 [*Productivity Commission Report*].

[45] Ibid at 1.

[46] Ibid at 247, cautiously suggesting the extension of mutual recognition principles to the use of goods.

[47] Mutual Recognition Act 1992 (Cth).

territories.[48] All State laws provided for termination of the reference or adoption of the legislation,[49] although the Agreement that underpinned the scheme was expressed to require unanimity to bring it to an end.[50]

Application of the mutual recognition principles was relatively straightforward in Australia because of the degree of commonality of standards. Nevertheless, there were difficulties, which fall broadly into three categories. First, it was acknowledged from the outset that there were some areas in which circumstances or policy differences between jurisdictions meant that mutual recognition was not acceptable. Examples included quarantine and the sale of firearms, fireworks and gaming machines.[51] Secondly, it was inevitable that problems would arise over time when differences in standards in particular areas were considered to threaten the legitimate interests of individual jurisdictions. The interests recognised for the purposes of the scheme were protection of health and safety and the control of environmental pollution.[52] Thirdly, it could also be foreseen that questions about whether occupations truly were 'equivalent' would arise in the context of the mutual recognition of occupations.

The first of these difficulties initially was met by excluding certain products and laws from the operation of the scheme in schedules to the legislation referred to and enacted by the Commonwealth.[53] All three categories, however, required an ongoing process through which problem areas could be examined and disputes could be resolved. The primary tool for this purpose is the Ministerial Council network, with the Council of Australian Governments (COAG) at its apex, exercising decision-making authority in accordance with the Mutual Recognition Agreement. The Commonwealth Act provides a mechanism whereby any jurisdiction can temporarily exempt goods from recognition within that jurisdiction on health and safety or pollution grounds for a maximum period of 12 months.[54] During that period, under the Agreement, the relevant Ministerial Council is expected to examine the issue, to determine whether a standard can be set and if so what the standard should be.[55] In performing this function, since 1997, Ministerial Councils have been expected to prepare a regulation impact statement and to comply with a set of principles and guidelines developed by

[48] Power was referred to the Commonwealth to amend the legislation only in terms which are approved by the designated person for each of the participating jurisdictions': Mutual Recognition (New South Wales) Act 1992 (NSW) section 4(b).

[49] The Western Australian adoption Act also fixes a 'termination day' at 28 February 2011, if not before: Mutual Recognition (Western Australia) Act 2001 (WA) section 7.

[50] Agreement relating to Mutual Recognition 1992 cl 7.1.3.

[51] Ibid cl 6.1.1.

[52] Mutual Recognition Act 1992 (Cth) section 15.

[53] Schedules 1 and 2.

[54] Mutual Recognition Act 1992 (Cth) section 15. The Act leaves it to the participating jurisdictions to implement a temporary exemption by Act or by regulation.

[55] Clause 5.1–5.5. The Agreement also provides for a party to refer a question of standards to a Ministerial Council, whereupon the same procedure applies.

COAG.[56] A standard can be determined by a weighted majority of six or more members of the Ministerial Council representing participating jurisdictions.[57] It can be disapproved by three or more of the Heads of Government of the participating jurisdictions; in the absence of disapproval, however, the parties are required to 'take such action, as soon as practicable … to implement the recommendation'.[58] If no standard can be set, permanent exemption is a possibility. This, however, requires the unanimous agreement of Heads of Government, leading to amendment of the schedules to the Commonwealth Act.[59]

The procedures for handling disputes over the equivalence of occupations are somewhat different. The scheme envisaged that disputes would be likely to arise in the context of concern by regulatory authorities over whether an applicant from another jurisdiction was registered to perform an equivalent occupation, justifying mutual recognition. For this purpose also, the position of the Commonwealth as a jurisdiction with paramount authority in Australia proved convenient. The legislation referred to and enacted by the Commonwealth confers jurisdiction to deal with disputes about equivalence of occupations on the Commonwealth Administrative Appeals Tribunal (AAT). If the AAT decides that an occupation is effectively equivalent and orders registration, the regulatory authority is bound to comply.[60] Equally, however, the AAT may declare either that occupations are not the same or that mutual recognition should not apply because registration of a person who did not meet local jurisdictional standards could threaten the health or safety of people in that jurisdiction or cause significant environmental pollution.[61] A declaration takes effect for 12 months and triggers a Ministerial Council inquiry similar to that for a temporary exemption for goods. In relation to occupations, however, the legislation also provides that Ministers from two or more participating jurisdictions can declare the equivalence of occupations, with effect in their jurisdictions,[62] and that such a declaration will prevail over that of the AAT.[63]

Mutual recognition was designed to preserve the integrity of the decision-making processes of the participating jurisdictions. In the words of the Productivity Commission, it offers 'an attractive reconciliation of political sovereignty

[56] COAG, *Principles and Guidelines for National Standard Setting and Regulatory Action by Ministerial Councils and Standard-Setting Bodies* (Barton, ACT, The Council, 1997), summarised in *Productivity Commission Report*, above n 44 at 107–8.

[57] Clause 5.2.2.

[58] Clause 5.10.2.

[59] Under section 47 the Schedules can be amended by a regulation made by the Governor-General. Section 47(2) provides that a regulation cannot be made 'unless the designated person for each of the then participating jurisdictions has published a notice in the official gazette of the jurisdiction setting out the terms of the proposed regulation and requesting that it be made'.

[60] Mutual Recognition Act 1992 (Cth) section 31.

[61] Ibid, section 31.

[62] Ibid, section 32.

[63] Ibid, section 30.

and economic efficiency'.[64] The mutual recognition principles leave local standards in place. Where new, harmonised standards are required, they are set by each jurisdiction, albeit pursuant to a decision of a Ministerial Council.

On the other hand, mutual recognition requires each jurisdiction to accept goods and occupations that may not meet its standards. The grounds on which a temporary exemption may be sought are relatively limited. The disagreement that triggers a temporary exemption may not be resolved in a manner favoured by the initiating jurisdiction, which may have voted against the decision in both the Ministerial Council and COAG, but which nevertheless is bound by the terms of the Agreement to put it into practice. A permanent exemption requires unanimity, which is even more difficult to achieve. Withdrawal from the mutual recognition scheme is a drastic last resort that is both politically and legally complicated. The political risk in withdrawing from an arrangement designed to enhance economic efficiency is significant and may be heightened further by the perception that withdrawal would breach an intergovernmental agreement, albeit one that is not enforceable in law.[65] There is also some, admittedly small, room for uncertainty about whether a reference can be repealed in law[66] and an even greater margin of uncertainty about whether, in this case, the Commonwealth legislation that originally was based on the reference thereby would cease to have effect.[67]

The allowance that the mutual recognition arrangements make for the decision-making processes of individual jurisdictions minimises the problems of accountability and transparency that often accompany intergovernmental arrangements. Inevitably, however, there are some. The first derives from the fact that the operation of the scheme depends on both the Commonwealth legislation and the intergovernmental agreement. The former prescribes matters that are deemed to be required as a matter of law; the latter provides the framework within which governments collectively take decisions for the purposes of the arrangements. The division is unexceptionable; the difficulty is that one is impossible to understand without the other and that they are not published together. It is now high time that intergovernmental agreements in Australia were regularly published, if not as a schedule to relevant legislation then at least as a

[64] *Productivity Commission Report*, above n 44 at 28.

[65] Typically, the nature of the obligations under Australian intergovernmental agreements suggests that they are not intended to be legally enforceable: *South Australia v Commonwealth* (1962) 108 CLR 130 (High Court). The Mutual Recognition Agreement is clearly unenforceable on this basis.

[66] The issue was not finally resolved in *Airlines Pty Ltd of New South Wales v New South Wales* (1964) 113 CLR 1 (High Court), although the better view now is that a reference can be revoked. The provision in the Western Australian adoption Act providing for its automatic termination is directed to overcoming this uncertainty.

[67] R French, 'The Referral of State Powers' (2003) 31 *University of Western Australia Law Review* 19.

category on the Commonwealth Register of Legislative Instruments.[68] A second issue for the accountability and transparency of decisions taken under the scheme is the reliance on weighted majority voting. Majority voting is a technique for deepening integration and enhances the effectiveness of the scheme from the standpoint of economic efficiency. On the other hand, it necessarily disturbs the traditional lines of accountability of governments to Parliaments and the relative lack of transparency of ministerial council decision-making exacerbates the problem further still. A third issue concerns accountability for decisions taken under the legislation that effectively create law, and in particular a declaration about the 'equivalence' of contested occupations by two or more Ministers.[69] The juridical character of a decision of this kind is unclear. Such declarations are exempted from the disallowance procedures that normally apply to legislative instruments under Commonwealth legislation.[70]

3. Trans-Tasman Mutual Recognition

The Trans-Tasman Mutual Recognition Arrangement (TTMRA) is a product of CER. The possibility of developing mutual recognition arrangements that would also include New Zealand was recognised in the concluding clause 9.1 of the Australian Mutual Recognition Agreement. A discussion paper on the issue was released by the two national governments in 1995, in which both expressed support for the idea.[71] An 'Arrangement' between all jurisdictions, including New Zealand, was signed in 1996 and implementing Trans-Tasman Mutual Recognition Acts were enacted by both the Commonwealth and New Zealand in 1997, to bring the arrangement into operation in 1998.

The scope and concept of the TTMRA were broadly comparable to the mutual recognition arrangements already operating in Australia.[72] Like the MRA, the TTMRA applied only to the sale of goods and the registration of occupations. In relation to these, it obliged the parties to accept and recognise each other's standards. It thus assumed sufficient commonality of standards, on which such an arrangement might be built. In fact, as the Productivity Commission noted, 'New Zealand as a sovereign nation with its own history, regulatory framework and policy environment, has developed its own set of regulations, many of which

[68] Australian Government: Attorney-General's Department, 'Incorporating the Federal Register of Legislative Instruments", Commonwealth of Australia Law <http://www.comlaw.gov.au/> accessed 28 September 2008.

[69] Mutual Recognition Act 1992 (Cth) section 32. The power to add new categories of permanent exemptions to the schedules by regulation requires evidence of the agreement of each of the participating jurisdictions. This is a point of interest, but the procedure appears to raise no questions of principle.

[70] Legislative Instruments Act 2003 (Cth) section 44.

[71] *Productivity Commission Report*, n 44 at 4.

[72] Recital F to the Arrangement described it as a 'natural extension' of the 1992 Agreement and expressed the intention of the parties that the former should be as consistent as possible with the latter.

are different to those in Australia'.[73] In the circumstances, mutual recognition between the Australian jurisdictions and New Zealand ought to have presented greater challenges than mutual recognition within Australia alone. As the Productivity Commission also noted, however, perhaps wryly, this is not always the case. The long period over which the regulatory structures and philosophies of the Australian States have developed has also given rise to inconsistent standards, which present considerable impediments to inter-jurisdictional trade and can be almost as difficult to bring into line.[74]

The independent statehood of New Zealand nevertheless required departure from the Australian arrangements to some extent, in relation both to the coverage of the mutual recognition principles and to the manner of their implementation.

In some respects, the coverage of the two mutual recognition schemes is much the same. Like the MRA, the TTMRA exempts certain goods and laws permanently from the arrangement where there is no prospect of agreement on the mutual recognition of standards;[75] provides a procedure for temporary exemptions when difficulties arise in relation either to goods or to occupations;[76] and puts in place procedures to resolve questions about whether particular occupations are equivalent in different jurisdictions.[77] The permanent exemptions listed are of a similar kind to those under the MRA although inevitably there are some additions. Those initiated by New Zealand include the Radiation Protection Act 1965 and the Antiquities Act 1975. The concept of temporary exemptions also is much the same in the two schemes, in the sense that an exemption must be justified on health and safety grounds or on grounds that exemption is necessary in order to control environmental pollution[78] and that a maximum limit of 12 months applies to a temporary exemption, during which an inquiry into the practicability of identifying agreed standards is expected to take place.

The scope of the application of the mutual recognition principles is further limited under the TTMRA, however, in ways that reflect the addition of a distinct national partner. First, four areas that the Productivity Commission described as raising "nation state" issues are excluded from the operation of the scheme.[79] These comprise customs controls, intellectual property, taxation, and specified international obligations, to the extent that these apply to the sale of goods and might otherwise attract mutual recognition principles.[80] Secondly, TTMRA provides for special exemptions in six areas where national standards differ so significantly that it could be seen from the outset that the parties needed time to work out satisfactory solutions, through mutual recognition, harmonisation of

[73] *Productivity Commission Report*, above n 44 at 2.
[74] Ibid at 30.
[75] TTMRA pt VIII, sch 2.
[76] TTMRA pts IV-V.
[77] TTMRA cls 5.8.1–5.8.10.
[78] TTMRA cl 4.2.1.
[79] *Productivity Commission Report*, above n 44 at 169.
[80] TTMRA pt VII, sch 1.

standards or permanent exemption from the scheme.[81] Examples include therapeutic goods, consumer product safety and gas appliances. The co-operation programs put in place to resolve these issues have had mixed success, in the sense that some progress has been made but not sufficient to enable any of the special exemptions to be removed. The difficulties in achieving deeper harmonisation in areas of this kind will be described later by reference to therapeutic goods.

Techniques for implementing the mutual recognition arrangements necessarily also vary under the TTMRA. As with the MRA, the TTMRA is based on an agreement between all participating jurisdictions, which is given effect through implementing legislation. From the outset, however, there was a question about the character of the agreement. The involvement of New Zealand made it an international agreement, but the involvement of the Australian States and territories, as entities without international legal personality complicated its characterisation as a treaty. In the event, the agreement was termed an 'Arrangement' and is understood as having less than treaty status.[82] On this basis, the agreement is not enforceable at international law and is closer in character to the non-enforceable executive agreements that are a feature of Australian intergovernmentalism.[83]

A second necessary variation in the techniques used to implement the TTMRA concerns the legislation on which it is based. Once New Zealand was involved, there was no possibility of overarching Commonwealth legislation of the kind that conveniently keeps the MRA in place. Necessarily therefore, the TTMRA is based on legislation enacted by both national Parliaments. Both Acts seek to give the mutual recognition principles priority over other inconsistent national legislation.[84] The New Zealand Act states the requirement in direct terms: 'Every law of New Zealand must, unless it or this Act otherwise expressly provides, to be read subject to this Act'.[85] In deference to the involvement of the Australian States and territories, the Commonwealth Act also is based on the reference power, relying on authority supplied by States that have referred power to the Commonwealth or that subsequently adopted the Commonwealth Act. Given the international character of the arrangement, it may be that the Commonwealth might have relied instead on its legislative power over 'external affairs' in section 51 (xxix) of the Constitution, pointing to the trade arrangements between Australia

[81] TTMRA pt IX.

[82] In its introduction to the TTMRA, the New Zealand Ministry of Economic Development describes it as a 'non-treaty' arrangement: <http://www.med.govt.nz/templates/StandardSummary____334.aspx> accessed 29 September 2008.

[83] C Saunders, 'Intergovernmental agreements and the executive power' (2005) 16 *Public Law Review* 294.

[84] Trans-Tasman Mutual Recognition Act 1997 (Cth) section 5(1); Trans-Tasman Mutual Recognition Act 1997 (NZ) section 5(1).

[85] The equivalent Commonwealth provision uses the language of statutory construction, although in practice it is likely to have a similar effect.

and New Zealand as a matter of international concern.[86] The collaborative nature of the mutual recognition arrangements, both in Australia and between Australia and New Zealand made a provocative step of this kind unnecessary and inappropriate in this case. The extent to which wide variety of arrangements between Australia and New Zealand attract the operation of the Australian external affairs power remains an interesting but largely unexplored question.

The involvement of New Zealand also made the constitution of a tribunal to deal with disputes over the equivalence of occupations less straightforward than under the MRA. It may have been possible to create a joint tribunal by enacting mirror legislation, following the model used by the Commonwealth and New South Wales to create a joint Coal Industry Tribunal, which successfully ran the gauntlet of an Australian constitutional challenge in *Duncan's* case.[87] A single tribunal would create other difficulties, however, at the point of review or appeal and the TTMRA provides for two tribunals instead, constituted to encourage collaboration. The Arrangement requires the Australian AAT and the New Zealand Trans-Tasman Occupations Tribunal to have regard to each other's decisions and to consider the desirability of cross-membership.[88] These undertakings are underpinned by legislation, in the interests of consistency in decision-making between the two bodies.[89]

One final implementation issue concerns the choice of forum for the ongoing resolution of problems that emerge in the course of the application of mutual recognition principles. It was assumed from the outset that the TTMRA arrangements would rely on the Australian ministerial council network in the same way as the MRA, giving New Zealand full membership rights in any relevant Council, including COAG itself, for the purpose.[90] The procedure here is almost exactly the same as for the MRA, with the minor exceptions that two-thirds of the members of a Ministerial Council representing participating jurisdictions is required to resolve the outcome of a temporary exemption and such a decision can be disapproved by one-third of the members of COAG.[91] The procedures are somewhat different for the new TTMRA category of special exemptions for

[86] Given the 'non treaty' status of the Arrangement it is not possible to rely on the use of the external affairs power to implement a treaty, which is a much more secure constitutional base. The difficulty of relying on the external affairs power for the purpose of legislating for a matter of 'international concern' is evident from observations of the Justices of the High Court in *XYZ v Commonwealth* (2006) 227 CLR 532, 542 (Gleeson CJ), 572–3 (Kirby J), 607–8 (Callinan and Heydon JJ).

[87] *R v Duncan; Ex parte Australian Iron and Steel Pty Ltd* (1983) 158 CLR 535 (High Court). A tribunal would not raise problems from the standpoint of the Australian separation of judicial power, as would a single court. On the latter issue, see M Kirby and PA Joseph, 'Trans-Tasman Relations—Towards 2000 and Beyond' in PA Joseph (ed), *Essays on the Constitution* (Wellington, Brooker's, 1995) 152 [Kirby and Joseph, 'Trans-Tasman Relations'].

[88] Clause 5.7.4.

[89] Trans-Tasman Mutual Recognition Act 1997 (Cth) section 35; Trans-Tasman Mutual Recognition Act 1997 (NZ) ss 45–6.

[90] TTMRA cl 6.1.

[91] TTMRA cls 6.3, 6.5, 11.1.

which a vote supported by two-thirds of the heads of government is required to remove laws from the special exemption category, to extend a special exemption or to create a permanent exemption.[92]

As with the MRA, the TTMRA is designed with the sovereignty or at least jurisdictional autonomy of its participants in mind. As with the MRA also, however, each also surrenders autonomy to a degree. The extent of the surrender derives additional significance from the fact that New Zealand is a separate state. Mutual recognition requires the Australian jurisdictions not only to accept each other's standards but also to accept those of New Zealand. For its part, New Zealand accepts not only Commonwealth standards but those of each Australian State and territory. In the event of a dispute, it is theoretically possible that an outcome would be reached under the decision-making processes of the scheme with which New Zealand does not agree but with which it would be morally and politically bound to comply.

Some questions of accountability and transparency also arise under the TTMRA. The Arrangement sets out the core structure for the scheme but is not published with the relevant legislation in either country, compounding the problems of comprehension to which a scheme of this kind inevitably gives rise. Much of the scheme relies on executive action in ministerial councils for which there is no tradition of reporting, diminishing the extent of parliamentary oversight and public accountability. The schedules to both Acts can be altered by regulations made by the enacting jurisdiction, but this authority in turn is conditioned on the need to establish that the requisite majorities within the ministerial council system have approved the change.[93]

The TTMRA offers an instructive illustration of the issues that arise in extending intergovernmental arrangements of an essentially domestic kind to include another sovereign state. The nature of the mutual recognition scheme, however, ensures that the issues manifest themselves in a relatively benign form. The challenge becomes greater if the goal of integration requires the parties to move beyond mutual recognition to harmonisation. If harmonisation is understood to involve complete legislative uniformity, it may be necessary to design such a scheme in a way that provides a mechanism for joint political decision-making about legislative change that automatically triggers change in each jurisdiction. Depending on the depth of uniformity sought, it may also be necessary to provide for a single regulator to ensure consistency in the administration of the scheme. In either case, a host of questions for legal and political accountability arise.

Techniques of this kind are familiar features of Australian intergovernmentalism. So far, they are relatively rare in Trans-Tasman relations. They are not unknown, however. In particular, the Joint Food Standards System for Australia

[92] TTMRA cls 9.2.2–9.2.3.

[93] Mutual Recognition Act 1997 (NZ) ss 75–87; Mutual Recognition Act 1997 (Cth) ss 43–8.

and New Zealand has created what is effectively a single food code through a process supported by a single regulator, Food Standards Australia and New Zealand, based on a treaty between the two countries.[94] And another attempt, which sought to harmonise the regulatory treatment of therapeutic goods, thus resolving one of the special exemption categories under the TTMRA has only recently failed.[95] The therapeutic goods arrangements would also have been based on a treaty;[96] would have involved a single regulator, established under Commonwealth law but invested with power by New Zealand and responsible to both governments; and would have enabled binding rules to be made by both a ministerial council, representing the two countries and by the Therapeutic Products Authority. It was the most ambitious intergovernmental regulatory scheme between the two countries to date. It is inevitable that further such schemes will be proposed over time, as pressures for market integration increase, if only in the context of resolving the areas currently subject to special exemptions from the TTMRA.

An Affair of State

1. What is it?

The changing relationship between New Zealand and Australia is the consequence of globalisation, which is characterised by the mobility of people, goods and capital, increasing the interdependence of national and sub-national communities. The emergence of what Ahdieh has described as 'intersystemic governance'[97] challenges traditional assumptions about the organisation of government to which established theories of democracy, legitimacy and political and legal accountability correspond. Multi-level government; overlapping jurisdictions; the blurring of the public and the private; greater reliance on voluntary co-operation; and erosion of the authority of the state produce conditions in which it is more difficult to regulate by general rules applied to individual cases within a constitutional framework that draws its legitimacy from a single people

[94] Agreement between the Government of Australia and the Government of New Zealand concerning a Joint Food Standards System 1995, as amended in 2001. The treaty status of the Agreement presumably reflects the fact that the other Australian jurisdictions are not parties to it, although this agreement also is an extension of an existing Australian arrangement.

[95] At the time of writing, the website is still available, although now labelled as 'historical information': Australia New Zealand Therapeutic Products Authority <http://www.anztpa.org/about/fs-structure.htm> accessed 29 September 2008.

[96] Agreement between the Government of Australia and the Government of New Zealand for the Establishment of a Joint Scheme for the Regulation of Therapeutic Products 2003.

[97] RB Ahdieh, 'From Federalism to Intersystemic Governance: the Changing Nature of Modern Jurisdiction' (2007) 57 *Emory Law Journal* 1 [Ahdieh, 'Intersystemic Governance].

by whom decision-makers are held to account.[98] Observers of these changes question whether the model of an all-powerful state in charge of the law was an 'historical one-off'[99] and argue that, in a world in which 'polyphony' is the norm it may be necessary to develop new conceptions of legitimacy and new modes of accountability.[100] They differ, however, over the extent to which it is either feasible or desirable to break with theories and practices developed in the context of the state as opposed to adapting these to the suit the new reality above and below the level of the nation state.[101]

Much, although not all,[102] of this reflection has been prompted by the development of the European Union and accelerated by the debate on its constitutional future. Famously, the European Union has progressed from a series of communities centred primarily on markets through a phase of 'functional integration'[103] to become a polity of a distinctive kind, prepared to tackle even questions of "high politics" of which a shared currency is a classic example.[104] In the course of this transition it has moved from an international organisation to one that is recognised as supranational in character, with governing arrangements that are closer to the constitutional than to the international end of the traditional spectrum of possibilities.[105] The distinguishing features of supranationalism lie in the existence of distinct European institutions, and in particular the European Community, the European Parliament and the European Court of Justice; the direct effect of European law[106] and the supremacy of European law.[107] They also include the use of majority voting, putting Member States 'in a situation of facing binding norms, adopted wholly or partially against their will, with direct effect in their national legal orders'.[108]

[98] KH Ladeur 'Towards a Legal Theory of Supranationality—the Viability of the Network Concept' (1997) 3 *European Law Journal* 33.

[99] Ibid at 44.

[100] Ahdieh, 'Intersystemic Governance, note 97 at 11, quoting R Shapiro, 'Federalism as Intersystemic Governance: Legitimacy in a Post-Westphalian World' (2007) 57 *Emory Law Journal* 115 at 122.

[101] For a survey of a variety of approaches to constitutionalism in the context of the European Union see M Avbelj, 'Questioning EU Constitutionalism' (2008) 9 *German Law Journal* 1 [Avbelj, 'EU Constitutionalism']. For an analysis of the need to develop arrangements specifically for global governance see N Krisch and B Kingsbury, 'Introduction: Global Governance and Global Administrative Law in the International Legal Order' (2006) 17 *European Journal of International Law* 1.

[102] Two other debates also are intertwined here: on globalisation and internationalisation generally and on the structure and operation of federalism, particularly in the United States. There is a vast literature on both. For the former, however, see Krisch and Kingsbury ibid and for the latter Ahdieh, 'Intersystemic Governance', above n 97.

[103] von Bogdandy, 'Supranational Federation', above n 27 at 33, citing Hans-Peter Ipsen, *Europaisches Gemeinschaftsrecht* §8/24, §54/124 (1972).

[104] Ibid.

[105] Avbelj, 'EU Constitutionalism', above n 101 at 3.

[106] J Weiler, 'The Transformation of Europe' (1991) 100 *Yale Law Journal* 2403 at 2413 [Weiler, 'Transformation'].

[107] Ibid at 2414.

[108] Ibid at 2462.

The European Union thus has emerged as a new form of polity that is difficult to accommodate to traditional understandings. This manifests itself in three connected ways that are relevant for present purposes.

The first concerns the character of the Union, as it becomes more deeply integrated. The burning question here is whether the Union is, or could conceivably become, a federation. Opinion is divided between those who argue that Europe takes a federal form[109] and those for whom Europe must be conceived as a new mode of political organisation, for which a new theoretical framework must be developed.[110] Even the former, however, must develop a new, or partly new, conception of federalism, which does not depend on a relationship between jurisdictions within a single state.[111]

A second manifestation of the challenge presented by Europe to traditional notions of governance concerns the nature of the rules that govern its operation. The story here is more complicated. There is a sense in which the rules for the design of the European Union and its operation in practice have been constitutional, rather than international in character for a long time.[112] The debate has centred on the question whether, in this case, the arrangement should formally be characterised as constitutional, by developing a Constitution for the European Union. Even those who favour a written Constitution, however, accept that it must involve some departure from the traditional conception of a Constitution, insofar as this involves a 'people' and frames a government for a state. At the other extreme are those who deny the need for a written European Constitution, on the grounds that a new conception of constitutionalism is required, not only to provide a framework for a very different type of polity but to enable it to realise its capacity to overcome the drawbacks of the state system, bringing 'the Romantic identity of the people and the state to an end'.[113] In between are gradations of views, opposing formal constitutionalisation of Europe for a variety of reasons but accepting the characterisation of its arrangements as essentially constitutional in nature.[114] In the circumstances, it is not surprising that the instrument that emerged from the constitutional convention that followed the Treaty of

[109] For example, von Bogdandy, 'Supranational Federation', above n 27.

[110] Ladeur (note 98); A Somek, 'On Supranationality' (2001) 3 *Florida Coastal Law Journal* 23 [Somek, 'Supranationality'].

[111] von Bogdandy, 'Supranational Federation', above n 27, describing the Union as a 'non-state federal polity', at 32.

[112] Avbelj, 'EU Constitutionalism', above n 101 at 5.

[113] Ibid at 21, citing O Gerstenberg and CF Sabel, 'Directly-Deliberative Polyarchy: an Institutional Ideal for Europe?' in C Joerges and R Dehousse (eds), *Good Governance in Europe's Integrated Market* (Oxford, Oxford University Press, 2002) 291.

[114] Joseph Weiler, for example, who argues that Europe has unique advantages under its informal constitutional arrangements based on treaty: Avbelj, 'EU Constitutionalism', above n 101 at 11.

Nice[115] bore the hybrid characterisation of a 'Treaty establishing a Constitution for Europe'.[116] It may also be that confusion about the identity of the document is one reason why the enterprise failed.[117]

A third challenge presented by the European Union to traditional conceptions about government concerns legitimacy. The challenge exists at two distinct levels.[118] At one level, there is a question about the legitimacy of the arrangements that constitute the Union itself. If these are regarded as essentially international in character, familiar notions of legitimacy can be satisfied with a conclusion that the Union derives its legitimacy through each of the Member States. Greater difficulty arises, however, if the arrangements are conceived as constitutional, particularly if the legitimacy of constitutional arrangements is perceived as dependent on popular consent in some form.

A more familiar level of difficulty for the legitimacy of the European Union concerns the decisions made within its governance framework. On one view, these also draw their legitimacy, ultimately, from the voluntary participation of the several Member States. This view is difficult to justify, however, in the face of the features of supranationalism, including distinct institutions and majority voting. By traditional standards, therefore, there is a democratic deficit inherent in the design of the European Union, which calls for extension of the powers of the European Parliament and normalisation of the lines of accountability to the Parliament from the other institutions, including the European Commission. Neither of these developments is likely to be acceptable to the Member States and neither may be practicable, in a polity of the size and complexity of the European Union.

If traditional standards are not determinative, however, or at least are less important, it is possible to draw on other sources of support for the legitimacy of the Union. Legitimacy may also be measured in terms of the outcomes of governance, for example; and on any view the European Union has achieved levels of security and prosperity for its citizens that exceed the capacities of the individual Member States.[119] This somewhat shallow approach to legitimacy does not necessarily overcome the problem of the democratic deficit but it suggests that all is not necessarily lost if democracy is not secured in the traditional way. The experience of the European Union shows that there are other ways in which a supranational arrangement can develop a connection with people: creating a form of supra-national citizenship; enhancing the protection of individual rights;

[115] The process of institutional reform is outlined in Europa, 'The main stages in the institutional reform of the European Union' <http://europa.eu/institutional_reform/index_en.htm> accessed 1 October 2008.

[116] *Official Journal of the European Union* 2004/C310/01.

[117] The fate of the next step in European institutional reform, the Lisbon Treaty, remains in the balance after the rejection of the Treaty at referendum in Ireland.

[118] von Bogdandy, 'Supranational Federation', above n 27 at 47.

[119] Ibid at 44.

and creating opportunities for participation in decision-making.[120] It also shows, however, that appropriate opportunities for transparency and accountability may be missed as a novel form of polity develops above level of the nation-state.[121] Arguably, the purpose of both the Treaty establishing a Constitution for Europe and the Lisbon Treaty was to fill these gaps, enhancing the accountability and transparency of the Union both directly and through its Member States.[122]

These questions of the character of supra-national arrangements, the nature of the rules that govern their operation and the sources of legitimacy on which they rely are presently unresolved in relation to Europe itself. They are relevant to the relationship between Australia and New Zealand only to the extent that they show how traditional theories and institutional forms are in flux in the face of the challenge of intersystemic government. Like the European Union, the relationship between New Zealand and Australia lies somewhere on the spectrum between domestic and international forms of government. Like the European Union also, the relationship between New Zealand and Australia has progressively widened and deepened in terms of both the subjects that it covers and the way in which decisions are made, transforming it from an international arrangement to one of a distinctive kind. But the relationship between Australia and New Zealand is not supranational, at least if the European Union is taken as a prototype. There are no general institutions dedicated to the arrangements. The ministerial council system is an instrument of intergovernmentalism. Adjudication still takes place in separate jurisdictions, although the effects of dualism are moderated by considerable collaboration. Both the arrangements for food standards and the proposed arrangements for therapeutic goods involve, or would have involved, a joint regulator. In both cases, however, the design of the arrangements requires a regulator to be established by Commonwealth legislation and invested with authority by New Zealand and other participating jurisdictions, if any. Decisions made in the course of the Australia-New Zealand relationship do not have direct effect, although the TTMRA arrangements were drafted to prevail over inconsistent law. As yet there is no significant erosion of state sovereignty, at least from a legal point of view. As a result, there is no debate about legitimacy, which is assumed to be dependent on the legitimacy of the participating states themselves.

Australia and New Zealand are participants in a sui generis relationship that involves two nation states but is no longer entirely international in character. One of its distinctive characteristics is that it involves two states one of which is larger and more powerful and which is also a federation. As a result, as the relationship

[120] Ibid.

[121] Weiler, 'Transformation', above n 106 at 2466–71.

[122] P Craig, 'European Governance: Executive and Administrative Powers under the New Constitutional Settlement' (2005) 3 *International Journal of Constitutional Law* 407 [Craig, 'European Governance']; C Saunders, 'Democracy, Transparency and the Apparent Demise of the Treaty establishing a Constitution for Europe' (2006) 8 *Cambridge Yearbook of European Legal Studies* 9 [Saunders, 'Democracy, Transparency'].

between Australia and New Zealand has deepened, New Zealand has been drawn into arrangements of a hitherto entirely domestic kind, developed for the purposes of Australian co-operative federalism. From one perspective, New Zealand is merely another player in these arrangements. From another, however, the involvement of New Zealand has added a new dynamic, in consequence of its independent statehood. In the absence of any more nuanced possibilities, arrangements between Australia and New Zealand are international in character, from a jurisprudential point of view, offering a potential trigger to the Commonwealth's external affairs power, capable of enabling the Commonwealth to circumvent the need for complex intergovernmental negotiations within Australia. The Australian jurisdictions represent the same people, differently organised for federal purposes. The involvement of New Zealand brings in a new constituency, whose interests are represented by New Zealand alone. In principle, New Zealand has a greater option to withdraw from these arrangements than the Australian sub-national jurisdictions, whose withdrawal might be met by an adventurous exercise of Commonwealth power or a referendum to extend Commonwealth power. The inclusion of New Zealand in some deep forms of intergovernmental decision-making encounters difficulties under the Commonwealth Constitution even greater than those already encountered within Australia itself.

Finally, differences in the governing arrangements within New Zealand and the Commonwealth respectively add a new dimension to intergovernmental arrangements to which New Zealand is a party. The MMP electoral system makes decision-making in the Parliament of New Zealand less predictable than in the Parliaments of most Australian jurisdictions where governments generally have clear majorities as a consequence of preferential voting. More specifically, over time New Zealand has developed different parliamentary procedures in relation to, for example, the scrutiny of delegated legislation. An intergovernmental scheme that relies on delegated legislation, as proposed for the therapeutic goods scheme, must necessarily make provision for whether and if so how instruments of a legislative character will be subject to parliamentary scrutiny. Other Australian jurisdictions generally are content to leave the scrutiny of delegated legislation under intergovernmental schemes to the processes of the Commonwealth Parliament. This is not an option in New Zealand, where the Parliament represents a different people.[123] Where the two sets of procedures have evolved

[123] Although see the cautionary note in the New Zealand Cabinet Circular enabling exceptions to be made to the general rule of parliamentary disallowance where 'it is desirable in the interests of international uniformity to adopt verbatim rules formulated in another country or in an international forum': New Zealand, Department of the Prime Minister and Cabinet, 'Cabinet Office Circulars CO (08) 4' 12.3 (14 March 2008) <http://www.dpmc.govt.nz/Cabinet/circulars/co08/4.html> accessed 1 October 2008.

differently, however, as is the case with the scrutiny of delegated legislation,[124] finding a solution that satisfies both states without compromising the efficiency of the scheme can be a delicate matter.

2. Where is it Going?

On the "bicycle" theory of integration, the relationship between New Zealand and Australia can be expected to continue to widen and deepen.[125] At this still relatively early phase of its development it is useful to take stock of its speed and direction and to pay some attention to the framework within which it operates.

Some of the issues that may arise in the course of development of the relationship can deduced from the experience of relationships across jurisdictional lines within the Australian federation. Whatever the advantages of intergovernmental co-operation, it also has created a series of problems for systems of accountability that originally developed by reference to discrete jurisdictions. The most obvious of these concern their effects on Parliaments. Intergovernmental arrangements affect accountability to legislatures for undertakings given in ministerial council meetings, which may encompass commitments to enact legislation; for the administration of joint schemes; for expenditure; and for delegated legislation. All Parliaments are affected, but the impact of intergovernmental co-operation on the Parliaments of the States is significantly greater than its impact on the Commonwealth, due to the central role of the latter in most intergovernmental schemes. Typically, in Australian intergovernmentalism, template legislation is enacted by the Commonwealth Parliament, pursuant to agreement with the States; joint regulators are established as Commonwealth authorities; and regulations are promulgated by the Governor-General. In these circumstances, there is at least the possibility that Commonwealth accountability mechanisms will apply. Indeed, criticism of lack of accountability sometimes drives reliance on Commonwealth mechanisms alone to the exclusion of a role for other participating jurisdictions thus, perversely, detracting from the co-operative character of the scheme.[126]

Intergovernmental schemes also present some difficulties for legal as well as political accountability. Hybrid bodies such as ministerial councils or regulators

[124] Legislative Instruments Act 2003 (Cth); Regulations (Disallowance) Act 1989 (NZ). The former provides strict time limits within which instruments may be disallowed by either House of the Parliament. The latter places no time limit on disallowance.

[125] Somek, 'Supranationality', above n 110 at 23, citing JH Jackson, *The World Trade Organisation, Constitution and Jurisprudence* (London, Royal Institute of International Affairs, 1998) 24. The theory, according to Somek, is that '[f]alling down can only be avoided by constantly moving forward'.

[126] Graeme Hill gives as an example the change in the co-operative corporations scheme in the 1990s whereby the regulator was made responsible to the Commonwealth Parliament alone, despite exercising authority conferred on it by the Parliaments of the participating jurisdictions: 'Reviewing Decisions by Commonwealth Bodies made under State or Territory Legislation' (2006) *Public Law Review* 112 at 130.

exercising authority derived from multiple jurisdictions are unlikely to be caught neatly by procedures for judicial or merits review or other scrutiny or public interest mechanisms that have been designed for a single jurisdiction. In practice the problem has been ameliorated over time as far as judicial and merits review in Australia is concerned by judicial decisions accepting that, for example, joint regulatory authorities are 'The Commonwealth' for the purposes of the jurisdiction of the High Court in section 75(iii) of the Constitution, even when exercising State authority,[127] in a splendid example of the end justifying the means. Difficulties of this kind are latent in arrangements that cross jurisdictional boundaries, however. The resulting jurisprudence is highly complex. And solving the problem of review by equating a joint body with the Commonwealth is less likely to be appropriate when New Zealand is a party than when the arrangement is an entirely Australian domestic affair.

Occasionally, intergovernmental arrangements in Australia also encounter constitutional problems. This has occurred less often than it might have done: the High Court has accepted, for example, that adoption of Commonwealth legislation as amended from time to time pursuant to a decision of a ministerial council in which each jurisdiction has one member is not an abdication of power on the part of a Parliament of a participating State.[128] More serious difficulties have been encountered in the context of the transfer of authority to the institutions of other jurisdictions without a clear constitutional warrant. Thus in *Wakim*[129] the High Court held that federal courts could not exercise State jurisdiction and in *Hughes*[130] the Court suggested that there were limits to the extent to which State executive power could be conferred on Commonwealth ministers and agencies. There is currently a debate in Australia about whether a constitutional amendment should be sought to reverse the effect of these two decisions and if so what the terms of the amendment should be.[131]

Theories of intersystemic governance are helpful for understanding both intergovernmental relations in Australia and relations between Australia and New Zealand. They show that overlapping jurisdictional arrangements and the stresses that they produce are normal, in the sense that they are part of a wider change affecting countries elsewhere. They highlight the importance of seeking the rationale for such arrangements in terms of benefits for the peoples of all participating jurisdictions which could not be secured by a single jurisdiction

[127] *Macleod v Australian Securities and Investments Commission* (2002) 211 CLR 287 (High Court). For a complete analysis of the various ways in which intergovernmental schemes might be subjected to judicial and merits review in Australia see Hill, ibid.

[128] *Byrnes v R* (1999) 199 CLR 1.

[129] *Re Wakim; Ex parte McNally* (1999) 198 CLR 511.

[130] *R v Hughes* (2000) 202 CLR 535.

[131] *Harmonisation 2006*, above n 17 at 22–26.

acting alone. They acknowledge the impact of intersystemic processes on traditional mechanisms for democracy and accountability and identify the need to compensate for their loss, although there is as yet no clear view about how that might best be done.

In crafting compensating mechanisms, it is necessary to understand the character of the intergovernmental system to which they will apply. In the case of the relationship between New Zealand and Australia, the supranational dimension is underdeveloped. As a result, these arrangements derive their legitimacy almost entirely through the processes of the participating states. On the other hand, the degree of integration is relatively deep and increasing and there are pressures for the adoption of new intergovernmental forms that will make it deeper still. This somewhat lopsided result is explicable by the fact that, in many cases, arrangements between Australia and New Zealand are an extension of existing intergovernmental arrangements and procedures that have been in place within Australia for some time and in which the Commonwealth typically plays a lead role. The character of the relationship is unlikely to change in this respect, however, and if anything there are signs that it will intensify. One indication lies in the recommendations in the *Harmonisation 2006* report of the Standing Committee of the House of Representatives on Legal and Constitutional Affairs. The Report shows few signs that the Committee recognised the important differences in principle between the position of New Zealand in intergovernmental arrangements and the position of the Australian States. The Committee thus recommended that "wherever possible" the "joint regulator model" as developed in Australian intergovernmental relations should be used for legal harmonisation between Australia and New Zealand;[132] and that the governments investigate 'the feasibility … of a referred legislative responsibility mechanism … whereby … one Parliament can voluntarily cede legislative competency on a specific matter to the other Parliament … and the resulting regulatory framework could apply in each country'.[133] In the event, both recommendations were rejected by the Commonwealth government.[134] The fact that they were made in the first place is, however, an indication of how the relationship is viewed in some Australian political quarters.

As the relationship between New Zealand and Australia has developed, there are signs that the participating governments have been conscious of the need to try to ensure accountability for decision-making under arrangements that by nature are inclined to be complex and opaque. The government of New Zealand in particular has insisted on the distinction between co-ordination and harmonisation, requiring good reasons, grounded in the interests of New Zealanders, for pursuing the latter, more challenging, course. There are some signs in the operating procedures for the most integrated arrangements for which the key

[132] Ibid at 53, recommendation 6.

[133] Ibid at 56, recommendation 7.

[134] *Harmonisation Response, 2008*, above n 20.

agency is Food Standards Australia New Zealand that attention has been paid to the need for accountability and transparency in both jurisdictions.[135] More might be done, however. Some possibilities are set out below, in the hope that they might stimulate debate on how this small but important intergovernmental relationship might develop in the future.

The first concerns the treatment of intergovernmental agreements. The *Harmonisation 2006* report recommended that COAG consider the circulation of draft agreements for public scrutiny and comment; the parliamentary scrutiny of agreements in all jurisdictions; and the inclusion of all agreements requiring legislative implementation on the COAG website.[136] This is an idea that is long overdue. Many intergovernmental agreements represent a form of soft law, which affect the operation of legislation. The reality of their number and significance should be recognised by making them available in a systematic way. Where agreements are linked with legislation, as in the case of the mutual recognition arrangements, this should be made clear and the documents should be made available together.

Secondly, there is a case for all Parliaments to become more involved in the processes of intergovernmental decision-making. Some insight into how this might be done is provided by the proposals for the European Union in both the Treaty for a Constitution and the Lisbon Treaty. The former, for example, provided procedures to alert the Parliaments of the Member States to pending European legislation; entitled the Parliaments to receive a wide range of European documents including proposed legislation and the agendas for and outcomes of meetings of the Council of Ministers; and enabled them to comment on the compliance of proposed arrangements with the subsidiarity principle.[137] The detail of these procedures is not necessarily appropriate for an arrangement of such a different kind, but attention to the principle of the appropriate involvement of the Parliaments of the participating jurisdictions is important.

A third possibility also draws inspiration from European developments. The Treaty for a Constitutional for Europe would have recognised a distinction between the legislative and non-legislative functions of European Ministers acting in a Council formation, requiring the Council to sit in public when performing its legislative role.[138] In the context of the relationship between Australia and New Zealand, the role of ministerial councils in law making is confined to agreements to make law and, sometimes, to the making of delegated legislation. Nevertheless, in a parliamentary system, the former translate quickly into legislation enacted by the respective parliaments and the common law places

[135] Food Standards Australia New Zealand, 'About FSANZ' <http://www.foodstandards.gov.au/aboutfsanz/> accessed 2 October 2008.

[136] *Harmonisation 2006*, above n 17 at 171, recommendation 26.

[137] Saunders, 'Democracy, Transparency', above n 122.

[138] Craig, 'European Governance', above n 122 at 416–17. A similar proposal appears in the Lisbon Treaty para 17.

few if any restrictions on the scope of the rules that may be made by delegated legislation, as long as they fall within the empowering Acts. Drawing on the European example, it may be appropriate to recognise the significance of the role that ministerial councils play in law making, by providing greater transparency for these parts of their proceedings.

Fourth, if intersystemic governance is now, if not the norm, at least a normal dimension of governance it should not be treated as an exception in scrutiny legislation and procedures. Provisions designed to protect international and domestic intergovernmental relations should be kept to the minimum necessary to protect the workability of the arrangements themselves.[139]

Finally, in the event that an amendment is attempted to the Commonwealth Constitution to deal with the difficulties presented to forms of intergovernmental arrangements by the decisions in *Wakim* and *Hughes*, consideration should be given to whether this amendment should be extended to authorise Australian participation in integrative arrangements with other countries and in particular with New Zealand. An amendment of this kind would remove impediments to the design of such arrangements from the Australian end without compromising the sovereignty of New Zealand. It would thus give both countries greater flexibility in the design of collaborative arrangements, including the provision of accountability procedures. By providing a constitutional basis for such arrangements it could also make a contribution towards a more transparent relationship.

The Ironies of History

At the turn of the 20th century, New Zealand declined to join the Australian federation. With the passage of time, both the federation of the six Australian colonies and the decision by New Zealand not to participate in it have come to appear unremarkable. Neither, however, was inevitable. New Zealand did not participate in the Australasian Federal Convention of 1897–98, but neither did Queensland; and the very name of the gathering suggests that there was an expectation that New Zealand might take part. The first referendum on the draft Constitution failed in New South Wales as a result of the inflated majority required for its passage.[140] Western Australia postponed its decision to participate until after the Commonwealth Constitution had been enacted by the British

[139] An example of such provisions is Freedom of Information Act 1982 (Cth) ss 33, 33A, dealing respectively with international and Australian intergovernmental relations. Both provisions in fact are relatively tightly drawn. Varying approaches have been taken to the breadth of this and comparable provisions in State legislation: cf *Cyclists Rights Action Group and the Department of Transport* (1994) 35 ALD 187 (Commonwealth Administrative Appeals Tribunal) and *Re Cyclists Rights Action Group and Department of Transport,* [1995] WAICmr 16 (20 June 1995) (Office of the Information Commissioner (WA)).

[140] The NSW Enabling Act was amended in 1897 to increase the required minimum vote from 50,000 to 80,000. The referendum achieved a majority, but was 8,405 votes short of the prescribed minimum: National Archives of Australia, 'Federation: The Guide to Records' <http://www.naa.gov.

Parliament and thus is not listed amongst the colonies agreeing to the Constitution in the preamble to the Constitution Act. Many of the reasons attributed to New Zealand's hesitation about federation were shared by one or more of the Australian colonies as well, including the threat of the loss of autonomy.[141] And both sides kept open the possibility of New Zealand participation for a period after federation. New Zealand made representations in London during the passage of the Constitution Bill to try to ensure that it could join the Commonwealth later on the same terms as the original States, although these were unsuccessful.[142] The Government of New Zealand also appointed a Royal Commission to look further into the question of federation in 1901. Finally, however, this reported in adverse terms, concluding that 'merely for the doubtful prospect of further trade with the Commonwealth of Australia, New Zealand should not sacrifice her independence as a separate colony'.[143] From the Australian side, there may be some significance in the fact that the first electoral legislation enacted by the Commonwealth Parliament in 1902 preserved the right to vote of Maori, alone of all indigenous people,[144] thereby dealing, at least in part, with another objection by New Zealanders to the Australian constitutional arrangements.[145] For at least a decade after federation, there are signs of a continued expectation in Australia that New Zealand eventually would join.[146]

In one sense at least, by the turn of the 21st century, New Zealand's decision not to do so has been vindicated. The autonomy of the Australian States has progressively declined over more than one hundred years of federation. Both the States and the mainland territories are subordinates in the intergovernmental process, although they retain a certain amount of constitutional authority and political influence. New Zealand has options to withdraw from intergovernmental arrangements in the name of the people for whom New Zealand representatives alone can speak. The Australian States have less flexibility in this regard,

au/naaresources/Publications/Research_Guides/fedguide/chronology/chron6.htm> accessed 3 October 2008. Philip Joseph notes that the eventual decision of New South Wales to enter the federation, through a second referendum in 1899, forced New Zealand to consider its position (although not to change its mind): PA Joseph, 'Introduction' in PA Joseph, *Essays on the Constitution* (Wellington, Brooker's, 1995).

141 FLW Wood, 'Why did New Zealand not join the Australian Federation in 1900–1901?' (1968) 2 *New Zealand Journal of History* 115, 122. More recent historical scholarship has drawn attention to the importance of growing national sentiment in Australia and by inference also in New Zealand: PM Smith and P Hempenstall, 'Australia and New Zealand: Turning shared pasts into a shared history' *History Compass* 1 (2003) AU 031, 001–008 <http://www.nzac.canterbury.ac.nz/docs/hico031.pdf> accessed 3 October 2008.

142 Kirby and Joseph, 'Trans-Tasman Relations', above n 87 at 132.

143 Ibid at 133.

144 Commonwealth Franchise Act 1902 (Cth): 'No aboriginal native of Australia Asia Africa or the Islands of the Pacific except New Zealand shall be entitled to have his name placed on an Electoral Roll …'

145 Tapp, 'Federation', above n 5 at 255–56. Tapp notes the Royal Commission's concern about section 127 of the Commonwealth Constitution, which then provided that 'aboriginal natives' would not be counted in reckoning population numbers for the purposes of the Constitution: at 256.

146 Ibid.

more directly exposed as they are to the possibility of political or legal retaliation. To some extent, the involvement of New Zealand counters the Commonwealth's dominance of intergovernmental negotiations with indirect benefit to the Australian States. On the other hand, the States are threatened by the international character of the relationship between Australia and New Zealand insofar as it provides a potential trigger for the exercise of the Commonwealth's external affairs power (sec 51(xxix), further diminishing the constitutional authority of the States.

Nevertheless there also are dangers in the present arrangements for New Zealand, as its relationship with Australia has evolved. The adaptation of Australian intergovernmental processes to the relationship between New Zealand and Australia, coupled with the imbalance in the size and economic power of the two countries, puts New Zealand at some risk of becoming a seventh State de facto, without the benefit that formal statehood brings and without the relative clarity of a constitutional framework. Securing the benefits of intersystemic government without surrendering the autonomy of the participants to an unacceptable degree becomes a particular challenge in these circumstances, which is likely to require determination, insight and public understanding in the years that lie ahead.

14

Early Days

SIR STEPHEN SEDLEY

ALTHOUGH I LOOK with envy at young lawyers who swim with ease in the great sea of modern public law where as a young barrister I struggled from day to day, sometimes to get into the water at all, at other times to escape being swamped by waves or carried off by the undertow, it was still a piece of luck to have been called to the Bar of England and Wales as long ago as November 1964.

It would have been July, in fact, if I had not miscounted the number of dinners I had eaten in what should have been my final term and been refused call by the Inner Temple until I had eaten my way through a full further term. My first chambers clerk, Walter Berry, had clerked one of the great Privy Council sets of chambers between the wars but now, in his eighties, was clerking the small set in which I became a tenant at the end of my pupillage. When Walter had started as a boy in the Temple in the 1890s, there were no typewriters and it was the junior clerk's job to write out the governors' pleadings and opinions in a clear hand for signature. When our solitary chambers typist, Miss Green, was on holiday or unwell, Walter would write out my pleadings in copperplate with his steel-nibbed pen and I would sign them. I must be the last member of the Bar to have sent their work out like this.

But this is not the only sense in which I feel on occasion like a time traveller. In 1964 neither administrative law nor public law was part of the Bar's curriculum or practice. Its jejune examinations (it was still a non-graduate profession) included constitutional law, but that was all. My generation entered the courts with at best a dim awareness that there were prerogative writs with Latin names that were used for purposes too obscure to recall. The government ran the country; judges ran the courts.

I started in practice doing everything that came my way. You could take briefs from the day after you were called to the Bar, and an alarming proportion of your learning was done at your client's expense. But two groups of clients became quickly more significant than the rest. One was the Kentish gypsies; the other was low-income tenants in Notting Hill and in East London. Neither would have come my way but for the legal aid system, now mostly history, which since 1949 had enabled poor people to obtain advice and representation and which solicitors were finally realising was not a form of charity but a worthwhile source of work and income.

***

The pressure on England's gypsies had been growing since the passing of legislation[1] which gave local authorities power to close the commons on which they had traditionally stopped, with a concomitant power to open permanent campsites for them. Local councils had begun energetically exercising the first power, fencing and ditching their remaining commons, while not a single one had used the power to open a site for the nomads they were depriving of their stopping places. Gypsies, who were consequently having to camp on the grass verges of arterial roads, now found that it was a crime to be a gypsy encamped on a highway[2], and the police were securing regular convictions and sometimes heavy fines.

Brian Richardson, an amiable anarchist architect, knew some of the travellers who moved through his part of Kent—still at that time thick with the hop-fields that afforded gypsies and East Enders an annual spell of convivial and well-paid work. He persuaded a group of thirty two of them who had just been convicted and fined by the Sevenoaks Justices to go and see a local solicitor, Peter Kingshill, who lived near Sevenoaks. Peter, who had reached this country as a teenage refugee from Nazi Germany and whose heart was in work of this kind, gave notice of appeal to the Croydon Quarter Sessions and sent me the brief.

All quarter sessions appeals were de novo hearings. The prosecutor, having called the local police sergeant who recounted from his notebook that he had observed each of the accused encamped with his family and animals on the grass verge of a highway, closed his case. Nervously (the chairman of the court was Fitzwalter Butler QC, the editor of Archbold) I submitted that the Crown had failed to prove that the accused were gypsies. The chairman, visibly pleased to have something out of the ordinary to deal with, upheld the submission, and all 32 convictions were quashed.

The police did not give up. They prosecuted most of my clients again, this time calling evidence about their way of life in order to prove that they were gypsies. On one occasion a local preacher, Pastor George Lywood, volunteered to give evidence in mitigation. Not yet having learned the first two rules of magistrates' court advocacy (never call the solicitor, never call the parson), I sanguinely put Lywood in the box and asked him what he could tell the court about the difficulties faced by nomads in the Sevenoaks area. Lywood (who I later learned had served with legendary bravery as a tail-gunner in Wellington bombers

[1] Caravan Sites and Control of Development Act 1960.

[2] Highways Act 1959, s127: the ban covered only hawkers, other itinerant traders and gypsies.

throughout the war) launched into a hellfire sermon on the fate awaiting magistrates who persecuted the poor. Neither the chairman nor I could stop him; the fines were colossal.

But a different bench upheld my submission that one of the thirty two, Abe Cooper, was now *autrefois acquit*, preventing the police from trying to prove again what they had failed to prove before. The police appealed to the High Court. Legal aid paid for a leader—Basil Wigoder QC—who reckoned that we were going to be the ones who got issue estoppel into criminal law. He had not reckoned with the presence on our court of Lord Justice Diplock, who spent the first fifteen minutes mining Basil's path with bland questions, each of which turned out to be a landmine on which Basil duly spent the next two hours stepping.[3]

But what made my first appearance at the bar of the Lord Chief Justice's court memorable was not our predictable forensic defeat. It was that the same court was hearing a case brought by Margaret Lain, the widow of a police officer, against the Criminal Injuries Compensation Board for having failed to make an award in accordance with the White Paper under which ministers had set up the ex gratia scheme. The Crown's case, argued by the Treasury Devil, Nigel Bridge, was that the entire scheme was a discretionary exercise of prerogative power over which the courts had no jurisdiction.

The Lord Chief Justice, Lord Parker, gave the first judgment. He was followed by Diplock, reading, as he always did, in a barely audible monotone from a manuscript held up in front of his face (the court's shorthand writer told me in later years that she could neither hear the one nor read the other). Straining to hear, it became apparent even to me that something epoch-making was being decided. Nigel Bridge, sitting intently forward on the seat reserved for the Treasury Devil on counsel's bench, listened poker-faced as government's last historic bastion against judicial review fell:[4]

> The question of jurisdiction raised by this application is one of novelty and importance …
>
> The jurisdiction of the High Court as successor of the Court of Queen's Bench to supervise the exercise of their jurisdiction by inferior tribunals has not in the past been dependent on the source of the tribunal's authority … The earlier history of the writ of certiorari shows that it was issued to courts whose authority was derived from the prerogative, from Royal Charter, from franchise or custom as well as from Act of Parliament. Its recent history shows that as new kinds of tribunals have been created, orders of certiorari have been extended to them too and to all persons who under authority of the government have exercised quasi-judicial functions. True, since the victory of Parliament in the constitutional struggles of the seventeenth century, authority has been generally if not invariably conferred upon new kinds of tribunals by or under Act of Parliament and there has been no recent occasion for the High Court to

[3] *Mills v Cooper* [1967] 2 QB 459.

[4] *R v Criminal Injuries Compensation Board, ex parte Lain* [1967] 2 QB 864 at 883–84.

> exercise supervisory jurisdiction over persons whose ultimate authority to decide matters is derived from any other source. I see no reason, however, for holding that the ancient jurisdiction of the Court of Queen's Bench has been narrowed merely because there has been no occasion to exercise it. If new tribunals are established by acts of government, the supervisory jurisdiction of the High Court extends to them if they possess the essential characteristics upon which the subjection of inferior tribunals to the supervisory control of the High Court is based.

Although it has become conventional for academic writers to ascribe this turning point to the GCHQ case almost two decades later,[5] it was Diplock in *Lain* who had seen the point and done the job. Significantly, Mrs Lain lost: it was held that the Board had made no error. But instead of ducking the jurisdiction issue on this ground, the court took the opportunity to make it the foundation of its decision.

The sense I got, sitting there as a very junior barrister, stayed with me: times were changing; government was not beyond law as I had been taught to believe it was; a penetrating and educated judicial mind with a strong sense of history had begun the process of restoring and renovating the proper relationship between the executive and the law.

In the late 1960s the Crown Office list, which today typically keeps a Divisional Court and 6 or more single judges busy every day of the legal year, was ordinarily slotted into the Wednesday morning list of the Lord Chief Justice's criminal appeal court, which turned itself into a divisional Queen's Bench court for the purpose. Lord Parker would refuse leave to move wherever he could, and the workload was correspondingly light. A case as difficult and important as *Lain* was very rare. But by the early 1970s I was turning up in the Chief's court from time to time and occasionally getting somewhere.

The cases were coming from the poor parts of east and west London, where tenants were often at the mercy both of unscrupulous private landlords and of neglectful local authorities—the latter not only as landlords but as the statutory enforcement agencies for housing standards. There were also now independent rent-setting tribunals. We were increasingly finding that these statutory agencies, with which our clients had no relationship either in contract or in tort, were acting unlawfully or unfairly. But our training gave us no equipment for bringing them to book.

When I say we, I am speaking not only of the handful of lawyers who became involved in this work but—importantly—of the law centres which, from 1969 onwards, began to be set up with public or charitable funding, taking on the worst of the housing providers first in London and then in the other big cities. To our aid came some independent environmental health officers and surveyors who could give the expert evidence that was needed. Between us we started

[5] *Council of Civil Service Unions v Minister for the Civil Service* [1985] AC 374.

working out how the cobwebbed mechanisms of judicial review could be deployed to make local justices, councils and tribunals do their job properly.

In 1971 Lord Widgery succeeded Lord Parker as Lord Chief Justice. Widgery was regarded by the profession as a dull and conservative figure, a wartime brigadier and former planning lawyer who would always kick for touch if he saw trouble approaching. That was not how, as a young barrister, I found him. He was no pushover, but it became clear after a few sallies into his court that if I could show him a worthwhile issue of principle, he would do what he could to help. He was especially good on natural justice issues, which were probably the ones we were most regularly encountering. It was Widgery who chose to preside regularly in the Divisional Court because he sensed the need for a policy-guided hand on the tiller, and it was he who early in the 1970s stopped fooling about with a *Wednesbury* test of fairness ("Could any rational tribunal have refused to adjourn this case?") and started simply deciding whether what had happened was plainly unfair.[6]

***

The Child Poverty Action Group, still today a leading voice in the area of social security, set up its Citizens' Rights Office towards 1970[7] and began taking on central government in a series of cases picked to test issues affecting large numbers of people in scenarios uncluttered by eccentric facts. After a time the department of state against which the cases were being brought began to see the positive value of such a strategy, and their principal solicitor, Charles Blake, began to work with the CPAG in finding useful test cases to clarify difficult points of law.

Other public authorities, especially cash-strapped local councils, were much more intransigent, and I got a bloody nose on several occasions when cases went wrong. On one occasion, after two days of a protracted judicial mugging in the Court of Appeal which drove me at one stage to say that I would only answer the court's question if I was given two uninterrupted sentences in which to do so (which, to be fair, they gave me before launching the next barrage) and which culminated in a judgment that seemed to me to come close to insult, I wrote to the chairman of the Bar's professional conduct committee—Peter Taylor, the future Lord Chief Justice, as it happened—to ask what protection the Bar Council was prepared to give against this kind of judicial behaviour. Peter's reply—that there was absolutely nothing the Bar could do—had a PS: "If this is the worst thing that's happened to you, you're not doing too badly."

The case was one of the many public housing standards cases which law centres were taking on, and which provoked very differing reactions both from local benches and in the High Court and Court of Appeal. Some courts were

[6] See *R v SW London Supplementary benefits Appeal Tribunal, ex parte Bullen* (1976) 120 *Solicitors Journal* 437.

[7] Headed up by the solicitor Henry – now Mr Justice – Hodge.

appalled at the conditions in which poor people were expected to live. Others thought them greedy and ungrateful. In one case we had to get an order from the Divisional Court requiring local magistrates to convict a local authority: they had dismissed the only expert evidence—ours—because it came from a (male) environmental health officer with a pony tail and an earring. In another the local bench refused to believe that the High Court had granted an order of prohibition against them, and my instructing solicitor, Larry Grant, had to travel out to the suburbs, go into the witness box and swear to the magistrates that he had witnessed the order being made.

***

For the growing number of cases involving central government, Nigel Bridge, who in 1968 set off on his judicial path to the Lords, was succeeded as Treasury Devil by Gordon Slynn. One could not have had an opponent from whom it was possible to learn more about intellectual rigour in analysis and fairness in argument. It was a pleasure to argue cases against him and his successors, Harry Woolf (whom Slynn talent-spotted and recommended for the job), Simon Brown and John Laws, each of whom contested—or occasionally conceded—my applications month after month for two decades without a hint of rancour or impatience, until finally in 1992, with our climactic case *M v Home Office*[8] frustratingly stood out of the Law Lords' list to allow a 9-judge panel to rehear *Pepper v Hart*,[9] Laws and I both accepted appointment to the bench.

***

What proved more intractable over these years was being allowed to challenge anything which central government regarded as a matter of high policy. This was not usually formally articulated as a ground of public interest immunity: it was simply that, if civil servants decided to categorise an issue as one of high policy formation, you could not get disclosure of the materials that would show whether the challenge was well-founded or not. Much of the change that has come about in this regard has been because it has been realised that it is in government's own interests to account in detail for the formation of its policies, not infrequently in order to show legislation to be compatible with the European Convention on Human Rights.[10]

But the first breach in the wall as I experienced it was rather more comical. Early in the 1980s a county council, wanting to close one of its secondary schools, applied to the Department of Education for permission to do so. The application sat in someone's in-tray for months until finally the county council pointed out to the department that the school holidays were coming to an end and nobody

[8] [1994] 1 AC 377.

[9] [1993] AC 593.

[10] See eg, *Evans v Amicus Healthcare* [2004] EWCA Civ 727, paras 42–56. See *Williams v Home Office* [1981] 1 All ER 1151 for an early example of court-enforced disclosure of the policy-making process.

knew whether the school was going to reopen. A day or two later a senior official phoned the county education department to say the minister had agreed that the school could be closed and that a letter would be in the post that night to confirm it—but please would the council say nothing to anyone until the letter arrived. When the letter arrived, however, it said the opposite: the school could *not* be closed. Blow that, said the county council, they told us it could be, and they went ahead with the closure.

The parents—who had been almost unanimously opposed to closure—came to me, and we shot off to the High Court with an application for an order of prohibition, with the Department of Education joined as a respondent. At that stage we knew no more than I have so far recounted. But the judge presiding in the Divisional Court that heard the case was Tasker Watkins LJ who, having won the Victoria Cross as a subaltern, had little fear of central government or anyone else.

> "Where's the department's file?" said Tasker Watkins to Treasury counsel at the end of the first day's hearing.
>
> "It concerns high policy formation, my Lord," said John Laws. "It is not the practice to disclose this kind of material."
>
> "Here, on my desk, by 10.30 tomorrow morning," said Tasker, and rose.

And out it all came. Within half an hour of the phone call requesting silence until the letter arrived, the local press had the news and a reporter phoned the local MP in London for his reaction. The MP, a member of the governing party who not only had children at the school but whose majority was smaller than the number of parents there, raced round to the department, collared the Secretary of State, told him the local press had somehow got wind that departmental permission was coming to close the school and pointed out to him that it could cost them the seat. The Secretary of State summoned the minister, who said he'd only done what his civil servants advised (the file, many inches thick, had a sheet pinned to the front of it reading "Minister: if you AGREE with the proposal, please tick here", accompanied by a large ministerial tick and an affidavit asserting that the minister had read the entire file before administering it), but the post had not yet gone and the letter could be retrieved from the out-tray.

So it was that, despite the ministerial tick, the letter which went into the post that night said the school could not be closed. Of such stuff, sometimes at least, is policy made. We won the case and the school stayed open.

***

One of the areas of public administration on which public law had made no impact at all by the 1970s was the prison system. In the handful of reported cases[11] Lord Goddard, Lord Denning and others had sent a clear message that prisoners, by definition undeserving, must put up with their conditions and not come complaining to the courts. It was thanks very largely to the work of the solicitors Gareth Peirce and Kate Akester and a young barrister named Edward Fitzgerald that prison law not only forced its way on to the public law agenda but became the force for human rights that it is today. My role was simply to present from the front bench the cases they assembled, using the learning and strategy that Edward Fitzgerald brought to them.

The mercurial Ed had been a pupil in first in my chambers and then in John Mortimer's at a time when Mortimer was brought in to give leading counsel's opinion on a difficult issue which I had advised was highly problematical—whether the Home Office could be sued for assault for administering virginity tests to women entering the country from the Indian subcontinent for arranged marriages. Mortimer, in an opinion half a page long, said he agreed with me. The Law Society, who at the time administered the legal aid system, expressed disappointment and asked him for something a little more substantial. Back came an opinion of colossal depth, breadth and learning, signed 'J.M.' but manifestly not his work. John, a fluent and enchanting advocate who found law a distraction[12], had wandered into Geoffrey Robertson's room looking for a pupil to do some of the research and had stumbled on Ed.

In the course of the 1980s Ed Fitzgerald was joined by Tim Owen[13], and on the footing of their hard work I was able to advance a succession of arguments—they can be tracked in Owen's now standard textbook on prison law—before which the walls of silence surrounding British prisons began to crumble. As early as 1979, in the wake of the Hull prison riots, the High Court had held the adjudicative functions of the boards of prison visitors amenable to judicial review for failures of due process.[14] But for many years the inner fortification—governors' adjudications—remained intact, the Court of Appeal likening them (the mindset was revealing) to decisions of a military commander in the field or the master of a ship at sea.[15] Thereafter in a succession of cases the Home Office, conscious that the bastion was vulnerable if the issue reached the Lords, brought forward prisoners' release dates in order to be able to submit to the Lords, successfully for a time, that leave should not be granted because each case was now moot.

The Joshua whose trumpet brought the wall down was a prisoner named Mark Leech. Leech, now a reformed character running the charity Unlock for ex-prisoners and editing the annual *Guide to the Penal System of England and*

[11] See eg, *Becker v Home Office* [1972] 2 QB 407: "If the courts were to entertain actions by disgruntled prisoners, the governor's life would be made intolerable" (Lord Denning MR at 419).

[12] He used to call himself an Old Bailey hack. It is not widely known that Rumpole of the Bailey started life as John Mortimer's self-parody.

[13] Both of them now in silk, and Ed with a CBE for his services to human rights law.

[14] *R v Board of Visitors, Hull Prison, ex parte St Germain* [1979] QB 425.

[15] *R v Deputy Governor Camphill Prison, ex parte King* [1985] QB 735.

Wales, was at the time not only a professional con artist but the ablest barrack-room lawyer in the prison system. It was on him, as luck would have it, that a deputy governor decided to practise a textbook breach of natural justice. The prison system still had adjudications recorded in longhand by a long-suffering prison officer, and the official record of Leech's adjudication went (from memory) something like this:

> PO: On a search of the prisoner's cell, sir, a biro adapted for smoking cannabis was found concealed in the ceiling tiles.
>
> DG: Right, I find the case proved.
>
> Prisoner: Hang on, you haven't heard my defence.
>
> DG: I'm not interested in your defence.

With this on the record, there was no answer other than non-justiciability, and the argument that making governors' adjudications justiciable would bring prison discipline to its knees was given its quietus by the case that accompanied Leech's. A prisoner named Prevot, whose good-looking wife used to visit him regularly, had been found guilty on an adjudication of enjoying a degree of conjugal comfort in the course of a visit under cover of the wife's fur coat. Prevot had been refused permission to call either his wife or any of the sixteen other prisoners who were having visits at the same time at tables in a single large room, to say that if anything untoward had occurred they would have been better placed to see it than the two prison officers at the far end of the room. It was not exactly likely that they would be believed, but that was not the point.

One of my more memorable moments at the bar was watching Nigel Bridge, by then a Law Lord, trying to keep a straight face as the facts were described. Another was watching as John Laws, always a fine advocate but at his best when he had his back to the wall, fought for his forensic life as Bridge led the judicial pack at him. The daylight that has entered the prison and parole systems, intensified since 2000 by strong messages coming from Strasbourg, has been an important element in the renewal of our public law.[16]

***

The story of the gypsies of England and Wales is more sombre. In 1968 a Liberal MP, Eric Lubbock, got a private members' bill enacted to make the power of local authorities to open sites for homeless travellers into a duty. For the next 25 years, until the Thatcher administration repealed it, the duty was ignored or evaded by most local authorities. When we tried to obtain coercive orders or declarations against them, they successfully pleaded that the Act gave the enforcement function to central government. But central government sat on its hands

[16] *Leech v Deputy Governor, HMP Parkhurst; Prevot v Deputy Governor, HMP Long Lartin* [1988] AC 533.

and, apart from issuing circulars, did nothing to enforce the duties. Attempts at judicial review failed to shift it. Although Peter Kingshill and I won some reprieves and forced some authorities to think again,[17] such protection as gypsies have managed to secure against constant eviction and harassment has come from Strasbourg.[18]

***

It was on the back of this work that, in May 1991, I was brought in by a leading immigration practitioner, David Burgess, to represent a client of his, a young Zairean teacher, anonymised as M, who had fled after being imprisoned and tortured by Colonel Mobutu's police, but been refused asylum here. He consulted Burgess, who reckoned that his case had been wrongly presented and that, if M could be kept here for a short while, the Court of Appeal might well intervene. Counsel had accordingly gone before Garland J, who understood the Home Office's counsel to have given him an undertaking that M would not be removed pending application to the Court of Appeal. Despite this, M, with two guards, was put on a plane for Kinshasa, his holdall helpfully packed with copies of his asylum application for the attention of Mobutu's police. Garland J that evening issued an injunction ordering the Home Secretary to secure M's immediate return. The plane was at that stage on the tarmac in Paris, but neither then nor on arrival in Kinshasa was any attempt made to bring him back. The injunction was ignored until late the following afternoon, by when M was in the hands of the Zairean police.

The Home Office restored the case before Garland J, showed him the passage in Lord Bridge's speech in *Factortame Ltd v Secretary of State for Transport*,[19] which (erroneously) asserted that injunctions could not be made against the Crown, and got the order discharged. But there had meanwhile been a valid order which had been breached, and the only remedy was to impeach the Home Secretary for contempt of court. Here, at last, was the big issue. On the day of the directions hearing a large man in a black suit approached me shortly before the court sat and asked me if I could point out the contemnor to him. It was the court tipstaff hoping to finger the Home Secretary's collar.

The full history of the case can be found in the law reports[20] and elsewhere.[21] I mention it here because Sir William Wade, who gave us advice and encouragement in the contempt proceedings, considered it the most important constitutional decision of the last two hundred years. I have mentioned that John Laws and I, who had argued it against each other at first and second instance, both left

[17] See eg, *R v Secretary of State for the Environment, ex p Lee* [1985] JPL 724.

[18] See *Chapman v United Kingdom* (2001) 33 EHRR 18.

[19] [1990] 2 AC 85.

[20] [1994] AC 377

[21] See S Sedley, 'The Crown in its own courts', in C Forsyth and I Hare (eds) *The Golden Metwand and the Crooked Cord, Essays in Honour of Sir William Wade* (Oxford, Clarendon, 1998) at 253.

the bar for the bench while the government's final appeal was still pending. To my pleasure, my brief was taken by the great South African advocate Sydney Kentridge, who enlarged the majority I had secured in the Court of Appeal into a unanimous vindication of the rule of law and the amenability of ministers in virtue of their office to the coercive powers of the courts.

The implications of the shift from personal to official liability in contempt have not been fully explored, or perhaps even fully grasped; but if *M v Home Office* forms a landmark on the path to the common law's eventual acknowledgment of the state as an entity known to, and governed by, law, it is because it came in the wake of a renewal and reinvigoration of our public law in which it had been Mike Taggart's achievement and my good fortune to play a part.

15

The Killing of the Prisoners at Agincourt and a Movement from Contract to Status[1]

AWB SIMPSON

ONE OF THE features of Mike Taggart's scholarship has been his readiness to devote his attention to important subjects that are outside the orthodox and the mainstream, and in what follows I shall try to emulate him in a manner I hope he will approve. In a famous passage in *Ancient Law. Its Connection to the Early History of Society and Its Relation to Modern Ideas*, Henry Maine argued that the movement of progressive societies had hitherto, at least, been a movement from status to contract. What follows is an account of a movement in the other direction. It concerns the protection of prisoners of war. The story of some prisoners who notably did not enjoy protection is familiar to all through Shakespeare's *Henry V*, and through the Lawrence Olivier and Kenneth Branagh movies based on the play. It all happened at the battle of Agincourt which, in English culture, still enjoys an iconic status as a famous victory against all the odds. The phenomenon with which this essay is concerned can be illustrated from the story of the battle and the killing of the French prisoners.

It was fought on 25 October 1415, and is, as medieval battles go, extremely fully documented.[2] Yet there is virtually no aspect of the battle which is not, to

[1] I am grateful to Dino Kritsiotis and Grace Tonner for reading a draft of this essay and commenting on it.

[2] A Currie, *The Battle of Agincourt. Sources and Interpretations* (Woodbridge, Boydell Press, 2000) [Currie, *Battle of Agincourt*] reproduces most of them, translated into English where needed. Her *Agincourt. A New History* (Stroud, Tempus, 2006) [Currie, *A New History*] is the most recent scholarly study, which appeared soon after J Barker's highly readable and scholarly, *Agincourt. Henry V and the Battle that Made England* (New York, Little Brown, 2005). These books refer back to the very considerable literature, which I do not list here. JH Wylie and WT Waugh, *The Reign of Henry the Fifth* (Cambridge, Cambridge University Press, 1929) provides in three volumes a mass of somewhat undigested information. H Nicolas, *History of the Battle of Agincourt* (London, H Pordes, 1970 reprint of edition of 1832) [Nicolas, *History of the Battle*] is the earliest scholarly history; it is unlikely that he

some degree, shrouded in uncertainty. Two things are, however, quite clearly established. The first is that Henry V and his army won a dramatic victory, the third major victory in the Hundred Year's War after Crecy (1346) and Poitiers (1356), leaving the score three nil. And although the precise number of deaths on each side is not and never will be known, there is no doubt that far more French died than English, with something of the order of 7,000 French dead.[3] This means an extraordinary death toll of between 35% and 58%, depending on what the combatant size of the French army was; I take the most likely figure to be somewhere between 12,000 and 20,000.[4] At most there were 500 English dead, 8% or perhaps less.[5] So this was one of those battles, other examples being Omdurman (1898), and Navarino (1827), in which one side utterly trounced the other.[6] Such victories are often, but not always, the consequence of an imbalance of fire power, and the lethal efficiency of the English longbow certainly played a large part at Agincourt. The second is that a considerable number of French prisoners were deliberately killed. A high proportion of the French who died at Agincourt were aristocrats, or persons of superior social status, rather than common soldiers.[7] How many of them were killed as prisoners, and how many simply died in battle, or died later from their wounds, is not known. On the English side there were few dead of superior social status: the Duke of York and the Earl of Suffolk, two persons who had been dubbed as knights on the eve of the battle,[8] and some nine or ten others;[9] quite where the English Chaplain, who

ever visited the area. Sir John Woodford visited the battlefield, mapped the area, preserved some local traditional information, and dug in the grave pits in 1818. His map is reproduced, but poorly, in Currie, *The Battle of Agincourt* at 362; original in the British Library Add MS 16368 C.

[3] There is evidence of the burial of 5,800 or more on the site, and there were other burials elsewhere. The author of the *Ruisseauville Chronicle*, who lived at a nearby abbey, and may well have been involved in the burials, gives the number quoted as a minimum. The location of the French grave pits is known through both tradition and investigation by Sir John Woodford, in 1818. There has been no modern archaeological investigation.

[4] See below text to n 40.

[5] Currie, *A New History*, above n 2, App C lists the various figures. The Berry Herald, who was not there but as a herald would have access to information on the count of the dead gives a figure of three to four hundred. Currie, *Battle of Agincourt*, above n 2 at 182.

[6] The defeated army at Omdurman suffered about 10,000 killed, the English 48. At Navarino the allied fleet suffered 181 killed and no ships sunk; the Ottoman fleet around 3,000 dead and 70 out of 78 ships sunk or destroyed. In some battles the losing army has been annihilated, but Agincourt was not such a battle.

[7] Thus the *Ruisseauville Chronicle* (Currie, *Battle of Agincourt*, above n 2 at 127) says that of the 7,600–7,800 dead between 1600 and 1800 were entitled to coats of arms, and that an unspecified further number were gentlemen. Roughly speaking a quarter of the casualties were of very high social status.

[8] Richard Kyghley and Daffyd ap Llewellyn (known as Davy Gam, Gam being a nickname indicating that he had a squint).

[9] Some 112 English who died at the battle can be identified, according to Barker, *Agincourt* 304. But see Currie, *A New History*, above n 2 at 281, giving figures of 17 archers, 3 men at arms and 90 others with no indication whether they were archers of men at arms. The English dead were mainly burned near the battlefield; the two leading aristocrats (and perhaps some others) were boiled and their sanitised remains returned to England.

was present and wrote *The Deeds of Henry V*, giving this figure, drew the line of social division is obscure, but these nine or ten would probably have been either knights or esquires.[10]

The killing of the prisoners has come to be viewed as a blot on the record of Henry V; indeed in France some have given him the nickname cutthroat, *coup gorge*. In present day international humanitarian law it is of course wholly unlawful, except in special circumstances by way of exception, for example as an extreme and necessary measure to prevent escape, to kill prisoners. This general principle was adopted in the *1907 Hague Convention IV*[11] and is now further elaborated in the *1949 Geneva Convention III Relative to the Treatment of Prisoners of War* and the *Protocol* of 1977.[12] Although thus embodied and elaborated in international instruments, the prohibition on killing prisoners is today properly viewed as a rule of customary international law.[13] In war, or armed conflict as it is now called, it is of course not infrequently violated even by soldiers from armies in which in general the rights of prisoners are respected. Thus in Max Hastings' *Armageddon, the Battle for Germany 1944–5*,[14] there are numerous accounts of the unlawful killing of prisoners, and this on both sides. Furthermore to acquire the status of a prisoner, entitled to protection, and cease to be an opponent who can lawfully be killed, you have first to be captured, and attempts to make this transition by surrender, or, to use the traditional old expression, by laying down your arms, are in real life extremely hazardous. Military memoirs are full of examples,[15] and one reason why soldiers continue to fight even in desperate conditions is no doubt that it often seems safer than trying to surrender. Under the 1949 Geneva Convention the protection of prisoners begins "from the time they fall into the power of the enemy", but no legal provision can legislate away the inevitable uncertainty as to precisely when this moment has arrived.[16] The *1977 Geneva Protocol I* uses a more elaborate concept of being *hors de combat* which also covers a person who has expressed an intention to surrender, or is unconscious, or unable to engage in combat because of wounds or illness.[17] But the dangerous uncertainty of the moment of transition remains.

[10] Only two other men at arms can be identified; see Currie, *A New History*, above n 2 at 281

[11] See A Roberts and R Guelff, *Documents on the Laws of War* (Oxford, Oxford University Press, 3rd edn, 2000) 73 [Roberts and Guelff, *Documents*].

[12] Roberts and Guelff, ibid at 243 and 419. The modern law distinguishes between lawful and unlawful combatants; the former are eligible for prisoner of war status whilst the latter are entitled to a lesser degree of protection.

[13] See by way of illustration Roberts and Guelff, ibid at 177–78, providing excerpts from the *Judgement of the International Tribunal at Nuremberg*, which takes this view.

[14] London, Macmillan, 2004. See 101, 241–42, 287, 499, 553–54, 558.

[15] See for examples J Keegan, *The Illustrated Face of Battle* (New York, Viking Press, 1989) 103 quoting the conventional brutal preliminary remark of the English soldier "Too late, chum".

[16] See Article 5 of the *1949 Geneva Convention*; Roberts and Guelff, *Documents*, above n 11 at 243.

[17] For the text see Roberts and Guelff, ibid at 443.

What was the position back in 1415?[18] We need first to place the killing of the French prisoners into its context. To this end I shall first give a brief account of the character of the two armies that met there, and of the course of the battle. I shall then give an account of the reason why the prisoners were killed, and the way it was gone about. To simplify this I shall say at the outset that modern knowledge on all this is both patchy and variable in certainty, and the chief sources for the battle itself, the chronicles, are far from consistent. Five of the accounts of the battle were by persons actually present—an English Royal Chaplain, whose name is not known,[19] John Hardyng[20] and Jean Le Fèvre (on the English side),[21] Jean Waurin[22] and Ghillebert de Lannoy[23] on the French. But as the Duke of Wellington, who knew a thing or two about battles, pointed out long ago, even those who are present at a battle never have a comprehensive picture of what has gone on, any more than does a person present at a ball.[24]

Henry V's army comprised, first of all, 900 men at arms, that is to say cavalry, all of whom would wear some form of full armour. Notions about the wearing and character of armour are distorted because much evidence comes from the funeral effigies of the wealthy, and from artists depictions; little information exists as to what the less wealthy men at arms wore, and hardly any armour from this period has survived.[25] Henry V's helmet, preserved in Westminster Abbey, is not a battle helmet, but one worn for jousting. The more wealthy men at arms would certainly have worn very expensive modern plate armour, also called white armour, since it was polished and gleaming, but the less wealthy probably wore chain mail armour, perhaps mixed with some plate, some of it quite old.[26] For horsed combat they carried lances, which could be as much as fourteen feet long. These weapons were also used for foot combat, for which they might be shortened, as they were on the French side at Agincourt, and probably on the English too. They would in addition possess at least one war horse or *destrier*, or a rouncy, a war horse of lower quality, always a stallion, both being expensive

[18] Today Azincourt.

[19] Currie, *Battle of Agincourt*, above n 2 at 22.

[20] Ibid at 78.

[21] Ibid at 135. Le Fèvre was present as some sort of herald or perhaps trainee herald; he was aged 19 at the time.

[22] Ibid at 136. He was fifteen at the time of battle at which his father and half brother were killed. Waurin and Le Fèvre collaborated with each other and with one Enguerrand (or Enguerran) de Monstrelet in producing the fullest account of the battle, though their accounts differ. Monstrelet was not present.

[23] His *Oeuvres* were not included in Currie's *Battle of Agincourt*, above n 2. He was captured at the battle and placed in a building that was set on fire; he escaped. He only recorded an incident in the battle.

[24] Quoted Keegan, *Face of Battle* 103.

[25] A considerable amount of armour has been recovered from the grave pits of the battle of Wisby (1361), but this was out of date even then, thus providing no evidence relevant to Agincourt. See B Thordeman, *Armour from the Battle of Wisby* (Highland Village Texas, Chivalry Bookshelf, 2007). This reprints the original Stockholm edition of 1939.

[26] Archers did not wear full armour of any kind, though they sometimes wore cap helmets and protective jerkins.

pieces of equipment,[27] and swords, daggers, and a variety of other weapons, such as forms of club, or forms of axes. At Agincourt, as earlier at Crecy and Poitiers, they fought dismounted. The major body of Henry's fighting men were, however, the archers, 5,000 of them, many but not all of whom had horses. But they too all fought dismounted. In addition there were a considerable but uncertain number of non-combatants, called in my military days "the odds and sods"; chaplains, cooks, farriers, grooms, pages, surgeons and so forth. Aristocrats in particular traveled in considerable style with numerous attendants and servants. Although some of the men at arms would be of relatively low social status, many were persons of gentle birth and independent means, and some were nobles. The archers were virtually all of plebeian status. The army was created by a system of contracts between the Crown and persons willing or eager to serve in the wars; the soldiers were not there in discharge of feudal obligations of service. For aristocrats and gentlemen war was what they did, and many would consider themselves as under an obligation to their monarch to support him in war. They contracted to bring a retinue to the war, of which they would serve as the captain. Retinues were of very varied size. Thus Thomas, Earl of Arundell, contracted to bring 100 men at arms (including 7 bannerets,[28] 3 knights[29] and 89 esquires[30]) and 300 mounted archers. Philip Leche, himself a knight, contracted to bring 3 men at arms and 9 archers.[31] Under these contracts the soldiers were to be paid, their wages being, for the less socially elevated, often better than they could earn in other ways. A massive body of information has survived on this system of contracts;[32] the scholar who has made the fullest and most brilliant use of it is Anne Currie. Unfortunately it sheds relatively little light on the actual conduct of operations; you cannot obtain a clear picture or indeed any picture at all of the Battle of Alamein from the records of the Pay Corps. But the records of the Pay Corps would still tell us a lot about who was there and why, and historians have

[27] Stallions alone were thought to be courageous enough for war; they "had the balls for it". Men at arms would have one or more riding horses; the more wealthy might have a considerable number of war horses, as well as pack horses to carry baggage; carts do not seem to have been used on the march to Agincourt. The number of horses with the army would have been 7,000 or more.

[28] Bannerets exercised a command function in battle under the captain of the retinue; they bore rectangular banners. See M Prestwich, *Armies and Warfare in the Middle Ages. The English Experience* (New Haven, Yale University Press, 1996) 13–15 [Prestwich, *Armies and Warfare*]; his account does not however match the evidence for Agincourt, and largely relates to an earlier period.

[29] That is persons who had gone through the ceremony of knighthood; relatively few of the men at arms were knights in this sense. All would be armigerous, that is entitled to a coat of arms, which would be displayed in battle on tunic known as coat armour worn over protective armour. The outstanding book on these evolving social distinctions is M Keen, *Origins of the English Gentleman. Heraldry, Chivalry and Gentility in Medieval England 1300–1500* (Stroud and Charleston SC, Tempus Press, 2002).

[30] Esquires, who by 1415 would in the main be armigerous, belonged to a social grade below that of the knights, though some would in due course become knights. Below them came persons of gentle birth who were "mere gentlemen".

[31] Nicolas, *History of the Battle,* above n 2 at 373 and ff.

[32] This survives in the records of the Exchequer preserved in the National Archives.

to make the best use possible of what records there are. The main source of information on the conduct of the battle has to be the chronicles.

English armies were organized into three units called battles, and on the march would proceed in line ahead with one battle as the vanguard, then the second battle as the main body, and at the back the third battle as rearguard.[33] At Agincourt the three battles were certainly deployed close together in line abreast; there is much controversy about the positioning of the archers but it is likely that some were interspersed amongst the men at arms, whilst most of the archers were deployed on the wings. There is some evidence that the archers were organized for battle in units of 100 or 50, or conceivably in even smaller units of 20 (though there is no direct evidence for units of 20 at Agincourt). How precisely the men at arms were organized in battle is not clearly known. It is clear that the retinue was the basic unit of organization, and its members kept together on the march, and in camp.[34] But since the retinues varied in size from some hundreds down to two or three, and comprised both men at arms and archers, this provided a ridiculously bad system for control in battle. One might expect to find evidence of a subsidiary system of battle control, under which the soldiers were organized in a hierarchy of smaller units, as is the modern English army, with its battalions, companies, platoons and sections, each with its commander. But the evidence for this at Agincourt is scanty indeed, though presumably bannerets and knights did perform a command function within each retinue.[35] Furthermore for this period there is no evidence whatever of the holding of general collective field exercises, in which deployment and movement of all three battles, or even just one, was rehearsed. Men at arms and archers did, however, go through arduous training in individual skills, and for aristocrats individual mounted combat was practiced by jousting, a mock battle between two individuals, when they charged each other with blunted lances separated by a barrier.[36] Such individual mounted combats, the ideal of the romanticized vision of war known as chivalry, hardly ever happened. Archers had to spend much time in practice; where I live in Sandwich, near the coast east of London, The Butts, where the archers practiced at the time of Agincourt, is now the town cricket ground. Trumpet calls, cries,[37] and banner movements were used for control, but virtually nothing is known about the details of this. Henry's army had a structure which brought it together, and controlled it out of battle, and one that enabled it to be deployed for battle in an

[33] Units called wings were also placed on the flanks, and of course scouts ranged widely.

[34] See for this M Keen 'Richard II's Ordinances of War of 1385' in RE Archer and S Walker (eds) *Rulers and Ruled in Late Medieval England* (London and Rio Grande, Hambledon Press, 1995) 33 and especially 38–39

[35] The practice of knighting soldiers on the eve of battle, well attested in the Agincourt campaign, may have been intended to improve the command structure.

[36] Earlier tournaments were held in which groups of knights fought mock but dangerous battles, but this had by our time passed out of use. See M Keen, *Chivalry* (New Haven and London, Yale University Press, 1984) Ch V [Keen, *Chivalry*] and generally, Prestwich, *Armies and Warfare*, above n 28 at 224–27.

[37] Members of retinues may have used the name of their captain as a rallying cry.

organized way, as we know happened at Agincourt, where the deployment was supervised by Sir Thomas Erpingham. Once close combat began the men at arms at least apparently functioned in the main as a collection of belligerent individuals, over which it was extremely difficult to exercise any further general control. We can have no clear picture of what it was like. We know how Roman legionaries typically engaged in close combat, first throwing javelins, and then closing to engage with short swords, but whether a similar sequence was the norm in Henry's army is not known. Were lances thrown, or simply used to jab at opponents? All we do know is that there was a great deal of what Brigadier Ritchie-Hook would have called "biffing".[38] The archers, if the practice of firing volleys was used, must have been under some form of decentralized control, but there is no evidence of them practicing firing drills collectively.

The size of the French army is not known; figures given in the sources differ wildly. It was considerably larger than the English army, and a figure of between 12,000 and 20,000 fighting men is possible.[39] Its character was different; it was mustered through the system of feudal obligation, under which a local lord would go to war with his men, and form part of the military force of his superior lord. The retinues of the French army were not constructed through a system of contracts entered into for a campaign, though the soldiers were of course paid. It is likely that it comprised a higher proportion of persons of elevated social status. There were also present a considerable number of archers, some with longbows and some with cross bows; they would be hired mercenaries under contract. The French army, like the English, was divided into three battles.

The English army was heading towards Calais, and had spent the night in or near the village of Maisoncelles. The French army had on the previous day passed it at quite a short distance to the east, and Henry had anticipated a battle, and had drawn up his army to withstand a French attack. But there was no attack, for the French army had continued it's march northwards, and by nightfall was encamped in an area which is today called *La Plaine du Moulin*, south of Ruisseauville, east of Senecoville, and near Agincourt.[40] This meant that the roads to Calais were effectively blocked. From Maisoncelles there were a number of possible routes to Calais; those which are today metaled were not the only ones which could have been used, and the main road to Calais, which ran from Hesdin to Fruges, was to the west of Agincourt, so far as can today be judged. It was not the present day D104 that passes across the supposed site of the battle.

[38] See Evelyn Waugh's *Men at Arms* for elucidation of this concept.

[39] Currie, *New History* 228, inclines to around 12,000 combatants, with two thirds or more being men at arms. It must be noted that the total size of the French army, which was on its own soil, could easily, if non- combatants are included, have been twice this figure. If the lower figure is correct then the percentage of fatal casualties (for which we have slightly better figures) is hardly credible; see above text to n 3. Hence I incline to the higher figure

[40] The windmill from which this area got this name no longer exists, but its location is given on the map of 1818; see Currie, *Battle of Agincourt*, above n 2 at 362.

The precise location of the battlefield is not entirely clear.[41] However, it is likely that the English army was initially deployed between the villages of Agincourt and Tramecourt.[42] The name endings—*court*—indicate that there was in each a seigneur's residence. In Agincourt this was a castle, remains of which survive. No chronicles mention the castle as playing any part in the battle; presumably the fighting took place some distance away from it, or perhaps it was already ruinous. At Tramecourt the existing manor house is eighteenth century, and may be on the site of the earlier one; the same family as was there is 1415 still owns it. Both today have churches, but that in Agincourt is sixteenth century, probably on the site of an earlier church which was the mother church for those at Tramecourt and Maisoncelles.[43] Between these villages was a hamlet known as Gacogne; it is not known if this existed in 1415. Modern writers have generally agreed a site north of a field which is today called *La Cloyelle*, with English initial deployment some distance, perhaps as much as 800 yards, to the south of the road between the villages, and more or less in line with the church at Tramecourt; this may well be correct.[44] The main area of combat would be north of this, somewhere near the road which links the two villages today, and would have done so in 1415. To the south is Maisoncelles[45]. The villages are today surrounded by enclosed and fenced areas, or the remains of them, beyond which are open cultivated fields. This is the typical pattern in this area, and there are also large isolated farmsteads outside the villages, but no way of being sure if these existed back in 1415. There is absolutely no reason to believe that the village layout was radically different back in the early fifteenth century, though of course the fenced areas, used for

[41] There is some evidence from the 18th Century Cassini map of the area (reproduced in Nicolas, *History of the Battle,* above n 3 between 264 and 265 and in Currie, *Battle of Agincourt,* above n 2 at 365 Figure 4) that the battle actually took place to the west of Agincourt. This has been overlooked by modern historians but explains the plate in Nicolas, *History of the Battle* between 112 and 113 (which is at odds with the text at 111) which locates the battlefield near the main road from Hesdin to Fruges. Cassini was a reliable cartographer, the Cassini family produced the first accurate triangulated maps of France. The location given was presumably derived from local tradition. This map also shows the Chapel at Gacogne, built in 1734 on the site of the French grave pits, but destroyed in the Revolution.

[42] T Sutherland, 'The Battle of Agincourt: An Alternative Location' in *Journal of Conflict Archaeology* (2005) I 246 suggests a site well to the north of the accepted site. This is based in part on the failure to find any arrowheads in a metal detector survey, but unfortunately does not say what precise area was searched. The arguments presented confuse chronicle accounts of what happened on 24 October with what happened on 25 October.

[43] The location between these two villages depends of the chronicles of Waurin, Le Fèvre and Monstrelet, who collaborated; see n 22 above. Other chroniclers either give no location or are more vague about it. Since the local peasantry would normally flee, even those present might be unable to ask them the names of villages; Henry V himself had to ask the French herald after the battle the name of the nearby castle at Agincourt. Hardyng, who was present, wrongly thought he had spent the night before the battle in Agincourt. The Chaplain gets the name of the river the army crossed the day before wrong, calling it the River of Swords; it was and is *La Ternoise.*

[44] The current *Institut Geographique National* 1:25000 map of the area (Number 2205E) is reproduced in Currie, *New History* as plate 124.

[45] The present day church at Maisoncelles is post-1945; the village was destroyed by bombing during the war, since there was a V 1 launching site there, which can still be seen.

orchards, vegetable plots or farm stock, may have been enlarged or contracted.[46] On the Tramecourt side there are today considerable areas of woodland, but none on the Agincourt side; accounts of the threatened confrontation between the two armies on the day before the battle make it clear that there was woodland in 1415; the 1818 map shows woodland broadly corresponding to what exists today.[47] The English deployment must have been on a front of about 1000 yards.[48] The French army originally deployed some distance, somewhere between 500 and 1000 yards, to the north, perhaps in line with the castle at Agincourt. Wherever it was there, or further to the north, there would not have been enough open space to deploy in line abreast, though there would have been if the deployment had been much nearer Ruisseauville. Hence the deployment of the French army was radically different from that of the English army, for the three battles were deployed in line or column ahead. Since the French men at arms were anxious to be positioned where the fighting was going to take place, the numbers in the leading battle were greater than those in the main body and rearguard. The archers were placed at the rear, in a position that did not allow them to play any part in the battle. Probably the reason for this was a wish to enable as many as possible of the more aristocratic men at arms to engage in combat with the English men at arms. Back at Crecy the crossbowmen were viewed with such disdain by the upper class French men at arms that they were even ridden down and killed for having put up a bad show. They appear to have been viewed in something of the same way at Agincourt.

The English after some considerable time advanced, so as to come within effective bowshot range—about 250 yards or so—of the French. The French men at arms were, like their English equivalents, mounted cavalry men, and probably it was just after this that a relatively small force of them attempted to ride down the English archers.[49] But this attack achieved nothing except to create confusion amongst the main body of men at arms when the cavalrymen, or their riderless

[46] The earliest large scale map of the area so far as I am aware is that of 1818 by Sir John Woodford; it depicts the area as very much the same as it is today. See n 2 above.

[47] See n 2 above. The 1818 map does show a small area of woodland on the Agincourt side, which had in the past been larger. The Cassini map also shows woodland north of Tramecourt and some woodland west of Agincourt. On the Tramecourt side the woods did not immediately surround the village; what immediately surrounded it was enclosures.

[48] Simple arithmetic indicates that if deployed four deep (there is some evidence for this) the men at arms would have needed about 225 yards, leaving around 775 yards for the archers, who would, if in lines, be between six and seven deep. One can juggle with the figures but no clear conclusion emerges. There is some pictorial evidence for deploying of archers in front of men at arms. A portrayal of the battle, reproduced on the dust-jacket of P Reid, *Mediaeval Warfare* (New York, Carrol and Graf, 2007) from a MS in the *Bibliotheque Nationale* in Paris has them so deployed. It is difficult to know what to make of such pictures; produced for aristocratic patrons often with experience of war, one might expect them to be at least plausible in their depiction of soldiers, arms and modes of combat. The backgrounds to all early pictures of Agincourt are wholly fanciful.

[49] A French written battle plan for such an operation survives, but it was probably composed some time earlier when there had been a possibility of a battle near Monchy-Lagache which never happened.

horses, no doubt pin-cushioned with arrows, fled back towards where they had started.[50] One reason for the failure of this attack was the fact that the archers fought behind a screen of pointed stakes, hammered into the ground, angled forwards at forty five degrees or so.[51] Thereafter the French men at arms fought on foot; horses were far too vulnerable to the English archers, as had long been obvious. The French men at arms, rather than remaining in position as the passive recipients of showers of arrows, which even at this range could cause serious injuries, now advanced to contact the English line. Only by doing so did they become able to kill or injure the English soldiers. Thus the French were induced to make the attack; in medieval military thought it was always best to be the attacked rather than to be the attacker. So it was that the battle began.

Quite quickly the French were in utter disorder; the reasons for this seem to have been general lack of discipline, overcrowding, caused in part by the narrow front[52] and in part by those who were not at the front of the column pressing forward in enthusiasm to get to where the action was, the muddy condition of the ground which, given the crowding, made it easy to loose footing, and the devastating effect of the English longbows. If as seems likely the French men at arms, originally deployed over a front of around 1000 yards, concentrated on attacking only the English men at arms, deployed on a front of only about 225 yards, this would have aggravated the confusion.

There is a tendency to think of longbows as a long range weapon, which they were, and there has been much discussion of their effective maximum range. I suspect however that it was their devastating effect at close range, at which armour could readily be pierced, or the man at arms knocked down by the shock, which was critical. On the English side the archers, even when they had run out of arrows (there must have been some system of resupply, but nothing is known about it[53]), were more nimble than heavily armoured men at arms, and were apparently able easily to attack and kill or wound the French, using a variety of weapons, including the mallets with which they hammered in their protective stakes. Once a man at arms had lost his footing he would be unable to defend himself effectively; the whole aim of personal combat was to bring one's

[50] For accounts see Currie, *A New History*, above n 2 at 245–48, Barker, *Agincourt* 280–83. In the time taken for the cavalry to charge 100 yards (and there seem to have been only about five hundred of them) each archer could have fired three or four arrows, and at the end of the charge the archers, protected by stakes, could hardly have missed.

[51] In later warfare pikes and bayonets were used to perform the same function.

[52] There have been attempts to explain the confusion in part by the funneling effect when soldiers advance into a narrower place, and by somewhat imaginative claims that the very moderate slope of the ground seriously aggravated this effect. You have only to visit the place to see that the latter claim is absurd.

[53] Archers carried twenty-four arrows, and would have rapidly run out of arrows unless there was resupply; eventually they did run out, but by then the French were in utter confusion. It is known that during his French campaigns between 1418 and 1422 as many as 1,350,000 arrows were bought, but no figures seem to exist for the Agincourt campaign. See C Allmand, *Henry V* (New Haven and London, Yale University Press, 1992) 216.

opponent to the ground. We are even told that bodies piled up as high as a man and that other French men at arms clambered over them in their attempts to come to grips with the English; one writer, Keegan, has doubted this, but the evidence comes from someone who, unlike Keegan, was present.[54] The chronicles suggest that it was mainly the archers rather than the men at arms who wreaked destruction on the French. As for the French archers, they had been deployed at the tail of the column, and took little or no part in the action. Artillery also played no part, though it is known that one English archer was killed by a gun, presumably a handgun. We do not know how long the *melée* lasted, but it cannot have been very long, given the energy expended in face to face combat;[55] quite soon the English appeared, as the saying goes, to be in possession of the field. Prisoners may well have been taken during the *melée*,[56] but it is more likely that most were taken after the fighting had stopped, when there would be disabled men at arms on the field, and some unwounded but trapped under fallen bodies.

Sometimes a collapse of the enemy's line of battle was followed in medieval warfare by a pursuit, or rout. This happened, for example, in the Wars of the Roses after the battle of Towton in 1461, when the defeated forces were pursued for some eight miles or so up to the outskirts of York. So long as men at arms were in line, each gave his neighbours protection; once the line broke this was no longer so, and a soldier running away was not well positioned to defend himself if pursued either on foot or, worse, on horseback. For obvious reasons it was during the rout that most casualties were suffered and most prisoners taken. The point of the pursuit was indeed in part that it gave an opportunity to take prisoners. After Agincourt, as after Crecy,[57] there was no pursuit, and the exceptionally large number of casualties was suffered on the field of battle itself.[58] One reason why there was no pursuit may have been a decision by Henry that in view of the fact that there were still substantial French forces in the area a pursuit would have been dangerous. Another may have been that the soldiers did not want to engage in pursuit, since there were plenty of potential prisoners still on the field of battle. There is simply no evidence, so we can only speculate. For Crecy there is evidence that the King forbade pursuit on the day of the battle, which ended towards

[54] Keegan, *Face of Battle* 93.

[55] An approximate and speculative timetable would go as follows. Daylight about 6 a.m., armies in position by about 8 a.m., armies remain stationary (and some negotiations take place) 8–11 am., English advance 11–11.15 a.m., archers open fire on French line 11.15 a.m., cavalry charge 11.20, *melée* begins 11.30 a.m. English in possession of the field 12.30 p.m. Currie *NH* at 240 has the battle (not the *melée*) begun by about 10 a.m. which is about an hour or so earlier than my guess. One chronicle, the *Chronique de Ruisseauville*, whose author lived nearby, says that the battle (perhaps meaning the *melée*) lasted only half an hour; other chronicles disagree, but it all depends on what you count as the start.

[56] For discussion see Currie, *A New History*, above n 2 at 256–59.

[57] See A Ayton and P Preston (eds), *The Battle of Crecy 1346* (Woodbridge, Boydell Press, 2007); R. Mathews, *The Battle of Crecy* (Stapleton, Spellmount Press, 2007).

[58] The location of the French grave pits at Gacogne may indicate the area where there were most killings, and hence most bodies lying about, or it could be that this was a piece of then unused land.

nightfall. The soldiers were permitted the next day to break ranks and plunder. At Poitiers (1356) there was a rout on the day of the battle.

What triggered the killing of the prisoners? There are essentially two different explanations in the sources. Both agree that after the men at arms at the front of the French column, the vanguard, had been comprehensively defeated the remains of the French army for a while took no further part in the fighting. Some retinues may have begun to withdraw. So there was a lull in the conflict, though for how long we have no idea. During this period, and perhaps in some cases earlier, the English soldiers busied themselves in taking prisoners, and also in searching for loot, for example on the bodies of the dead and wounded.[59] Then, according to one account in the chronicles, there were indications that the French to the front of the English were reforming and might renew the attack. It was fear of a renewed attack from these French forces which triggered the killing of prisoners.[60] According to the other account, which was used by Shakespeare,[61] the killing was triggered by an attack on the baggage, which was held to the rear of the army.[62] There certainly was such an attack, led by Isambart d'Agincourt, the local seigneur, and Robert (or Robinet) de Bournoville, and it was this attack, together in some accounts with the reforming of units of the main army, which was the trigger; the English feared that they would be again attacked, possibly from the rear as well as the front. There is no doubt that this raid on the baggage occurred, but there are discrepancies over precisely when; the Chaplain, who was with the baggage, says it took place shortly after the armies engaged.[63] There are other discrepancies. According to some sources the killing of the prisoners was a spontaneous reaction from the English soldiers; a cry was raised warning of a possible attack, and this triggered the killings.[64] Other sources more plausibly say that Henry ordered them to be killed, and that the order was given either by, or after, a trumpet call. This seems at first puzzling since it would suggest that there was an appropriate trumpet call, "Kill Prisoners", like modern day calls: "Officers Dress for Dinner", or "Last Post" of "Come to the Cookhouse Door". This does not seem likely, but conceivably there was a call that meant "Give No Quarter". Alternatively the call may simply have been a call to reform in battle order, "Reform Ranks".[65] Jean le Fèvre and Jehan de Waurin, both of whom were present, and who collaborated with Enguerand de Monstrelet, who was not, in writing up what happened, said there was reluctance to obey the order because it

[59] Upper class men at arms would carry wealth, for example gold or silver coins, around with them.

[60] For example the Chaplain (Currie, *Battle of Agincourt*, above n 2 at 37), Elham (ibid at 47), Tito Livio (ibid at 62), the Monk of St. Denis (ibid at 108).

[61] Shakespeare relied on Raphael Holinshed's *Chronicles*, printed 1586–87, and these give this account.

[62] For example, Pierre de Fenin (Currie, *Battle of Agincourt*, above n 2 at 118), Enguerrand de Monstrelet, ibid at 163).

[63] Currie, *Battle of Agincourt*, above n 2 at 35.

[64] For example the Chaplain (Currie, ibid at 37), Elham (ibid at 47), and Tito Livio (ibid at 62).

[65] See Currie, *Battle of Agincourt*, above n 2 at 125.

entailed loss of ransoms. Henry, therefore, had a man at arms put in charge of two hundred archers who were to carry out the killings, and did. One text says that it was threatened that disobedience to the King's order meant death. Soldiers engaged in guarding prisoners or taking them to the rear[66] would be deflected from their principal duty, and such prisoners might escape and themselves join in the fighting; it would be natural for Henry to want his soldiers to reform and prepare to resist a new attack. Then, according to some sources, heralds[67] were sent to the French to warn them that if fighting were resumed it would be without quarter. Quite how many were killed is not known, but it was a considerable number, and the killings may explain the large number of persons of high rank who died, for these were the most desirable persons to capture and hold to ransom. R. de Belleval in his *Azincourt* (1865) identifies some 387 princes, seigneurs and knights who died. It also explains why many of the dead at Agincourt could not later be recognized, since they had been cut about their heads and faces and stripped naked by plundering peasants; the killings would have been carried out by blows or slashes to the head or neck, the prisoners being without their helmets.[68] Keegan has suggested that the mechanics of mass slaughter are such that the number killed cannot have been large, which may be true, though I do not find it convincing.[69]

There is some chronicle evidence of the number of prisoners who survived and accompanied Henry's army on its march from Agincourt to Calais after the battle; thus the *Chronical of Ruisseauville* gives a figure of 2,200,[70] the *Chronicle* by the Monk of Saint-Denis 1404, le Fèvre, who was present, and because of his heraldic connections fairly reliable, 1600.[71] Of the English chronicles that written by the monk Thomas Walsingham, who was not present, gives the highest figure in English sources of up to 700.[72] The Chaplain, who was present, names only six prisoners[73] and adds that there were few others of gentle birth; he does not however give a total figure. This suggests that those who survived to be taken to

[66] We know that one French prisoner, Ghillebert de Lannoy, had been taken off the field of battle with a number of other prisoners and put in a barn, which was set on fire so as to kill them; he managed to escape.

[67] Heralds, who wore a distinctive dress, were immune from violence. One herald, Jacques de Heilly, is said to have died at Agincourt; he did, but he was not a professional herald.

[68] See, eg, Currie, *Battle of Agincourt*, above n 2 at 164, 126 (where it is said that the English disfigured the dead as well).

[69] Keegan, *Face of Battle* 95–96.

[70] Currie, *Battle of Agincourt*, above n 2 at 127. Currie, *New History* in Appendix C tabulates the wildly discrepant figures given in the *Chronicles.* R. de Bellevall *Azincourt* (Paris, 1865) identifies 50 taken prisoner.

[71] Currie, *Battle of Agincourt*, above n 2 at 169, though this may be a figure for those taken on the day of battle, not those who were taken to Calais. One of the duties of heralds was to count the dead and discover what had happened to combatants.

[72] Ibid at 53.

[73] The Dukes of Orleans and Bourbon, the Counts of Richemont, Vendôme and Eu, and the Marshal of France, Jean le Meingre Boucicaut.

Calais were in the main socially less elevated persons.[74] I suspect that the Chaplain, who was in the business of glorifying his King, was explaining the fact that only a small number of prisoners were later brought back to England and put on show, and only six of those were of very high status.[75] After such a total victory this small number might seem odd. The reason was surely that most of those of slightly less exalted status had been killed; we have direct evidence that the prisoners to be killed did not include the really top people such as the two Dukes and the Marshal of France. In addition, some prisoners were not brought back to England because they were sold to enterprising citizens of Calais, their captors preferring ready discounted cash to a ransom that might not be paid for many years.

In the medieval world men went to war for various reasons, but there were two which predominated: the pursuit of honour and reputation, and the pursuit of the spoils of war.[76] Hence, to place the killing in an historical context, the first point which needs to be made is that the function of taking prisoners was the pursuit of economic gain through the extraction of ransoms, a function which of course no longer motivates the taking of prisoners today. So far as I am aware there is no evidence of a regular practice in the Hundred Years War of making prisoners of common soldiers. There was no point. They had no value; they could not be held to ransom since they did not come from wealthy families, and it was no longer the practice to turn them into economic assets as slaves, which is what was done in the ancient world.

One form taken by mediaeval warfare was the *chevauchée*, the plundering, slaughtering, fast moving raid on horse back;[77] essentially it was a form of economic warfare, in which speed of movement was used to avoid the risk of confrontation in battle. The most normal confrontational form taken by medieval warfare was the siege, and at the conclusion of a siege if the besieged city had not surrendered and negotiated terms, common soldiers and indeed all other males were normally killed, the women raped, and the city plundered.[78] A very recent example at the time of Agincourt had been the sacking of Soissons in 1414, where even the nuns were raped, and the churches plundered; in the theory of the

[74] Currie, *Battle of Agincourt*, above n 2 at 38.

[75] Those known to have been imprisoned in England include the Dukes of Orleans and Bourbon, the Counts of Richemont, Vendôme and Eu, and the Marshal of France, Jean le Meingre Boucicaut, George de Clere, Jean de Ligne, Jennett de Poix and David de Poix, and Rauol de Gaucourt (captured at Harfleur). See Currie, *A New History*, above n 2 at 288–89 and note at 322 where it is pointed out that the names of a number of prisoners turn up in papers in the National Archives. There is apparently a University of Nottingham MA thesis by one Rémy Ambühl on the subject, which I have not myself seen.

[76] KB McFarlane 'The Investment of Sir John Fastolf's Profits of War', *Trans. Royal Hist. Soc.* 5th Series vii (1957) 91 gives a good picture of the huge profits made by Fastolf (1380–1459). See also M Keen, *Chivalry*, above n 36 at 228–37 for the lack of fit between the ideals of chivalry and the realities of the devastation caused by the passage of a mediaeval army in pursuit of loot.

[77] For accounts see Prestwich, *Armies and Warfare*, above n 28 at 10, 200–5.

[78] See generally Prestwich, *Armies and Warfare*, above n 28 Ch 12, and for the law governing the matter see MH Keen, *The Laws of War in the Later Middle Ages* (Oxford, Oxford University Press, 1965) at 119–23 [Keen, *Laws of War*].

time women and the church should have been immune.[79] Even if terms were negotiated this might well not save all the surrendering soldiers from being killed. So no prisoner of war camps had to be provided to house the defeated garrison. If the city surrendered and made terms, as happened for example just before Agincourt in the case of the city of Harfleur, those members of the garrison who were worth it might be held to ransom. Indeed before setting out on the march which led him to Agincourt Henry released some such prisoners, who gave undertakings to report back to him when he reached Calais, as indeed they did.[80] It was sometimes the practice to let common soldiers go in return for an undertaking not to fight again against the King in the current campaign, but it is uncertain if this was done in the case of any members of the Harfleur garrison.[81] The reason for these apparently humane practices was in reality severely practical: they encouraged surrender. A garrison of a besieged city knew exactly what the alternatives were likely to be unless the siege was relieved: surrender and with a bit of luck save your life, fight on to the end and die. Individual acts of surrendering achieved nothing; the surrender of a besieged city was negotiated with the captain of the garrison and the city fathers. There were numerous sieges during Henry V's campaign to secure control of Normandy—first Harfleur, then, after Agincourt, Caen (1417),[82] Rouen (1418–19)[83] and following that a number of castles such as La Roche-Guyon, Gisors and Ivry. During Henry V's last campaign in France in 1421 there was the siege of Dreux, which surrendered after brief resistance, and Henry's last major siege, that of Meaux, which lasted from October 1421 until May 1422. The terms on which Meaux surrendered were harsh, quite a number of the defenders being hanged, but most of the defenders were spared.[84] One who was not spared was a person who "blewe and sounded an Horne during the siege"; he had, for some reason, enraged Henry V.[85] I wonder if he made flatulent noises on his trumpet when the King was in sight from the walls.[86] Henry, like most successful generals, was not a nice man, and you did not insult a warrior King with impunity.[87]

[79] Soissons was the place where the martyr cobblers, Crispin and Crispianus, had died for their faith; the battle was fought on their saints' day.

[80] Currie, *Battle of Agincourt*, above n 2 at 39 noting their arrival on 16 November.

[81] Currie, *A New History*, above n 2 at 99 and note 47 at 310.

[82] Which was brutally plundered; not surprisingly Bayeux shortly afterwards surrendered.

[83] Rouen surrendered; thereafter a number of other cities, such as Mantes, Dieppe and Honfleur surrendered either without resistance, or after a short resistance. For an account of the siege of Rouen, a massive military operation, see J H Wylie and W T Waugh, *The Reign of Henry the Fifth* (New York, Greenwood Press, 1968) Vol. III Ch LVII. Under the terms of capitulation nine defenders were placed at the King's mercy; most apparently redeemed their lives for money.

[84] See Wylie and Waugh, ibid Ch LXXI.

[85] T Rymer's *Foedera etc* (1739–45), Vol X 212, quoted A Burne, *The Agincourt War* (London, Eyre and Spottiswoode, 1956) 175.

[86] See Burne, ibid at 175–76 for another explanation.

[87] Sir Edgar (Bill) Williams (1912–1995), Warden of Rhodes House in Oxford, had been General Montgomery's intelligence officer. He much admired his general as a general, but once told me that "Montgomery was not a nice man".

In the case of battles, which were relatively uncommon, there appears to have been no regular practice of taking common soldiers of low social status, such as archers, as prisoners. There was no point in doing so; they had no economic value. During the battle proper they were, if possible, killed; if there was a pursuit they were again, if possible, killed, and if they were later found wounded they were finished off, as happened the morning after the battle of Agincourt to some wounded Frenchmen. Those who escaped simply did not fall into the hands of the victors, so even had there been prison camps of some kind (which there were not) there would have been virtually nobody to put in them. If defeated common soldiers wanted to survive, as they must have done, the best course was to get as far away from the battlefield as possible as quickly as possible. If wounded the best thing was to crawl or drag oneself into some sort of cover and hope not to be found. The situation was not so much that prisoners could be killed. It was rather that combatants could be killed, and there was no right to choose to cease to be a combatant and become instead a prisoner through an act of surrender.

The possibility of becoming a prisoner was a luxury only enjoyed by those who were of sufficiently high social status as to belong to the warrior class.[88] Indeed the practice of wearing armour, coupled with the practice of taking defeated opponents as prisoners and holding them to ransom, can be viewed as ways in which the European warrior class significantly reduced the risks to them of participation in war. In battle members of the warrior class could readily be identified from their clothing and accoutrements. Displaying a coat of arms, for example, was a little like having an insurance policy.

It was a long established practice for English Kings to issue *Ordinances of War* whose principal aim was to establish cohesion and discipline in their fragmented contract based armies.[89] Henry V followed this practice, and we have the text of his *Ordinances* issued in 1419[90] and one other incomplete text which may belong to his reign, or more probably to 1430 in the reign of Henry VI, then an infant.[91] Those issued for the Agincourt campaign have not survived, but will have been similar to those issued in 1419, for it was the practice to reissue with modification earlier *Ordinances*; the earliest surviving model comprises the *Ordinances* of 1385 issued by Richard II. One subject addressed in them was the problems caused by pursuit of the spoils of war.[92]

[88] Under the code of chivalry war was an activity only fully appropriate for those of gentle birth; members of the proletariat really had no business to be on the battlefield at all, though for practical reasons their presence had to be tolerated.

[89] What follows is principally based on Keen 'Richard II's Ordinances of War of 1385' and Keen, *The Laws of War* Ch X 'The Law of Ransom'.

[90] Reproduced in Nicolas, *History of the Battle*, above n 3 Appendix No. VIII from a MS in the College of Arms; also in print in T Twiss (ed) *The Black Book of the Admiralty* (London, HM Stationery Office, 1871) Vol 1 at 453.

[91] British Library MS. Add. 33191a; I have not inspected this.

[92] In addition to the regulations mentioned below the *Ordinances* specifically forbade plundering the Church, or meddling with the holy sacrament, and protected women, particularly women on

One such problem was the risk that soldiers would break ranks and become a disorderly mob bent on plunder, either in the form of tangible assets, such as gold or silver, or through the pursuit of potential prisoners. So one provision provided the death penalty for anyone who raised, on his own initiative, the cry of "Havoc"—the cry which licensed uncontrolled plundering.[93] Another provision dealt with other "unlawfull Scryes", meaning cries, in particular the cry called "Mount", meaning "To Horse". This would be the cry used after an engagement on foot to initiate a pursuit on horseback. The basic system for the division of the spoils of war was that one third of the spoils, including ransoms, acquired by a member of a retinue went to the captain of the retinue, and one third of the captain's spoils went to the King.[94] There were numerous problems in operating this system and inducements to cheat. So the taking of prisoners was closely regulated. For example the taking of a prisoner had to be reported to the captain, and also to the King, or to the Constable or Marshall of the army.[95] Another provision forbade the taking of children under fourteen years old as prisoners unless they were the sons of a lord, or of a worshipful gentleman, or of a captain; such children were then to be brought to their father, presumably himself a captive. The point must have been both that they should not be separated from their father and not themselves be held for individual ransom.[96] Obviously the taking of prisoners involved soldiers moving about out of line, as reports were made, prisoners moved to a safe location, and perhaps wounds dressed (a dead prisoner was of no value); the activity disrupted battle lines. Safe conducts for prisoners, and their sale, for they were treated as a form of property, were also closely regulated. A number of provisions set out the principles which identified the person whose prisoner the captive was and therefore the person entitled to the ransom.[97] Another provision forbids the practice of one soldier coming to another and threatening to kill his prisoner unless granted a share.[98]

childbed, merchants, and labourers. There was also a provision restraining the pillaging of lodgings assigned by the harbingers, who were the soldiers whose job it was to find lodging for the soldiers when on the march.

[93] The article 'For theim that crye Havoke' in Nicolas, *History of the Battle,* above n 2 at 33. Those who acted on the cry were to lose horse and harness (ie, armour and equipment) until they had paid a fine.

[94] The *Ordinances* include an article 'For the payyng of Thyrdes' (Nicolas, *History of the Battle,* above n 2 at 34) which only partially reflects the system. Very high-ranking prisoners would be treated as prisoners of the King, though the soldier who made the capture might be compensated.

[95] See the clause 'For to bringe in p'soners in to the Kings knowledg, Counstable and Marishall'.

[96] 'A statut for Children within the age of xiiij yeres'. The lawfulness of holding children to ransom is discussed by Bonet (cited below n 106) at Book IV c. xciv, who thought it unlawful if the child was innocent, meaning not engaged in any way in warfare.

[97] See Nicolas, *Laws of War* 32 'For takinge of Prisoners', and 34 'For Prysoners'.

[98] Nicolas, ibid at 34, a second article 'For Prysoners'.

From this text and earlier ones the whole system can, broadly speaking, be understood.[99] Soldiers who were worth taking prisoner could be identified on the battlefield by their accoutrements, and heraldic devices. The process of becoming a prisoner involved what amounted to an offer and an acceptance. The prospective prisoner would normally, as the 1419 *Ordinances* puts it, have been "borne to the earthe"; if he was on his feet he would still be fighting. Since he would be in full armour, and battle was noisy, conversational opportunities would be limited. So although he might try to make a verbal proposal, more usually he would make an appropriate gesture, typically by holding out his gauntleted hand, which would be less dangerous than removing and offering his helmet, for some protection was still retained. The offer could be accepted either verbally, or by a suitable gesture, such as that of taking the offeror's gauntlet. Either way the captor had to take a tangible pledge from the prisoner, normally a gauntlet or a helmet, or I suppose both.[100] He would surely have been disarmed, but this does not seem to have any evidentiary function. The captor also had to accept the prisoner's pledge of faith; in some conditions I suppose this could be done at once, but in combat there might have to be a delay. I imagine that the offer of surrender in the course of the battle was as hazardous as is putting your hands up in modern warfare. Indeed one illustration of this at the battle of Agincourt is recorded. The Duke of Alençon, who was engaged in an attempt to kill Henry himself, was brought to the ground, and raised his hand to the King in the gesture of surrender, but before the King could take his pledge of faith the King's bodyguard killed him.[101] The pledge of faith used the prisoner's hope of eternal life as a security for performance. If he violated the pledge he ran the risk of damnation. Once the fighting ended there would be an opportunity to place matters on a more regular footing, as by the execution of a formal legal document,[102] but this was not necessary. A purely verbal contract was all that was required.

Such a contract conferred on the captor a property right which could, for example, be sold or inherited, and it gave rise to obligations between captor and prisoner which resembled those between a lord and his vassal. The basic obligation of the prisoner was to be a good and loyal prisoner to his new master. The basic obligation of the captor certainly included an obligation to spare his life, for this was the whole point of the transaction, but beyond this it seems difficult to be very precise, since the conditions in which captives were held

[99] The system is described by Keen, *Armies and Warfare*, above n 28 Ch X and by Prestwich, *Armies and Warfare*, above n 28 at 100–9 on which I rely; the account in the text is simplified since the details are not relevant to the basic points being made.

[100] There is pictorial evidence for the practice of tying the hands of prisoners, and at Agincourt the archers would have spare bowstrings which could be used for this; possibly this was done before a solemn contract was entered into. See the picture reproduced as Plate 27 in Barker from Martial d'Auvergne's *Vigiles de Charles VII*, a MS in the *Bibliothèque Nationale.*

[101] This story is in the *Le Chronique d'Enguerren de Monstrelet*, Currie, *New History* 258, Currie, *Battle of Agincourt*, above n 2 at 168.

[102] See Keen, *Armies and Warfare*, above n 28 at 167–68.

varied widely, and were affected both by negotiations, and by such factors as the status of the prisoner. Thus a very high status prisoner, such as Charles, Duke of Orleans, who was to remain a captive in England until release in November 1440, devoted his time to aristocratic pursuits such as hunting and hawking, and to the writing of poetry. Those of less elevated status would not have fared so well, and much would depend on who their new master was. There were no clear rules governing the size of the ransom, which might take many years to collect.

It is against this background that we have to comprehend the killing of the prisoners at Agincourt. The taking of prisoners and other plundering activities, such as searching and stripping the dead and wounded, interfered with the responsibilities of soldiers as combatants and therefore had to be controlled. We do not know, for there is no evidence, whether official permission was given at some point after victory seemed to have been achieved for the soldiers to start pursuing the spoils of war, for example by an officially sanctioned cry of "havoc", or perhaps by a trumpet call. I think it likely that this is what must have happened, for this was an army which we know was in general strictly controlled. But there is no direct evidence. Once a renewed attack was feared it would be natural for Henry V to forbid further pursuit of plunder; his army would need to reform, and prepare to resist the French attack. But if the soldiers were encumbered with large numbers of prisoners this would be unlikely to happen, or at least happen quickly. Also there was a risk that the prisoners would, even if they had been disarmed, pick up weapons, of which there must have been many lying about, and rejoin the fray, though if they had pledged their faith they would risk damnation for doing so. As we have seen the sources differ in that some present the killing of the prisoners as a spontaneous reaction to the fear of a renewed attack; others more plausibly say that an order to kill was issued by the King. Simply not taking prisoners was not a violation of the laws of war, especially if a decision to give no quarter was communicated, as may have happened after the killing had begun, when Henry sent heralds to the French, also warning them that the remaining prisoners would also be killed. Since the French did not renew the attack the threat of no quarter was never acted upon.[103] But the killing of prisoners by their captors to whom they had made a pledge of faith was unlawful, and it was unlawful not because it violated some basic principle of the medieval equivalent of international humanitarian law, but because it was a breach of contract. Even then there were two exceptions. One was where the prisoner committed treason against his captor.[104] The other, mentioned very briefly by

[103] There is some evidence that when the French sacred banner known as the *oriflamme* was carried in battle this signaled a decision to take no quarter; see Prestwich, *Armies and Warfare*, above n 28 at 314 discussing the battle of Crecy, at which an English dragon banner was unfurled in response to convey the same message. However it has been argued by Currie, *A New History*, above n 2 at 272 that although the custodian of the *oriflamme* died at Agincourt, the banner itself was not present there. Barker, *Agincourt* 288 has it that the *oriflamme* was destroyed in the battle; I am however persuaded by Currie.

[104] See Keen, *Armies and Warfare*, above n 28 at 179.

Honoré Bonet[105] in *The Tree of Battles* in which he discusses the question whether a captor can lawfully kill his prisoner, was if there was "a risk of his escaping with the result of prolonged war, damage or mischief"[106] Bonet also insists that a decision to kill a prisoner in such circumstances must be made by the sovereign prince, not by the captor; the prince would not be a party to the pledging of faith of the prisoners. Taking "prolonged war" to include a resumption of fighting, this more or less completely exonerates those who killed the prisoners at Agincourt, so long as the order to kill was given by Henry V, as some of the sources say it was. It is a fact which several writers have noticed that none of the contemporary writers, whether from the English or the French side, criticize Henry V for the killing of the prisoners.[107] If, as some evidence suggests, the killings were carried out by some of the archers, who had not themselves taken a pledge of faith from their victims, this would have had the advantage of not imperiling the souls of their captors.

Over the following six centuries there has been, in this instance, and perhaps in others, a movement, notwithstanding Maine, from contract to status. For today, under international humanitarian law, prisoners, so long as they count as lawful combatants, enjoy a special and very favourable status simply from the fact that they have become prisoners of war, and even unlawful combatants are to some degree protected. And in the modern world the transition from combatant to prisoner is not achieved by contract. In the medieval period the taking of prisoners of war was principally motivated by the pursuit of private profit,[108] and the protection of such prisoners of war as were taken rested not on status, but on contract, a contract which was in its turn embedded in the customs of the age of chivalry which governed the pursuit of the spoils of war.

[105] Also appears as Bouvet.

[106] *Tree of Battles: English Versio*n by GW Coopland, ed (Cambridge, Mass, Harvard University Press, 1949) 152. The author (1343-c1405) completed this work on the laws of war in 1387.

[107] The fullest discussion of the legalities is by T Meron in his fascinating *Henry's Wars and Shakespeare's Laws. Perspectives on the Law of War in the Late Middle Ages* (Oxford, Clarendon Press, 1993) Ch 9. His view is the same as mine, but he argues that the threat to give no quarter and kill the remaining prisoners if battle was resumed was unlawful. As late however as 1863 the Lieber Code by Article 60 conceded that no quarter might be ordered by a commander "In great straits when his own salvation makes it impossible to cumber himself with prisoners".

[108] Sometimes there might be other motives, such as the hope of obtaining useful information from the prisoner.

The Writings of Michael Taggart*

Books:

(ed) (with Pearson, L and Harlow, C) *Administrative Law in a Changing State: Essays in Honour of Mark Aronson* (Oxford, Hart Publishing, 2008)

(ed) *An Index to Common Law Festschriften: From the Beginning of the Genre up to 2005* (Oxford, Hart Publishing, 2006)

(ed with Huscroft, G) *Inside and Outside Canadian Administrative Law: Essays in Honour of David Mullan* (Toronto, University of Toronto Press, 2006)

Private Property and Abuse of Rights in Victorian England: The Story of Edward Pickles and the Bradford Water Supply (Oxford Studies in Modern Legal History) (Oxford, Oxford University Press, 2002) (awarded JF Northey Memorial Prize for the best book published on New Zealand law or by a New Zealand lawyer in 2002)

(ed) *The Province of Administrative Law* (Oxford, Hart Publishing, 1997)

(ed) *Judicial Review of Administrative Action in the 1980s: Problems and Prospects* Auckland, Oxford University Press in association with the Legal Research Foundation, 1996)

(with Eagles, I and Liddell, G) *Freedom of Information in New Zealand* (Auckland, Oxford University Press, 1992) (awarded JF Northey Memorial Prize for the best book published on New Zealand law in 1992)

Chapters in Books:

"Common Law Price Control, State-Owned Enterprises and the Level Playing Field" in L Pearson, C Harlow and M Taggart (eds), *Administrative Law in a Changing State: Essays in Honour of Mark Aronson* (Oxford, Hart Publishing, 2008) 185–204

* Thanks to Mary-Rose Russell, the Manager of the Davis Law Library at the University of Auckland, for her help in compiling this bibliography, and to Carolyn McKenna, for her research assistance. This bibliography is select in the sense that it does not include publications in popular or non-scholarly fora.

"Some Impacts of the PBRF on Legal Education" in C Geiringer & D Knight (eds), *Seeing the World Whole: Essays in Honour of Sir Kenneth Keith* (Wellington, Victoria University of Wellington Press, 2008) 250–59

"Commentary: 'Dialogue' as Inter-Branch Communication" in C Geiringer & D Knight (eds), *Seeing the World Whole: Essays in Honour of Sir Kenneth Keith* (Wellington, Victoria University of Wellington Press, 2008) 340–46

"*Associated Provincial Picture Houses Ltd v Wednesbury Corporation* (1948)" in P Cane & J Conaghan (eds), *The New Oxford Companion to Law* (Oxford, Oxford University Press, 2008) 55

(with Dyzenhaus, D) "Reasoned Decisions and Legal Theory" in Douglas E Edlin (ed), *Common Law Theory* (New York, Cambridge University Press, 2007) 134–67

(with Huscroft, G) "David Mullan: In Appreciation" in G Huscroft and M Taggart (eds), *Inside and Outside Canadian Administrative Law: Essays in Honour of David Mullan* (Toronto, University of Toronto Press, 2006) 3–8

"Globalisation, 'Local' Foreign Policy, and Administrative Law" in G Huscroft and M Taggart (eds), *Inside and Outside Canadian Administrative Law: Essays in Honour of David Mullan* (Toronto, University of Toronto Press, 2006) 259–95

"Rugby, the Anti-apartheid Movement, and Administrative Law" in R Bigwood (ed), *Public Interest Litigation: The New Zealand Experience in International Perspective* (Wellington, LexisNexis NZ Ltd, 2006) 69–98

(with Klosser, J) "Controlling Persistently Vexatious Litigants" in M Groves (ed), *Law and Government in Australia* (Sydney, Federation Press, 2005) 272–300

"The Tub of Public Law" in D Dyzenhaus (ed), *The Unity of Public Law* (Oxford, Hart Publishing, 2004) 455–79

"Reinventing Administrative Law" in N Bamforth and P Leyland (eds), *Public Law in a Multi-Layered Constitution* (Oxford, Hart Publishing, 2003) 311–35

"The Nature and Functions of the State" in P Cane and M Tushnet (eds), *The Oxford Handbook of Legal Studies* (Oxford, Oxford University Press, 2003) 101–18

"'The Peculiarities of the English': Resisting the Public/Private Law Distinction" in P Craig and R Rawlings (eds), *Law and Administration in Europe: Essays in Honour of Carol Harlow* (Oxford, Oxford University Press, 2003) 107–21

"*Ultra vires* as Distraction" in C Forsyth (ed), *Judicial Review and the Constitution* (Oxford, Hart Publishing, 2000) 427–29

"What Role for Judges?" in C James (ed), *Building the Constitution* (Wellington, Institute of Policy Studies, 2000) 382–87

"Tugging on Superman's Cape: Lessons from Experience with the New Zealand Bill of Rights Act 1990" in J Beatson, C Forsyth and I Hare (eds), *Constitutional Reform in the United Kingdom: Practice and Principles* (Oxford, Hart Publishing, 1998) 85–97

"Expropriation, Public Purpose and the Constitution" in C Forsyth and I Hare (eds), *The Golden Metwand and the Crooked Cord: Essays on Public Law in Honour of Sir William Wade QC* (Oxford, Clarendon Press, 1998) 91–112

"The Contribution of Lord Cooke to Scope of Review Doctrine in Administrative Law: A Comparative Common Law Perspective" in P Rishworth (ed), *The Struggle for Simplicity in the Law: Essays for Lord Cooke of Thorndon* (Wellington, Butterworths, 1997) 189–219 (awarded Sir Ian Barker Prize for the best published contribution to New Zealand law in 1997)

"The Province of Administrative Law Determined?" in M Taggart (ed), *The Province of Administrative Law* (Oxford, Hart Publishing, 1997) 1–20

"Public Utilities and Public Law" in P Joseph (ed), *Essays on the Constitution* (Wellington, Brookers, 1995) 214–64

(with McLean, J and Rishworth, P) "The Impact of the New Zealand Bill of Rights Act 1990 on Administrative Law" in *Essays on the New Zealand Bill of Rights Act 1990* (Auckland, Legal Research Foundation, 1992) 62–97

"The Rationalisation of Administrative Tribunal Procedure: The New Zealand Experience" in R Creyke (ed), *Administrative Tribunals: Taking Stock* (Canberra, Centre for International and Public Law, Australian National University, 1992) 91–120

"*Osmond* in the High Court of Australia: Opportunity Lost" in M Taggart (ed), *Judicial Review of Administrative Action in the 1980s: Problems and Prospects* (Auckland, Oxford University Press in association with the Legal Research Foundation, 1986) 53–69

"Rival Theories of Invalidity in Administrative Law: Some Theoretical and Practical Consequences" in M Taggart (ed), *Judicial Review of Administrative Action in the 1980s: Problems and Prospects* (Auckland, Oxford University Press in association with the Legal Research Foundation, 1986) 70–102

"Freedom of Information in New Zealand" in NS Marsh (ed), *Access to Government-Held Information* (London, Sweet & Maxwell in association with the British Institute of International and Comparative Law, 1987) 211–47

Guest Editorships:

Special issue on Administrative Law (with co-guest editors H Arthurs, D Dyzenhaus and M Loughlin) in (2005) 55 *University of Toronto Law Journal* 311–887 (Summer issue)

Special issue on "New Zealand Public Law" in (2004) 15 *Public Law Review* 77–161 (June issue)

Special issue on "Corporatisation" in (1995) 6 *Public Law Review* 5–95 (March issue)

Editorial, "Perspective" (1995) 6 *Public Law Review* 5–6

Journal Articles:

"Acting Judges and the Supreme Court of New Zealand" (2008) 14 *Canterbury Law Review* 122–139

"Proportionality, Deference, Wednesbury" [2008] *New Zealand Law Review* 423–481

"'Australian exceptionalism' in Judicial Review" (2008) 36 *Federal Law Review* 1–30

"Vexing the Establishment: Jack Wiseman of Murrays Bay" [2007] *New Zealand Law Review* 271–340

"[Review of Developments in] Administrative Law" [2006] *New Zealand Law Review* 75–103

"Mark Aronson: An Appreciation" (2006) 50 *Australian Institute of Administrative Law* 10–13

"Ruled by Law?" (2006) 69 *Modern Law Review* 1006–25

"The Impact of Apartheid on Commonwealth Administrative Law" [2006] *Acta Juridica* 158–208 (also published in the separately published book version of the journal – H Corder (ed), *Comparing Administrative Justice Across the Commonwealth* (Juta & Co Ltd, Cape Town, 2008) 158–208)

"Turning the Graveyard of Legal Scholarship into a Garden: The Indexing of Common Law *Festschriften*" (2006) 17 *Public Law Review* 90–96

(with Risk, RCB) "The Published Work of John Willis" (2005) 55 *University of Toronto Law Journal* 887–90

"From 'Parliamentary Powers' to Privatization: The Chequered History of Delegated Legislation in the Twentieth Century" (2005) 55 *University of Toronto Law* Journal 575–627

"Prolegomenon to an Intellectual History of Administrative Law in the Twentieth Century: The Case of John Willis and Canadian Administrative Law" (2005) 43 *Osgoode Hall Law Journal* 223–67

"Alexander Chaffers and the Genesis of the Vexatious Actions Act 1896" (2004) 61 *Cambridge Law Journal* 656–84

"The New Zealandness of New Zealand Public Law" (2004) 15 *Public Law Review* 81–86

"[Review of Developments in] Administrative Law" [2003] *New Zealand Law Review* 99–120

"Gardens or Graveyards of Scholarship? *Festschriften* in the Literature of the Common Law" (2002) 22 *Oxford Journal of Legal Studies* 227–52

(with Dyzenhaus, D and Hunt, M) "The Principle of Legality in Administrative Law: Internationalisation as Constitutionalisation" (2001) 1 *Oxford University Commonwealth Law Journal* 5–34

"[Review of developments in] Administrative Law" [2000] *New Zealand Law Review* 439–60

"Reinvented Government, Traffic Lights, and the Convergence of Public and Private Law: Review of Harlow and Rawlings: *Law and Administration*" [1999] *Public Law* 124–37

"Judicial Review in 'the Olive Grove of Academe'" [1999] *New Zealand Law Journal* 171–74

"Déjà Vu All Over Again" [1998] *New Zealand Law Journal* 234–36

"Tugging on Superman's Cape: Lessons from Experience with the New Zealand Bill of Rights Act 1990" [1998] *Public Law* 266–87 (revised version of a conference paper published also in the conference proceedings)

"Introduction to Judicial Review in New Zealand" [1997] *Judicial Review* 236–40"

Legitimate Expectation and Treaties in the High Court of Australia" (1996) 112 *Law Quarterly Review* 50–54

"Outside Canadian Administrative Law" (1996) 46 *University of Toronto Law Journal* 649–61

"Corporatisation, Contracting and the Courts" [1994] *Public Law* 351–58

"State-owned Enterprises and Social Responsibility: A Contradiction in Terms?" [1993] *New Zealand Recent Law Review* 343–64

"The Impact of Corporatisation and Privatisation on Administrative Law" (1992) 51 *Australian Journal of Public Administration* 368–73

Taggart, M "Corporatisation, Privatisation and Public Law" (1991) 2 *Public Law Review* 77–108 (revised version of inaugural lecture published by Legal Research Foundation Inc. as occasional paper no. 31, Auckland, 1990)

(with Dyzenhaus, D) "Judicial Review, Jurisprudence and the Wizard of Oz" (1990) 1 *Public Law Review* 21–52

"Courts, Ombudsmen and Freedom of Information: The Empire Strikes Back" (1990) 20 *Victoria University of Wellington Law Review monograph series no. 2* 1–47

"The Impact of Freedom of Information Legislation on Criminal Discovery in Comparative Common Law Perspective" (1990) 23 *Vanderbilt Journal of Transnational Law* 235–98

"The Official Information Act 1982 in the Courts" [1989] *New Zealand Recent Law Review* 195–206

"Freedom of Information and the University" (1988) 6 *Otago Law Review* 638–63

"Copyright in Written Reasons for Judgment" (1984) 10 *Sydney Law Review* 319–29

"The Binding Effect of Decisions of the Privy Council' (1984–85) 11 *New Zealand Universities Law Review* 66–68

"Should Canadian Judges be Legally Required to Give Reasoned Decisions in Civil Cases?" (1983) 33 *University of Toronto Law Journal* 1–44

"Should Administrative Tribunals be Required to State Findings of Fact?" (1980–81) 9 *New Zealand Universities Law Review* 162–93 (Awarded the Legal Research Foundation's Prize for the best article published on New Zealand law in 1981)

"*Levison v. Patent Carpet Cleaning Co.*" (1978) 3 *Auckland University Law Review* 330–33

"Contributory Negligence: Is the Law of Contract Relevant?" (1977) 3 *Auckland University Law Review* 140–55

Book Reviews:

J Getzler *A History of Water Rights at Common Law* in (2005) 25 *Legal Studies* 337–40

GB Baker and J Phillips (eds), *Essays in the History of Canadian Law in Honour of R.C.B. Risk* in (2001) 51 *University of Toronto Law Journal* 188–91

C Graham and T Prosser, *Privatizing Public Enterprises: The State and Regulation in Comparative Perspective* in (1993) 4 *Public Law Review* 271–76

AJ Harding *Public Duties and Public Law* in (1990) 10 *Windsor Yearbook of Access to Justice* 277–79

LA Hallett *Royal Commissions and Boards of Inquiry* in (1982–83) 10 *New Zealand Universities Law Review* 403–4

F Dawson and DW McLauchlan *The Contractual Remedies Act 1979* in (1982) 20 *University of Western Ontario Law Review* 366–73

PS Atiyah *The Rise and Fall of Freedom of Contract* in (1980) 70(9) *Harvard Law Record* 13 (April 25)

Index

Introductory Note

References such as '178–9' indicate (not necessarily continuous) discussion of a topic across a range of pages. Wherever possible in the case of topics with many references, these have either been divided into sub-topics or only the most significant discussions of the topic are listed. Because the entire volume is about the 'common law', the use of this term (and certain others occurring throughout the work) as an entry point has been minimized. Information will be found under the corresponding detailed topics.